CIPS Study Matters

Level 5

Advanced Diploma in Purchasing and Supply

COURSE BOOK

Sustainable Procurement

Printed and distributed by the Chartered Institute of Purchasing & Supply

Easton House, Easton on the Hill, Stamford, Lincolnshire PE9 3NZ

Tel: +44 (0) 1780 756 777

Fax: +44 (0) 1780 751 610

Email: info@cips.org

Website: www.cips.org

First edition October 2009
Reprinted with minor amendments October 2010

Contents

Preface

Welcome to your new Study Pack.

For each subject you have to study, your Study Pack consists of three elements.

*   A **Course Book** (the current volume). This provides detailed coverage of all topics specified in the unit content.

*   A small-format volume of **Passnotes**. For each learning objective, these highlight and summarise the key points of knowledge and understanding that should underpin an exam answer. Use your Passnotes in the days and weeks leading up to the exam.

*   An extensive range of **online resources**. These include a **Quick Start Guide** (a rapid 40-page overview of the subject), practice questions of exam standard (with full suggested solutions), notes on recent technical developments in the subject area, and recent news items (ideal for enhancing your solutions in the exam). These can all be downloaded from the study resources area at www.cips.org. You will need to log in with your membership details to access this information.

For a full explanation of how to use your new Study Pack, turn now to page xvii. And good luck in your exams!

A note on style

Throughout your Study Packs you will find that we use the masculine form of personal pronouns. This convention is adopted purely for the sake of stylistic convenience – we just don't like saying 'he/she' all the time. Please don't think this reflects any kind of bias or prejudice.

October 2010

The Exam

The format of the paper

The time allowed is three hours. The examination is in two sections.

Section A — case study scenario, with two compulsory application questions based on the case study, each worth 25 marks.

Section B — questions to test knowledge and understanding. Candidates will be required to answer two questions from a choice of four, each worth 25 marks.

The unit content

The unit content is reproduced below, together with reference to the chapter in this Course Book where each topic is covered.

Unit characteristics

This unit is designed to provide students with a working knowledge of sustainable procurement: what it is, how it aligns with overall organisational strategies, policies and operations and how to recognise, apply and successfully manage sustainable procurement activities to achieve future improvements and benefits and mitigate risk.

Through the exploration and evaluation of external and internal sustainability factors, drivers, barriers and trade-offs, students will cover a wide range of situations across sectors and industries.

By the end of the unit, students should be able to recognise and implement appropriate sustainable specifications, sourcing and whole-life contract management for products and services and evaluate how sustainable procurement impacts on business performance. They will be equipped with supplier audit, assessment and development tools to measure and increase sustainable procurement activity in the global supply chain. They will furthermore be encouraged to develop and implement policy and engage stakeholders, acting as catalysts for change in the internal and external environment in which their organisations operate.

Statements of practice

On completion of this unit, students will be able to:

* Compare definitions of sustainable procurement in relation to sustainable development and apply them appropriately to different business sectors within local, national and global markets

* Evaluate the key internal and external factors, in particular legislation, which influence the achievement of successful sustainable procurement across different business sectors, organisations and geographic regions, taking into account both current and emerging global trends

* Analyse the importance of aligning sustainable procurement policy and operations to overall business strategy of the organisation

* Assess the main criteria for sustainable procurement specifications, sourcing and whole-life contract management of products and services

* Apply supplier audit, assessment and development tools to the supply chain in order to measure and improve sustainable procurement

* Evaluate the drivers, barriers, conflicts and trade-offs to achieving sustainable procurement within the organisation

* Evaluate ways in which procurement personnel could act as catalysts for change in engagement with the internal and external environment to mitigate risk, secure supply and ensure sustainable supply chains.

Learning objectives and indicative content

1.0 Defining and developing sustainable procurement
(Weighting 20%)

1.1 Define sustainable procurement in relation to the concept of sustainable development

• Sustainable development and sustainable procurement in context	1
• Brundtland Commission definition	1
• Sustainable consumption and production	1
• Differing definitions of sustainable procurement	1
• The United Nations Environment Programme for Sustainable Consumption	1
• European Union sustainable development strategy	1
• Sustainable Procurement Task Force	1
• How sustainable procurement supports sustainable development	1
• Why sustainable procurement should be good for business	1

1.2 Analyse current and emerging global trends in the field of sustainable procurement

• Innovation and the successful implementation of sustainable procurement ideas	2
• Worldwide demographic trends	2
• Overall production and service capacity and capability	2
• Corporate social responsibility (CSR)	2
• A changing skills base	2
• Alternatives to fossil fuels and rising energy costs	2
• Availability, use, and depletion of diminishing natural resources	2
• Sustainable procurement as a qualifier for all purchasing decisions	2

1.3 Evaluate the external factors influencing sustainable procurement and apply the PESTLE model in the context of different organisations and sectors, including the public, private and third sectors and their tiers:

• The 'triple bottom line' of environmental, social and economic factors	1
• International and local influences on sustainable procurement	3
– Political (eg government policies, targets and incentives – workforce structure, waste management, conservation and protection of natural resources, land use, water management, Local Government Act 2000, Local Agenda 21, Special Development Areas)	3

How to Use Your Study Pack

Familiarisation

At this point you should begin to familiarise yourself with the package of benefits you have purchased.

*   Go to www.cips.org and log on. Then go to Study and Qualify/Study Resources. Browse through the free content relating to this subject.

*   Download the Quick Start Guide and print it out. Open up a ring binder and make the Quick Start Guide your first item in there.

*   Now glance briefly through the Course Book (the text you're reading right now!) and the Passnotes.

Organising your study

'Organising' is the key word: unless you are a very exceptional student, you will find a haphazard approach is insufficient, particularly if you are having to combine study with the demands of a full-time job.

A good starting point is to timetable your studies, in broad terms, between now and the date of the examination. How many subjects are you attempting? How many chapters are there in the Course Book for each subject? Now do the sums: how many days/weeks do you have for each chapter to be studied?

Remember:

*   Not every week can be regarded as a study week – you may be going on holiday, for example, or there may be weeks when the demands of your job are particularly heavy. If these can be foreseen, you should allow for them in your timetabling.

*   You also need a period leading up to the exam in which you will revise and practise what you have learned.

Once you have done the calculations, make a week-by-week timetable for yourself for each paper, allowing for study and revision of the entire unit content between now and the date of the exams.

Getting started

Aim to find a quiet and undisturbed location for your study, and plan as far as possible to use the same period each day. Getting into a routine helps avoid wasting time. Make sure you have all the materials you need before you begin – keep interruptions to a minimum.

Begin by reading through your Quick Start Guide. This should take no more than a couple of hours, even reading slowly. By the time you have finished this you will have a reasonable grounding in the subject area. You will build on this by working through the Course Book.

Using the Course Book

You should refer to the Course Book to the extent that you need it.

- If you are a newcomer to the subject, you will probably need to read through the Course Book quite thoroughly. This will be the case for most students.

- If some areas are already familiar to you – either through earlier studies or through your practical work experience – you may choose to skip sections of the Course Book.

The content of the Course Book

This Course Book has been designed to give detailed coverage of every topic in the unit content. As you will see from pages vii–xv, each topic mentioned in the unit content is dealt with in a chapter of the Course Book. For the most part the order of the Course Book follows the order of the unit content closely, though departures from this principle have occasionally been made in the interest of a logical learning order.

Each chapter begins with a reference to the learning objectives and unit content to be covered in the chapter. Each chapter is divided into sections, listed in the introduction to the chapter, and for the most part being actual captions from the unit content.

All of this enables you to monitor your progress through the unit content very easily and provides reassurance that you are tackling every subject that is examinable.

Each chapter contains the following features.

- Introduction, setting out the main topics to be covered

- Clear coverage of each topic in a concise and approachable format

- A chapter summary

- Self-test questions

The study phase

For each chapter you should begin by glancing at the main headings (listed at the start of the chapter). Then read fairly rapidly through the body of the text to absorb the main points. If it's there in the text, you can be sure it's there for a reason, so try not to skip unless the topic is one you are familiar with already.

Then return to the beginning of the chapter to start a more careful reading. You may want to take brief notes as you go along, but bear in mind that you already have your Quick Start Guide and Passnotes – there is no point in duplicating what you can find there.

Test your recall and understanding of the material by attempting the self-test questions. These are accompanied by cross-references to paragraphs where you can check your answers and refresh your memory.

Practising what you have learned

Once you think you have learned enough about the subject, or about a particular topic within the overall subject area, it's good to practise. Access the study resources at www.cips.org, and download a practice question on the relevant area. Alternatively, download a past exam question. Attempt a solution yourself before looking at our suggested solution or the Senior Assessor's comments.

Make notes of any mistakes you made, or any areas where your answer could be improved. If there is anything you can't understand, you are welcome to email us for clarification (course.books@cips.org).

The revision phase

Your approach to revision should be methodical and you should aim to tackle each main area of the unit content in turn. Begin by re-reading your Quick Start Guide. This gives an overview that will help to focus your more detailed study. Then re-read your notes and/or the separate Passnotes accompanying this Course Book. Then return to question practice. Review your own solutions to the practice questions you have had time to attempt. If there are gaps, try to find time to attempt some more questions, or at least to review the suggested solutions.

Additional reading

Your Study Pack provides you with the key information needed for each module but CIPS strongly advocates reading as widely as possible to augment and reinforce your understanding. CIPS produces an official reading list of books, which can be downloaded from the bookshop area of the CIPS website.

To help you, we have identified one essential textbook for each subject. We recommend that you read this for additional information.

The essential textbook for this unit is *Sustainability Handbook* by William Blackburn, published by Earthscan (ISBN: 978–1–84407–495–2).

CHAPTER 1

Sustainable Development and Procurement

Learning objectives and indicative content

1.1 Define sustainable procurement in relation to the concept of sustainable development

- Sustainable development and sustainable procurement in context
- Brundtland Commission definition
- Sustainable consumption and production
- Differing definitions of sustainable procurement
- The United Nations Environment Programme for Sustainable Consumption
- European Union sustainable development strategy
- Sustainable Procurement Task Force
- How sustainable procurement supports sustainable development
- Why sustainable procurement should be good for business

1.3 External factors influencing sustainable procurement...

- The 'triple bottom line' of environmental, social and economic factors

Chapter headings

1 The concept of sustainable development

2 Sustainable consumption and production

3 Sustainable procurement

4 The 'triple bottom line'

5 The broad argument for sustainable procurement

6 Sustainable development agendas

Introduction

We begin our Course Book, as the syllabus begins, by explaining some of the concepts and inter-related terminology surrounding 'sustainability' and its applications to economic activity (sustainable development) and corporate policy and practice (sustainable production, consumption and procurement).

Although sustainability issues have recently been added to several CIPS syllabuses, we assume no substantial prior knowledge, and use this chapter to give a broad overview of how the concept of sustainability has emerged, what it means in various contexts, and why it has grown in prominence in both public and private sector procurement.

A key thread of this narrative is the broadening of the perceived responsibilities of economic activity in general, and businesses in particular, beyond the primary goals of economic development and performance: firstly, embracing the responsibility of achieving these goals without compromising or damaging the natural environment; and, more recently, extending this responsibility to the protection and promotion of human rights and social justice. We therefore introduce the concept of the 'triple bottom line' (economic, environmental and social factors) in this chapter.

1 The concept of sustainable development

Introduction

1.1 Let's start at the beginning. 'Development' is a shorthand term for a cluster of activities aimed at improving human and social well-being, through the creation and maintenance of wealth, social infrastructure, equity, education, employment, enabling technologies and so on. It thus embraces a range of social, economic, industrial and technological activity, with the broad aim of bettering conditions for human life.

1.2 As a starting point, therefore, we may say simply that sustainable development is development activity that can be sustained, or kept up, over the long term; that does not undermine or put at risk the conditions and resources required to preserve well-being into future. Perhaps the most obvious example is the need to conserve or replace non-renewable resources, exhaustion of which would impact on the well-being and further development of future generations.

1.3 The Scottish Executive website describes sustainable development as follows.

'The fundamental aim of sustainable development is to secure the future. We have seen how actions in the past have made life more difficult for us today. Developing sustainability means ensuring that our actions today do not limit our quality of life in the future.'

The emergence of sustainability as a political and corporate issue

1.4 According to Blackburn (2007), the concept of sustainability first emerged into mainstream discourse in 1972, during the United Nations Conference on the Human Environment. At a time when serious environmental concerns were beginning to be raised in relation to industrial development and practices (on issues such as deforestation, pollution and the use of toxic pesticides, for example), the conference delegates debated which was more important: economic development or environmental protection? A series of high-profile environmental disasters (such as the Exxon Valdez oil spill and the Chernobyl nuclear reactor explosion) subsequently raised the public and political profile of environmental issues.

1.5 At the same time, issues of social justice also became a matter of widespread concern, with a particular focus on the apartheid (racial segregation) policies of South Africa, which attracted popular activism and economic sanctions. Public bodies, in particular, were urged to be 'socially responsible' and 'ethical' in their investments, in order to bring financial pressure to bear on companies to recognise issues such as human rights and equal opportunity.

1.6 Through its discussions, the UN had recognised that economic development and environmental protection were inextricably linked – and potentially, mutually reinforcing. Economic development would be required to raise living and working conditions, and to support investment in environmental conservation and viable technologies. At the same time, any attempt to improve human well-being that threatened the environment was doomed to failure in the long run – because the depletion of resources, the degradation of environments and the pollution of air and water (for example) would impact on the well-being and development potential of future generations.

1.7 This essentially two-dimensional view of sustainable development can be seen in the following UK definition.

'Most societies want to achieve economic development to secure higher standards of living, now and for future generations. They also seek to protect and enhance their environment, now and for their children. Sustainable development tries to reconcile these two objectives.' (HMSO, 1994)

1.8 The UN therefore appointed a think-tank, under the chairmanship of Gro Harlem Brundtland, to come up with strategies to enable continuing economic development without threatening the environment. The Brundtland Commission (reporting in 1987) focused on the need to develop a stable relationship between human activity and the natural world, which would not reduce the prospects of future generations to enjoy a quality of life at least as good as that of the present generation.

1.9 These ideas were refined by the 1992 Rio Declaration on Environment and Development (issued by a UN Conference held in Rio de Janeiro), in which social justice and human rights issues (such as peace, poverty, child labour, the role of women and the plight of indigenous peoples) were explicitly added to the mix.

1.10 This three-dimensional (economic-environmental-social) view of sustainability subsequently became widely adopted, and in 1997, the term 'triple bottom line' (TBL) was coined by John Elkington to highlight the need for nations and organisations to measure their performance in all three areas.

1.11 In recent years, these three dimensions have formed a framework for a range of issues broadly related to business ethics and corporate social responsibility, including corporate governance, fair trade, labour relations, diversity, transparency – and an increasing number of existing and emerging environmental concerns: climate change, renewable energy, pollution, genetic modification and so on. They have been variously expressed as:

- Profit (economic performance), People (social sustainability) and Planet (environmental sustainability)
- Economics, Environment and Equity (social justice)
- Resources (the wise use and management of economic and natural resources) and Respect (for people and other living things). Note that this two-dimensional 2Rs model, proposed by Blackburn, still encompasses the triple bottom line.

1.12 By now, there are thousands of different published definitions of sustainability and sustainable development. Herman Daly (1991) has nevertheless argued that:

'Lack of a precise definition of the term "sustainable development" is not all bad. It has allowed a considerable consensus to evolve in support of the idea that it is both morally and economically wrong to treat the world as a business in liquidation.'

The Brundtland Commission definition of sustainability

1.13 The Brundtland Commission's report, *Our Common Future,* was published in 1987, and contained a general definition of sustainable development which is still widely used:

'Development that meets the needs of the present without compromising the ability of future generations to meet their own needs.'

1.14 This definition introduces two key concepts:

- Needs: in particular the needs of the world's poor, to which overriding priority should be given; and
- Limitations: imposed by the state of technology and social organisation on the environment's ability to meet present and future needs.

1.15 Essentially, humanity must take no more from Nature than Nature can replenish or repair. There needs to be a balance between improving human and social wellbeing and preserving natural resources and ecosystems.

1.16 There are thus five guiding principles in the Commission's recommendations for a sustainable development strategy.

- Living within environmental limits
- Ensuring a strong, healthy and just society
- Achieving a sustainable economy
- Promoting good governance
- Using sound science responsibly.

1.17 For development to be sustainable, it must satisfy the following criteria.

- *Long-term decision-making.* Sustainable development requires the use of a long-term horizon for decision making, in which society pursues long-term aspirations (and recognises the long-term impacts and consequences of its actions), rather than making short-term, reactive responses to problems.
- *Interdependence.* As outlined above, sustainable development recognises the interdependence of economic, environmental, and social well-being. It promotes actions designed to expand economic opportunity, improve environmental quality and increase social wellbeing.
- *Participation and transparency.* Sustainable development depends on decision-making that is inclusive, participatory, and transparent. It recognises the importance of process in decision-making and implementation, including the consultation and involvement of stakeholders.
- *Equity.* Sustainable development promotes equity between generations and among different groups in society, aiming to reduce disparities in access to the benefits (and sharing of the risks and costs) of development.
- *Proactive prevention.* Sustainable development is anticipatory: it promotes efforts to prevent problems as the first course of action.

Sustainability and the organisation

1.18 You should already be able to see how the basic principles of sustainable development apply directly to the activity of business organisations – and other social stakeholders, such as governments, regulatory bodies, academic/scientific institutions and public interest groups (NGOs).

1.19 Blackburn (2007) argues that the aim of sustainability or sustainable development from an organisation's perspective is 'long-term well-being, for society as a whole, as well as for itself.' Note that this emphasises the place of economic performance within the concerns of sustainability: the continuing financial viability of an organisation supports human and social well-being, by creating and maintaining employment, and stimulating investment. Meanwhile, human and social well-being supports organisational survival, by maintaining the flow of skilled/willing labour, spending and investment: the two ideas, as for 'sustainable development', are potentially mutually reinforcing, rather than conflicting. We will return to this idea as we make the business case for sustainability and sustainable procurement.

1.20 It is also worth noting the varying use of terminology in this area.

- 'Corporate social responsibility' (CSR) is often used as an umbrella term for attempts to balance economic performance (or the financial viability of the business) with environmental responsibility and social responsibility (also related to areas such as corporate ethics, citizenship and philanthropy).

- However, terms such as 'social responsibility' and 'corporate citizenship' may also be used to refer specifically to the social dimension of the triple bottom line (labour relations, community involvement, human rights and so on) – or, more generally, to the social and environmental (as opposed to economic) concerns of organisations.

- Moreover, specific organisations may express their goals and commitments in these areas in their own ways.

1.21 In the exam, you will need to note the implications of any terminology used in case studies – and clarify your own use of terms. It is also worth noting that such terms will need to be explained clearly to employees and other stakeholders when recommending the introduction of sustainability policies and programmes!

2 Sustainable consumption and production

2.1 Economic systems depend on two basic processes: demand (arising from the consumption of goods and services) and supply (arising from the production of goods and services).

2.2 For an industrialised society to be sustainable, it must therefore seek to attain the economic, environmental and social sustainability of both consumption or demand-side processes and production or supply-side processes. 'Sustainable Consumption and Production' (SCP) is a term used to describe this aspect of sustainable development.

2.3 SCP is one of the four priority areas for UK action set out in the Sustainable Development Strategy Securing the Future (2005), based on a programme of measures to support:

- The design and production of more sustainable products and services, which reduce environmental impacts from the use of energy, resources, or hazardous substances

- Cleaner, more efficient production processes, which strengthen competitiveness, and

- A shift in the pattern of consumption towards goods and services with lower impacts, for more sustainable lifestyles.

Sustainable production

2.4 The term 'production' can be used to describe a wide range of activities undertaken in the process of transforming raw materials, resources and other inputs into goods and services, including: product/service design; procurement and supply; logistics (including the transport of inputs and products); resource consumption; extraction, processing, manufacturing, assembly or service delivery; waste management; technology management; facilities management; human resource management; outsourcing and off-shoring of production; and so on.

Example: Defra

The website of the UK Department for the Environment, Food and Rural Affairs (Defra) offers a useful insight into government policy and action in the area of SCP, as part of its 'business and the environment' policy.

'Most environmental impacts and some social impacts can be attributed to products and services we produce and consume. The greatest pressures now come from the impacts of homes, household goods, food and travel. Changing lifestyles and growing consumption bring even greater demands.

'Sustainable Consumption and Production (SCP) is about reducing our environmental impacts, while maintaining or improving economic outputs and standards of living. Business and consumers can also save money by doing more with less, and using resources such as water, energy and raw materials more efficiently.'

Some of the ways in which Defra seeks to achieve these aims include:

- Providing education, advice and guidance to consumers and businesses on the environment and 'greener' living (its Guide to Environment and Greener Living, for example, is downloadable from DirectGov at http://www.direct.gov.uk)

- Supporting innovation to bring through new products, materials and services: for example, through the technology programme administered by the Department for Business, Innovation and skills

- Promoting the use of environmental management systems and reporting

- Leading by example by working to embed sustainable procurement into the public sector. (Defra was a key sponsor of the Sustainable Procurement Task Force, whose recommendations were the basis of the UK Government's Sustainable Procurement Action Plan 2007.)

2.5 Each of these activities has the potential to create negative environmental (and social) impacts. You should be able to think through a typical production cycle of a product or service you know well — or to think through our list of general processes — and come up with a corresponding list of sustainability issues. Some examples of key concerns include the need to:

- Minimise environmental pollution, damage and degradation from industrial activity

- Manage waste products (often referred to as the 3Rs: reduction, re-use, recycling) from production, packaging, end-of-life products and so on

- Reduce greenhouse gas (GHG) emissions, or reduce the 'carbon footprint' of organisational activity (eg by reducing energy consumption and transport, utilising renewable energy sources and so on)

- Minimise the use of non-renewable materials and resources, and develop design specifications using renewable, recyclable, clean or sustainably produced materials

- Design products which are environmentally-friendly in their materials, production processes, consumption and end-of-life disposal

- Design or adapt production processes to be environmentally 'clean', resource-efficient, safe for workers

- Minimise negative impacts on communities and social amenities from business activity (eg traffic congestion, noise, dirt, loss of employment)

- Ensure the ethical and responsible treatment of labour, supply chains and communities (eg labour conditions, fair trading)

- Build and manage sustainable production capacity, through education, training, environmental management systems, monitoring and reporting and so on.

2.6 We will look at sustainable design specifically in later chapters, but just thinking through some basic economic-environmental-social factors, we might expect a 'sustainable product' to be:

- Fit for purpose and providing value for money

- Energy and resource efficient
- Made with maximum use of sustainably managed, renewable or post-consumer (recycled) materials
- The cause of minimal pollution, waste and GHG emissions in its supply, production and usage
- Durable, easily upgraded and repairable
- Re-usable, recyclable or safely disposable (with minimum waste impacts)
- Ethically sourced, produced and supplied.

Sustainable consumption

2.7   Sustainable consumption is closely linked to sustainable production.

2.8   Firstly, producers are themselves consumers (buyers and users) of labour, materials, components, products and services: sustainable production implies the sustainable procurement and use of these resources.

2.9   Secondly, the nature of market economies is that producers supply what consumers demand: unless the market is willing to engage in sustainable consumption, there will be no business benefit to sustainable production. (Conversely, sustainable consumption is only possible where sustainable products are available.)

2.10 Thirdly, the idea of sustainable consumption imposes a responsibility on producers to think beyond the sustainability of their own inputs and processes, to how their outputs will be used, maintained and disposed of – so that sustainable production actively supports sustainable consumption.

2.11 It is a key strand of the strategy of governments and pressure groups (and corporations already committed to sustainability) to educate and motivate consumers to engage in sustainable consumption, in order to create a demand-side stimulus for sustainable production. As we will see later, some of the main pressures for corporate sustainability come from increasing consumer demand for sustainable brands, the reputational capital available from developing them – and the reputational risk of not developing them!

2.12 A wide variety of published and online guidance is now available for consumers, to help them make 'green' and ethical choices and lifestyle changes. In addition, product labelling, British and international standards certification, and product endorsement by pressure groups provide consumers with information on the sustainability of particular products and brands. Examples of sustainable consumption which can be applied by organisations (as well as individual consumers) include the following.

- Buying energy efficient equipment and appliances (eg as identified by certified energy efficiency rating systems) and reducing energy consumption (eg by raising awareness and switching off appliances not in use)
- Reducing unnecessary transport mileage, fuel usage and carbon emissions (eg using public transport or cycling, buying fuel-efficient and clean-fuel vehicles, telecommuting, reducing unnecessary air travel)
- Re-using and recycling, and purchasing re-usable/recyclable and biodegradable products, and products with recyclable (and ideally, less) packaging. (Waste plastic bags are a major environmental problem, for example, and many countries now impose taxes, fines or outright bans on their use.)
- Purchasing local, seasonal materials and produce (to minimise transport miles, a major contributor to GHG emissions)

- Carbon 'offsetting': compensating for domestic or corporate carbon emissions, if they cannot be reduced, by purchasing 'offsets' (or 'credit carbons') on the carbon credit market, or independently investing in renewable energy, energy efficiency, reforestation and other carbon-reducing projects. (This is generally regarded as a last resort.)

- Buying ethically sourced and produced goods (eg cosmetics not tested on animals, certified Fair Trade products which guarantee the ethical treatment of labour and suppliers). This is a major trend, with increasing demand for Fair Trade cotton, coffee, tea and chocolate brands, among others. Organisations such as The Body Shop have built high-profile brands on ethical sourcing and production.

- Using local, small and diverse suppliers where possible (to support communities and equal opportunity, and to reduce transport miles)

- Consuming less. (This is a controversial area, since – understandably from the point of view of producers – would-be sustainable consumers are more often urged to buy more environmentally-friendly or ethical products than actually to buy less 'stuff' altogether... Nevertheless, consumption may be reduced without jeopardising the economic sustainability of producers: for example, by placing a premium on durability, 'less-goes-further' and so on.)

Example: Marks & Spencer's Plan A

According to a 2006 survey commissioned by Marks & Spencer, 90% of consumers think retailers should ensure their products are manufactured in a fair and humane way – and 31% said these considerations had actively influenced a purchase decision. In 2007, M & S launched a cutting-edge Corporate Social Responsibility programme called 'Plan A' (so called because 'There is no Plan B'), built on five 'pillars' of CSR, reflecting a spectrum of sustainability commitments.

- Climate change: eg reducing energy-related CO2 emissions from stores and offices; supporting farmers who are investing in small-scale renewable energy production; piloting 'eco-stores'; monitoring the carbon footprint of the food business; and encouraging consumers in more eco-friendly washing of clothing products.

- Waste: eg engaging customers in reducing plastic bag usage and recycling clothing; reducing packaging; increasing use of recycled materials; improving recycling of construction waste and coat hangers. (The target is to send zero waste to landfill.)

- Sustainable raw materials: eg promoting animal welfare in fashion and food production; increasing use of Fair Trade and organic cotton and recycled polyester; increasing sales of organic food.

- Fair partner: eg extended use of Fair Trade certified products; supporting local farmers; raising money in the community for charitable projects; updating commitments on labour standards and working with overseas suppliers to help them identify and share best practice.

- Health: eg removing artificial colourings and flavourings from 99% of food products; reducing salt levels and introducing front-of-pack Food Standards Agency 'traffic lights' to identify salt levels; and training employees as 'healthy eating assistants'.

Note how M & S is involving stakeholders, including employees, suppliers and customers (using 'pledges' of commitment to each of the five pillars) in Plan A. The programme therefore addresses sustainable production, procurement (upstream activity involving the supply chain) and consumption (downstream activity involving consumers).

---

3 *Sustainable procurement*

How sustainable procurement supports sustainable development

3.1 It should be clear, from our discussion above, that the procurement function has a key role to play in any organisation's contribution to national (and international) sustainable development strategy and commitments.

3.2 The procurement function is responsible for sourcing the inputs to organisational processes. As such, it can contribute to sustainable consumption by the organisation: ensuring that inputs are environmentally-friendly and ethically sourced. Of course, this is also a key contribution to sustainable production, which includes the sustainability of its inputs and sourcing processes.

3.3 Sustainable procurement is, as you might by now have come to expect, an approach that takes economic, environmental and social sustainability into account when making purchasing decisions. It's about looking at what purchased items are made of, where they come from, how they are made and by whom, how they will be used – and whether they are in fact necessary – to ask:

- Does procurement, in all these aspects, meet the present needs of the organisation, its customers and its wider stakeholders, without compromising the ability to continue to do so in future – by degrading the environment, depleting resources, undermining trading relationships and so on?

- Does procurement, in all these aspects, protect or enhance the economic viability of the organisation (by adding value, controlling costs, securing supply continuity, meeting the needs of internal and external customers, building beneficial supply chain relationships and so on), without negative environmental or social impacts?

Definitions of sustainable procurement

3.4 *Supply Management* made a major feature of 'sustainability' in its issue of 21 June 2007, covering a wide variety of issues – and triggering a lively correspondence as to the value of the terminology and practice, in subsequent issues. One survey, cited in the feature, suggested that more than 80% of purchasers believe the profession lacks a clear understanding of the term.

3.5 Sustainable procurement (the phrase generally used by the UK government and CIPS) goes by many different names: 'green procurement', 'environmental procurement', 'affirmative procurement', 'responsible procurement', 'socially responsible procurement' (CIPS Australasia) – and so on.

3.6 Some definitions focus primarily on environmental concerns, although social aspects are gaining prominence in the business-focused literature, particularly because of growing awareness of the reputational risk faced by organisations which ignore issues such as child labour and workforce or supplier exploitation in their supply chains. In addition, global financial crisis has renewed the former emphasis on economic and financial viability concerns: maintaining profitability to support corporate survival, jobs, the efficient use of public funds and so on – according to sector and circumstances.

3.7 The United Nations' procurement website emphasises the full spectrum of economic, environmental and social criteria in its definition and explanation of sustainable procurement.

'Procurement is called sustainable when it integrates requirements, specifications and criteria that are compatible and in favour of the protection of the environment, of social progress and in support of economic development, namely by seeking resource efficiency, improving the quality of products and services and ultimately optimising costs.

Through sustainable procurement, organisations use their own buying power to give a signal to the market in favour of sustainability and base their choice of goods and services on:

- Economic considerations: best value for money, price, quality, availability, functionality;

- Environmental aspects, ie green procurement: the impacts on the environment that the product and/or service has over its whole lifecycle, from cradle to grave; and

- Social aspects: effects of purchasing decisions on issues such as poverty eradication, international equity in the distribution of resources, labour conditions, human rights.

3.8 The EU's Sustainable Development Strategy similarly recognises the need to take into consideration economic, environmental and social factors in analysing the impact of sustainable procurement on the purchasing and supply chain environment.

3.9 Meanwhile, CIPS itself has adopted the definition of sustainable procurement used by the Sustainable Procurement Task Force (SPTF). In *Procuring the Future*, the report of the Sustainable Procurement National Action Plan, sustainable procurement is defined as:

'A process whereby organisations meet their needs for goods, services, works and utilities in a way that achieves value for money on a whole-life basis in terms of generating benefits not only to the organisation, but also to society and the economy, whilst minimising damage to the environment.'

3.10 The phrase 'on a whole-life basis' is explained as implying that: 'sustainable procurement should consider the environmental, social and economic consequences of design; non-renewable material use; manufacture and production methods; logistics; service delivery; use; operation; maintenance; re-use; recycling options; disposal; and suppliers' capabilities to address these consequences throughout the supply chain.' In other words, sustainable procurement takes into account the whole lifecycle of a purchase and purchased items – and the chain or network of supply relationships.

3.11 A similar view is suggested by Alan Knight (*How Green is my Kitchen?*), who defines the sustainable supply chain simply as:

'The management of raw materials and services from suppliers to manufacturer/service provider to customer and back, with improvement of the social and environmental impacts explicitly considered'.

3.12 Knight argues that the greatest sustainability benefits come from applying sustainability goals as far as possible upstream in the supply chain (towards the extraction or production of raw materials) and as far as possible downstream (towards the ultimate consumer) – and back again through reverse logistics, and the recycling or disposal of products and wastes.

3.13 In your own further reading – and the policy statements of your own organisation – you may come across other definitions. Try to discern, in each case, the scope and emphasis of the concerns expressed by each definition, and the orientation to supplier or supply chain management that is implied.

The procurement function's contribution to sustainability

3.14 Broadly, the procurement function is well placed to exercise influence on sustainability because of its position at a crucial interface between the organisation and its external environment. It may have input to, or responsibility for, activities such as the following.

- The development and implementation of sustainable procurement strategies and policies
- The design and development of sustainable products and services (especially in situations where early buyer involvement is used, or where procurement can act as the interface with suppliers to develop early supplier involvement)
- The definition of requirements (in specifications, tender documents, contracts, purchase orders and service level agreements) to include sustainable materials, components, supplies and services

- The sustainable and ethical sourcing of products and services, building sustainability considerations into sourcing strategy – and each stage of the sourcing cycle (including supplier selection)

- The management of supply and logistics processes to minimise waste, transport and other environmental impacts, and to support reverse logistics, recycling, re-use and other measures. (This may, for example, include the development of lean supply.)

- The monitoring, management and development of suppliers (and supply chains) throughout the life of contracts and supply relationships, to support sustainability performance and improvement

- Monitoring, measuring and reporting on the sustainability of procurement (and related production and logistics issues), to help raise awareness, make the business case for sustainability, and manage overall corporate sustainability performance.

3.15 Each of these activities will be explored in detail in later chapters of this text.

3.16 The Sustainable Procurement National Action Plan argues that sustainable procurement 'is something the best of the private sector is already doing – whether through enlightened leadership or shareholder pressure'. However, along with other major international agencies, it also notes that because of its vast purchasing power and influence, public sector procurement is a key tool in changing unsustainable patterns of consumption and production – and presenting a persuasive case to the private sector.

4 The 'triple bottom line'

4.1 One of the earliest and most respected advocates of corporate sustainability is John Elkington. In 1987, he co-founded SustainAbility, a strategic consultancy, research and advocacy organisation, 'offering a range of services and undertaking advocacy in order to create financial value at the same time as addressing environmental, social and governance issues in an integrated manner'. (There is lots of great case study material available at the organisation's website: http://www.sustainability.com.)

4.2 Elkington was looking for a new language to express what was seen as an inevitable expansion of the environmental agenda to embrace wider sustainability concerns. In 1994, he coined the term 'triple bottom line'.

4.3 Based on the accounting concept of 'the bottom line' (profit), the term was designed to engage business leaders, raising awareness that corporate activity not only adds economic value, but can potentially also add environmental and social value – and, more importantly, create environmental and social costs (previously regarded as 'externalities', not accounted for in the performance measurement of organisations). Traditionally, these have been borne financially by governments and experientially by communities: in TBL thinking, businesses which cause costly social and environmental impacts should share (or at least recognise) these costs.

4.4 The triple bottom line (also called TBL, 3BL, and later 'People, Profit, Planet') recognises the need for businesses to measure their performance not just by how well they further the interests of their primary stakeholders (shareholders) through profitability (the 'economic bottom line'), but also by how well they further or protect the interests of their secondary stakeholders (including wider society), in relation to social and environmental sustainability. TBL accounting means expanding the traditional reporting framework of a company to take into account ecological and social performance, in addition to financial performance.

4.5 SustainAbility now works with many influential corporations (including Shell) which have adopted TBL frameworks. With the ratification of a United Nations standard for urban and community accounting in 2007, this has become the dominant approach to public sector 'full cost' accounting, reflected in UK public sector sustainability targets.

Profit (economic measures)

4.6 Profit is the original bottom line. However, in a sustainability framework 'profit' implies the ongoing impact the organisation has on its economic environment. This is not the conventional, internal business measurement of profit, but a quantified, comparable measure of the lasting value added to the host society.

4.7 Beyond this strict definition, however, economic sustainability can embrace a number of commercial considerations such as: ethical trading, corporate governance, value for money, adding value, sustainable pricing and supplier negotiation, resource efficiency, risk-managed capital purchasing, and responsible budgetary control.

People (social measures)

4.8 The social dimension of sustainability, as we have seen, relates to fair and beneficial business practices towards labour, the community and the region(s) in or with which a company conducts its business. A TBL organisation seeks to benefit many constituencies, and not to exploit or endanger them.

4.9 This may include issues such as: the preservation of the living conditions and amenities of communities; ethical treatment of labour (health and safety, fair pay and conditions); monitoring of subcontractors for labour exploitation (and child labour or slave labour, in developing countries); support for small and local businesses; support for diversity and equal opportunity in employment; development of skills; support for the use of local labour and the long-term unemployed; equitable gain sharing with supply chain members; and 'giving back' to communities (eg through investment, charitable giving and sponsorship).

Planet (environmental measures)

4.10 This relates to the more established area of sustainable environmental policies and practices, which seek either to benefit the natural environment or to minimise harmful impacts upon it.

4.11 This may involve: reducing pollution, waste and energy/resource consumption; minimising or repairing environmental damage (eg deforestation); controlling the disposal of harmful wastes; using renewable or recyclable materials and designs; reducing greenhouse gas (GHG) emissions and 'carbon footprint'; educating supply chains and customers to support environmental practices; investing in 'green' projects such as renewable energy, land reclamation and reforestation; and so on.

Drivers for TBL

4.12 In his book *Cannibals with Forks: Triple Bottom Line of 21st Century Business* (1999) Elkington suggested a number of emerging disciplines and methods that will drive sustainability forward: Table 1.1.

Table 1.1 *Seven drivers for sustainability revolutions*

Driver	Old paradigm	New paradigm
1. Markets	Compliance	Competition
2. Values	Hard	Soft
3. Transparency	Closed	Open
4. Lifecycle technology	Product	Function
5. Partnerships	Subversion	Symbiosis
6. Time	Wider	Longer
7. Corporate governance	Exclusive	Inclusive

4.13   Unpacking these 'revolutions' one by one:

- *Markets.* With increased global competition, growing numbers of companies are finding themselves challenged by customers and financial markets regarding their sustainability credentials: over the long term, those with sound foundations, built on a TBL model, will have the best chance of survival.

- *Values.* With a global shift in human and societal values towards environmental and social concerns, companies that fail to embrace TBL thinking may find themselves compromised.

- *Transparency.* Information on companies' sustainability plans and activities is increasingly demanded by governments, regulators, investors and consumers. Initiatives such as the Global Reporting Initiative (discussed in Chapter 13) illustrate this trend.

- *Lifecycle technology.* Stakeholder expectations now span whole business processes, supply chains and product lifecycles. Sustainability must be managed not just in product design and manufacture, but through supply, finance, usage, reverse logistics, end-of-life disposal and so on.

- *Partnerships.* There is an increasing degree of collaboration in sustainability initiatives, including industry alliances (for best practice sharing), and partnerships with public and third-sector organisations (such as Greenpeace), which are able to provide information, guidance, accountability, resources and credibility.

- *Time.* Most politicians and businesses find it hard to think in time-frames longer than two or three years, but the emerging agenda requires thinking across decades or even centuries. All stakeholders in sustainability need to view things over a far longer time-frame.

- *Corporate governance.* In the USA the Sarbanes-Oxley Act and in the UK the Stock Exchange Combined Code have laid the foundations for sounder governance. What is a business for? Who should have a say in how it is run? What is the appropriate balance between the interests of shareholders and other stakeholders? What balance should be struck at the level of the triple bottom line?

Limitations of TBL

4.14   The triple bottom line concept has been hugely influential in bringing sustainability to the fore. It is, however, not without its detractors, and the main arguments against it are as follows.

- Specialisation promotes efficiency, knowledge management, development and (in international trade) comparative advantage. Companies need to focus on their distinctive, value-adding competencies: to 'stick to the knitting' (as Peters and Waterman put it, in *In Search of Excellence*).

- Concern for environmental issues is a luxury for corporations in less affluent economies: the need to survive inevitably takes precedence over global, long-term concerns.

- Nationalism – the view that you look after your own citizens first – may get in the way of consensus on sustainability (which is seen as a global issue).

- Sustained economic downturn or recession inevitably refocuses businesses on economic indicators, in the interests of survival.

- Application, in monetary-based economic systems, is a major weakness of TBL, according to *The Challenge of TBL: A Responsibility to Whom?* (Fred Robin). It is difficult to make a genuine business case for TBL, when the costs of sustainability improvements are tangible – and their value is difficult to measure.

4.15 TBL (along with many of the issues and some of the science of sustainability) is still the subject of debate. As long as this is the case, there will be considerable corporate inertia – or active resistance – to sustainability policies and programmes. Advocates for sustainable procurement will need to develop convincing business case arguments to promote their agenda, as discussed in Chapter 6.

The TBL for procurement

4.16 Profit, People, Planet considerations can be applied specifically to procurement activities, to illustrate the dimensions of sustainable procurement. Table 1.2 summarises some of procurement's key potential contributions in each area.

Table 1.2 *Potential for procurement to add value to the TBL*

Profit: adding economic value	Securing value for money
	Effective investment appraisal and capital purchasing
	Cost management and budgetary control
	Added value (through sourcing efficiencies, supplier involvement, quality improvement)
	Ethical trading to support the long-term financial viability of suppliers and supply markets (including sustainable pricing, ethical tendering and negotiation, payment on time)
Planet: adding environmental value	Input to design and specification of green products/services
	Sourcing of green materials and resources
	Green sourcing, including selection, management and development of suppliers with environmental capability and commitment
	Reducing the waste of resources throughout the sourcing cycle
	Managing logistics (including reverse logistics) to minimise waste, pollution, GHG emissions and environmental impacts (and to support re-use, recycling and safe disposal)
People: adding social value	Encouraging purchasing team and supplier diversity
	Monitoring supplier practices to ensure observance of human rights and labour standards (eg re slavery, child labour, conditions of work, health and safety, equal opportunity)
	Input to health and safety of products/services (design, specification, supplier quality management)
	Fair and ethical trading (fair pricing, ethical use of power, ethical business practices)
	Local and small-business sourcing

4.17 Some purchasing contributions may add value across all three measures. Examples include: risk management; compliance with legislation, regulation and standards; sustainable supplier management and development; and monitoring and reporting activity (eg purchase audits).

4.18 Other examples will no doubt occur to you. Challenging purchase requisitions and specifications by internal customers, for example, may help to reduce unnecessary purchases, variety and stock-holding (leading to waste through obsolescence, deterioration and damage). This adds value both economically and environmentally.

4.19 Such activities may offer 'quick wins' – and demonstrable benefits – for a TBL programme. However, there will also be a need for 'trade-offs' between the three measures in many cases. Local sourcing, for example, is a good way of promoting both social sustainability (supporting community employment and investment) and environmental sustainability (lower 'carbon footprint' from reduced transport) – but may attract higher prices. We will discuss some of these trade-offs, and how they can be managed, in Chapter 15.

5 The broad argument for sustainable procurement

5.1 We will look at the drivers for sustainable procurement in later chapters, but it is worth making a general business case as part of this introductory overview.

5.2 The public sector has particular reasons for demanding greater levels of sustainability from its supply chain: it is directly and explicitly responsible for ensuring that public money spent on goods and services (€150 billion per annum in the UK) is applied in such a way as to maximise benefits to society.

5.3 Sustainable procurement worldwide is heavily driven by public procurement agendas, and is often viewed as a public sector initiative. This view is slowly changing as legal and commercial pressures are raising the priority of corporate social responsibility in the private sector. The fact remains, however, that private sector firms are accountable primarily to their shareholders, and the prime objective of business organisations is economic performance.

5.4 Milton Friedman and Elaine Sternberg famously took the view that 'the social responsibility of business is profit maximisation': to give a return on shareholders' investment. Spending funds on objectives not related to shareholder expectations is simply irresponsible: regard for shareholder wealth is a healthy discipline for management, providing accountability for decisions. The public interest is, in any case, already served by profit maximisation, because the State levies taxes.

5.5 'Consequently,' argued Friedman, 'the only justification for social responsibility is enlightened self interest' on the part of a business organisation. So how does sustainable procurement serve the interest of the firm, or the supply chain as a whole?

Why should sustainable procurement be good for business?

5.6 Different organisations and sectors will have different drivers for sustainability in different areas of their activity. However, a number of general arguments may be advanced for sustainable procurement policies and practices: see Table 1.3.

Table 1.3 *Potential benefits of sustainable procurement*

Compliance	Law and regulation impose certain social and environmental responsibilities on organisations (eg in relation to workplace health and safety, employment protection, consumer rights and environmental care). There are reputational, financial and operational penalties for failure to comply (eg 'polluter pays' taxes, closure notices and so on).
Reputational benefits and reputational risk management	Voluntary measures and standards accreditation on sustainability may enhance corporate image and reputation, enabling the organisation to attract and retain quality suppliers, employees and investors.
	The risk of reputational damage extends to 'responsibility by association' in supply chains: buying organisations are increasingly held responsible for unsustainable behaviour by their suppliers. A 'good' example is the embarrassing exposure of the exploitative labour practices at one of Oxfam's suppliers of Make Poverty History wristbands.
Brand proposition, differentiation and competitive advantage	Sustainable product design, and sustainably sourced inputs, can create a differentiated and competitive brand proposition, which is increasingly valued by consumers. Examples include the sustainability strategies adopted by The Body Shop and Marks & Spencer. High-profile listings and awards now recognise and promote responsible brands (eg the Medinge Group's Brands with a Conscience: http://www.medinge.org).
Workforce and supply base commitment	Above-statutory provisions for the treatment of employees and suppliers (and more general sustainability credentials) may be necessary to attract, retain and motivate them to provide quality service and commitment – particularly in competition with other employers/purchasers.
Supply continuity	Support for the financial viability and sustainable practices of suppliers protects the ongoing security of supply, which might otherwise be put at risk. (The squeezing of supplier profit margins, for example, may risk supplier failure, corner-cutting on quality, refusal to supply and so on.)
Minimisation of failure costs	Significant costs may be incurred to rectify failures: eg environmental clean-up, rectification, fines, compensation claims and so on – as well as the cost of lost sales, disruption to supply or production while problems are sorted out, loss of employee morale and so on. As in quality management, prevention costs are potentially less than failure costs...
Cost management and efficiency	A retained emphasis on economic performance, and particularly, a whole-life costing approach (encouraged by the lifecycle focus of sustainability), can contribute to cost management and profitability.
	The environment-friendly focus on resource-efficiency and the reduction or elimination of waste products and processes can lead to measurable efficiencies and cost savings. Videoconferencing, for example, is both 'green' (avoiding travel) and a cost-reducing approach to meetings.
Improvement and innovation	Sustainable procurement initiatives often require increased supply chain communication, and investment in problem-solving and innovation: this may open up new avenues for performance improvement, cost reduction, enhanced collaboration, supplier development and product/service innovation, with flow-on benefits.
Shareholder value	In terms of shareholder returns, the companies listed in the Dow Jones Sustainability Group Index (DJSI) have been shown to outperform the general Dow Jones Index over time.

5.7   In the public sector, the UK government has outlined eight good reasons for buying sustainable products.

- To achieve best value for money (eg by lifecycle costing)
- To fulfil the government's commitment to sustainable development
- To be able to withstand increased public scrutiny

- To meet international obligations (such as the Kyoto Protocol)
- To stimulate the market for sustainable technologies
- To maintain and improve our standard of living
- To improve health and the environment
- To save money

5.8 Of course, business also needs to remember the 'enlightened' part of the 'enlightened self-interest' equation! Profit maximisation and performance improvement does not, by itself, always imply (or lead to) sustainable behaviour – as recurring examples of economic, environmental and human exploitation show. (High-profile past examples include: environmental degradation caused by Shell oil refineries in Nigeria; child labour used by Nike and other Western clothing manufacturers; fraudulent reporting by Enron; etc.)

Example: Shell Global

In the mid-1990s Shell Oil's plan to dispose of the Brent Spar oil rig in the North Sea, together with long-term allegations about the environmental (and resulting social) damage of its operations in Nigeria, brought social and environmental responsibility onto the world stage. The negative consumer response hit Shell's reputation and market value – and the Shell Group Business Principles now include explicit sustainable development policies:

'Contributing to sustainable development for us means helping meet the world's growing energy needs in economically, environmentally and socially responsible ways. It is the right thing to do, and it is good for business... Integration of sustainable development in the business is potentially a source of competitive differentiation, positioning Shell as the Partner of Choice, enabling value growth and thereby increasing Total Shareholder Return'.

This makes a great case study. See: http://www.shell.com/home/content/responsible_energy – and browse links such as 'Our sustainable development journey' and 'The business case for sustainable development'.

Is there a case against sustainable procurement?

5.9 We mentioned, more or less in passing, the arguments of Friedman and Sternberg that the prime social responsibility of organisations is profit maximisation. Playing devil's advocate, one could certainly argue this case: where profit maximisation conflicts with social and environmental principles, it is the task of society or the State, not company directors, to set things right.

5.10 As an example, we could suggest that recycled materials, 'green' and locally-produced goods, and the use of small local suppliers, means higher prices. Use of low-cost labour can likewise increase corporate profits – some of which will be reinvested to create employment opportunities and so on (the so-called 'trickle down' effect: what is good for corporations is, eventually, good for society). And similar examples could be multiplied.

5.11 In many cases, these arguments can be countered on their own terms, as being fundamentally incorrect in their cost assumptions. The Sustainable Procurement Task Force, for example, argues that:

- Sustainable development is an investment, not just a cost. Impacts may fall outside the normal budgetary cycle – but this needs simply to be reflected in indicators, targets and benchmarks for performance management.
- Environmental, economic and social responsibility need not be incompatible with efficiency targets
- Purchasers need to think about whole-life costs – and be more imaginative in seeking added value. 'Energy efficient light-bulbs, for example, may cost more upfront but the savings will come further down the line.'

- Purchasers tend to focus attention on high-value, high-risk areas, where the greatest differences can be made. 'For example, construction contracts with high environmental considerations are very relevant. But at the same time you have to focus on contracts for, say, recycled paper, as people… can associate with this and it will help to raise the profile of sustainable procurement internally.' In other words, a strategy of 'small wins' is effective in changing attitudes over time.

5.12 It must be recognised that there are indeed significant barriers, trade-offs and challenges involved in sustainable procurement – as discussed in Chapters 14–16. Some of the key barriers have been summarised by a study reported in *Supply Management* ('Breaking through the barriers', 21/6/2007): Table 1.4.

Table 1.4 *Barriers to sustainable procurement in the private sector*

External barriers	Internal barriers
Newly identified:	*Newly identified:*
• Volume of sustainability information	• Lack of knowledge/skills
• Language and cultural differences	• Resource limitations
• Lack of supplier commitment	• Weak processes
• Limiting standards	• Poor communication
	• Scope of audits too wide
Previously identified:	*Previously identified:*
• Customer desire for lower prices	• Lack of roadmap or strategy
• Competitive pressures	• Lack of management commitment
	• Cost reduction focus
	• Other procurement targets
	• Purchasers' abilities
	• Accounting methods

5.13 Ultimately, however, these arguments take place within a moral framework: society, in the form of legislators and opinion formers, has simply decided that certain practices are undesirable, even if in some cases they might maximise corporate profits. Fundamentally, it is not an option for supply chain managers to ignore the requirements of legislation and ethical codes. Such matters are genuinely – and intentionally – a constraint on supply chain decision-making and relationships.

6 *Sustainable development agendas*

The Bruntland Commission

6.1 The Brundtland Commission (and its 1987 report, *Our Common Future*) was primarily concerned with securing global equity: redistributing resources towards poorer nations whilst encouraging their economic growth. The report also argued that equity, growth and environmental maintenance are not mutually exclusive concepts, but that each country is capable of achieving its full economic potential while at the same time conserving its resource base.

6.2 As we saw earlier, the report highlighted three fundamental components to sustainable development: environmental protection, economic growth and social equity (the three E's). The environment should be conserved and our resource base enhanced, by gradually changing the ways in which we develop and use technologies. Developing nations must be allowed to meet their basic needs of employment, food, energy, water and sanitation. Achieving these aims would require major technological and social change.

The European Union Sustainable Development Strategy (EU SDS)

6.3   In June 2006, the European Council adopted an ambitious and comprehensive renewed EU SDS for an enlarged EU, building on the initial Gothenburg strategy (2001).

6.4   The renewed EU SDS sets out a single, coherent strategy on how the EU will more effectively live up to its long-standing commitment to meet the challenges of sustainable development. It recognises the need to gradually change our current unsustainable consumption and production patterns and move towards a better integrated approach to policy-making. It reaffirms the need for global solidarity and recognises the importance of strengthening our work with partners outside the EU, including those rapidly developing countries that will have a significant impact on global sustainable development.

6.5   The overall aim of the EU SDS is to identify and develop actions to enable the EU to achieve a continuous long-term improvement in quality of life through the creation of sustainable communities able to manage and use resources efficiently, able to tap the ecological and social innovation potential of the economy, and in the end able to ensure prosperity, environmental protection and social cohesion.

6.6   The strategy sets overall objectives and concrete actions for seven key priority challenges for the coming period until 2010, many of which are predominantly environmental.

- Climate change and clean energy
- Sustainable transport
- Sustainable consumption and production (including procurement)
- Conservation and management of natural resources
- Public health
- Social inclusion, demography and migration
- Global poverty and sustainable development challenges.

6.7   Education, research and public finance are stressed as important instruments in facilitating the transition to more sustainable production and consumption patterns. And because monitoring and follow-up are crucial for effective implementation, the renewed strategy contains a strong governance cycle. Every two years (starting in 2007), the Commission is to produce a progress report on the implementation of the strategy. This report is to form the basis for discussion at the European Council, which will give guidance to the next steps in implementation.

Sustainable Procurement Task Force

6.8   Government has a crucial role in furthering sustainable development through its own large-scale procurement of goods, services, labour, property and other resources. With a budget of some £150bn, the UK public sector can transform market values and practices.

6.9   The Sustainable Procurement Task Force was established in 2005, jointly funded by Defra and HM Treasury, and charged with drawing up an action plan to bring about a step-change in public procurement to put the UK among the sustainability leaders in the EU by 2009. Task force chairman, Sir Neville Simms, said of sustainable procurement:

'Future generations will neither excuse nor forgive us for ignoring the signals we see today. They will not accept that it was too difficult or too costly to keep our economic aspirations in balance with the impact of the environment and the effect our decisions will inevitably have on society'.

6.10 The task force drew on a range of governmental and non-governmental organisations to analyse the key barriers to sustainable procurement and presented a National Action Plan for overcoming them. The report *Procuring the Future* delivered its findings and recommendations in June 2006.

- *Lead by example.* The lack of consistent leadership on sustainable procurement emerged as a key barrier. Many public sector procurers lack clear direction from the top of their organisation on the priority to be given to delivering sustainable development objectives. To address this, a clear commitment from government should be cascaded down through both government targets and performance management systems that are independently monitored.

- *Too much guidance.* Procurers complained of guidance and information presented in an incoherent manner – a 'one size fits all' approach. The proposal was to rationalise policies into a single integrated framework which meets the needs of procurement.

- *Raise the bar.* The existing minimum standards for central government should be properly enforced and extended to the rest of the public sector. The task force recommends working with suppliers to identify future needs and to phase out products and services that fall below minimum standards.

- *Build capacity.* The public sector must develop its capabilities to deliver sustainable procurement. Sustainable procurement cannot be undertaken effectively unless procurement activities are carried out professionally and effectively; all procurement should be carried out by people whose skills have been developed appropriately.

- *Remove barriers to sustainable procurement* – whether actual or perceived. Whole-life costing was not being implemented in practice, the focus being on lower upfront costs. Rules, budgetary constraints, entrenched viewpoints were all barriers. All public organisations were called upon to examine their budgeting arrangements to make sure they encourage and support sustainable procurement.

- *Innovation.* The public sector must capture opportunities for innovation and social benefits and must manage risk better through smarter engagement with the market. Many suppliers questioned felt that it was difficult to penetrate the public sector with innovative solutions and that there were missed opportunities.

6.11 The Task Force put forward three building blocks for moving the sustainable procurement agenda forward.

- *A flexible framework* that guides public sector leaders in actions to make sustainable procurement happen: this will be discussed in Chapters 7 and 8, as we look at the development and implementation of sustainable procurement policies.

- *Prioritisation of spend.* Ten priority areas were identified for action nationally.

- *Toolkits* providing expert advice and support to public sector procurers.

6.12 The plan for action requires 'determined effort from the top down throughout both central and local government, the NHS, indeed everyone who either spends money from the public purse or on behalf of the public'.

The UN Environment Programme for Sustainable Consumption

6.13 UNEP works to promote more sustainable forms of industrial development, raise awareness, build capacities and demonstrate practical applications within businesses in developing economies. It is a 'lead body' in the sense that it sets the agenda for other countries and organisations to follow and/or to adapt as appropriate to their circumstances.

6.14   Key activities of UNEP in sustainable consumption and production include initiatives in partnership with Governments and civil society groups to develop new public policies and improved application of policy tools in support of sustainable consumption and production. It offers a range of programmes and activities designed to further research, develop initiatives and provide support for sustainability planning.

6.15   The Sustainable Consumption and Production (SCP) Branch of UNEP focuses on achieving increased understanding and implementation by public and private sector decision makers of policies and actions for SCP. Given the breadth of the challenges and actions required to achieve SCP, activities are focused on specific tools, encompassing policies, market-based instruments and voluntary approaches, with emphasis given to some specific economic sectors.

- *Cleaner production*: conserving raw materials, water and energy, eliminating toxic and dangerous raw materials, and reducing the quantity and toxicity of all emissions and wastes at source during the production process

- *Environmental management tools*: a variety of procedures, methodologies and instruments are available to assist individuals and organisations to undertake various environmental management tasks

- *Waste management*: preventing pollution and minimising waste

- *National programmes and action plans*. The development of comprehensive and workable national programmes or action plans on sustainable consumption and production is seen as a prime factor in ensuring a shift to sustainable policies and lifestyles.

Chapter summary

- Sustainability has come to be seen as an important influence on economic activity within both public and private sectors. This was reflected in the Brundtland Commission of 1987, among other initiatives.

- Sustainable consumption and sustainable production are closely linked. Taken together (SCP), they are a priority area identified in the UK Sustainable Development Strategy.

- Sustainable procurement has an important contribution to make to SCP. Procurement staff stand at a vital interface between the organisation and the environment and have wide scope to promote SCP.

- The triple bottom line emphasises that a single (economic) indicator of success is insufficient. Apart from profit, organisations must also pay attention to people (social factors) and planet (environmental factors). Procurement staff can make an important contribution in all three of these areas.

- A case can be made against sustainable procurement (and has been made by such authorities as Friedman and Sternberg). However, the arguments against can often be countered on their own (usually economic) grounds – and even if they could not, many authorities believe that unsustainable development is simply unacceptable.

- There are now many national and international agendas for sustainable development. These include the EU SDS, the UK government's Sustainable Procurement Task Force, and the UN Environment Programme for Sustainable Consumption.

Self-test questions

Numbers in brackets refer to the paragraphs above where your answers can be checked.

1   How was sustainable development defined by the Brundtland Commission? (1.13)

2   What criteria must be satisfied for development to be sustainable? (1.17)

3   List some of the key concerns in sustainable production. (2.5)

4   Give examples of sustainable consumption practices. (2.12)

5   Give a definition of sustainable procurement. (3.7, 3.9, 3.11)

6   List activities that procurement staff may be involved in to promote sustainability. (3.14)

7   What are the three elements in the triple bottom line? (4.4–4.11)

8   Outline arguments against the triple bottom line. (4.14)

9   The UK government has outlined eight good reasons for buying sustainable products. List as many of them as you can. (5.7)

10   List potential benefits of sustainable procurement. (Table 1.3)

11   Outline economic arguments to counter the case against sustainable procurement. (5.11)

12   List barriers to sustainable procurement in the private sector. (Table 1.4)

13   List findings of the 2006 report *Procuring the Future*. (6.10, 6.11)

Further reading

Chapter 1 of Blackburn *The Sustainability Handbook* gives a readable introduction to the subject.

CHAPTER 2

Global Trends in Sustainable Procurement

Learning objectives and indicative content

1.2   Analyse current and emerging global trends in the field of sustainable procurement

- Innovation and the successful implementation of sustainable procurement ideas
- Worldwide demographic trends
- Overall production and service capacity and capability
- Corporate social responsibility (CSR)
- A changing skills base
- Alternatives to fossil fuels and rising energy costs
- Availability, use and depletion of diminishing natural resources
- Sustainable procurement as a qualifier for all purchasing decisions

Chapter headings

1   Overview of current and emerging trends

2   Innovation and implementation

3   Global demographic trends

4   Sustainable resource issues

5   Corporate social responsibility

6   Sustainable procurement as a qualifier for purchasing decisions

Introduction

In Chapter 1, we gave an introductory overview of sustainable development and the ways in which sustainable development strategies cascade down to sustainable production and consumption (which in turn flow down to sustainable procurement).

In this chapter, we continue the syllabus's focus on a general/background orientation to the subject, by examining some of the key trends affecting sustainable procurement. This is potentially a vast – and constantly changing – area of study, and one in which you may need to do some wider reading (although we will provide us much updating material as possible via the CIPS student website, as trends emerge and develop).

The recommended textbook by Blackburn uses the phrase 'sustainability trends' as a catch-all heading for a summary of the wide variety of issues or areas of concern which currently appear on sustainability agendas (or should do so): urbanisation, child labour, climate change, deforestation and so on. This is, in fact, one of the few areas of the syllabus which give an opportunity to survey these issues/concerns: the content of sustainability and sustainable procurement policies, rather than the process of developing and implementing them.

We summarise Blackburn's survey in an appendix to this chapter, and then focus on the areas mentioned in the syllabus content. A range of issues will then be followed up in more detail as part of the learning objective on 'external influences on sustainable procurement', in Chapter 3.

1 Overview of current and emerging trends

1.1 As noted in our introduction, the *Sustainable Procurement* syllabus mainly focuses on 'process' issues in developing and achieving sustainability. The indicative content for this learning objective raises a number of process trends: emerging concepts such as corporate social responsibility which support sustainable procurement; the adoption of sustainable procurement values in purchase decision-making; the increasing pace of 'green' innovation and the implementation of sustainable procurement ideas – and so on.

1.2 However, alongside these themes, the syllabus also picks out certain topics and issues which are the focus of environmental or social sustainability concern. These may be called 'trends' because they reflect repeated events, effects or findings over time (so that year-on-year statistics on population weight suggest a trend towards growing obesity, for example) – and/or because they reflect increasing focus and concern (that is, they are 'trendy' topics).

1.3 A broad overview of some of the key trends, summarised from Blackburn (2007), is set out in an appendix to this chapter. You should browse through this before proceeding further.

1.4 Reading the appendix should equip you with a broad awareness of trends and issues, which you can follow up in areas that interest you, if you wish.

- Corporations will need to monitor these kinds of issues, as they impact on their business (and procurement) activities: they may form part of a sustainability or reputational risk assessment, for example.
- Public sector organisations (such as government departments and agencies and local government authorities) may well have direct responsibility for furthering the agenda, developing and implementing public policy, in a range of these areas.
- Similarly, third-sector organisations (such as charitable, interest, pressure and advocacy groups) may have one or more of these issues as the focus of their activity.

1.5 Obviously, some of these issues will be of more direct concern to sustainable procurement in some nations, industry sectors and business types than others. It would be a useful exercise to consider, for each identified trend: (a) for what types of organisation/industry it would be of most immediate concern; and (b) what might be the key implications for procurement and operations management. Consider how each of the trends identified may present opportunities for business, product or market development – as well as challenges, constraints, potential for business and reputational risk and so on.

1.6 In this and later chapters, we will explore in more detail those trends most directly relevant to sustainable procurement – and mentioned explicitly in the syllabus content.

2   *Innovation and implementation*

Increasing innovation support for sustainability

2.1   Innovation and implementation will be discussed in later chapters, as something organisations need to do in order to further sustainable procurement. As 'trends in sustainable procurement', they basically amount to one thing: momentum.

2.2   The Austrian economist Joseph Schumpeter distinguished three stages in the process by which new technologies develop and become adopted by an industry or market.

- *Invention*: scientifically or technically new ideas are devised for a product or process.
- *Innovation*: the ideas are developed into marketable products and processes, which are introduced to the market. Innovation or product development includes prototyping, feasibility studies, technical and market testing and so on.
- *Diffusion (or dissemination)*: the innovation proves successful and gradually comes to be widely available for use, through increasing adoption by individuals and organisations – which makes them increasingly cost-effective over time.

All three stages are required for what we call 'technological change', resulting in the cumulative economic and environmental impacts of new technology.

2.3   The term 'sustainability-driven innovation' is sometimes used for the creation of products, services, processes and new markets, driven by economic, social and environmental sustainability issues.

2.4   Technical innovations, in products and processes, are enablers for sustainable procurement, production and consumption: organisations are able to do things more sustainably, because more cost-efficient, energy-efficient and environmentally-friendly options are available. As such innovations are successfully diffused and brought to market, there is increasing impetus for sustainable new/modified products, services and processes.

2.5   Early adopters may be able to secure price premiums, as sustainability represents a valued differentiating factor in their own offerings. As more sustainable options become available, however, it becomes easier and less costly for organisations to incorporate them, creating wider adoption. Late adopters are then pressured to conform, because their competitors are doing so – and because market expectations have been lifted.

2.6   Meanwhile, on the supply side, increasing demand acts as a continual spur to further innovation and problem-solving. Lucrative potential markets have opened up for sustainable solutions to increasingly urgent problems such as climate change and resource depletion. There is major investment in scientific and technical research and innovation, in areas such as alternative energy sources, machine and process design to reduce pollution and emissions, and environmentally friendly synthetic materials.

2.7   This investment is also supported by impetus from the following sources.

- National and trans-national sustainable consumption and production (SCP) policies, such as: the Marrakesh process (developing a framework of programmes to be discussed at the UN Commission on Sustainable

Development in 2011); the United Nations Environment Programme (UNEP); and the UK's Sustainable Development Strategy

- Product policy initiatives and regulation, such as the EU Energy Using Products Directive (rules for the eco-design of electrical and electronic devices), or the EU's Integrated Product Policy (targeting environmental impacts at all stages of the lifecycle of a product from raw materials, through manufacture, to disposal); or legislation on the use of plastics and packaging (eg Denmark's packaging tax, and Taiwan's fines for businesses giving away plastic bags, utensils and plastic containers).

- Government investment in innovation research and infrastructure – and encouragement of the private sector to do the same – in order to boost national competitiveness. In the UK, for example, HM Treasury offers tax incentives for investment in research and development activity. Knowledge Transfer Networks (KTNs) were set up by government, industry and academia to facilitate the transfer of knowledge between the industrial and scientific sectors.

- In addition to direct investment in technology development, governments can create demand for technology products and innovation – for example, by public spending on sustainable products such as energy-saving light bulbs – which will stimulate private sector research and development.

- Private sector firms also stimulate invention and innovation in various ways: by providing experts to innovation think tanks, by inviting contributions from independent inventors, and by making innovative products and processes available in the market.

Example: Fuji Xerox

'In 1969, when Xerox introduced the first printer capable of printing on both sides of a piece of paper, terms such as "carbon footprints" and "green offices" were not in the vernacular. Four decades later, the printer and photocopier giant now known as Fuji Xerox has an enviable reputation as a corporate leader through its efforts to reduce electronic waste.

'Between 1995 and 2007 alone, the company estimates it avoided almost 100,000 tonnes of carbon emissions and cut its requirements for raw materials by 17,400 tonnes courtesy of a product design process and business philosophy that promotes remanufacturing and recycling.

'The showpiece of Fuji Xerox's green efforts is an eco-manufacturing centre in the Sydney suburb of Zetland that remanufactures and redesigns failed electronic parts that otherwise would have been thrown on the scrapheap...

'For Fuji-Xerox, environmental and bottom-line benefits aside, the other big advantage of its anti-waste campaign is that it helps keep customers happy. 'We find that our customers are including environment in their procurement positions more and more. We receive tender documents from government agencies and large corporate organisations and their questions are getting more and more sophisticated about what our environmental performance is.' Technology providers are increasingly expected to aid customers' environmental targets...

'Fuji Xerox has created tools such as carbon calculator for office document systems. It has also produced a sustainability report outlining the company's performance against key areas of stakeholder accountability across economic, social and environmental areas (following Global Reporting Initiative guidelines). The 2009 report, which is independently verified, highlights key achievements such as strong financial performance; sourcing and delivering more responsible and environmentally-friendly solutions; helping customers achieve more sustainable outcomes; improving customer experience; and strengthening employee engagement.'

Cameron Cooper 'Fuji Xerox leading on e-waste', *The Australian*, October 8 2009

2.8 Obviously, it would be beyond the scope of the syllabus to discuss specific technical innovations in detail, but you should watch out for examples that interest you in the quality press. Shimo-Barry (*The Environment Equation*) notes that: 'There are plenty of new products out there for the eco-friendly consumer... New corn-based plastics (polylactic acid, PLA or corn plastic) which biodegrade and don't leach toxins, and are increasingly used to make water bottles, containers, labels, electronics casings, clothing fibre and ball-point pens... Low-VOC paints and varnishes (volatile organic compounds are chemicals that contribute to the chemical formation of ozone, which is a greenhouse gas)...'.

2.9 The flavour of the diffusion of sustainable innovation is captured by Shimo-Barry's comment on corn plastic that: 'Currently, only certain stores stock the new material and only for certain products, but it is rapidly making inroads as retailers respond to environmentally aware consumers. Buying corn plastic products will help speed that process along.'

2.10 Sustainable procurement will therefore play a part in supporting sustainable innovation, by:

- Sourcing innovative products, services and processes (including new ways of thinking about procurement), as they become available and viable options
- Selecting, supporting and leveraging the capabilities of suppliers who are innovating, or have the potential to innovate, in pursuit of greater sustainability
- Supporting the organisation's own innovation capability, by promoting sustainable options in design, specification and sourcing.

Forward Commitment Procurement

2.11 The Sustainable Procurement Taskforce advocates a Forward Commitment Procurement (FCP) model for public sector procurement: 'a commitment to purchase, at a point in the future, a product that does not yet exist commercially, against a specification that current products do not meet at a sufficient scale, to make it worthwhile for suppliers to invest in tooling up and manufacture'.

2.12 FCP evidences to the market that there is a need for improved products and allows the supply chain to consider these needs and design a product and/or service to meet the FCP specification. Some of the public and private sector examples of FCP highlighted in the Taskforce report are shown in Table 2.1.

Successful implementation of sustainable procurement ideas

2.13 Like the successful market adoption of innovative products and services, the successful adoption of sustainable procurement ideas and policies – with demonstrated business benefits – also creates momentum. Organisations which have led the way in sustainable procurement are confirmed in their policies by positive stakeholder response and (triple) bottom line benefits. Laggards are increasingly encouraged to emulate them, by:

- The demonstrated potential benefits of doing so
- The realistic potential for doing so – especially given the increasing body of information and guidance on how to develop and implement sustainable procurement and how to pursue cost-effective Quick Wins
- The potential risks of not doing so, given rising customer expectations.

2.14 We will not cover examples of successful implementation separately here: rather, examples will be given throughout this Course Book, in the context of specific policy areas and developments. Just be aware, in the context of sustainability trends, that there are an increasing number of major organisations successfully implementing sustainable procurement, across all sectors – and promoting the fact heavily to stakeholders – and that this creates an impetus for other organisations to follow.

Table 2.1 *FCP driving sustainability innovation*

Organisation	Actions	Outcome
London Borough of Lewisham	A partnership agreement to supply 'green' wind power electricity on a 12 year or longer contract, from a named wind farm.	Would enable additional investment to be found for development of wind turbines and there could be a discount for the authority.
HM Prison Service	HMPS is currently market sounding on a specification to create a zero waste prison mattress system that meets or exceeds current operational requirements in terms of health and safety.	HMPS wants all its mattresses and pillows not classified as hazardous waste to be recycled or reused instead of going to landfill; and to reduce to 2% pa the number of mattresses disposed of as hazardous or clinical waste.
Wal-Mart	Installing solar power equipment at a yet to be determined number of its stores, the retailer has also asked bidders for expansion plans, including projected prices and costs, over the next five years.	It could amount to a significantly large solar installation, much greater than anything currently in existence – in the order of 100 megawatts of power over the next five years.
Starbucks	Starbucks will work with its suppliers to develop a paper coffee cup that contains 10% post-consumer recycled paper. A first for this industry.	The cup has created a new greener product which other companies can now purchase and has the capacity to become the new market standard.
Unilever and 'Refrigerants, Naturally'	A commitment to replace hydrofluorocarbons (HFCs) with hydrocarbons (HCs) in point-of-sale cooling applications. Suppliers were pre-warned as to the future purchase of HFC-free cabinets up to three years before substantial orders were placed.	All ice cream cabinet suppliers in Europe are now capable of producing HC refrigerated units.

3 Global demographic trends

Demographics

3.1 Demography is the study of population and population trends. Demographic data relate to population size, structure (eg breakdown by age or ethnic group), distribution (eg density and movements) and characteristics (eg education and employment). Demographic data is useful for procurement (and business in general) because populations represent the source of demand for goods and services (and hence input requirements). They also represent the source of skilled labour, which may affect purchasing recruitment – and also supply prices (as a cost of production for suppliers) and supply risk (as a contributor to supplier quality, delivery and viability).

3.2   We identify a number of global demographic trends in the appendix to this chapter. How might they impact on sustainable procurement?

Population size

3.3   If a country's population is too small, it may have insufficient labour and skills to exploit its resources and provide necessary services. If it is too large, it may make excessive demands on the physical environment and resources, or may create a demand for public services that the public or private sector may not be able to supply. Changes in the rate of population growth are caused by factors such as changes in the birth or fertility rate, changes in the death or mortality rate and changes in the rate of emigration (people leaving the country) and/or immigration (people coming into the country).

3.4   Long-term growth in the world's total population has been due mainly to the reduction in the mortality rate: improved medicine and hygiene have reduced early loss of life through disease and childbirth. This has contributed to an increasingly ageing population, which puts pressure on health and welfare services (with fewer taxpayers per pensioner).

Population distribution

3.5   We are also seeing a change in *population distribution*: less developed countries have a high birth rate, while developed countries have a declining birth rate (in some countries, below the 'replenishment' rate of two children per couple). Statistics published by the Population Reference Bureau (Washington DC) show that each year world population grows by 90 million, with 97 out of every 100 new births occurring in the developing world. Developed countries are therefore facing a situation in which they will need to import labour, in order to maintain productivity and taxation revenue: a key driver for immigration. Net immigration is now the major source of population growth in developed nations.

Distribution of wealth and opportunity

3.6   The distribution of wealth and opportunity is also a global issue.

- Overall, the gap between rich and poor is widening, in terms of gross domestic product (GDP) per capita, and incomes.

- Access to economic benefits and workforce participation (or 'equal opportunity') varies widely. The participation of women and ethnic minorities in some areas of economic activity (particularly at managerial levels) is still an issue, even in developed nations.

- Meanwhile, many workers worldwide continue to be engaged in forced labour, or on exploitative terms, or in unsafe working conditions.

- Many people lack access to educational opportunities, basic skills (including literacy and numeracy) and technological infrastructure and tools (such as telephone, internet and even electricity) that would enable them to aspire to economic participation on more equitable terms.

Implications for procurement

3.7   Some of the key issues, risks and opportunities arising for sustainable procurement from these factors may be summarised as follows.

- There may be a growth in the overall customer base, creating increased demand for inputs. However, since the bulk of this growth will be in developing countries, there will also be drivers for increased international marketing and sourcing, and for the adaptation of product/service specifications to meet the needs and cultures of specific regions.

- There will also be a growth in particular market segments, such as older consumers. So, for example, durability may replace fashion as the key attribute of product design and the purchasing of materials and components; distribution systems may increasingly favour home delivery; renewed emphasis may be placed on value-for-money products, with a pressure on purchasing to reduce costs – and so on. Immigration will also increase the racial, ethnic, religious and cultural diversity of market segments, requiring attention to the diversity of product/service offerings, workforces and supply bases.

- Increasing population, and resulting consumption, creates pressure on the environment: more pollution, waste, resource depletion and so on. Sustainable procurement by private and public sectors will be a key contributor to minimising the environmental effects of this increased consumption.

- There may be business opportunities for organisations in meeting the challenges of higher populations and population densities (particularly with the complementary trend of increasing urbanisation in developing nations): for example, in innovative, sustainable and low-cost housing, food supply, communications infrastructure and so on. Buying organisations may also help to counter urbanisation, for example by paying fair prices and supporting employment opportunities in rural areas (using regional suppliers or distribution centres, say).

- Business may share responsibility for doing its part to reduce disparities in global mortality rates and life expectancy: eg by developing health products, investing in social infrastructure in developing nations (and especially in supply market communities) – and eliminating labour and environmental practices which entrench poverty and endanger health.

- Organisations will need to develop policies to co-opt workers in developing regions (eg using 'virtual organisation' via ICT links, or outsourcing) or to attract immigrant workers – with related challenges of supporting and assessing education and skill-training in both domestic and international labour supply markets. An ageing population (and related age discrimination legislation in the UK) may also impact on labour supply: forcing firms to pay more for young workers, or to retrain and retain older workers.

- Supplier selection, monitoring and development should be used to reinforce sustainable and ethical labour practices: putting pressure on suppliers to avoid forced and child labour, workforce exploitation and poor conditions – and providing incentives and support for female participation, supplier diversity, fair trading and so on.

4 *Sustainable resource issues*

The issue of fossil fuel and other resource consumption

4.1 Consumption of resources is, in part, a social justice issue: 'Each year, it takes between 45 and 85 tons of natural resources per person to support the economy of a typical industrialised country. To provide that same level of consumption to the rest of the world... would take at least three Earths worth of resources' (Blackburn). More importantly, however, population growth and economic development together create accelerating resource consumption: increasing numbers of people consuming at increasing rates. Insofar as that consumption is of non-renewable resources, or outpaces resource renewal — there is a major sustainability problem!

4.2 Blackburn argues that 'to achieve sustainability of resources, the world must bring back into balance its consumption, technological development, resource re-use and recycling, and population growth'.

- For *non-renewable resources* (such as fossil fuels and minerals), the focus is on developing adequate supplies of alternatives — before the current resources are so depleted as to cause economic or social disruption.

- For *renewable resources* (such as wood, grain, cotton, fish and other biomass), the focus is on: (a) harvesting at a sustainable rate, not exceeding the rate of replenishment; and (b) consuming at a sustainable rate, not exceeding the combined rate of harvest, re-use and recycling of the resource.

4.3 Resource depletion can be delayed by reducing the consumption rate. This may involve measures such as support for recycling and re-use; increased resource efficiency (supported by technology); and government policies (eg tax penalties and incentives) for reduced consumption. Government and business can also provide incentives and support to accelerate the research and development of substitutes — and procurement functions have a key role in securing their adoption (initially, perhaps, at higher cost), to stimulate demand for innovation. Fundamentally, however, there may need to be a radical shift in cultural norms, to reverse the short-sighted drive for increasing consumption — before it's too late and we've 'cut down our last tree'.

Rising energy costs

4.4 Depletion of resources leads to intensifying competition for increasingly scarce supplies. In the long term, shortage or uncertainty of supply will act as a constraint on business growth. More immediately, it results in rising costs. We have seen this in the global energy market — the fossil fuels for which are both non-renewable and in high demand (especially from major consumers, the US and China).

- Global energy demand is expected to increase by 60% in the years to 2030. BP's Energy Report 2005 suggests that, using known reserves at current consumption rates, there is approximately a 160-year supply of coal, 70 years of natural gas — and 40 years before oil becomes scarce.

- Oil prices have been pushed higher, in part, by: China's increasing economic expansion and consumption of oil; continuing expansion of the automobile industry (a major oil consumer); and political instability in the Middle East (since 75% of all oil reserves are in OPEC nations).

- Coal consumption has been dampened by environmental concerns, but it remains the major source of power generation in the US, and usage is growing rapidly in China — and the depletion of oil reserves, and the emergence of 'clean coal', may create greater reliance in future.

- Natural gas has been increasingly adopted because of its low pollutant properties. New gas discoveries have generally kept pace with consumption, but this will not necessarily continue to be the case. There are also price issues arising from political issues and control of supply (eg via pipeline from Russia to Western Europe).

4.5 The 'up side' of rising energy costs is a renewed focus on improving energy efficiency – particularly because reduced energy consumption also reduces carbon footprints. Energy efficiency ratings (designed into products and services with the support of procurement) can be a source of competitive differentiation and advantage. Meanwhile, procurement functions with responsibility for energy purchases will be in a strong position to drive energy-saving policies in the workplace and supply chain.

Environmental issues in the use of fossil fuels

4.6 Apart from scarcity and price issues, the use of fossil fuels gives rise to a number of environmental concerns. They are seen as one of the main contributors to global climate change, as their burning releases greenhouse gas (GHG) emissions into the atmosphere. As vehicle ownership grows across the globe, and as developing countries further industrialise their economies, coal and oil (and its derivatives, petrol and diesel) are increasingly viewed as environmentally unsustainable – especially in the face of national commitments to reducing carbon emissions (eg under the Kyoto Protocol).

4.7 In addition to carbon footprints, the use of fossil fuels is often associated with environmental damage in the form of oil spills, pipeline leakage, explosions, and soot, smog and other forms of air pollution.

Alternative fuels and energy sources

4.8 Examples of alternative (renewable) energy sources already available, and being further developed, include the following.

- *Biomass fuels*: made from renewable living (plant and animal) matter. Current options include traditional wood burning (although this releases GHGs), and newly developed fuels including: biodiesel (produced from rapeseed or waste cooking oils); bio-ethanol (produced from starchy plants such as corn and sugar); and biogas (using methane from landfill sites). Such products are claimed to result in 60–95% reduction in carbon emissions. Brazil, with one of the largest renewable energy programs in the world, produces ethanol from sugar cane, providing 18% of the country's automotive fuel. There is a large biomass plant in Sweden, while in the UK attempts are being made to develop a power station that will run solely on wood from a nearby farm. However, there is not enough farmland worldwide to produce sufficient bio-fuels to meet current automotive demand – and there is resistance on social sustainability grounds to diverting food crops for fuel use.

- *Hydrogen fuel cells*: these cells use hydrogen and oxygen to produce electricity (currently used to power public buses in some European cities). The technology is still under development, but eventually promises an environmentally clean and sustainable fuel source if successful on a large scale.

- *Nuclear power*: despite ongoing safety and cost concerns, and negative public perceptions, nuclear power is increasingly regarded as a viable, clean energy option (which is cost-effective in the long term, compared to the 'full' cost of fossil fuels).

- *Hydro power* uses water flow to power turbines, currently accounting for almost one-fifth of the world's electricity generation. However, hydro projects are costly, and attract public opposition – partly on environmental grounds, where they involve the damming of rivers and submersion of habitats and communities.

- *Solar power:* using silicon-based photovoltaic cells to capture and store light energy to generate electricity. PV cells can be used in solar panels or film, which in turn can be incorporated in construction products such as cladding, roof tiles, louvers and glazing. Advantages of solar energy include: renewable, clean energy, with no pollution or GHG emissions; decreasing costs (with greater cell efficiency and government support) and low whole-life energy consumption costs; and a versatile range of applications in the built environment (especially being portable for use in remote areas). However, intermittency of sunlight can reduce efficiency, and solar energy is currently more expensive than traditional electricity.

- *Geo-thermal energy:* using the natural heat of the earth's core at 'hot spots', where the earth's crust is thin, and hot rocks and water are near the surface. In Southampton, there is a scheme whereby hot water (around 700°C) is pumped from 1,800 metres below ground to heat a number of houses and buildings. Clean and renewable, but geographically limited.

- *Wind energy:* huge wind turbines, whose rotation generates electricity, are clustered in 'wind farms' in coastal, mountainous and open areas with strong prevailing winds. (Small domestic equivalents are also being introduced.) Wind turbines are renewable, clean and increasingly efficient, and their use is growing at a rate of 30% annually: some states, such as Denmark and Hawaii, meet a significant proportion of their electricity needs from wind power. However, wind farms are considered unsightly and noisy, and often face objections from local residents.

- *Waves and tidal movements* can also be used to generate electricity, using turbines. A wave energy plant has operated on the island of Islay in Scotland since the early 1990s, for example. The rise and fall of tides are constant, and offer relatively cheap electricity: however, present designs do not produce a lot of power, and barrages across river estuaries can change the flow of water and, consequently, the habitat for birds and other wildlife.

4.9 In 2006, about 18% of global final energy consumption came from renewables, with 13% coming from traditional biomass such as wood burning, and hydropower providing 3%. Modern technologies, such as geothermal, wind, solar, and ocean energy together provided some 0.8% of final energy consumption. The technical potential for their use is very large, exceeding all other readily available sources.

4.10 Climate change concerns, coupled with high oil prices and increasing government support, are driving increasing renewable energy legislation, incentives, innovation and commercialisation. European Union leaders reached an agreement in principle in March 2007 that 20% of their nations' energy should be produced from renewable fuels by 2020, as part of their drive to cut carbon dioxide emissions.

A changing skills base

4.11 The syllabus caption 'a changing skills base' may refer to a number of issues in sustainability. As we saw earlier, it is in part a demographic trend, to do with the challenge of securing equitable access to employment for disenfranchised populations without access to basic skills (such as literacy and numeracy) or emerging in-demand skill sets, given increasingly IT- and knowledge-based employment markets.

Example: Exxon Mobil

Exxon Mobil – previously known as an oil company (with leading brands Esso and Mobil) – has changed its corporate brand to position itself as an innovator in alternative energies.

With the brand tag line 'Taking on the world's toughest energy challenges', a recent corporate advertising campaign stated:

'Oil, gas, coal, biofuels, wind, solar... to fuel the future we need them all.

Meeting future demand will take more than just oil. We'll need to tap every practical source of energy: including natural gas, coal and renewables. But whatever the source, we'll need technology to help us use it as efficiently as possible.'

The Exxon Mobil website (www.exxonmobil.com) contains extensive information about initiatives in the area of 'energy and the environment', aimed at (a) making more energy supplies available and (b) reducing the environmental footprint of energy development.

- ExxonMobil is committed to operating throughout the world in a way that protects the environment and takes into account the economic and social needs of the communities where we operate. Our goal is to achieve excellent environmental performance in each of our businesses to 'Protect Tomorrow. Today.' It is our objective to operate responsibly everywhere we do business by implementing scientifically sound and practical solutions that consider the needs of the communities in which we operate.

- Our commitment to operating in an environmentally sustainable manner is anchored in our environmental policy. Our policy emphasises individual responsibility; fosters appropriate operating practices and training; and requires our facilities to be designed, operated, and managed with the goal of preventing incidents, and controlling emissions and waste to below harmful levels. Not only is this our central commitment to environmental responsibility, but pursuing it year after year has helped ExxonMobil reduce operating costs, improve safety, and reduce impact to the environment.

- Understanding the full lifecycle of our operations is important to operating in an environmentally sustainable manner. There are four key steps, which are integral to the life cycle of our operations. The first step is to assess the surroundings prior to development. The second step is to design and construct facilities to minimise their environmental footprint. The third is to ensure the integrity of the facilities we operate, and the fourth is to restore the environment when operations are concluded. We have numerous examples of incorporating this full lifecycle concept into our projects around the world.

For a fascinating case study of environmental and sustainability policy, see: http://www.exxonmobil.com/corporate/energy_impact.aspx

4.12 However, this also makes it a resource issue. We have noted that businesses will increasingly rely on workers from developing countries (and, domestically, on women, immigrants and lower-income communities). Access to – and adequacy of – education and skills training is a major issue. Businesses may need to help develop learning and skilling, to ensure future labour quality.

4.13 There is also the emerging concept of 'green jobs' or 'sustainability-related hires', for which new skill and knowledge sets are required. Mechanical, electrical and chemical engineers are coming into high demand, as alternative energy and innovation projects proliferate. Finance sector experts with experience in mergers and acquisitions and the structuring of deals are expected to be heavily involved in new sustainable projects. Sustainability managers, officers and consultants will also be required.

4.14   In Australia, a 2008 CSIRO study, titled *Growing the Green Collar Economy* forecast that employment in sectors with high environmental impact (transport, construction, agriculture, manufacturing and mining) would increase substantially. However, it added that the transition to a sustainable economy would require 'a massive mobilisation of skills and training' to equip new workers, and to enable workers already employed in these key sectors to adjust their practices.

4.15   In the absence of a large existing pool of experts in the green field, employers have to think laterally about the skill-sets of prospective employees: developing innovation, initiative and TBL thinking. University graduates now entering sustainability and environmental science courses will form a key part of the future talent pool – but one which will not emerge for some years.

4.16   The skills base is also an issue for resourcing change and support for sustainable procurement. A 2007 survey reported in *Supply Management* indicated that over 80% of purchasers felt that the profession lacked a clear understanding of the term 'sustainable procurement'. The profession has arguably been slow to grasp the agenda and learn new skills – or perhaps to shift priorities, in the face of economic recession.

Overall production/service capacity and capability

4.17   We're not really sure what this syllabus caption refers to, as it doesn't seem to express a trend. However, we can note the following points (and if we get further clarification as to how examiners might interpret this topic, we will post additional material on the CIPS student website).

4.18   Industrialisation has brought a constant increase in the overall production capacity of the world's economies – and this clearly has an effect on the consumption of both non-renewable and renewable resources. As global capacity continues to rise, the rate of consumption is a critical issue.

4.19   Capacity and capability are increasingly globalised. Globalisation may be defined as 'the increasing integration of internationally dispersed economic activity' (Boddy). This integration may involve the globalisation of markets, economies and/or production. High domestic labour costs have, in particular, stimulated the growth of off-shoring by labour-intensive businesses: corporations in developed countries outsource the production of finished goods and components, and the delivery of services, to countries such as Taiwan, China, South Korea, Singapore, Sri Lanka and India. The media is now full of examples of companies offshoring their administrative work and telephone enquires (eg major banks) and product assembly (eg Hitachi, Compaq, Mattel).

4.20   Some of the sustainability implications of this are highlighted in the appendix to this chapter. Some agencies argue that globalisation supports sustainable development: prompting investment in infrastructure and skilling in developing economies; encouraging participation in economic activity and the reduction of poverty; promoting economic integration and international peace; and so on. Opponents argue that globalised capacity/capability encourages the exploitation of low-cost labour; disempowers small and local suppliers; 'exports' pollution and environmental degradation; erodes local cultures; and creates unemployment in the domestic labour market.

4.21　The onus will therefore be on trans-national corporations to conduct global sourcing and outsourcing in a responsible and sustainable manner. Which leads us to our next topic: corporate social responsibility.

5　*Corporate social responsibility (CSR)*

5.1　Society as a whole may have low direct influence on the policies and activities of an organisation. However, society's interests are organised, focused and represented in various ways: by government policy, legislation and regulation; by 'consumerism' or the consumer rights movement; by pressure and interest groups seeking to exert influence on behalf of particular constituencies or on particular issues; and by the fact that wider society is part of the environment within which the organisation operates – and within which it competes for labour, suppliers, customers, support and other key resources.

5.2　The term 'corporate social responsibility' is used to describe a wide range of obligations that an organisation may feel it has towards its secondary stakeholders, or the society in which it operates. One CIPS examiner has written that: 'CSR means the commitment to systematic consideration of the environmental, social and cultural aspects of an organisation's operations. This includes the key issues of sustainability, human rights, labour and community relations, and supplier and customer relations beyond legal obligations. The objective [is] to create long-term business value and contribute to improving the social conditions of the people affected by our operations.'

5.3　The term 'corporate social responsibility' is often used interchangeably with 'sustainability' (although sustainability adds a distinctive focus on the wellbeing of future generations), and covers the same broad range of economic, social and environmental issues. CIPS recognises ten key CSR issues, which are most relevant to supply chains: environmental responsibility, human rights, equal opportunities, diversity, corporate governance, sustainability, impact on society, ethics and ethical trading, biodiversity, and community involvement.

5.4　We discuss these issues (as 'sustainability' issues) throughout this text. The key point about CSR, in this context, is that for many corporations, it has already begun to establish a cultural and strategic platform for the development of sustainable procurement. Sustainable procurement policies will often be prompted by, and aligned with, corporate-level CSR policies (as we will see in Chapter 6).

5.5　The CIPS Practice Guide on CSR states that: 'It is an increasingly popular view that it is no longer acceptable that an organisation continues to operate in isolation without considerations of its environment and its stakeholders.' As we saw in Chapter 1, there is increasing demand from Non Government Organisations, stakeholder activists and consumers for organisations to be accountable for their impacts on their stakeholders. There has also been a broad recognition by organisations that such accountability is not only increasingly required to secure their legitimacy and 'licence to operate', but that it can be turned to the positive benefit of the organisation in many ways. (See Table 1.3, for example.)

5.6　The CIPS Guide states that: 'The [procurement professional] has a responsibility to at least be aware, if not have a thorough understanding, of CSR issues in purchasing and supply management, and to endeavour to ensure that P & SM practice does not have a negative social impact on all stakeholders concerned, and that any issues are addressed in a positive manner... CIPS encourages P & SM professionals to consider the long-term implications of their actions and to question objectives that may unintentionally have negative socio-economic consequences.'

Example: IKEA Group

Household goods and furnishings retailer IKEA expresses the idea of sustainability succinctly in its core responsibility statement: 'Low prices are the cornerstone of the IKEA vision and our business idea – but not at any price. The IKEA vision is to create a better everyday life for the many people – our customers, co-workers and the people who produce our products. Consequently, low prices at IKEA must not be achieved at the expense of people or the environment. That is a condition for doing good business.'

The group's corporate social responsibility statement (People and the Environment) covers commitments to:

- Product safety (for the environment and human health)

- Economy in the use of resources (minimising use of materials, designing for disassembly)

- Sourcing wood from sustainably managed forests, and cotton from sustainable sources; and partnering with the World Wildlife Fund in advocacy and supplier support for sustainable management

- Serving and selling certified Fair Trade coffee

- Using long-term supplier relationships and supplier development programmes to ensure that products are 'manufactured under acceptable working conditions by suppliers who take responsibility for the environment'

- A code of conduct (The IKEA Way on purchasing home furnishing products: IWAY) which specifies the minimum requirements placed on suppliers and describes what they can expect in return. IWAY requirements include: compliance with national legislation; no forced or child labour; no discrimination; payment of at least the minimum wage and compensation for overtime; a safe and healthy working environment; and responsibility for waste, emissions and the handling of chemicals.

- The IKEA Social Initiative, partnering with Unicef and Save the Children to support children in developing countries (including the abolition of child labour)

- Working actively to reduce carbon emissions from its operations: optimising packaging solutions; transporting goods with the least possible environmental impact; encouraging more customers and co-workers to leave their cars at home; cutting electricity consumption and reducing reliance on fossil fuels; partnering with WWF to create a casebook of best practice for suppliers

This is interesting and accessible reading – and the website also contains practical lists of continuous incremental improvements ('The never ending list') and other useful resources. See: http://www.ikea.com/ms/en_GB/about_ikea/our_responsibility/index.html.

5.7 From a CIPS perspective, CSR implicitly requires sustainable procurement. 'In the midst of the ongoing debate on how best to achieve good social and environmental performance, supply chains are becoming a defining factor. Few could have missed the furore that has erupted over unethical practices within global supply chains, such as child labour and exploitation of migrant workers, for example. However, while the supply chain does bring risks, it also brings opportunities: for example, organisations are working with suppliers to identify new energy sources, new power sources for vehicles and an increasing emphasis on minimal environmental footprints. These changes shake out markets and create opportunities in the supply chain.'

5.8 For our present purposes, therefore, it is sufficient to note that CSR is a significant driver and enabler of sustainable procurement policies and initiatives in the marketplace as a whole – and within a given organisation.

6 *Sustainable procurement as a qualifier for purchasing decisions*

6.1 The Scottish website Canny Buyer (www.cannybuyer.com) defines sustainable procurement as 'a process that embraces all the steps that could be taken by organisations to ensure that the acquisition of goods and services has as little adverse impact as possible (and as great a beneficial impact) on people and the environment'.

6.2 Throughout this text, we will discuss ways in which sustainability considerations and criteria can be built into purchasing decisions.

- Chapters 6 to 8 explore the ways in which sustainability values, targets and measures can be developed and implemented in an organisation, as part of a drive towards organisation-wide CSR or sustainability objectives.

- Chapter 9 suggests how sustainability considerations can be incorporated into purchase specifications.

- Chapter 10 traces the influence of sustainability issues on each stage of the sourcing cycle.

- Chapter 12 examines the implications of sustainability objectives for contract and relationship management, and supplier development.

6.3 The key point to recognise here, in the context of sustainability 'trends', is that – driven in part by the CIPS agenda on CSR, discussed earlier – sustainability is increasingly being embedded in procurement policy and practice at every stage. As it becomes a policy priority for an organisation, it will increasingly be a 'qualifier' for purchasing decisions: that is, a factor to be taken into account in making those decisions, and a criterion by which their success will be measured. In other words, sustainability is becoming a critical success factor for procurement.

Example: The London Borough of Camden

In 2005, the London Borough of Camden employed the UK's first sustainable procurement manager. Policy examples emerging from this initiative include:

- Environmental sustainability: increasing the use of environmental products and saving energy (eg recycled paper, recycled aggregate for highway maintenance)

- Social sustainability: reworking agency staff contracts so the workforce reflects diversity in the borough's population; encouraging the main supplier to use local and small businesses as second-tier vendors; supporting the use of local labour, the long-term unemployed and under-represented groups; re-contracting school dinner provision to meet goals for healthy, locally-produced and organic meals for pupils.

Chapter summary

- Organisations in all sectors are increasingly required to address trends in sustainability. The appendix to this chapter contains a large number of examples.

- Sustainability has been an important driver of innovation, leading to the creation of products, processes, services and new markets.

- In some cases, organisations have stimulated innovation by forward commitment to products not yet commercially available.

- Sustainable procurement is influenced by trends in population size, population distribution, and wealth distribution, among many other demographic factors.

- Resource depletion is a global problem. One element in a solution may be simply to reduce consumption. Another possibility is to develop alternatives to non-renewable fuel sources.

- The term 'corporate social responsibility' is used to describe a wide range of obligations that an organisation feels it has towards its secondary stakeholders. A commitment to sustainability is often seen as one element in a CSR orientation.

- Sustainability should be regarded as an important criterion in purchasing decisions.

Self-test questions

Numbers in brackets refer to the paragraphs above where your answers can be checked.

1   List some of the main trends in modern thinking on sustainability. (1.2 and appendix)

2   Describe Schumpeter's analysis of the stages in technology adoption. (2.2)

3   List sources of impetus for investment in innovation relating to sustainability. (2.7)

4   Give examples of forward commitment procurement (FCP). (Table 2.1)

5   Describe the implications for sustainable procurement of modern demographic trends. (3.7)

6   Resource depletion can be delayed by reducing consumption. List measures that might be adopted to achieve this. (4.3)

7   Give examples of alternatives to non-renewable energy sources. (4.8)

8   What is meant by corporate social responsibility? (5.2)

Further reading

From your 'Essential Reading' list, you might look at Blackburn (*The Sustainability Handbook*):

- Appendix 1: Summary of Sustainability Trends – to follow up on our brief survey in the appendix to this chapter.

Appendix: Overview of sustainability trends

Growth in global business competition	Over the last three decades, the share of total world output by transnational corporations has doubled. Large corporations are under pressure to deliver global expansion, profitability and brand strength – at the expense of small local businesses.
Opposition to globalisation	For critics and protestors, globalisation is a social justice issue: eroding local cultures and economies, degrading the environment, supporting over-consumption and giving excessive power to corporations. Businesses committed to global production and marketing must increasingly be prepared to justify the sustainability of their policies and practices.
Speed of communications; the 'digital divide'	The e-revolution has supported fast, efficient, knowledge-based business in countries with high income and developed infrastructure – but only 10% of the world's citizens have access to the internet: more than half have never used a phone. There is a need for a viable long-term business strategy to benefit disadvantaged markets.
Widening prosperity gap	The rich are getting richer; the poor, poorer. While poverty levels are improving worldwide (led by gains in China, India, Indonesia and Pakistan), they are projected to worsen in other parts of South Asia and sub-Saharan Africa. Developing meaningful opportunities for economic improvement (in the face of national debt, lack of infrastructure and skills, rapid population growth, political instability and trade restrictions) is a key issue.
Population growth; mortality rates	UN projections suggest that global population will rise by 50% by mid-century, creating pressure on the environment. This will also be an ageing population, due to increased life expectancy, creating pressure on health and welfare systems. Meanwhile, however, in some regions, high child and maternal death rates are still a concern.
Increased immigration, lower fertility in industrialised nations	A significant and growing proportion of the population growth in high-income countries is due to immigration: fertility rates are now below the replacement rate of 2.1 children per woman in Europe and the US. This may help reduce resource consumption – but also creates a shrinking domestic labour pool and product markets, and the need to attract employees and customers from developing regions.
Hunger and malnutrition	The number of undernourished people (consuming less than 1900 calories per day) is falling in industrialised countries, but the problem remains severe in southern Asia and sub-Saharan Africa.
Child and forced labour	Over 12 million people work as slaves or in some form of forced labour: women and girls make up more than half of those subject to economic exploitation. An estimated 250 million children aged 5–14 work in the developing world (many in agricultural harvesting and garment sweatshops).
Education needs for the disenfranchised	Given that business will increasingly rely on workers from developing countries (and, domestically, on women, immigrants and lower-income communities), access to – and adequacy of – education and skills training is a major issue. Businesses may need to help develop learning and skilling, to ensure future labour quality.
Urbanisation	Population growth in low-income countries will increasingly be in urban areas (and slums) – creating pollution and a range of social ills. Who will bear the costs, and solve the problems, of the urban population boom?

Over-consumption of resources	Major industrialised countries consume an inequitable proportion of the world's natural resources. Meanwhile, a growing population consumes resources at ever-increasing rates – and many of these resources are non-renewable (or not renewable at the current rate of consumption). 'To achieve sustainability of resources, the world must bring back into balance its consumption, technological development, resource re-use and recycling, and population growth.' (Blackburn)
Fossil fuel depletion	Protecting ongoing resource availability is a key priority for non-renewable resources in high demand, such as fossil fuels: oil, natural gas and coal. Companies will be expected to support the development and deployment of new energy technologies and renewable sources (eg nuclear power, hydropower, solar systems and biomass energy).
Climate change	There is broad (though debated) scientific consensus that the emission of carbon dioxide and other heat-trapping or 'greenhouse' gases, from the use of fossil fuels (among other processes initiated or supported by human activity), influences global average temperatures and climate patterns, with potentially devastating future consequences. There is increasing pressure on government and business to reduce GHG emissions and engage in proactive efforts to stabilise GHG concentrations (eg by investing in reforestation and renewable energy projects). As a signatory of the Kyoto Protocol, the UK is committed to national emission reduction targets.
Deforestation	Agricultural development, and harvesting for forestry products (wood, paper etc), has resulted in massive depletion of the world's forests. This diminishes the absorption of carbon emissions, exacerbating climate change – and also contributes to loss of habitat, species extinction, soil erosion, flooding and other damaging effects. There is an urgent need to promote Sustainable Forestry Practices – particularly in developing economies.
Threats to biodiversity	Deforestation and population growth (habitat destruction), pollution, climate change and introduced species have accelerated species extinction. Apart from the ethical issues, businesses may be deprived of valuable resources and research subjects (eg in areas such as pharmaceuticals).
Freshwater depletion; water contamination	Groundwater depletion and contamination are creating water shortages for agriculture, industry and human consumption: over 40% of the world's population currently live in 'water-stressed' areas. Water supply and management are key areas of business risk and opportunity – especially for large industrial users of water, such as beverages, textiles and agriculture.
Spread of hazardous pollutants	Contamination of soil, water, air and food stocks continues to raise health scares – despite legislation on the production, use, emission and disposal of POPs (persistent organic pollutants such as DDT and other pesticides), mercury and other substances. 'Companies need to determine if they generate or emit hazardous chemicals from their operations, and if so, properly handle, control and ultimately dispose of them in ways that won't harm people or the environment.'
Traditional air pollutants	National and international regulations have helped reduce and stabilise air contaminants such as sulphur dioxide (from power plants), nitrogen dioxide (from auto emissions), ground-level ozone (smog), carbon monoxide, lead and soot (in dust or smoke). However, air pollution remains a problem in rapidly developing countries such as China.
Ozone depletion	Emissions of ozone-depleting CFCs (chlorofluorocarbons) have reduced dramatically following the Montreal Protocol, banning their production and use, but ozone-depleting substances are still leaking into the atmosphere from equipment (eg refrigerators and air conditioners) manufactured before the agreement – and from companies using CFCs under treaty exemptions, and countries not bound by the treaty.

Low credibility of corporations	Surveys indicate that corporations are poorly rated for their credibility, trustworthiness on the environment, honesty in consumer and employee relations, and responsible use of power. 'The public really doesn't trust you to do the right thing. To overcome that bias, you must consistently demonstrate competent, trustworthy, caring behaviour with a wide range of stakeholders. You must be open and honest in your communications. You must align yourself with academics, NGOs and others who are trusted. And... you must never forget that a single corporate scandal can destroy the trust you have earned.' (Blackburn)
Extended producer responsibility (EPR) or product stewardship	EU regulators have embraced the concept of EPR: a manufacturer's responsibility for products does not end with delivery, but extends until ultimate disposal of materials after use. This implies a producer obligation to: minimise adverse effects; assume responsibility for take-back; provide hazard information; and assume legal liability for harm resulting from the proper use of the product, as well as from product defects.
Green products	There is a growing trend towards green products: 'variations of regular products that better address environmental or social concerns'. Successful examples include organic foods, microcredit financial institutions, energy-efficient equipment and recycled paper products. Although some consumers are willing to pay a premium for sustainable products, green products generally have to be competitive on performance, convenience and price. Meanwhile, products causing green concern (such as genetically modified crops) may be difficult to promote – or actively boycotted
Green marketing/labelling	There has been a rise in sustainability or green marketing, both in direct promotion of products, and in cause-related marketing (associating the brand with a social or environmental cause, through donation, endorsement or partnership). Consumers, pressure groups and governments have increasingly pressed for more consistent, credible and effective sustainability information about products and services.
Green product certification	Eco-labelling standards and certifying bodies geared to specific product areas have been increasingly popular. There is a range of certification programmes for forestry products, green buildings, energy-efficient equipment, coffee and other produce, and so on.
Rise in socially responsible investing (SRI)	SRI includes: screened investments (publicly traded securities selected for one or more ethical, social or environmental factors); community investing and social venture capital (investing in sustainability-oriented projects); and investor advocacy (highlighting sustainability issues in the financial media and shareholder meetings). 'Sustainability is not simply an issue of conscience: given the financial problems we have seen flow from the ethical mis-steps of companies, it's an issue of investment risk.' (Blackburn)
Investor concerns about corporate governance	Corporate governance involves the rules, policies and practices under which the company is managed by its board of directors. Attention to governance issues, following high-profile corporate scandals and collapses, has resulted in legislation (eg the Sarbanes-Oxley Act in the US), and codes of practice (eg the UK Stock Exchange Combined Code). Governance is increasingly seen as an issue of social and economic sustainability.
Increased demands for transparency, public reporting	There has been increasing pressure from stakeholders for corporations to provide clear, open and credible information about their sustainability policies, practices and performance. In some countries, this is now embodied in corporate financial reporting laws. The Global Reporting Initiative (GRI) is a coalition of advocates for transparency, which offers guidelines on sustainability reporting.

Growing power of NGOs	There has been an explosive increase in the number of active non-governmental organisations (NGOs): pressure and interest groups which use a wide variety of promotional, educational and lobbying techniques to influence public opinion, government policy and corporate practices. Business organisations may need to develop defensive public relations platforms to counter NGO influence – or develop proactive partnerships to harness NGO expertise and credibility for sustainability initiatives.
Increasing global terrorism	Terrorist organisations use violence, generally perpetrated against civilian targets, in their pursuit of political aims. Some of those aims may be seen as legitimate 'sustainability' issues of social equity or access to resources and respect. However, the means used are intentionally inhumane, inequitable (in so far as one believes in the innocence of civilian victims) and socially and economically destabilising – and therefore unsustainable.

CHAPTER 3

External Influences on Sustainable Procurement

Learning objectives and indicative content

1.3 Evaluate the external factors influencing sustainable procurement and apply the PESTLE model in the context of different organisations and sectors, including the public, private, and third sectors and their tiers.

- International and local influences on sustainable procurement

    - Political (eg government policies, targets and incentives – workforce structure, waste management, conservation and protection of natural resources, land use, water management, Local Government Act 2000, Local Agenda 21, Special Development Areas)

    - Economic (eg basic principles of supply and demand, costs, exchange rates, employment market, availability of materials and energy/fuels)

    - Social/ethical (eg availability of skills, working conditions and practices, corruption, corporate citizenship, CIPS ethical code, societal values, ethical farming, fair trade)

    - Technological (eg innovation, new technologies, materials and processes)

    - Legislative (eg environmental laws, workforce legislation)

    - Environmental (eg renewable vs non-renewable energy, waste management and reduction – landfill capacity, packaging, carbon footprint reduction, global climate change – availability of agricultural land, water, greenhouse gas/CO_2 emissions, pollution)

  - External stakeholder pressure and attitudes (eg BSE, bird flu, use of artificial colours and flavours, GM crops, animal testing)

  - Standards (eg labelling ISO 14023/25, environmental management systems ISO 14001, social accountability SA 8000)

Chapter headings

1   The PESTLE model

2   Political influences

3   Economic influences

4   Social/ethical influences

5   Technological influences

6   Legislative influences

7   Environmental influences

8   External stakeholders

9   Standards

Introduction

The syllabus at this point focuses on external factors (and in the following learning objective, internal factors) 'influencing sustainable procurement'. This is rather a vague phrase, which may include: drivers for (and constraints on) sustainable procurement; factors shaping sustainable procurement policy and practice (that is, 'process' factors in whether and what kind of sustainable procurement is adopted by an organisation); or issues in sustainable procurement (that is, 'content' factors dictating what areas of social and environmental concern are the focus of an organisation's sustainability efforts).

In this chapter, we give a broad survey of both process and content factors in the external environment, following the examples set out in the syllabus indicative content. The main value of this will be to introduce analytical tools such as the PESTLE model and stakeholder analysis, which you can apply to specific organisations or sectors, as required, in the exam.

You might also include the triple bottom line (TBL) among these tools of analysis, as it is included at this point in the syllabus. However, it sits oddly here: although it can be seen as a way of classifying external factors – as economic, social and environmental – it is more properly considered an internal influence on sustainable procurement, as a tool of organisational performance measurement. In any case, we have already discussed it as part of our overview of the emergence of the sustainability concept, in Chapter 1: you should re-cap that material if you need to.

Having looked at external factors in this chapter, we will give the same kind of analysis of internal factors in Chapter 4. In Chapter 5, we will look specifically at those factors (both internal and external) that constitute key drivers for sustainable procurement. The issue of constraints and challenges to sustainable procurement are reserved for the final section of the syllabus, although we will introduce some of them in passing.

1   The PESTLE model

The external environment

1.1   As you should be aware from your earlier studies, the open systems model of organisations emphasises the importance of taking the external environment into account. Firstly, because an organisation depends on its environment as the source of its inputs; the market for its outputs; and a key source of feedback information to measure and adjust its performance. And secondly, because an organisation also impacts on its environment, in the process of taking in inputs and creating outputs (both products, such as goods and services, and 'by products' such as waste, pollution or local employment).

1.2   The external environment will therefore exert a strong influence on an organisation's strategy, activity and performance (including sustainable procurement) in various ways.

- It presents threats (such as restrictive legislation, competitor initiatives, technology obsolescence or boycotts by pressure groups, say) and opportunities (such as growth in demand for green products and services, technological improvements or more skilled workers entering the labour pool). These will be key factors in the formation of sustainable procurement strategies and plans.

- It is the source of resources needed by the organisation (labour, materials and supplies, plant and machinery, energy, finance, information and so on). External factors determine to what extent these resources are, or are not, available in the right quantity, at the right time and at the right price.

- It contains stakeholders who may seek, or have the right, to influence the activities of the organisation. An organisation must comply with laws and regulations on sustainability, for example, in order to avoid legal and financial penalties, but it may also have to consider the demands of employees, suppliers and customers – or bow to media and public opinion which might jeopardise its market or reputation.

1.3 So procurement professionals, among other managers, must analyse and understand the environmental factors affecting their organisation. But that's only the beginning, because those factors are also constantly changing – and change in the environment often creates a need (or opportunity) for change in an organisation's plans and activities. Organisations will need to assess the degree of uncertainty in their environments, and identify trends or directions of change, in order to measure and manage threats and opportunities in relation to sustainability.

1.4 In addition, you should be aware of the potential for one-off 'catastrophic' events to pose corporate responsibility challenges: eg influenza epidemics, natural disasters (such as tsunami or earthquake), or the discovery of harmful effects of products (such as the emergence of BSE). What might be the economic, social and environmental impacts of such events? How might the risk of their happening be minimised or managed? What might be an ethical or responsible response to them, if they do happen? Get used to asking such questions of just about any headline you see in the quality press. What's going on here? How might this be relevant to the sustainability obligations of organisations of different types?

The PESTLE model

1.5 There are two basic tools available for classifying external factors and influences on sustainable procurement.

- The triple bottom line (TBL, 3BL or Profit People Planet) model, which uses a three-dimensional classification into economic, environmental and social factors. This is often used as the general basis for talking about sustainability issues, and was discussed in Chapter 1.
- The PESTLE model: a popular tool of environmental analysis, which specifies a number of categories under which the main external factors impacting on organisations can be analysed. These factors are: Political, Economic, Socio-cultural (including ethical), Technological, Legal and Environmental.

1.6 We will look at each of the PESTLE categories in turn, to suggest the kind of factors you might consider when applying the model in the context of specific organisations and sectors. However, a broad example of the kind of analysis that can be conducted, to support sustainable procurement planning and decision-making, is shown in Table 1.1. Obviously, more specific factors or changes would raise more specific questions.

1.7 The PESTLE model is also used to highlight external factors for further analysis, assessment and measurement, using tools such as SWOT analysis (strengths, weaknesses, opportunities and threats). We will discuss some of these applications in Chapter 13.

1.8 One final point about using the PESTLE or TBL models in exams: when you read or use the phrase 'environmental factors', you need to be clear whether it refers specifically to the natural environment or 'green' factors (in the sense in which people are concerned about 'the environment') – or whether it is referring to the business or purchasing environment as a whole.

Table 1.1 *PESTLE analysis*

Factor	Description	Analysis
Political	Government influence on your industry/sector	What are the likely implications of a change in government environmental, social or sustainability policy?
Economic	Growth trends; patterns of employment, income, interest/exchange/tax rates etc.	How might changes affect future demand for products/services, or future supply and cost of resources/labour? How can resource viability and equitable access to economic benefits be protected or enhanced?
Socio-cultural	Changing composition, attitudes, values, consumption patterns and education of the population	How might demographic and cultural trends affect the needs and expectations of customers, suppliers and other stakeholders in regard to products, services and corporate conduct? How might they affect skill availability?
Technological	Changing tools for design/manufacturing, information and communications etc.	Are there opportunities for more sustainable processes, products and services – and/or risks of unsustainable exploitation? Are competitors adopting sustainable offerings more quickly?
Legal	Law and regulation on business, employment, information etc.	How will the organisation need to adapt its policies and practices in order to comply with (or pre-empt) forthcoming measures?
Environmental	Resource depletion, needs for pollution/waste/impact management, carbon footprint issues, potential for 'green' products and processes	Which factors may cause supply or logistical problems, compliance issues, market pressure or risk to reputation? What opportunities are there in 'green' design, production and marketing?

2 *Political influences*

General political influences

2.1   Politics is, broadly, a term for the processes through which power and influence are applied to handle conflicts of interest between stakeholders – including processes, at the level of the State, for agenda-setting and policy-shaping, democratic decision-making, the formulation of law and regulation and so on.

2.2   Political factors affect businesses in a variety of ways.

- Local government authorities formulate policies and bye-laws which affect local infrastructure, land/building use and service delivery.

- At a national level, the political process includes legislation (which directly affects business activity) and the economic policy of governments (which influences labour availability, consumer spending and other important factors of business).

- The government controls much of the economy, as the nation's largest supplier, employer, customer and investor: policy shifts can transform markets.

- As businesses increasingly trade in international markets, the politics of other nations (such as government policy or political instability in an overseas supplier's or subcontractor's country) also create opportunities and risks.

- Political influences cross national boundaries: eg through international institutions such as the European Union (whose directives affect all member countries) and the World Trade Organisation.

- Political influence, in the wider sense, may be applied to organisations by pressure and interest groups, such as Greenpeace, Amnesty International or trade unions.

- Businesses are influenced by political factors – but they also exert some influence over them (or seek to do so): by lobbying government decision makers, making financial donations to political parties, influencing public opinion and so on.

2.3 Potential political influences on sustainable procurement therefore include factors such as the following.

- Sustainability policies and targets formulated by local and national governments and wider political bodies such as the EU. In addition to broad 'sustainability' and 'sustainable procurement' strategies and targets, there are specific policy measures in areas such as conservation, waste management, pollution and emissions, workforce diversity, equal opportunity and human rights.

- Sustainability agendas and commitments formulated under international agreements, such as the Kyoto Protocol on climate change (a political process, because of the element of international debate and consensus-seeking)

- State support and incentives for sustainable development: eg regional development grants; assistance offered to small firms; subsidies or tax incentives for sustainability initiatives and projects; 'polluter pays' taxes and emissions trading ('carbon offsetting') schemes

- The strength or weakness of trade unions, and their agenda to promote worker rights and broader social aims

- The influence and focus of sustainability-oriented lobbying groups, pressure and interest groups (NGOs), media and public opinion on government policy

- Problems of instability, authoritarianism, corruption and industrial exploitation in some governing regimes, potentially creating ethical, social and environmental issues in international supply markets.

2.4 We will briefly consider the areas of government policy, targets and incentives specifically mentioned by the syllabus – although you may be able to think of others, applicable to your own areas of interest.

Workforce structure

2.5 The UK and EU, among other developed economies, are progressively setting targets for workforce diversity. In order to promote equality of opportunity, the aim is for workforces (and by extension, supply chains) broadly to reflect the diversity of the overall population, in terms of sex; race and ethnicity; (dis)ability; and age.

2.6 We might also note that government policy in other areas – such as education and skills-training, immigration or retirement ages – impacts on the structure of the workforce.

Waste management

2.7 The *Environmental Protection Act 1990* defines waste as any substance which constitutes a scrap material, an effluent or other unwanted surplus arising from the application of any process; any substance or article which requires to be disposed of which has been broken, worn out, contaminated or otherwise spoiled; and anything which is discarded or 'otherwise dealt with as if it were waste'.

2.8 Each year in the UK, households, commerce and industry together generate about 100 million tonnes of waste, most of which currently ends up in landfill. Even biodegradable waste (previously regarded as desirable) generates methane, a powerful greenhouse gas and potential contributor to climate change.

2.9 It is recognised by the EU and member governments that the management of waste is a crucial element of environmental sustainability, and there is tight regulation on the management, movement and disposal of waste, particularly in areas of significant health, safety and environmental risk: hazardous waste, dangerous goods, waste electronic and electrical goods and so on. Ongoing targets have also been set for waste and landfill reduction, and the take-up of re-use and recycling programmes.

Conservation and protection of natural resources

2.10 Natural resources include air, soil, fresh water, ecosystems (such as wetlands, rainforests and marine environments) and living resources such as biodiversity, forests and fisheries. They also include public access – embracing issues such as cultural landscapes, rights of way and heritage architecture and design.

2.11 Government policy and activist pressure alike recognise that human and environmental health and wellbeing are dependent on the quality of our air, water, soils and biological resources. Natural and built environments are often bound up with valued identity and culture. And, ultimately, economic activity is directly or indirectly reliant on functioning ecosystems.

2.12 Political pressure and government policy may be applied in areas such as the following.

- Development approvals, zoning and land use restrictions (administered by local authorities), to prevent over-development of areas of natural value

- The designation and preservation of 'green belts' and urban wildlife/habitat corridors within urban and developed areas (local); cultural heritage sites, National Parks and Sites of Special Scientific Interest (national); Special Areas of Conservation and Special Protection Areas (EU); and World Heritage Areas (international)

- Activity by a wide range of NGOs (such as the National Trust, the Woodlands Trust or the Wetlands Conservation Society) to promote the preservation of cultural and natural heritage. NGOs are also increasingly seeking to purchase and manage land of unique value, such as rainforest, wetland and old-growth forest, as the only way to preserve them, while offering existing owners (particularly in poorer countries) an equitable share of their economic value.

- The protection and management of biodiversity, habitats and endangered species. This may involve in situ conservation measures such as conservation of habitats and species where they naturally occur: eg under the UK's national Habitat Action Plans; and international agreements such as the moratorium on whaling (still frequently in the news, with strong governmental and pressure group opposition to continuing activity by Japanese whaling fleets). It also involves the ex situ conservation of species, eg in zoos, botanical gardens and seed banks. The issue of biodiversity may seem comparatively remote from procurement, but it is a strong political issue (and one of the ten principles of CSR promoted by CIPS). In addition to the ethical aim of avoiding human-accelerated species extinction, the conservation of biodiversity secures valuable natural resources for future generations, and protects the viability of important eco-system functions.

- Requirements for corporations to deliver environmental impact statements as part of development proposals

- Equitably balancing considerations such as biodiversity and conservation with the legitimate needs of poor societies to reap livelihoods and economic value from land and other natural resources.

Special Areas of Conservation

2.13 The EU Habitats Directive (1992) requires member states to create a network of protected wildlife areas, known as Natura 2000, across the European Union. The network consists of Special Areas of Conservation (SACs) and Special Protection Areas (SPAs), and is part of a range of measures aimed at conserving important or threatened habitats and species. Such an integrated approach allows for the more effective sharing of information, and more effective biodiversity management.

2.14 SACs and SPAs have an established and protected status, whereby owners or occupiers must obtain permission before carrying out any potentially damaging environmental operations. (Many SACs in England are also nationally designated Sites of Special Scientific Interest.)

Land use

2.15 Land use implies the transformation of natural environments into environments that meet human needs: fields, pastures, housing, recreational/commercial/industrial applications and so on. Significant effects of land use include deforestation, soil erosion, soil degradation, salination and desertification. Changes to land use (including clearing land for agriculture, increased irrigation, and de- or re-forestation) also contribute to climate change, according to a recent NASA report.

2.16 Land use concerns are likely to continue to grow in the face of continuing population growth. According to a report by the United Nations Food and Agriculture Organisation, land degradation has been increased where there has been an absence of land use planning or its orderly execution. Locally and nationally applied land use policies are therefore a key strand of sustainability.

Water management

2.17 Water is becoming increasingly scarce on a global scale. Drought, salination, contamination, population growth and increasing consumer, agricultural and industrial water consumption are all contributing factors. A recent report by the International Water Management Institute (IWMI) suggests that one third of the world population faces some form of water scarcity, whether physical (when resources cannot meet demand) or economic (poor infrastructure and unequal distribution, due to lack of investment).

2.18 The UK government recently launched a new water strategy for England: Future Water. The framework for water management includes: sustainable delivery of secure water supplies; an improved and protected water environment; fair, affordable and cost-reflective water charges; reduced water sector greenhouse gas emissions; and more sustainable and effective management of surface water.

Local Agenda 21

2.19 The Rio Earth Summit (the 1992 UN Conference on Environment and Development) expanded on the Brundtland Commission's proposals under the name 'Local Agenda 21', recognising the need to work out local agendas for sustainable living into the 21st century. Signatory nations were urged to develop a Local Agenda 21 strategy driven by the community (rather than by central or local government): governments, NGOs industry and the general public are all encouraged to become involved. Signatories are monitored by the International

Commission on Sustainable Development, and encouraged to promote Agenda 21 at local and regional levels.

Local Government Act 2000

2.20 The UK Local Government Act 2000 enacted a number of provisions relevant to sustainability, including the following.

- A duty for local authorities to develop a comprehensive 'community' strategy for promoting wellbeing, including environmental wellbeing
- Broad powers for local authorities to promote the economic, social and environmental wellbeing of their communities, including powers to establish local strategic partnerships
- A new ethical framework for council members.

2.21 Meanwhile, it is worth noting that the economic sustainability of public sector procurement has also become a policy priority, driven by central government efficiency guidelines (arising from the Gershon Review) and financial imperatives (the need to cut costs in order to improve stakeholder value). Many councils are pooling their procurement on a regional or category basis, for example, in order to gain economies of scale through consolidated buying. Others are developing or joining shared electronic procurement systems (such as e-Procurement Scotland).

Example: Liverpool City Council

Liverpool City Council's *Community Strategy* is summarised as follows.

Liverpool 2024: Vision, Drivers & Outcomes

Competitiveness:

1   Increased wealth creation, jobs and businesses, particularly in the knowledge economy

2.   A larger, more skilled workforce through improved skills and qualifications

Connectivity:

3.   Connecting Liverpool as an international gateway for goods, people and information

4 .   Improving public transport, reducing congestions and enhancing pedestrian movement

Distinctive sense of place:

5 .   Cultural, tourist, business and retail destination of choice

6.   Improved housing standards, choice and availability

Thriving neighbourhoods

7 .   A cleaner, greener environment, delivered by efficient, effective and locally responsive services

8 .   Reduced crime, fear of crime, disorder, anti-social behaviour and substance misuse

9 .   Cohesive, open communities that value diversity

Health and wellbeing:

10.   Improved health and wellbeing, and reduced health inequalities

11.   Improved opportunities for independent living and for children and families to thrive

12.   Shared action to address climate change and environmental sustainability.

---

3   *Economic influences*

General economic influences

3.1   The macro-economic environment embraces the general level of activity and growth in the economic system; the market mechanism of supply and demand (and its effect on the viability and price of products and services); and the effect of economic 'boom and bust' cycles. These factors may pose issues of economic performance and sustainability (especially for sustainable products and services), as well as social impacts (eg on local and national employment and income levels) and environmental impacts (eg on resource consumption and waste products).

3.2   This 'big picture' is related to more detailed economic factors such as a government's fiscal (tax) and monetary (money supply) policy; interest and foreign exchange rates; inflation; consumer spending; labour costs and unemployment levels; international trade agreements; and the fluctuating availability and price of materials, commodities, energy resources; and so on.

3.3   These factors may influence sustainable procurement in various ways.

- The amount of economic activity determines the wealth of a nation, which influences the amount of disposable income – which in turn influences the demand for 'discretionary' (including sustainable) goods and services, the prices at which they can be sold, and therefore whether or not they are sufficiently profitable to attract producers. In times of recession, there may be low demand for sustainability if it involves extra cost. On the other hand, economic growth results in higher consumption and waste, which impact on overall social and environmental sustainability.

- Employment and unemployment levels may affect the availability of labour and labour costs, as well as disposable incomes and demand. High long-term unemployment is economically and socially unsustainable for a number of reasons. Unemployed workers do not produce anything, reducing national income. They may also lose their skills over time, creating a loss of productive capacity, and incurring costs of retraining. Rising unemployment is costly for governments because it means less tax coming in – and more benefits going out. And, of course, there are personal and social costs: personal hardship and its knock-on effects in increased crime and family breakdown.

- Rates of inflation affect prices, and therefore supply costs. They may also make imports relatively expensive or inexpensive, altering a firm's sourcing strategy in regard to international/local sourcing.

- The overall rate of taxation affects the level of demand in an economy (less tax means more disposable income). The taxation of specific products (such as alcohol and tobacco) may be used to drive sustainable consumption – in the same way that tax incentives and penalties may influence firms' sustainability policies (eg 'polluter pays' taxes).

- Exchange rate fluctuations create risk in international sourcing, potentially making foreign currency purchases (imports) more expensive, again influencing sustainability decisions about local/international sourcing, fair prices for overseas suppliers and so on.

- Macro-economic factors (as well as availability) contribute to fluctuating availability and prices in commodity, resource and other supply markets.

3.4   Organisations also operate within the more immediate economic environment of a business sector, industry and market – including key stakeholders such as customers, suppliers and competitors. This raises additional sustainability issues such as ethical trading and marketing and fair competition.

3.5   Again, we'll look briefly at some of the key economic influences raised by the syllabus (others have been mentioned above), but it's worth bearing in mind that this will depend on your own up-to-date reading. The pressures and constraints created by the 2009 economic recession, for example, are not specifically mentioned (other than in the general area of 'costs') – yet this is likely to be a major influence on sustainable procurement policy and implementation, as highlighted by Supply Management's special issue on embedding sustainable procurement (27 August 2009).

Basic principles of supply and demand

3.6   As you should know from your previous studies:

- Demand is the quantity of goods that consumers are willing and able to buy. It varies with price: in general, as the price of a good goes up, demand goes down – because some people will cut down on their purchases, or switch to cheaper substitutes. (This depends in practice, however, on other factors such as the price of substitute and complementary goods, the amount of disposable income, consumer preferences and price sensitivity.)

- Supply is the amount that firms are willing and able to produce and sell. This too varies with price: in general, as the market price of a good rises, supply also rises – because higher prices mean greater profitability, increasing the willingness of firms to produce more. (Again, this depends in practice on other factors such as production costs, technology, the number of suppliers in the market and business expectations.)

3.7   For the private sector, the business case for sustainable products and services depends on there being sufficient demand for them to create and sustain a market, and to bear prices which will make them both affordable for the consumer and viable (profitable) for the producer. A market economy assumes that people will purchase goods and services to satisfy their wants and needs, at a price they are able and willing to pay. Commercial organisations have to offer goods and services which are in demand, at prices which maintain that demand, in order to compete with others in the market. In other words, consumer choice ultimately decides whether sustainable goods and services are a market priority, and at what price they can be sold.

3.8   For the public sector, a different set of sustainability issues arises. Some goods and services are perceived as essential for the wellbeing of individuals and society – such as health, education, utilities and security services – even if commercial organisations don't want to produce them. In such circumstances, government must step in to control and subsidise production, so that basic goods and services are made available and affordable. The public sector, in a mixed economy, therefore performs important sustainability functions.

- Providing essential goods and services which might not be provided by the private sector, owing to 'market failure'

- Redistributing wealth, via taxation, in order to provide financial support for non-wage earners such as the sick, pensioners and the unemployed

- Protecting the public interest, by regulating private sector activity – and, where necessary, 'bailing out' private enterprises (as we have seen during the current financial crisis, for example).

Costs

3.9   Costs are a key influence on sustainable procurement, both externally (in the form of fluctuating market costs of labour, resources, commodities and other supplies) and internally (in the form of pressures on procurement functions to secure reductions in materials and sourcing costs, particularly in the face of global recession).

3.10 On the one hand, the issue of costs (and pressure for cost management and reduction) create a constraint on sustainability. An August 2009 Supply Management survey found that 64% of purchasers have 'not secured substantial financial benefit from sustainability' (in the short term), and that the issue is 'not a high priority in the current economic climate' (Supply Management, 27 August 2009).

3.11 On the other hand, there are positive opportunities for cost efficiencies from sustainable procurement.

- The rising costs of energy from non-renewable sources is a positive driver for sustainability initiatives aimed at reducing energy consumption – at the same time as reducing the organisation's carbon footprint. The SM survey found that energy and water costs were the chief areas where outlay had been reduced.

- The tangible value of sustainability may emerge from a more holistic approach to whole-life costs. 'Up-front' costs of sustainability may pay for themselves later, in reduced compliance, usage, maintenance, failure, disposal and other costs – and in enhanced reputational capital and sales revenue from sustainable branding.

Economic recession

3.12 While economic recession raises cost and budgetary constraints for sustainable procurement, it also raises key issues of social sustainability.

- Costs may need to be reduced to maintain profitability, particularly if the firm has to reduce the price of products/services in order to stimulate demand and maintain sales. However, this may be regarded as a sustainability measure: maintaining the affordability of products and services; and preserving the financial viability of the firm (and related employment livelihoods and so on).

- Recruitment may need to be suspended in advance of recession, to allow the workforce to be reduced by natural wastage rather than redundancies. In highly cyclical industries, companies might be more proactive in developing a numerically flexible workforce (eg by subcontracting and outsourcing) – to which procurement functions may contribute.

4 Social/ethical influences

4.1 The socio-cultural environment embraces a wide range of the 'people' aspects of the society in which the organisation operates and from which it draws its suppliers, customers and workers. Socio-cultural factors include: demographic characteristics and trends (discussed in Chapter 2); cultural norms, values and customs (including increasing concern about sustainability issues); lifestyle and fashion trends (including 'green' consumerism); social infrastructure (structural support for education, communications, economic participation and other civil activities); and human resource management (attitudes and policies about how people should be employed and managed in organisations).

4.2 These factors reflect the needs and expectations of the organisation's target market (customers), and will obviously be taken into account when developing sustainable products, services and marketing plans. However, they also reflect other stakeholder groups: affecting the availability of skilled labour, for example – and shaping the kinds of relationships and responsibilities the organisation has (or needs to develop) towards its employees, suppliers and host communities.

4.3 'Ethical' factors more specifically embrace a range of issues to do with corporate social responsibility and business ethics: what constitutes 'right conduct' for an organisation in its context. They inevitably overlap with legal and environmental factors, since compliance and environmental protection are generally regarded as ethical responsibilities. However, they also include corporate policies, industry and professional Codes of Practice, and stakeholder pressure in areas such as: fair trading and the ethical treatment of suppliers; the fair and humane treatment of employees (over and above legal minimum requirements); the upholding of societal values (eg avoiding corruption); supporting local communities (eg with investment and employment); and selecting and managing suppliers so that they comply with good practice in these areas.

4.4 Let's look at the specific areas mentioned by the syllabus.

Availability of skills

4.5 Demographic trends, government education and skilling policies and infrastructure investment all influence the availability of skills in the labour market. As discussed in Chapter 2, this may in turn influence organisational strategy and policy in regard to:

- The sourcing of human resources and suppliers from international labour markets (eg by virtual organisation, outsourcing or off-shoring)
- Workforce and supplier diversity, with the need to attract, deploy and retain women, mature and immigrant workers
- Proactive investment and support for education and skilling initiatives in the community, in order to develop and sustain the pool of quality labour: apprenticeships and work experience programmes, co-investment in vocational skills training and so on. (The same may be said of supplier development programmes.)

Working conditions and practices

4.6 Labour conditions are a key area of corporate social responsibility, embracing employee and human rights issues not just within the organisation's own workforce, but across supply chains and in supply market communities. Human rights and labour organisations have helped to highlight abuses, raise worker awareness and expectations, and organise legitimate protest in pursuit of healthy, safe and equitable working conditions. Meanwhile, an alerted media has put the spotlight on global brands whose off-shored production facilities or supply chains exploit slavery, child labour, sweatshops (eg in the clothing and sporting goods industries), unsafe working conditions and low wages. This has sparked widespread public outrage and consumer boycotts, raising organisations' awareness of the significant reputational risks.

4.7 According to the International Labour Organisation (ILO), nearly half of the world's 2.8 billion workers are unable to earn enough to lift themselves and their family members above the US$2-per-day poverty line. This is a sustainability issue for developed nations, because cycles of poverty and inequity create long-term threats to global stability, security and supply.

4.8 Procurement functions will therefore have to pay attention to issues such as: human rights (including the abolition of forced labour, slavery and child labour); equal opportunity; healthy and safe working conditions; and employment rights (eg to fair or minimum wages, trade union membership, protection from unfair dismissal); in the workforce policies and practices of suppliers and supply chains. This may require 'drilling down' to lower levels of tiered supply chains. The importance of such measures was illustrated in a recent high-profile case concerning the global charity, Oxfam. It suffered severe embarrassment when it emerged that its overseas suppliers of 'Make Poverty History' wristbands were themselves exploiting their workers.

Corruption

4.9 Corporate corruption may take the form of: bribery, extortion, fraud, deception (eg knowingly false financial reporting), collusion and other anti-competitive practices, and money laundering (exploiting the proceeds of crime or funding terrorist activity). This type of activity is generally considered unethical, and in many cases will be illegal in a given jurisdiction – although there are cultural differences around the ethics of business gifts and inducements, nepotism (favouritism directed at relatives and personal connections) and so on.

4.10 These issues have been re-ignited by high profile exposés of bribery, and surveys showing that bribery and corruption are widespread in some overseas supply markets. The 2007 Corruption Perceptions Index (published by NGO Transparency International) revealed that more than 40% of 180 countries examined were perceived to have 'rampant corruption' in their public sector procurement.

4.11 Corruption is a sustainability issue, as it causes serious economic damage, interferes with fair competition and destroys confidence in the integrity and functioning of financial and political systems. It is, specifically, an issue for sustainable procurement, as the subject of legislation (on fraud, money laundering, inducements in public procurement and so on) and industry and professional codes of practice.

Corporate citizenship

4.12 The term 'corporate citizenship' is often used to express the social dimension of sustainability and/or more general corporate social responsibility: the willingness of organisations to work within (and together with) local, national and international communities to 'do the right thing', as co-stakeholders in society.

4.13 Insofar as an organisation recognises its obligations as a corporate citizen – or aspires to do so, or is forced to do so by pressure from consumers and other stakeholders – it will adopt sustainable procurement as part of its corporate social responsibility strategy. A Corporate Citizenship Statement sets out what an organisation understands by corporate citizenship and how it shapes the way in which the organisation seeks to operate. It provides an introduction to the policies, codes and positioning statements that shape the organisation's commitment to corporate citizenship in specific areas of activity, including procurement.

The CIPS ethical code

4.14 The CIPS Professional Code of Ethics is likely to be a direct influence on sustainable procurement, as the ethical standard and disciplinary framework (the basis of best conduct) for purchasing professionals in the area of purchasing ethics. The Code sets out key ethical principles including: upholding the standing of the profession; maintaining high standards of integrity in all business relationships; rejecting business practices which might be deemed improper; avoiding the use of position or authority for personal gain; acquiring, maintaining and fostering technical competence; seeking to maximise benefit for the employing organisation; and complying with all relevant laws and contractual obligations.

4.15 The Code specifically addresses issues such as: impartiality and declaration of interests; maintaining the confidentiality and accuracy of information; constructing contracts and supply relationships which support deliveries and benefits and promote fair competition; avoiding the acceptance of business gifts and hospitality which might be perceived as inducements; and how to seek advice on ethical issues and dilemmas.

Societal values

4.16 The term 'societal values' simply means the prevailing (and shifting) values, norms and assumptions held by a given society at a given time: literally, what is 'valued' by a society. Sustainable procurement is likely to be significantly influenced by the values, attitudes, demands and expectations of consumers, employees and other key stakeholders; pressure and interest groups; and their reflection in media and public opinion.

- Values are reflected in consumption: a generation of increasingly 'green' and 'ethical' consumers will stimulate demand for sustainable products – and the erosion of demand for (or active boycott of) products perceived to be environmentally damaging or unethical.

- The emerging concept of corporate reputation management argues that a positive reputation, in the perceptions of a range of stakeholder publics, is an important intangible resource for an organisation: a form of reputational capital. Organisations with strong positive reputations in areas valued by stakeholders (including sustainability) reap benefits of customer, employee and supplier loyalty; increased profitability; and resilience in the face of recession and public relations crises. We discuss this concept further in Chapter 4.

4.17 There have been major shifts in societal values since the 1950s, in regard to issues such as equal opportunity for women, diversity, environmental sustainability, social justice, expectations in regard to employment rights and corporate transparency – driving consumer and pressure group demand for corporate social responsibility in these areas.

Ethical farming

4.18 Raising animals and growing crops, for food, clothing and other applications, are practices that date back to ancient times. Methods of performing these functions (and public perceptions and expectations around them) have changed significantly in recent decades. There is now a dual focus on both increasing productivity and yield (to meet the social obligation of meeting human needs), and avoiding negative, unsustainable or inhumane impacts on land, soil, water, seed quality and the wellbeing of animals.

4.19 Large-scale agri-businesses have tried to use the same management style for raising livestock and growing crops as for assembling cars or other modern conveniences: aiming to get products to market as quickly and cheaply as possible, maximising profits at every stage of the process. Public concerns about the practice of 'factory farming' in particular, however, have created a movement towards a code of conduct for the humane treatment and slaughter of livestock.

4.20 Compassion in World Farming (CWF) is one of the leading global organisations developing the ethical farming agenda. Within many parts of the world, 'free range eggs' (avoiding battery housing of chickens) and 'dolphin friendly tuna' (avoiding the use of indiscriminate catches) are now accepted products, for which consumers are demonstrably prepared to pay premium prices. The same may be said of 'cruelty free cosmetics' (not tested on animals) and 'non-genetically modified foods'.

Fair Trade

4.21 'Unfair' trading arises when large buyers exert their bargaining power to force down the prices of small suppliers, to levels that bring economic hardship to producers, exacerbating poor wages and working conditions for their workers, and bringing no economic benefit to their communities. In the UK, there have been recent calls for formal regulation of the relationship between large supermarket chains and their suppliers, for example, because of the allegedly unfair 'squeezing' of prices. More commonly, however, fair trade issues arise in developing economies: the media has recently highlighted the plight of coffee and tea growers, and textile and garment trade workers.

4.22 Started over sixty years ago, Fair Trade has developed into a worldwide concept, seeking to ensure decent living and working conditions for small-scale and economically disadvantaged producers and workers in developing countries. It involves an alliance of producers and importers, retailers, labelling and certifying organisations – and, of course, consumers willing to pursue ethical consumption by support for certified Fair Trade products. Meanwhile, the comparatively new discipline of 'fair trade marketing' involves 'the development, promotion and selling of fair trade brands and the positioning of organisations on the basis of a fair trade ethos' (Jobber, 2007).

4.23 Fair Trade products are marketed in two different ways. The traditional or integrated route is where goods are produced, imported and/or distributed by specialised Fair Trade organisations, under standards developed by the International Fair Trade Association (IFAT). The other route to market is through Fair Trade labelling and certification, whereby goods (mainly food products) are certified by an independent third party verification body, to guarantee that their production chains respect the International Fair Trade standards developed by FLO (Fair Trade Labelling Organisations International).

4.24 Recent years have seen a significant increase in both awareness and sales of Fair Trade goods, with sales showing annual growth rates of 20% to 30% – and this is likely to provide a strong influence on sustainable procurement policies.

Example: the rise of Fair Trade

The Body Shop has long cultivated a fair trade ethos as part of its brand positioning, with a policy of assisting small-scale indigenous communities and supporting small business development by offering fair prices (a policy called 'Trade Not Aid').

Other major organisations have launched fair trade brands as part of their brand portfolio: eg Nestlé's Partners Blend fair trade coffee, and Marks & Spencers' range of fair trade clothing.

In August 2009, Cadbury and the Fair Trade Association announced that major brand Cadbury's Dairy Milk Chocolate would go Fair Trade certified in Australia within a year. A media release by the Stop the Traffik Coalition affirmed: 'This is great news for impoverished cocoa farmers in West Africa and will help greatly in the efforts to end child slavery on cocoa plantations. It is also great news for chocolate consumers expanding their choice of chocolate that has been certified to be free of child slave labour and labour that has been trafficked onto the cocoa plantations.'

---

5 Technological influences

5.1 The technological environment embraces the technological development or sophistication of the organisation's national or international markets, and more specific developments in the particular fields that are relevant to the organisation.

5.2 Technology factors become more important every day, as innovations and developments have the following effects.

- Enable 24/7 global communication and business activity, via the world wide web – supporting international sourcing and small business access to markets, and green, economically efficient procurement processes, but also widening the 'digital divide' which disadvantages less developed economies

- Support the development of new products (such as alternative energy and 'green' products) and business processes (such as e-commerce and recycling) which may offer sustainability gains, but also incur development costs

- Shorten product lifecycles, by increasing the pace of modification and obsolescence – creating opportunities for product innovation, but also pressures for over-consumption and increased waste

- Change industry structures and activities (eg with the automation of manufacturing and the rise of electronics products) – creating new business opportunities, but also issues of skill obsolescence, unemployment and/or overconsumption

- Creating 'virtual' teams and organisations, in which people share data and work together linked mainly by ICT, regardless of their physical location – supporting lower carbon footprints (by reducing travel), work-life balance and wider access to employment, but also creating issues such as the off-shoring of jobs.

Innovation

5.3   One major influence in the technological environment is the pace, direction and diffusion of innovation in the product and supply markets in which an organisation operates. Eco-innovation is the process of developing new products, processes or services which provide customer and business value but significantly decrease environmental impact. We discussed innovation for sustainability in Chapter 2 as a major trend for sustainable procurement.

New technologies, materials and products

5.4   Environmental technology (also known as green technology or clean technology) is the application of science and technology in a manner that (a) conserves the natural environment and resources, and (b) works to reduce or minimise the negative impacts of human activity on the natural environment.

5.5   Environmental technologies are being applied in a number of fields. Some are well known, such as solar power, alternative fuels, lean-burn engines etc. Others are less well known, such as anaerobic digestion (renewable energy from waste). New technologies are being constantly developed and refined, in the form of new materials, different applications for materials, better design processes and more efficient manufacturing processes.

5.6   The European Union has recognised that it needs to invest more in innovative ways to protect the environment whilst boosting competitiveness. The European Commission has developed a policy to stimulate the development and uptake of environmental technologies across Europe: the European Environmental Technologies Action Plan (ETAP).

5.7   As we saw in Chapter 2, eco-innovation is steadily building a consumer and supply market for 'green' materials and products, focusing on areas such as: health and safety benefits; 'natural/organic' agricultural products; recyclability and safe disposal; sustainable source management; reduction of chemical exposure, hazardous materials and wastes; and energy efficiency (Blackburn, 2007).

6   *Legislative influences*

6.1   Although the syllabus refers only to 'legislative' factors, the 'legal' environment also includes sustainability factors such as: the operation of the justice system (the law and how it is enforced) and the organisation's contractual relationships with various parties (including suppliers, customers and employees). In addition to provisions laid down by legislation or statute, there are also principles developed by judges' decisions in the courts (case law), which determine how the law is interpreted.

6.2 There is a wide range of national and trans-national (eg EU) law and regulation on areas related to corporate social responsibility and ethics such as: the rights of parties in commercial contracts; the rights of employers and employees in the employment relationship; health and safety at work; consumer protection; human rights; environmental protection; data and privacy protection; public sector procurement; and so on. Compliance with relevant legal provisions is essential both to demonstrate ethical behaviour (an important reputational and CSR objective for many organisations) – and to avoid penalties and sanctions for not doing so.

Environmental legislation

6.3 There has been increasing legislation, at the national and European level, on environmental protection issues, including: : air and water quality, climate change and GHG emissions, agriculture, biodiversity and species protection, pesticides and hazardous chemicals, waste management, remediation of environmental impacts, and conservation of public lands and natural resources.

6.4 Key UK legislation includes: the Environmental Protection Act 1990, the Environment Act 1995, the Climate Change and Sustainable Energy Act 2006, the Climate Change Act 2008, the Energy Act 2008 and the Environmental Damage (Prevention and Remediation) Regulations 2009 (implementing the Environmental Liability Directive 2004/35/CE).

Workforce legislation

6.5 The agenda on human and labour rights has similarly stimulated a wide body of legislation which affects an organisation's relationship with, and treatment of, its workers. Because of the compliance and reputational risk of labour rights violations by suppliers or sub-suppliers, such issues also extend to sourcing principles and supplier selection, monitoring and management.

6.6 Workforce or employment law covers a range of issues, including: discrimination and equal opportunity, health and safety, employment protection, employment rights, industrial democracy, employee relations and so on. There have been increasing legislative constraints on managerial decision-making in these areas, in recent decades. The social policy of the European Union has added momentum to this trend: European Directives are still being enacted into the law of member states.

6.7 Because legal issues are so pervasive, it is not possible to cite their relevance in every context. We have therefore drawn together all the relevant material in a separate chapter. Sustainability-related law, regulation and standards will be discussed in Chapter 11.

7 *Environmental influences*

7.1 The natural environment embraces factors such as: legislation, international obligations (such as the Kyoto agreement on climate change) and government targets in regard to environmental protection and sustainability; consumer and pressure-group demand for eco-friendly products and business processes; issues of pollution, waste management, disposal and recycling; the depletion of non-renewable natural resources and the development of alternatives; the protection of habitats and biodiversity from urbanisation and industrialisation; the reduction of greenhouse gas (GHG) emissions; and so on.

7.2 All these factors will impact on purchasing activity in areas such as materials specification; supplier selection and management (to ensure good environmental practice); logistics (eg environmental impacts of transport) and reverse logistics (eg take-back and recycling); and compliance and risk management. Specific industries and firms will also have particular concerns: you might like to think what 'green' issues might be a priority for a car manufacturer, an airline, a brand of canned tuna, a construction project or a hospital, say.

7.3   We have already mentioned a number of environmental issues and concerns, in Chapter 2 (among the 'trends' in sustainable procurement), and in this chapter (since environmental issues have often been the focus of political policy, societal value change and technological innovation). We will just draw together some key themes here.

Renewable vs non-renewable energy

7.4   We saw in Chapter 2 how resource depletion or over-consumption and rising costs have placed pressure on societies and organisations to reduce their reliance on non-renewable energy sources (fossil fuels), and to reduce their consumption of renewable energy sources to keep pace with supply. This drives a sustainable procurement focus on issues such as: the procurement of energy- and fuel-efficient plant, equipment and transport fleets; the application of supply market expertise to the design of energy-efficient processes and products; investment in renewable energy (eg solar, wind, bio-mass); promotion of programmes to reduce energy consumption patterns in the workplace and supply chain (contributing to the reduction of carbon footprint); and so on.

Waste management and reduction

7.5   We saw earlier in this chapter how waste management is a key area of UK government policy. This drives a sustainable procurement focus on issues such as: reduction of waste materials sent to landfill (due to limitations in landfill capacity); increase in the biodegradability of product and packaging materials used; reduction in the amount of packaging specification for purchases; reduction in packaging designed for products; design for disassembly, re-use and recycling; reverse logistics capability for take-back and disposal; and compliance with relevant waste management regulations.

Global climate change and carbon footprint reduction

7.6   As we explained briefly in Chapter 2, climate change or 'global warming' is perhaps the 'hottest' topic in environmental politics, with a number of major research reports and a major film raising the profile of the issue for governments and pressure groups worldwide – and therefore for sustainable procurement.

7.7   The science of climate change is still under debate, but there is fairly widespread political consensus on the prevailing theory. Essentially, 'greenhouse gases' (GHGs) in the atmosphere, including carbon dioxide (CO_2), fulfil an essential function in keeping the earth warm. Excess levels of these gases, however, can raise the temperature too far, causing the melting of polar ice-caps, the rising of sea levels and changes to global climate patterns. This may have a range of severe consequences, including the flooding of coastal areas and the displacement of communities; the disruption of agriculture and food production; and the increase in severe weather events such as hurricanes and droughts (which – among other ill effects – may disrupt supply).

7.8   In order to counter the threat of human-caused global warming, societies, corporations and households are urged to reduce greenhouse gas emissions, and to reduce their 'carbon footprint': that is, the total impact of their activities on the amount of carbon dioxide in the atmosphere, measured in tonnes of CO_2. Under the Kyoto Protocol, the UK has adopted binding targets to reduce emissions of greenhouse gases by 12.5% relative to 1990 levels over the period 2008 to 2012, and national regulations have been implemented to support these targets.

Example: emission reductions for individual firms

The following are some practical measures that can be taken by individual firms.

- Setting policies and targets for reducing carbon emissions and monitoring carbon footprint

- Minimising the use of non-renewable (fossil fuel) energy in all activities, and sourcing or generating 'green' (renewable) electricity

- Reducing business travel and the air freight of goods (and/or labelling air-freighted products to give consumers the choice); planning road haulage to minimise fuel use and emissions; moving towards the use of bio-diesel in lorry fleets; and using 'green' company car fleets

- Carbon offsetting (ideally, where no other method of reducing CO2 emissions is available). Individuals, companies or governments can purchase financial instruments called 'carbon offsets' (representing the fruits of emissions-reducing projects) to compensate for their own greenhouse gas emissions. (The Kyoto Protocol sanctioned offsets as a way for governments and private companies to earn 'carbon credits' which can be traded in a compliance market.)

- Carbon labelling: supporting the work of the Carbon Trust to develop the labelling of consumer products and services with their carbon impact

- Developing and selling products with a lower carbon impact (eg low-energy use household appliances, non-HFC-gas refrigerators and air-conditioning systems, clothes which can be washed at lower temperatures)

- Mobilising and supporting key suppliers and logistics providers in reducing their carbon emissions, and making this a criterion for supplier selection and evaluation.

- Mobilising and supporting customers in reducing their carbon emissions. Marks & Spencer, for example, are now educating their customers on carbon footprint reduction (in a joint campaign with the World Wildlife Fund, WWF), supporting the carbon labelling of their products, and siting retail outlets to encourage the use of public transport and cycling (to reduce car usage).

Land use and water management

7.9 We saw earlier in this chapter that land use and water management are important areas of government policy in environmental management. Issues of water availability and contamination, and the limitation of land available for agriculture, place pressures on sustainable procurement in areas such as: conservation of water in operational processes (and encouraging the supply chain in such measures); sourcing agricultural products from sustainably managed land; and location of industrial/commercial sites to avoid loss of agricultural land.

7.10 Blackburn (2007) notes that more and more companies are beginning to see water supply and management as an area of important business risk and opportunity. This is certainly true for some large industrial users of water, such as those in beverages and bottling, textiles and apparel, biotechnology, electronics, and agricultural and food processing. A business's water risks and opportunities may go beyond its own facility grounds, however, and extend up and down its supply chain, too. Anheuser-Busch found water shortages affecting its suppliers and hampering the company's brewery operations: a drought in Idaho limited irrigation for barley production. A product assessment by Proctor & Gamble revealed that 85% of their sales were associated with consumer water use. Consequently, the company identified water as an area of company focus under its sustainability programme.

Pollution

7.11 Pollution is the contamination of air, water, or earth by harmful substances. The use of cars and trucks, increased chemical wastes, nuclear wastes, and accumulation of rubbish in landfills have all been the subject of legislation specifically aimed at decreasing pollution.

- Air pollution is the release of chemicals and particles into the atmosphere causing harm or discomfort to humans or other living organisms, or damaging the natural environment. It is often identified with industrial factories, power stations and vehicles.

- Water pollution includes surface runoff particularly from agricultural production, leakage into groundwater, liquid spills, wastewater discharge and littering.

- Soil pollution occurs when chemicals are released by spill or underground leakage. The use of landfill sites contaminates land and is now the subject of increasing legislation that encourages local councils, in particular, to find alternative ways of disposing of waste.

Procurement's contribution to environmental sustainability

7.12 Areas of environmental concern in which purchasing staff have a role to play are summarised by Saunders (*Strategic Purchasing and Supply Chain Management*) as follows.

- Recycling and reusing of materials and waste products (which may require new reverse logistics processes to recover products from consumers)
- Safe disposal of waste products that cannot be recycled
- Supplier selection policies (and tender criteria) to support firms that conform to environmental standards (eg with regard to air, water and noise pollution)
- Supplier and product selection policies that reflect concern for conservation and renewal of resources
- Safe and animal-friendly testing of products and materials
- Concern for noise, spray, dirt, vibration and congestion in the planning and operation of transportation

7.13 We might also add:

- Acting as the interface between suppliers and product development/design departments, to encourage knowledge-sharing, research and innovation for 'greener' product specifications and collaborative processes
- Monitoring, managing and perhaps supporting the environmental performance of suppliers on an ongoing basis, to ensure their compliance with the buyer's environmental standards (in order to minimise the reputational risk of being associated with an environmental disaster)
- Sourcing materials and services for environmental protection and reclamation (eg re-planting trees or cleaning up polluted areas).

7.14 A commitment to avoiding materials that are harmful to the environment, if alternative products are available at a similar price and quality, shouldn't be controversial. However, cost has been a significant obstacle in the past: 'green' products have typically been more expensive than their 'non-green' equivalents. The last few years have seen radical changes in this situation, and in many cases actual savings are to be made in choosing a green or sustainable alternative. (Energy efficient light-bulbs, for example, may cost more upfront but the savings will come further down the line in reduced energy use.)

7.15 If no cost-effective or value-adding green alternatives are available, the buyer may need to work with suppliers to reduce the damaging environmental impact of a product – or with production colleagues to see if the product can be replaced.

Example: Coca Cola Enterprises

The Coca Cola Company is often cited as a case study for risk management and sustainability planning in the area of water management. Both Blackburn (2007) and Senge (*The Necessary Revolution*) focus on the long journey to put water sustainability at the centre of the beverage business.

'In the past, the emphasis has been on operational performance: efficiency, wastewater treatment, managing water within the plant. Traditionally, little attention was paid to where or how plants got water for their bottling operations, or overall conditions of water availability for the larger community. It took a real wake-up call before we started to think beyond the four walls and pay attention to the larger system.' (Senge)

Features of Coca Cola's sustainability approach included:

- Partnership with WWF. 'The expertise, stature and combined public and commercial influence of the two sectors working together may be crucial to fundamental sustainability challenges like water.'

- A comprehensive inventory and risks assessment to determine security of supply (including water sources and uses, and potential future government restrictions on water).

- An action plan for: water risk surveys and mitigation; water treatment, recycling and reclaim; water saving initiatives (eg using alternative 'rinsing' methods); and efficient waste water treatment.

Other issues in Coca Cola's CSR and sustainability policies include: reducing beverage calories in schools; calculating and reducing carbon footprint; expanding a hybrid (green energy) truck fleet; and internal and external recycling programmes.

8 External stakeholders

8.1 'Stakeholders are those individuals or groups who depend on the organisation to fulfil their own goals and on whom, in turn, the organisation depends' (Johnson & Scholes, *Exploring Corporate Strategy*). 'A stakeholder of a company is an individual or group that either is harmed by, or benefits from, the company or whose rights can be violated, or have to be respected, by the company. Other groups, besides shareholders, who typically would be considered stakeholders are communities associated with the company employees, customers of the company's products and suppliers' (Jobber, *Principles and Practice of Marketing*).

8.2 You should be familiar with basic stakeholder groups, and their influence and interests, from your studies in other modules. The key points of stakeholder theory for the purposes of this learning objective are as follows.

- External stakeholders include 'connected stakeholders' (or primary stakeholders), who have an economic or contractual relationship with the organisation: customers, investors, suppliers and intermediaries. They also include 'secondary stakeholders' who are not directly connected to the organisation, but who have an interest in its activities, or are impacted by them in some way: government, pressure and interest groups (or NGOs), the local community and wider society.

- External stakeholder groups have varying degrees of power to influence the organisation directly, arising from control over resources (materials, labour, money, support); involvement in implementing the organisation's strategies (eg suppliers); expertise (eg consultants, NGO partners); the power to threaten sanctions or negative consequences (eg consumer boycott or restrictive legislation); legislative protection of their rights (eg consumers); or the power to influence public opinion, government policy or consumer behaviour (eg NGOs).

- The 'weak' view of stakeholder theory holds that satisfying key, active or participant stakeholders, such as customers and suppliers, is a good thing – but only because it enables the business to satisfy its primary purpose, the long-term growth in shareholder value. The 'strong' view of stakeholder theory argues that each stakeholder in a business has a legitimate claim on management's attention, and management's job is to balance stakeholder demands. Either view is compatible with sustainability, but will influence the priority given to economic, social and environmental sustainability objectives.

Example: The Concerned Consumer Index

The Concerned Consumer Index is a monthly measurement of consumer attitudes, conducted by research organisation Populus, in association with Good Business and The Times. According to the Populus website (www.populuslimited.com):

The survey shows that nine out of ten people feel that companies have a wider responsibility than just delivering goods at the lowest possible price. Three quarters of the population claims to weigh-up a company's reputation before buying its products or services, and nearly three in five say they actively avoid purchasing from certain companies because of questions they have about their social, environmental or ethical track record.

What marks out the 'Concerned Consumer' is that they do all these things. They belong to that half of the adult population that not only cares about social, environmental and ethical issues but actually does so enough to change their purchasing behaviour. They make decisions based on values as well as value. They are prepared to reward companies that they feel care about more than just selling to them as cheaply as possible.

Concerned Consumers are prepared to act. 50% seek out information about companies before buying from them on a regular basis. They are also ready to urge others to follow their lead. Two in five of them say they recommend goods and services to others on a frequent basis, nearly half as many again as the rest of the population. They are also more likely to pick up on stories both good and bad about the way businesses conduct themselves, to register these and to translate them into future buying decisions.

8.3   As we saw in our summary of the business case for sustainability in Chapter 1, the attitudes, expectations and perceptions of stakeholders can influence organisational policy on sustainable procurement (and other issues) in various ways.

- Demands for sustainable products and services by customers – and for ethical investments by investors – place competitive pressure on organisations to step up their sustainability performance. The Body Shop is a famous example of an organisation which built a successful brand with sustainability as a key brand differentiator.

- Customers (and increasingly, investors) have shown themselves willing to boycott organisations and products perceived to be unsafe, unethical or irresponsible – as experienced by Shell, Nike and McDonald's, for example.

- There is a threat of increased media, regulatory and NGO scrutiny and activism as a result of poor sustainability performance (and/or lack of transparency), potentially leading to the mobilisation of consumer and investor opinion, and/or to regulation or legislation. Activist pressure on animal testing, for example, has finally given rise to an EU ban on the practice.

- There is positive potential to partner with suppliers, customers and business allies to develop and promote sustainable procurement – as, for example, in Marks & Spencers' Plan A Pledges.

- There is positive potential to partner with NGOs to harness their expertise and credibility in developing sustainable procurement – and in exploiting their reputations via cause-related product development and marketing. We have already cited the example of Coca Cola partnering with WWF, for example.

8.4   It is difficult to know how much detail you might be required to know in regard to the specific examples cited in the syllabus. Guidance published by CIPS for this unit merely states that: 'The food industry has come under extreme pressure over the past few decades over issues such as BSE, bird flu, use of artificial colours and flavours and genetically modified crops.'

8.5　Just in case, we will briefly outline the key point of each of these issues.

Bovine spongiform encephalopathy (BSE)

8.6　'Mad cow disease' was first identified in cattle in 1986. Ten years later, it was announced that the human brain disease CJD was probably linked to BSE, and it seemed possible that victims had caught the disease from BSE-infected cattle. A special BSE Inquiry was set up in 1998 to investigate what became a major public health scandal, which was a public relations disaster both for the meat industry and for the government (because it initially claimed that beef was safe to eat).

Bird flu

8.7　Avian influenza or 'bird flu' is a contagious disease of birds caused by the Influenza A virus and transmissible to humans via close contact. Domestic poultry flocks are particularly vulnerable to epidemics of a rapid, severe and fatal form of the disease, and this was the source of a significant outbreak in Asia and Europe at the end of 2003. As with the BSE crisis, public and media concern forced the mass extermination of livestock.

Use of artificial colours and flavours

8.8　This is perhaps a more straightforward example of a shift in consumer perceptions forcing food manufacturers to change their products. Food additives are found in the majority of the processed foods, drinks and medicines consumed in the UK: they are used to make food look and taste more attractive, and for the purposes of preservation.

8.9　However, additives have increasingly been of concern, due to intolerances, allergies and other adverse health reactions, with some substances being associated with hyperactivity in children, asthma and so on. Once the issue was identified, increasing pressure was brought to bear to control the use of additives, and to ensure that they are separately listed in packaging.

Genetically modified (GM) crops

8.10　GM crops are crops that have been modified through genetic engineering. The first commercially grown and marketed GM crop was a tomato called Flavr Savr, which was made more resistant to rotting. This was released on the US market in 1994 without any special labelling, and a variant of the product was used to produce tomato paste that was sold in Europe in 1996.

8.11　When scientific studies appeared to demonstrate severe health damage in rats as a result of genetic engineering, there was a strong activist, consumer and public backlash. Leading food chains in Europe such as Nestlé and McDonald's committed themselves not to use GM modified products, and there have since been widespread bans on their use. However, GM has secured widespread acceptance in the USA, for example, where it is argued that GM is safe, commercially viable – and a potential solution to sustainability issues (eg creating pest- and disease-resistant crops, or less water-demanding crops in developing countries).

Animal testing

8.12　Animal testing is the use of animals in scientific experimentation and research. It is estimated that up to 100 million vertebrate animals are used annually, in addition to a much larger number of invertebrates (including insects). Animal testing has been used in the development of pharmaceuticals, household products, agricultural and industrial chemicals, paint, food additives and cosmetics.

8.13 There has been intense debate and activism concerning this issue over decades. Opponents among animal-focused NGOs question the necessity for animal testing, and argue that animals have an intrinsic right (as 'voiceless' stakeholders) not to be exploited or used with cruelty. Most governments throughout the world adopt the stance that animal testing is necessary to advance scientific and medical research, but that this should be carried out in a way that minimises suffering to the animal. (English law currently states that any new drug intended for humans must be pre-tested on at least two different types of live mammal.)

8.14 The jury is still out on this, although there appears to be a strong market for cosmetics and other products certified as being 'cruelty free' – and organisations occasionally face protests, boycotts or direct action (including sabotage) by radical activist groups.

9 Standards

9.1 In addition to legislation, included in the PESTLE factors, various international and governmental agencies, NGOs and commercial organisations have developed a range of voluntary regulatory codes of practice, and benchmark standards.

9.2 As with legislation, rather than discuss these standards here (and repeatedly as they apply to different topics), we will draw together our coverage in Chapter 11: Sustainability Standards and Legislation. For the purposes of this learning objective, you should just be aware that:

- As more and more industry leaders adopt standards, and encourage their suppliers to adopt them, there will be increased competitive pressure to conform.

- Sustainable procurement can benefit from the availability of standards: by using them to benchmark and improve internal performance; by gaining accreditation and therefore wider credibility with stakeholders; and/or by using them as a tool of sustainability management in the supply chain (eg using certification to standard as a supplier appraisal criterion, or using benchmarks as guidelines for supplier development and continuous improvement planning).

Chapter summary

- The external environment affects organisations in various ways: presenting threats and opportunities; providing resources; containing stakeholders.

- The environmental factors affecting organisations may be classified using the PESTLE model: political; economic; socio-cultural; technological; legal; and environmental (in the sense of 'green' issues).

- Political influences include local government policies and bye-laws, legislation and economic policy, international factors, and the activities of pressure groups.

- Macro-economic factors include the general level of economic activity, the market mechanism of supply and demand, and the effect of 'boom and bust' cycles.

- Micro-economic factors include the government's fiscal and money supply policies, rates of interest, foreign exchange and inflation, consumer spending levels, unemployment levels etc.

- Socio-cultural influences include demographic factors, cultural norms, lifestyle and fashion trends, social infrastructure etc.

- Technological influences have led to 24/7 global communication and business activity, the development of new products and services, shorter product lifecycles, changes in industry structures, and the creation of virtual teams.

- Legislative developments have had far-reaching effects on environmental law and human resource management.

- Environmental developments have included the issues of renewable vs non-renewable energy, waste management and reduction, global climate change, carbon footprint reduction, land use and water management, and pollution.

- Pressure from external stakeholders has surfaced in such incidents as the outbreak of BSE, the outbreak of avian flu, the use of artificial colours and flavours, the growth of GM crops and the use of animal testing.

- Sustainable procurement can be advanced by the use of standards such as the ISO 14000 series of standards.

Self-test questions

Numbers in brackets refer to the paragraphs above where your answers can be checked.

1   In what ways does the external environment impact upon an organisation? (1.2)

2   What six groups of factors are summarised in the PESTLE model? (1.5)

3   In what ways do political influences affect organisations? (2.2)

4   How can government policy assist in the conservation and protection of natural resources? (2.12)

5   What are the provisions of the Local Government Act 2000 in relation to sustainability? (2.20)

6   How do economic factors influence sustainable procurement? (3.3)

7   Describe the functions of the public sector in promoting sustainability. (3.8)

8   How can procurement functions help to improve working conditions along the supply chain? (4.8)

9   Explain what is meant by the Fair Trade initiative. (4.21–4.24)

10   Describe the effects of technological innovations in recent decades. (5.2)

11   Briefly outline current thinking on global climate change. (7.7)

12   In what ways can external stakeholders influence organisational policy on sustainable procurement? (8.2)

Further reading

We think this chapter has probably given you enough food for thought. Browse some of the websites cited, and the quality press, for further case study examples, if you have extra time. We will post up-to-date articles and case studies on the CIPS student website from time to time, to keep the 'influences' and 'issues' up to date…

CHAPTER 4

Internal Influences on Sustainable Procurement

1.4 Evaluate the internal factors influencing sustainable procurement in the context of different organisations and sectors, including the public, private, and third sectors and their tiers.

- Performance improvement (eg competitiveness, profitability, growth potential)
- Organisation strategy, policies and procedures
- Corporate social responsibility (CSR) policy
- People development policy
- Risk management (eg securing supply)
- Management attitudes
- Internal stakeholder positions and attitudes
- Availability of sustainable resources in the areas of labour, materials and processes (eg population demographics, skill levels in the supply chain, new materials, products and processes – textiles, plastics, farming)
- Brand reputation (eg use of child labour – clothing industry, CO_2 emissions – aviation, automotive and travel industries)
- Product and service design criteria and impact on the environment
- Internal capacity and capability (eg more efficiency through waste reduction – Ohno's 7 wastes)

Chapter headings

1 Internal influences on sustainable procurement

2 Performance improvement

3 Brand reputation

4 Organisational mission, strategy and policy

5 Organisational culture and attitudes

6 Resources, capacity and capability

7 Product and service features

Introduction

Having explored the external influences on sustainable procurement in Chapter 3, we now turn to the internal influences.

Again, we note that such 'influences' may include: drivers for (and constraints on) sustainable procurement within an organisation; internal 'process' factors shaping sustainable procurement policy and practice (which will be followed up in Chapters 7 and 8 on the development and implementation of sustainable procurement); and 'content' issues in sustainable procurement (which will be followed up further in Chapters 9–12 on sustainable specifications, sourcing, standards and contract management).

1 *Internal influences on sustainable procurement*

1.1 What kinds of internal factors will impact on whether an organisation develops sustainable procurement; how (and how effectively) it goes about this; and what kinds of areas and emphases it adopts?

1.2 Let's start with a broad overview of the factors mentioned in the syllabus.

- *Performance improvement.* To the extent that organisations believe that performance improvements are genuinely available from sustainability initiatives, this will act as a major driver for policy development, implementation and senior management 'buy in'. In the private sector, the 'hard' business case for sustainability may be based on enhanced profitability (from increased sales and reduced costs), competitive advantage (from differentiated branding) and growth potential (with innovation leading to new products and markets). In the public sector, it may be based primarily on the requirement to meet efficiency and sustainability targets.

- *Corporate reputation and brand strength* are key factors in making a business case for sustainability. Many organisations now recognise the importance of maintaining a positive reputation with a range of stakeholder publics (including customers/consumers, suppliers, employees and investors) on whose goodwill and support they depend. Many more organisations recognise the importance of avoiding reputational risk and damage, which can cause significant loss to immediate sales, share price and market share – as well as longer-term credibility and stakeholder loyalty.

- *Organisational mission, strategy and values*, and their flow-down into *policies and procedures* influence all organisational activity. Sustainability needs to be embedded from the top down (or 'vertically aligned') in order to secure meaningful support and compliance at all levels of the organisation.

- The existence of a strong *corporate social responsibility policy*, as discussed in Chapter 2, will support sustainable procurement, as a natural strategic 'fit'.

- The organisation's *people development policies* will have a strong influence, in building capability and continuity for sustainability: developing skills in innovation and partnering, a knowledge bank of sustainability issues, and a plan for management succession which embeds sustainability as a key value.

- The existence of a strong *risk management orientation and processes* will support sustainability, which can be viewed fundamentally as a risk management process: assessing reputational, compliance and supply risks and seeking to eliminate or manage them through sustainable practices. (Maintaining supplier viability and goodwill, through fair and ethical trading practices, for example, is a way of maintaining security of supply.)

- The *attitudes and values of internal stakeholders* will be crucial in whether sustainable procurement is successfully accepted and embedded in the organisation. The procurement function will have to secure the 'buy in' of internal customers (including senior management, and clients and partners in internal supply chains and cross-functional projects) to sustainability initiatives.

- *Resources* may or may not be available to support sustainable procurement initiatives. There may or may not, for example, be 'greener' materials, products or processes available in the supply market – or diverse supply partners with ethical labour practices – and the cost and time-scale to develop them may be prohibitive.

- Internal resources – in terms of *capacity and capability* – may or may not support sustainable procurement. The organisation may or may not, for example, have innovation capabilities for more sustainable design and production; or financial resources for investment in 'greener' plant and processes; or logistics capability for take-back and recycling; or potential for waste reduction and continuous improvement, to improve efficiency.

- Finally, the potential for sustainability will depend on the organisation's *products and services*: whether they pose immediate or high-priority sustainability issues and reputational/compliance risks (such as negative impacts on the environment); the extent to which greater sustainability can be attained without compromising key design or performance features; and the extent to which the total 'bundle of benefits' that make up the offering to the consumer includes sustainability values. The orientation of a firm producing high performance cars, plastic bags or cigarettes, for example, is likely to be different from one producing solar panels or offering ethical investment advice.

1.3 Clearly, these factors will vary across different sectors, industries and businesses. Public sector organisations are less likely to be concerned with profitability and shareholder value than are business corporations. Third-sector organisations are perhaps likely to place a premium on stakeholder attitudes and reputational value. A school, an airline, a forestry products business and an online gambling site face very different sustainability issues. We will make some of these distinctions, and discuss the characteristics of different sectors, industries and businesses in the context of sustainable procurement, in Chapter 5.

Focus and priority

1.4 Meanwhile, however, it is worth grasping the general point that sustainability is essentially a matter of focus (what does the organisation want to achieve) and priority (what is more or less important to it).

1.5 In Section 2 of this chapter, we will look at the 'hard' business case for sustainability: namely, that attention to sustainability issues can create economic value for the business in the form of profits, a strong share price (capital value) and shareholder dividends (shareholder value). For some organisations, this may be the first and perhaps only justification for investment in sustainability programmes – or for not investing in them. In order to be financially sustainable, businesses have to consider the primary interests of their investors: without profits and cashflow, they would go out of business.

1.6 However, as we argued in Chapter 1, 'enlightened self-interest' by business still needs to be 'enlightened'! Wider stakeholder needs – even where they impose extra burdens and costs on the organisation – cannot be dismissed: businesses also need to maintain their 'licence to operate', in the form of goodwill and co-operation from the customers, suppliers, workers and the general public.

1.7 As we saw in Chapter 3, companies rely on stakeholders for the resources and support they need to survive and prosper. Stakeholders, in return, have certain needs and expectations of companies. Insofar as a company's senior management believe in and are committed to this *quid pro quo* or mutual adjustment model, its approach to sustainability will embrace wider goals than a 'hard' business case.

1.8 Moreover, proactive moves in the area of sustainability and ethics – even where they do not directly promote economic value for the firm – can lead to business benefits in the long term. As a strong guiding value, they can enhance culture, morale and unity of direction. They can motivate employees to explore and innovate for further sustainability projects – which may be more economically attractive. And so on.

1.9 Blackburn emphasises that organisations need not do everything on sustainability all at once. They can develop and readjust sustainability priorities over time.

'The problem is that pursuing sustainability is not just about going after one issue... It's really about many issues, each with a different priority and business justification. For example, reducing waste for the purpose of cutting cost – something with visible short- and long-term financial benefits – is almost always more attractive to a business than furthering biodiversity. It is hopeless to search for overarching arguments that support aggressive advancement on all sustainability topics. Instead, one must first define a Sustainability Operating System, which enables a company to comb through topics, applying evaluation criteria to determine which topics deserve attention and which do not. In other words, with an SOS, one has a way of examining the business case for sustainability on a topic-by-topic basis from the unique viewpoint of each company...

'In early years, the SOS may point to productivity, legal compliance and high-risk issues. Later, after the top issues have been mastered, action can be taken on those of lower priority. These actions may well involve programs to control lower-level risks or enhance or protect the company's new-found reputation for social consciousness. At this later stage of the SOS, a 'save-the-whales' program may be considered. Such an initiative may fit nicely with the theme, culture and reputational goals of a company in the fishing industry, but not with one manufacturing farm equipment. All companies cannot take on all sustainability issues.'

2 *Performance improvement*

2.1 Economist Milton Friedman argued, as we saw in Chapter 1, that the sole responsibility of business executives is to maximise returns for their shareholders. Assuming that this is the sole or primary objective of business – although, as we mentioned above, this is not the case for all businesses – the main internal influences on the development and acceptance of sustainable procurement will be factors which drive profitability and shareholder value.

2.2 Blackburn illustrates this 'Show-Me-The-Money' business case for sustainability as shown in Figure 4.1. He summarises the business case for each element as follows.

- *Reputation and brand strength:* sustainability performance determines reputation, and reputation has a significant effect on sales and stock price. Studies show that one-fourth to one-third of a company's public reputation is based on social and environmental performance.

- *Competitive, effective and desirable products and services, and new markets:* companies can spur innovation by incorporating sustainability considerations into their design processes. By coupling these 'green' design processes with careful market assessments, a company can better address customer needs, produce products and services that are more competitive, and tap new markets. The result is increased sales and profits.

- *Productivity:* many aspects of sustainability, if properly addressed, can help improve business efficiency, which bolsters profits.

- *Operational burden and interference:* a company that neglects sustainability concerns invites public distrust, which can lead to greater regulation, operational burden and cost. By proactively addressing these concerns, a company can often ease this burden.

- *Supply chain costs:* by working proactively on sustainability issues with their suppliers and contractors, a company can help ensure that critical supplies and services will be available on an ongoing basis and that supply chain costs are properly controlled.

- *Cost of capital (lender and investor appeal):* a significant and growing number of investors and lenders are making investment and lending decisions based not only on traditional financial analysis, but on an evaluation of social and environmental performance as well. In order to remain attractive to these money providers and keep the cost of capital low, companies should properly manage their sustainability risks.

- *Legal liability:* companies guided by sustainability principles are less likely to incur crippling legal liabilities which can wipe out profits.

Figure 4.1 *How sustainability benefits can be argued to help determine business value*

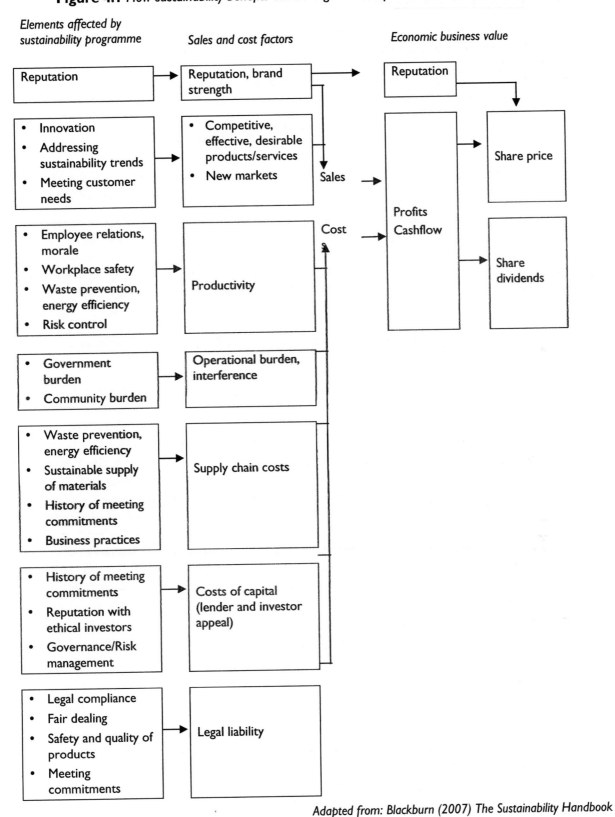

Elements affected by sustainability programme

Sales and cost factors

Economic business value

Adapted from: Blackburn (2007) The Sustainability Handbook

Profitability and 'eco efficiencies'

2.3   The imperative of profitability (especially in the private sector) may influence sustainable procurement in several basic ways.

- If an organisation is not securely profitable, financial sustainability will be the overriding objective, and wider sustainability concerns may be seen as an unaffordable luxury in the short term.

- A business case for sustainability may be made on the basis of profitability, as suggested by Figure 4.1 above.

- If a sound business case for sustainability is not made (or taken seriously) on the basis of profitability, senior management may fail to buy in to wider sustainability proposals.

2.4   Sustainability can contribute to improvements in profitability and added value by increasing sales revenue. Sustainable products and services, and a positive reputation and brand profile based on sustainability, can result in: increased sales of sustainable products/services valued by consumers; enhanced customer loyalty (higher life-time purchase value, and opportunities for cross-selling and up-selling); potential to charge premium prices for innovative/valued products and services; and potential for growth through new product/market development.

2.5   Sustainability can also contribute to improvements in profitability and added value by reducing costs.

- Production costs can be reduced through sustainability-driven productivity gains (eg from improved health and safety, workforce stability and morale); waste reduction and energy efficiency; and a reduced burden of regulation and compliance (eg from voluntary measures).

- Supply and materials costs can be reduced through sustainability-driven waste reduction and resource/energy efficiency; streamlined procurement processes; improved supplier relations (resulting in collaborative efficiencies and improvements); reduced supply risk and failure costs; and whole-life cost efficiencies (taking into account factors such as quality, durability, low maintenance/usage costs and re-use/recycling potential).

- Costs of capital can be reduced through sustainability-driven enhancements to corporate governance and CSR performance, increasing appeal to lenders and investors (particularly those focused on ethical and sustainable investments): increasing the availability of loan and share capital.

- Costs of compliance, liability and contract disputes can be reduced through sustainability-driven compliance, fair dealing, health and safety, product safety/quality and contract management processes.

Example: 3M Corporation

3M initiated a Pollution Prevention Pays programme in 1975. Since then, it has implemented over 5,000 initiatives aimed at eliminating or reducing pollution, involving product and process modification, equipment redesign and the re-use and recycling of waste materials. It is estimated that such projects have prevented more than 1.1 million tons of pollutants entering the environment, and offered the company over US$950 million in savings.

For a fascinating insight into the sustainability values and programmes of a major innovator, explore the sustainability pages on 3M's website:

http://solutions.3m.com/wps/portal/3M/en_US/global/sustainability

---

2.6   Blackburn also highlights the potential cost savings to be gained from designing products, services and production processes with 'green' considerations in mind.

- Reducing material intensity (less material used per unit of production)
- Reducing energy intensity (less energy per unit)
- Reducing the dispersion of toxic substances into the environment (reducing the degree of hazard and quantity of substances per unit)
- Improving recyclability (ease of disassembly, avoiding mixed materials)
- Increasing the service intensity of products and services (increasing functional value per unit of product or service hour)
- Improving the quality and durability of products (reducing defect and repair rates, lengthening product life; increasing number of uses per product)
- Maximising the percentage of resources from renewable sources (with long-range cost savings due to secure supply)

Competitiveness and growth potential

2.7   Sustainable procurement is ultimately about making 'greener' and more ethical products, services, processes and brand propositions. By investigating sustainability issues, supply market innovation potential and customer/market perceptions and expectations in regard to sustainability, an organisation can:

- Improve the appeal of its products and services to sustainability-aware consumers (and/or industrial buyers who are themselves seeking to develop sustainable procurement) – both immediately and in the long term, by building environmental monitoring and ongoing innovation and improvement into the process
- Enhance or maintain its competitiveness in customer markets, to the extent that it can outdo (or at least match) competitor initiatives in sustainability, and/or develop core (distinctive, non-replicable, value-adding) competencies in sustainability and innovation
- Develop a more competitive supply chain, through investment in sustainable relationships; innovation and improvement programmes; supplier development; sustainability monitoring, management and certification; and so on
- Create growth potential through the exploitation of new markets for sustainable (greener, healthier, energy-efficient, ethically sourced) brands, products and services
- Develop innovation capabilities (via supply networks, investment in research and development, improvement-seeking, customer research and so on) which may enable further product and market development.

Risk management

2.8   The whole point about sustainability – as we saw in Chapter 1 – is that it addresses an identified risk to the future wellbeing of society, and, from the point of view of organisations, to the social and environmental 'eco-system' which supports their activity. Lack of sustainability poses risks to an organisation in several key areas.

- Reputational risk: exposure of unethical, socially irresponsible or environment-damaging activity by the organisation and/or its supply chain, potentially damaging the organisation's image, brand and credibility in its customer, investor, labour and supply markets. (This important area is discussed in more detail in the next section.)
- Compliance risk: exposure of non-compliant or illegal activity by the organisation, incurring reputational, operational and financial penalties

- Supply risk: arising from supplier failure (eg as a result of unsustainable sourcing practices or excessively 'lean' supply chains) or supply failure (eg as a result of over-consumption of scarce commodities and resources).

- Financial risk (eg as a result of poor corporate governance, investment or financial management)

- Marketing risk (eg as a result of failure to recognise or meet market demand for sustainable brands, failure to match competitor initiatives on sustainability)

- Health, safety and liability risk (eg as a result of unsafe working conditions or products)

- Environmental risk (eg as a result of climate change or resource depletion disrupting supply or affecting supply prices).

2.9 Sustainable procurement will therefore be influenced by the risk management policies of the organisation, and its general 'risk appetite' or tolerance for risk. A more 'risk-averse' organisation will seek to develop sustainability in order to minimise or mitigate risks.

2.10 In fact, sustainable procurement can legitimately be seen as a tool of corporate risk management, because significant risks to the security and continuity of supply (as well as the other risks listed above) may arise from unsustainable sourcing and procurement practices. The buyer may be over-consuming commodities or resources that are in short supply, or over-specifying requirements (creating wastes). Low-cost sourcing may be supported by the squeezing of supplier profit margins, the use of child labour or exploitative employment practices somewhere in the supply chain – and these in turn may pose reputational risks, or risks of strikes or supplier failures disrupting supply.

2.11 Conversely, positive sustainable procurement practices can support the security, continuity and 'five rights' of supply: eg through supplier and supply chain development; certification of quality and environmental management systems; collaboration on mutually beneficial specification/design and resource efficiency improvements; equitable risk, cost and gain sharing with suppliers; best practice sharing; reputational and brand enhancement from sustainable supply chain management; and so on.

2.12 In addition, of course, sustainability explicitly recognises and seeks to manage the risks to health, safety, viability and wellbeing posed by the organisation and its supply network to their natural and stakeholder environments.

Sustainability as 'good management'

2.13 Blackburn (2007) argues that, fundamentally, the processes required for sustainable procurement are equivalent to the processes of sound management. He suggests that the business case for sustainability can be built via a sequence of process-focused questions.

1. Should business operations and functions perform short- and long-term planning in a way that anticipates future trends and considers the needs of those who make a company successful?

2. Should this planning involve a process by which operational and functional groups identify business risks and opportunities and prioritise them for action?

3. Should business managers be accountable for setting and achieving performance goals designed to realise these identified, high-value priorities?

4. Should progress toward these goals be periodically measured and reported within the organisation?

5. Should the company use this collected information to its best advantage in enhancing its credibility with interested employees, customers, suppliers, investors, governments and communities?

2.14　The answer to all these questions should be: 'yes, obviously'. Sustainable production and procurement can be seen in terms of simply applying the processes and techniques of good risk, reputation and business management.

3　*Brand reputation*

Reputation (and reputational risk) management

3.1　Corporate reputation guru Charles Fombrun defines corporate reputation as: 'the overall estimation in which a company is held by its constituents. A corporate reputation represents the net affective or emotional reaction – good-bad, weak or strong – of customers, investors, employees and general public to the company's name' (*Reputation: Realising Value from the Corporate Brand*). Reputations are built up over time, as people have positive and negative direct experiences of the organisation, and receive positive and negative messages from it or about it. Positive reputations take years to build – and can be dented or destroyed in a moment...

3.2　It is increasingly recognised that reputation is an important intangible asset. A strong positive reputation is a key source of distinctiveness for an organisation, which can differentiate it from its competitors; produce support for and trust in the organisation and its products (which in turn may enhance its stability and resilience in times of change and crisis); and help it to attract and retain quality staff, suppliers, investors and allies.

3.3　Conversely, a negative reputation – or reputational damage – can erode support and trust for the organisation and its products; create negative expectations (which in turn encourage negative perceptions); attract hostile scrutiny from the media and pressure groups; and damage the organisation's relationships with its key stakeholders (which in turn can have negative effects on its productivity, profitability, share price and so on).

3.4　Until comparatively recently, many corporations made little attempt proactively to manage how they were regarded by their stakeholders, other than customers. Even when reputation-damaging crises arose (such as a product safety recall, exposure of unethical dealings or an incident of environmental damage), many attempted to 'ride out the storm' by ignoring criticism or making token attempts to put a positive 'spin' on the issue to selected audiences.

3.5　This picture has begun to change, as corporate scandals have demonstrated the importance of building, maintaining and defending reputation; as the public and other secondary stakeholders have demanded greater governance, accountability and responsibility from organisations; and as reputation has increasingly been seen as a key element of both asset and risk management. Attempts are now made to measure the 'reputational capital' of corporations.

3.6　With the rise in media, pressure group and public interest in sustainability issues, corporate ethics and environmental and social responsibility have become key dimensions in the development and defence of corporate reputations – and the winning and preservation of credibility, consumer trust and brand strength.

Brands and corporate brands

3.7　As you may know if you have studied *Marketing for Purchasers*, a brand is: 'a name, term, sign, symbol or design, or combination of them, intended to identify the goods or services of one seller or group of sellers, and to differentiate them from those of competitors' (Kotler). Brands are designed to create intangible, often emotional, associations in the perceptions of target audiences, over and above the physical properties of a product, symbol or name.

3.8 Increasing numbers of organisations now seek to create brand associations and identities around the corporation (or group of corporations) itself – in addition to their product or service brands. Van Riel and Fombrun (*Corporate Reputation Management*) define corporate brands as 'the features of a company that employees, investors, customers and the public associate with an organisation as a whole. The purpose of a corporate brand is to personalise the company as a whole...; to cast a favourable halo over everything the organisation does or says – and to capitalise on its reputation.' Non-profit organisations have also started embracing the concept, as a key asset for obtaining donations, sponsorships and volunteers.

3.9 Again, sustainability has become a key dimension on which corporate brands seek to position themselves in the perception of their target audiences and markets, in relation to competitors. The strength of a brand's sustainability positioning may be based on elements such as the following.

- Heritage: the background 'story' to the brand (eg the long ethical and social justice involvement of Quaker companies such as Cadbury's)

- Values: the core values and characteristics of the brand (eg The Body Shop's ethical values)

- Reflection and identification: how the brand relates to stakeholder self-identity, or how stakeholders perceive themselves as a result of engaging with the brand (eg as an ethical investor or green consumer).

3.10 Various *Best Global Brands* and *Most Admired Companies* league tables are published annually, and you might like to browse some of these to see how they correlate with sustainability indices. A widely cited list of the top 100 global brands by financial value is produced by the Interbrand Corporation (www.interbrand.com): the website also offers a range of interesting brand-related articles, free to download, on subjects such as the impact of sustainability on corporate brand value. 'Not surprisingly, sustainability is driving brand value across all sectors – from automotive, to consumer products, to financial services. Auto-makers such as Honda (No 20) and Mercedes (No 11) are creating new, more efficient car models... Companies such as GE (No 4) and BP (no 84) increased their brand valuation by investing a substantial amount in sustainable business practices.'

3.11 As environmental issues and stakeholders change, and/or as the organisation changes, the brand may need to be repositioned. Oil company BP, for example, rebranded itself as a 'green' organisation by changing its brand to 'Beyond Petroleum' (investment in alternative greener and more sustainable energies) and its symbolism to create associations with the natural environment. Sustainable procurement may therefore be part of a marketing-led initiative to rebrand the organisation with ethical, green or CSR credentials.

Reputational risk management and sustainable procurement

3.12 Corporate reputations are constantly in danger of being eroded, undermined, damaged or destroyed. Regester & Larkin (*Risk Issus and Crisis Management in Public Relations*) argue that: 'Threats to reputation – whether real or perceived – can destroy, literally in hours or days, an image or brand developed and invested in over decades. These threats need to be anticipated, understood and planned for.'

3.13 According to ongoing consumer attitude monitoring by research firm Populus, three quarters of the UK population claims to weigh-up a company's reputation before buying its products or services, and nearly three in five say they actively avoid purchasing from certain companies because of questions they have about their social, environmental or ethical track record. Meanwhile, increasingly sophisticated awareness campaigns from a wide range of pressure and advocacy groups have contributed to heightened public sensitivity to a range of environmental and social issues, particularly targeting corporate activities.

3.14 Sustainable procurement is thus likely to be a cornerstone of reputational risk management and defence. Oxfam, for example, recently suffered a reputational crisis when a major overseas supplier of its 'Make Poverty History' wristbands was discovered to be exploiting its workforce with poor pay and conditions.

3.15 Corporations and whole industries can become negatively associated (often on the basis of one or two high-profile public relations crises) with unsustainable or unethical practices – attracting negative scrutiny, publicity, pressure group activism and consumer boycott. High profile examples include Wal-Mart in the US (using their size and price power to destroy small local competitors); McDonald's (contribution to child obesity and environmental damage); Nike (exploitation of workers in low-cost labour countries); Shell (environmental damage); and Microsoft (trouble with competition regulators). It should be noted that all these corporations continue to enjoy market success – but that all of them have taken significant steps to strengthen and communicate their CSR credentials, in order to 'manage the issues'.

Example: child labour and the clothing industry

To take the example cited in the syllabus, major players in the clothing and sporting goods sector, including Nike, have in recent decades had to address the issue of the use of child labour (and sweatshops, exploiting workers with poor wages and working conditions) by their suppliers in developing countries.

An article in *Supply Management* (7 June 2007) reported on Nike's unveiling of an 'updated' range of CSR goals.

'The firm, once famously criticised for poor conditions at supplier factories, says it wants to improve working conditions for the 800,000 people who manufacture its branded products. It hopes to eliminate the problem of excessive overtime by 2011.

'The company is also keen to increase the transparency of its supply chain operations by posting a list of the 700 factories it uses on the internet. The site will also explain the auditing tools it uses to examine its suppliers.

'It also intended to make its factories, shops and business travel climate neutral by 2011.

'[In May 2007], Nike signed a deal with a new supplier in Pakistan to make Nike footballs after problems with a different supplier last year. The contract has imposed strict guarantees on [the supplier] which is expected to meet nine workplace conditions, including making sure that employees are registered, paid hourly rates and eligible for social benefits, such as healthcare.'

In 2009, Nike was listed as one of the 'World's Most Ethical Companies' by the Ethisphere Institute.

3.16 Meanwhile, maintaining brand reputation has become increasingly difficult in business areas that are perceived as intrinsically environmentally or socially damaging: examples include forestry, mining, aviation, automotive, travel and tobacco. You should be aware from the quality press of how organisations in such areas are using sustainability programmes (and related corporate communications) to manage issues and counter negative perceptions: environmental rehabilitation and sustainable management; investment in alternative energy; promotion of carbon offsetting schemes; 'green' product development (such as the Toyota Prius and eco-tourism offerings); responsible health warnings; and so on.

Example: aviation and travel

To take another example cited by the syllabus, the aviation, travel and automotive industries are the focus of public and regulatory concern about carbon (CO_2) emissions and their contribution to climate change.

Airlines are well aware of sustainability issues. Willie Walsh, British Airways chief executive (*The Guardian*, 3 June 2008), has said that carriers are working 'every minute, every day' in order to reduce carbon emissions. This may involve investing in alternative fuel research (eg Virgin Airlines), negotiating new routes (to reduce stop-overs and flying time), and improving fuel efficiency (in airplane design and pilot training).

The International Air Travel Association (IATA) has issued a four-point 'road map' to make air travel more environmentally responsible.

- Investing more in fuel-efficient technology
- Sending out IATA's 'green teams' to advise airlines on cutting fuel use
- Urging governments to simplify air traffic control
- Persuading states to invest more research money into green plane and engine design.

Meanwhile, airlines and travel brokers are offering consumers carbon offsetting options – and consumers are being urged by pressure groups to avoid air travel where possible (eg for business travel, using video-conferencing instead) and to pick direct routes where available.

3.17 New sustainable procurement initiatives may, more proactively, represent an opportunity to reposition or re-brand the organisation on the basis of sustainability values likely to appeal to stakeholders. Marks & Spencer, for example, has significantly re-branded itself as a sustainability leader, with its Plan A Corporate Social Responsibility platform. Toyota has established itself as the market leader in energy-efficient hybrid (petrol-electric) car production, with its early-to-market Prius model: a strong position, with hybrids forecast to take 80% of the auto market by 2015.

4 Organisational mission, strategy and policy

Mission and vision

4.1 Organisations generally measure the relevance and value of any activity by whether and how far it will 'fit' (and ideally further) its overall purpose, goals and strategic plans. While Henry Mintzberg and others have demonstrated that organisational strategies and values can emerge from the bottom up – as the organisation comes to own and adopt ideas that 'catch on' with members, or work in practice at the front line – most organisations still pursue a top-down strategic management approach.

4.2 The organisation's mission (definition of purpose) and vision (strategic intent or desired future state) 'cascade' down to goals and objectives (targets or aims which the organisation will pursue in order to fulfil its mission and vision), and strategic programmes and plans to achieve them.

4.3 Corporate strategies (the general direction of the organisation and how value will be added over the long term) likewise cascade down to tactical or business level strategies (applied to particular divisions, functions or strategic business units, focusing on the tasks and objectives required to achieve the corporate strategies in the medium term). These in turn cascade down to operational strategies for functions and departments (focusing on the specific detail of tasks, targets, resources and actions needed to deliver business level strategies in the short term).

Sustainability as a guiding value

4.4　One of the key points arising from this 'hierarchy of objectives' is that, in order to secure widespread acceptance and support, sustainability will have to be championed and embedded in the guiding value system of the organisation, from the top down.

4.5　The concept of organisational 'mission' answers questions such as: who are we, what are we trying to do, whom do we serve or who or what determines our success? It generally comprises four elements (Campbell & Tawaday).

- *Purpose*: why does the organisation exist, and for whom (shareholders and other stakeholders)?
- *Strategy*: what business are we in? what do we do? how do we do it?
- *Values*: what do we value and believe to be important? what do we stand for?
- *Standards and behaviour*: what are the policies and norms that guide how we operate?

4.6　This kind of self-understanding shapes behaviour and decision-making. If sustainability isn't part of it – in some explicit form – the organisation may well struggle to secure widespread buy-in to sustainable procurement, because it isn't a priority 'fit' with the organisation's identity, purpose and direction.

4.7　Mission and value statements are concise 'word pictures' of the organisation. The following are some examples of statements which suggest a sustainability orientation.

- Wal-Mart: 'To give ordinary folk the chance to buy the same things as rich people.'
- The Body Shop: 'Tirelessly work to narrow the gap between principle and practice whilst making fun, passion and care part of our daily lives.'
- 3M: 'Our values: act with uncompromising honesty and integrity in everything we do; satisfy our customers with innovative technology and superior quality, value and service; provide our investors an attractive return through sustainable, global growth; respect our social and physical environment around the world; value and develop our employees' diverse talents, initiative; earn the admiration of all those associated with 3M worldwide.'

Sustainability and strategic alignment

4.8　If an organisation is to achieve its corporate objectives, the plans set for each unit and function – while specific to their own roles – must be co-ordinated with each other so that they contribute towards the overall objectives. This integration or alignment needs to happen in two directions.

- *Vertical alignment* is about ensuring that the goal of every activity contributes towards the overall or higher objectives of the business. So, for example, an organisation with a vision for CSR may set corporate objectives for sustainability, which will flow down to sustainable procurement objectives, and hence to operational targets for sourcing, specification and so on. Conversely, any sustainability objectives set for procurement will need to be in line with (and justified by their contribution to) overall corporate strategy.
- *Horizontal alignment* is about ensuring that the plans of every unit in an organisation are co-ordinated with those of others, so that they work effectively together – and present a consistent, coherent face to the world. So, for example, sustainable procurement plans will need to be co-ordinated with the needs of customers (defined by marketing plans), the requirements of production (defined by operations plans) and the availability of resources (eg through HR and financial planning) and so on.

Policies

4.9 Strategies are implemented via the development of policies, which communicate the requirements of the strategy for stakeholders. A policy is 'a body of principles, expressed or implied, laid down to direct an enterprise towards its objectives and guide executives in decision making' (Lysons & Farrington: Purchasing and Supply Management). Policies are generally set at a senior level, so that they have the force of direct authority: they must be adhered to by all people, in all activities to which they apply. Two key policy areas are mentioned in the syllabus: CSR policy and people development policy.

4.10 The corporate social responsibility (CSR) policy of an organisation will obviously have a strong influence on the subordinate policies and programmes established for sustainable procurement. If an organisation has a strong CSR policy in place, with environmental and social sustainability targets clearly articulated, this will require and support the development and implementation of sustainable procurement. If only vague lip service is paid to CSR at the policy level, it will be less easy to secure meaningful commitment and resources for sustainable procurement programmes.

4.11 On the other hand, the procurement function may have a strong role to play in championing and driving CSR policy: as the interface between the supply chain and internal customers (including the design and operations functions), it will bear much of the responsibility for the practicalities of CSR implementation.

4.12 A 2007 study of CSR across many countries (Baughn et al) found that currently, CSR policies tend to be focused on environmental rather than social aspects: as we saw in Chapter 1, environmental issues are more established, more readily measurable and manageable with purely technical solutions. The added emphasis on social issues, which is gaining ground, requires a more ethical and relational approach, which is particularly suited to the concerns of sustainable procurement and ethical sourcing.

4.13 People development means enhancing the skills, capability and performance of employees to ensure that they are given the opportunity to fulfil their potential and to maximise their contribution to the organisation and its customers. It embraces activities including career development, education and training, retention and empowerment. The people development policy of an organisation will therefore have an influence on sustainable procurement in various ways, by helping to determine:

- Managerial and workforce understanding of and commitment to sustainability values and issues, and the managerial and technical skills available to implement sustainable procurement (eg through the priority given to induction, education and training in sustainability; and the incorporation of sustainability criteria in employee selection, appraisal, reward and career development)

- Learning, knowledge- and best-practice-sharing, and knowledge retention within the organisation (eg if policies support management succession, employee retention, mentoring/coaching and so on, so that knowledge and practice for sustainable procurement grows and is maintained over time)

- Whether employees feel valued, and invited, empowered, resourced in such a way as to enable them to contribute meaningfully to sustainable procurement initiatives (harnessing their commitment and initiative)

- Whether employees and supply chains are fairly, ethically and responsibly treated, with support for diversity, equality of opportunity and a fair and responsible legal (and psychological) contract: all of these are themselves social sustainability issues.

4.14 We should also add that sourcing policies will be instrumental in directing sustainable procurement, in areas such as: the use of local or global sourcing; preference given to small or diverse suppliers; sustainability criteria used in the definition of requirements, appraisal of tenders and selection of suppliers; ethical/environmental monitoring of suppliers; and so on. We will discuss these issues in detail in Chapter 10.

Procedures

4.15 In order for policy to operate effectively it needs to be underpinned by systems and procedures: established methods, routines or sequences of activities laid down to accomplish operational goals. In implementing a sustainable procurement policy, for example, attention may have to be given to procedures for early supplier involvement, specification development, the management of tenders, supplier selection, negotiation of terms, contracting, contract management, supplier environmental monitoring or certification – and so on, at all stages of the sourcing cycle.

5 Organisational culture and attitudes

Management attitudes

5.1 Earlier, we argued that in order to secure widespread acceptance and support, sustainable procurement will have to be championed and embedded in the guiding value system of the organisation, from the top down. Managers are key instruments in this respect, as:

- The selectors and formulators of what the organisation's values, strategies and policy priorities will be (in the case of senior managers)
- The communicators and 'sellers' of corporate vision and values, and therefore the creators of corporate and departmental culture – which may, or may not, give value to issues such as environmental and social sustainability
- The implementers of sustainable procurement strategies and policies at the departmental level
- Potential champions and sponsors of sustainable procurement in their units and functions, and with the external stakeholders with whom they have contact on the organisation's behalf
- Potential sources of resistance, indifference or conflicting priorities, if they have not 'bought in' to sustainable procurement
- Potential facilitators or resistors of the cross-functional (and supply chain) communication and collaboration that will be required to support sustainable procurement.

5.2 The extent to which managers understand and own sustainable procurement values and principles – and are motivated, resourced and empowered to pursue them – will therefore be of crucial importance to the successful development and implementation of any sustainable procurement policy or programme. Managers may be a source of resistance or indifference, for example, if:

- Their performance is measured on purely financial or cost criteria, so that social or environmental sustainability is not a priority
- They feel threatened or insecure at the introduction of 'new' performance measures for which they do not have the skill/knowledge set
- The sustainable procurement agenda is perceived as political game-playing (eg an attempt by the procurement function to gain power over line managers)

- They have entrenched preconceptions about the costs of sustainable procurement, the difficulties of change and so on

- They lack understanding of the business case for sustainable procurement, and the urgency and significance of sustainability-related risks.

Internal stakeholder positions and attitudes

5.3 Managers are only one category of internal stakeholder: others include employees, and (from the point of view of the procurement function) other functions in the organisation. In the third sector, internal stakeholders will also include members (eg of a trade union, association or church) and volunteers.

5.4 Like external stakeholders, internal stakeholders exercise influence over the organisation in various ways (Johnson & Scholes, *Exploring Corporate Strategy*). They may have formal authority for decision-making (eg in the case of a manager); informal power (eg in the case of a charismatic team leader); control over key resources (eg information, rewards or labour); possession of valued knowledge or skills (eg sustainability, compliance or procurement specialists); control of the human environment (eg influencing or negotiating skills); and/or involvement in the implementation of policies and plans (eg exercising initiative or commitment to shape outcomes).

5.5 Internal stakeholders will therefore have an influence on how sustainable procurement policies are shaped – and how effectively they are implemented.

5.6 Employees in general may be indifferent or resistant to sustainable procurement, unless mechanisms are in place to secure their 'buy in' and commitment: communicating the vision; educating and consulting them on the issues; offering training where required; providing clear objectives, targets, guidelines and resources for implementation; allocating clear accountabilities; offering incentives and rewards/reinforcements; providing clear, ongoing progress and performance feedback; and so on. We will discuss all these issues in later chapters, when we look at the deployment of sustainable procurement policies.

5.7 Different functional interests may create different drivers for, and sources of resistance to, sustainable procurement. The procurement function may see it as a source of added value, credibility and status. The marketing function may likewise be broadly supportive of sustainability, as a potential source of competitive advantage and brand strength. Operational functions may be more resistant, if radical changes to processes and skills are required. The finance function may be resistant to measures which do not have potential for enhanced profitability and shareholder value. We will discuss these aspects further in Chapter 6, where we explore the implications of sustainable procurement for different functions in the organisation.

5.8 Internal marketing and communications will be an important part of the implementation of any sustainable procurement initiative.

Organisation culture

5.9 Organisation culture has been defined as 'a pattern of beliefs and expectations shared by the organisation's members, and which produce norms which powerfully shape the behaviour of individuals and groups in the organisation' (Schwartz & Davies). Deal & Kennedy have summed it up, popularly, as 'the way we do things around here'.

5.10 Corporate strategy is partly a matter of perspective: an expression of how an organisation sees itself, and what it values. Culture is therefore crucially important to the successful development and implementation of corporate strategy. What Mintzberg calls the 'cultural school' of strategic management emphasises that:

- Strategy formation is a process of social interaction, based on the beliefs and understandings shared by members of an organisation (though not necessarily clearly articulated)

- Culture and ideology tend to resist strategic change – and radical changes in strategy therefore have to be based on a fundamental change in culture and values

- Positive, dominant, widely-shared values (such as innovation, equality, or environmental and social sustainability) can be a powerful source of corporate direction and competitive advantage.

5.11 The good news is that cultures which are cynical about sustainability, short-termist, unsuited to changing requirements or otherwise unsupportive of sustainable procurement can be changed! Here are three key areas of leverage.

- Consistent expression and modelling of the new sustainability or CSR values by management (from the top down), leaders and influencers (who may need to be co-opted to the initiative by those in authority)

- Changing underlying values and beliefs, through communication, education and involvement; spreading new values and beliefs and encouraging employees to 'own' them (through incentives, co-opting people to teach others and so on)

- Use of human resource management mechanisms to reinforce the changes: including new values and behaviours in recruitment and selection profiles, appraisal and reward criteria; training and development planning; and so on.

6 Resources, capacity and capability

Availability of sustainability resources

6.1 In Chapter 3, we saw how external PESTLE factors impacted on the availability of resources to support sustainability (such as skills, investment and technology development), and on the pressures for sustainability arising from resource consumption and depletion. Internal factors similarly impact on the availability of labour, skills and competencies; new products, materials and processes; and capacity and capability for sustainability.

Labour and skills

6.2 Sustainability is a relatively new concept, and there is a recognised shortage of relevant skills – aggravated by a similar shortage of skilled procurement professionals. The need for more people with skills in both areas may act as a constraint on sustainable procurement – or a competitive opportunity for organisations which have sourced, retained and developed such skills.

6.3 Internal factors may influence the ability of the organisation and supply chain to attract, retain, deploy and harness the skills, knowledge and commitment required for sustainability. (The syllabus mentions 'population demographics' at this point, but that is more properly an external influence, as discussed in Chapter 3.)

6.4 Influences include: the HR policies of the organisation (in areas such as recruitment, diversity, motivation, retention, development, empowerment and employee relations); the extent of automation or computerisation of processes; the ability of the organisation to source expertise globally, through outsourcing and 'virtual' organisation; the employability and career mobility of staff members; policies and processes for supplier selection, management and development; and so on.

6.5 Research by the UK Confederation of British Industry (CBI) has suggested that employers can collaborate on skills and innovation, most commonly in local or sector clusters (and within supply chains) in order to enhance sustainability performance. Under a 'hub-and-spoke' approach, for example, a large employer can support learning and improvement activities among smaller firms (eg by opening their training facilities to suppliers). Small and medium-sized enterprise (SME) collaboration may involve the sharing of mentoring, skills or learning programmes, or the pooling of skills to compete more effectively for contracts.

New materials, products and processes

6.6 Sustainable procurement, design and materials management involves the increasing utilisation of materials that are abundant, non-toxic and recyclable. Ken Geiser argues that there are two overarching sustainable materials objectives.

- *Detoxification*: reducing the toxic characteristics of materials used in products and processes. This can be achieved by reducing the volume or strength of toxic materials used in the process of production, by substituting less toxic substances or re-designing the production method.

- *Dematerialisation*: increasing the intensity of the use and/or service derived from each unit of material used. This approach may involve recycling and reusing materials, re-designing products that use fewer materials or considering material usage at the design stage and ensuring the environmental sustainability of the product through all stages of its life.

6.7 Internal factors may impact on the ability of the organisation to adopt or develop new materials, processes and products to support sustainability. (Again, the syllabus mentions sustainable new or alternative products, materials, technology and methods becoming available for use in areas such as textiles, plastics and farming – but these are more properly external influences, as discussed in Chapter 3.)

6.8 Internal influences may include: infrastructure, skills and resources available to harness ICT (for video-conferencing, paperless transactions, and access to small/diverse supply markets, say); the ability to innovate and adapt in using new methods, equipment and materials (eg alternative energy sources); skills and resources available within the organisation or supply chain for research and development of new products (including early supplier involvement, purchasing research and sourcing); and so on.

Internal capacity and capability

6.9 Sustainability initiatives may initially be constrained by limitations in the organisation's capacity and capability, but one of the key arguments for sustainability programmes is that they act as an ongoing driver of enhanced capacity and capability.

6.10 Sustainable procurement objectives may spur the organisation to develop capabilities or competencies in supply chain development, environmental scanning, innovation, reverse logistics, 'green' design, ethical sourcing, stakeholder management and employee involvement, for example. The organisation may seek certification under one or more industry, national or international standards for environmental management systems or fair trading: learning from best practice and developing process capabilities.

6.11 Sustainable procurement programmes may also enhance productive capacity by increasing the efficiency and productivity of resources and processes. Productivity gains may come from:

- Enhanced employee loyalty, morale and commitment, as a result of ethical employment practices, employee involvement and sustainability values
- Reduced constraints and disruptions arising from poor or unsafe working conditions and accidents
- Enhanced continuity of supply, from sustainable supply chain management and risk management
- The reduction of wastes throughout sourcing and related business processes.

Waste reduction

6.12 One of the cornerstones of sustainable production and procurement is the reduction of wastes: the use of resources over and above what is required to produce value (as defined by the customer: if the customer does not need it or will not pay for it, then it is non-value-adding).

6.13 Taichi Ohno is credited with developing the Toyota Production System which laid the foundations of lean and world-class manufacturing. He identified seven categories of waste in production processes: Table 4.1.

Table 4.1 *Ohno's seven wastes*

Waste caused by ...	Comments
Over-production	Producing output which customers are not yet demanding leads to stockholding costs, product deterioration/obsolescence and scrap. This refers both to finished goods for external customers, and to work in progress for the next stage in the production process. Solutions include the use of 'pull' systems (such as *kanban*) to trigger production according to demand.
Transportation	Moving materials between different locations adds cost, and risks damage and deterioration. This may refer to moving materials from their source to our production facility, or to moving materials within the production facility. Either way, effective materials handling, transport and load planning can minimise movements.
Waiting	Delays or queues in processing mean that more time is taken than is really needed, without adding value. Waiting time may be minimised, or used for value-adding activity (such as training or maintenance).
Motion	Unnecessary motions (bending, reaching and so on) violate sound ergonomic principles. This can reduce productivity and cause fatigue (and possibly injury) to staff.
Over-processing	This can happen when unnecessarily sophisticated equipment is used to produce relatively simple goods, adding to their cost. It may also create inefficient facilities layouts and materials handling. Value analysis (and value engineering for new product design) is often used to remove non-value adding features and processes.
Inventory	Lean supply aims to eliminate the use of buffer stocks. Stockholding incurs cost without adding value, and can mask inefficiencies in production planning or processes. Just in time (JIT) systems are used to 'pull' inventory through the system in response to demand.
Defects/corrections	The costs of rework and scrap do not add value, but reduce bottom-line profit. Defects are regarded as opportunities for problem-solving and improvement, often using a *kaizen* or continuous improvement approach.

6.14 Others have added to Ohno's seven categories, including wastes with direct links to environmental and social sustainability in a wider variety of settings, such as:

- The waste of untapped human potential
- The waste of inappropriate systems
- Wasted energy and water
- Wasted materials
- Service- and office-generated waste.

7 *Product and service features*

7.1 Finally, the potential for sustainability will depend on the nature of the organisation's activities, products and services, their design criteria and impact on the environment. Here are some of the key issues.

- Whether they pose immediate or high-priority sustainability issues and reputational/compliance risks (eg plastic bags or toys containing lead paint)
- The extent to which greater sustainability can be attained without compromising key design or performance features (eg by designing a high-performance hybrid car, or a healthy food product that still tastes good!)
- The extent to which the total 'bundle of benefits' that make up the offering to the consumer explicitly includes (or excludes) sustainability values. Some products and services, for example, are inherently sustainability-supporting − like energy-saving light bulbs, or recycling services. Some are, arguably, inherently unsustainable: tobacco products and gambling services might come into this category, say.

7.2 Design issues have traditionally concerned themselves with aesthetics, function and profitability. However, decisions made during the design phase have a direct impact on the materials and energy used during manufacture and the energy consumed and pollution produced during the product's lifetime.

7.3 Design for the environment (DFE) is becoming increasingly important. Fiskel defines DFE as 'a systematic consideration of design issues related to environmental and human health over the lifecycle of a product'. This definition highlights the key areas of a systematic approach that reflects the whole life of the product, not just the design and development stages.

7.4 Blackburn similarly highlights two key issues in 'green design':

- 'Improving the efficient use of natural and economic resources all along the life cycle of the product, from material extraction to manufacture, use and post-use disposal. This means searching for ways to provide the customer the same function or service that the product was intended to perform, but at less cost and with less material and energy required in the manufacture and use of the product.'
- 'Providing greater respect and accommodation for the needs of people and other living things along the product lifecycle. This means designing products that are easier for customers to use and that pose less of a health and safety risk for them and for product manufacturers, transporters, disposers and other handlers. It also means developing products that minimise the potential harm to the environment along the product lifecycle, or even better, enhance the ability of the environment to repair and sustain itself.'

7.5 We will discuss issues in sustainable design further in Chapter 9 on purchasing specifications.

Example: BHP Billiton

Mining giant BHP Billiton has a strong sustainable development profile – not least, in response to widespread controversy in the Australian mining industry over issues such as: the environmental degradation caused by mining and transport operations; the dislocation of remote area communities due to a large 'fly-in-fly-out' labour force; the siting of mining operations in areas of cultural significance to indigenous people; the commercial exploitation of non-renewable mineral resources; and a large carbon footprint.

'For BHP Billiton, sustainable development is about ensuring our business remains viable and contributes lasting benefits to society through the consideration of social, environmental, ethical and economic aspects in all that we do.

'Working through complex operational issues associated with our operations has highlighted environmental and social performance as a critical success factor for the Company. We are well aware of the costs of getting it wrong; but more importantly, we recognise the value that can be created by getting it right. Consequently, we adopt a holistic approach to business strategy, seeking to realise value for our stakeholders through a sustainable business philosophy.'

The company's aspirational goal is stated as: Zero Harm.

Its website offers a wealth of information on sustainability issues in an extractive industry, including: health and safety risks; water conservation and recycling; and emissions reductions. There are published statements on: sustainability and sustainability reporting; Health Safety Environment and Community (HSEC) standards; stakeholders; health and safety; environmental commitment; social responsibility; and socio-economic goals – including supplier principles and standards – together with a number of case studies.

In 2006, the company launched an Emerging Markets Team, which currently leads a pilot Shanghai Procurement Hub, to help ensure that the company's procurement practices in China are responsible (in line with its Sustainable Development Policy and HSEC Management Standards), and to help foster a culture of HSEC in Chinese supply markets. The team engages only those suppliers that demonstrate that they maintain suitable HSEC standards and supports those suppliers' further improvement through ongoing audits and management, so that the company's purchases in China 'align mutual economic benefit with the encouragement of suppliers to adopt global best-practice HSEC standards.'

Chapter summary

- There are many internal influences on sustainable procurement policies. For most organisations, it is not practicable to address all issues simultaneously; the focus should first be on the high-risk issues.

- Blackburn and others argue that the benefits of adopting sustainable procurement include actual improvements in financial performance.

- Organisations are increasingly concerned with their brands and their overall corporate brand. A policy of sustainable procurement will lead to benefits in this area.

- Many organisations have integrated sustainable procurement into their core mission and values statements.

- Sustainable procurement will only be achieved with appropriate commitment from internal stakeholders; the organisational culture and attitudes must support it.

- A policy of sustainable procurement requires resources of labour, skills and materials. Minimising waste of resources is crucial.

Self-test questions

Numbers in brackets refer to the paragraphs above where your answers can be checked.

1   How do corporate reputation and brand strength make a contribution to adoption of sustainable procurement? (1.2)

2   List the sales and cost factors identified by Blackburn as benefiting from sustainability. (2.2)

3   How can sustainability reduce costs? (2.5)

4   How can sustainability contribute to competitiveness and growth potential? (2.7)

5   Define a brand. (3.7)

6   Why is sustainability important in reputational risk management? (3.12–3.15)

7   What four elements in an organisational mission are identified by Campbell and Tawaday? (4.5)

8   How does an organisation's people development policy influence sustainable procurement? (4.13)

9   List the roles of managers in a policy of sustainability. (5.1)

10   What three areas of leverage may be used to transform an organisation from cynicism about sustainability towards adopting sustainable policies? (5.11)

11   What is meant by detoxification and dematerialisation in the context of sustainable materials objectives? (6.6)

12   List Ohno's seven wastes. (6.13 and Table 14.1)

Further reading

From your 'Essential Reading' list, you might look at Blackburn (*The Sustainability Handbook*):

- Chapter 3: The Value of Sustainability

CHAPTER 5

Drivers for Sustainable Procurement

Learning objectives and indicative content

1.5   Identify which external and internal factors will drive sustainable procurement within an organisation and compare and contrast their relative importance across public, private, and third sectors and their tiers

- External and internal drivers
- Characteristics of the different sectors in the context of sustainable procurement
- Key drivers for different sectors, industries and businesses
- Sustainable procurement drivers as distinct from effects

Chapter headings

1   Sustainable procurement drivers and effects

2   The private sector

3   The public sector

4   The third sector

5   Different industries and businesses

Introduction

In Chapters 3 and 4, we have explored various external and internal factors 'influencing' sustainable procurement. Following the syllabus, we now consider which of these may act as positive driving forces for sustainable procurement within organisations of different types and within different sectors.

In the first section of the chapter, we highlight key drivers for sustainable procurement – and distinguish them clearly from the effects of sustainable procurement. The syllabus makes this distinction, in order to ensure clarity of analysis, and it is worth bearing it in mind when analysing the factors in exam case studies (and your own case examples): which are causes of, or contributors to, the introduction and take-up of sustainability initiatives, and which are effects of, or offshoots from, them?

In the following sections, we examine the distinguishing characteristics of the private, public and third sectors, and different industry and business types, in relation to sustainability issues. Obviously, we cannot cover all specific examples and permutations, but this discussion should offer a broad framework for considering which drivers are likely to have most relevance and impact for any particular sector, industry or case study organisation mentioned in the exam – or for any particular organisations you are interested in, which you might prepare to cite as case study examples, if invited to do so.

1 *Sustainable procurement drivers and effects*

Drivers

1.1 In Chapter 13, on tools of analysis to support sustainable procurement, we will discuss a technique called forcefield analysis: a technique for identifying forces for and against change, in order to diagnose some of the change management problems that will need to be addressed, and some of the resources and dynamics available to support it.

1.2 At any time in an organisation there exist both forces for change (pushing towards a preferred state) and forces for maintaining the *status quo* (pushing back towards the way things are). The interplay of these forces determines the pace and direction of change at any given moment.

- Driving forces (or drivers) are forces for change: encouraging people to give up old ways of doing things and to try new behaviours. Examples include: the desire to avoid the risk of customer boycotts and reputational damage; frustration caused by inefficient processes; new technology becoming available; legislation imposing compliance; or influence/support from senior management and influential stakeholders.

- Restraining forces are forces resisting change and supporting the *status quo*. Examples include: shortage of resources; opposition from influencers or cultural values; already-installed technology and established systems; managerial pre-occupation with short-term operational targets and so on.

1.3 In general, change may be driven by internal triggers or external forces.

- *Internal drivers* are factors that cause organisational disequilibrium: in order for equilibrium to be re-established, some element of the system will have to change. Internal triggers include: the questioning of leadership; poor performance (and pressure to become more competitive, innovative or profitable); the appointment of new senior managers or innovators; the change or re-ordering of organisational goals, values, processes or structures (eg the introduction of CSR objectives or a programme of business process re-engineering); or changes in knowledge (organisational learning) or resources, enabling the adoption of different processes and technologies.

- *External drivers* are factors in the organisation's competitive (micro) and wider (macro) environments. These may include: economic opportunities and threats; changes in a product, supply or labour market; increasing scarcity of natural resources; the emergence of ecological and ethical issues of concern to the organisation's stakeholders; technological developments; law and regulation; and consumer, public and pressure group pressure.

Drivers, enablers and effects

1.4 When analysing the internal and external factors influencing sustainable procurement, it may help to distinguish between two different types of positive influences.

- *Drivers*: forces which create pressure to develop and implement sustainable procurement strategies (eg by creating disequilibrium, opportunities or threats which must be addressed)

- *Enablers*: 'ecological' or support factors which create conditions favourable to the effective and efficient introduction, implementation and acceptance of sustainable procurement strategies.

1.5   Drivers *impel* action for sustainable procurement, which enablers serve to *facilitate*. So, for example, factors such as resource scarcity, legislation, reputational risk/opportunity and stakeholder pressure are likely to drive organisational measures for sustainability. Factors such as innovation capabilities, established risk management processes, a sustainability-educated management, the availability of sustainable resources and the development of industry-wide sustainability standards are likely to support such measures.

1.6   Here are some general enablers or ecological factors for sustainable procurement.

- Financial viability and stability (although change may also be more readily complied with if it is perceived to be a necessity for survival) and the availability of resources for change
- Adaptable (flexible, information-sharing) organisation structures and processes
- Vision, leadership and support from senior management
- Supporting policies and systems (eg for people/skills development, CSR, risk management and innovation)
- Available benchmarks, standards and best-practice sharing (eg sustainability and environmental management systems standards)
- A supportive culture, values and attitudes (eg willingness to learn and adapt, and adoption of sustainability values and positions by key stakeholders).

1.7   In analysing any situation or case study, it is also important to distinguish between the drivers/enablers of sustainable procurement and its effects. So, for example, legislation on waste and emissions reduction would be a driver for sustainable procurement – but policies and procedures for the reduction of waste, emissions and resource consumption would be the effect of introducing sustainable procurement in an organisation.

1.8   In general, you should be able to separate drivers and effects by chronology and cause-and-effect analysis. Drivers come before the introduction of a sustainability programme, as a contributing factor in it. Effects come after the introduction of a sustainability programme, as a result of it: improved labour practices or corporate governance; ISO 14001 and/or Fair Trade certification; sustainability-supporting strategies, policies and procedures; a positive employer/ investment brand; enhanced corporate reputation; cause-related and sustainable brand marketing; and so on.

1.9   This distinction will not always be clear cut. If an organisation's employees are educated and aware of sustainability issues, this might be a driver or enabler of sustainable procurement. On the other hand, the introduction of sustainable production should have the effect of creating a more educated and aware workforce. Similarly, an existing CSR or corporate citizenship policy may be a driver for more specific initiatives in procurement – but they may also be the effect of observable benefits gained by procurement-led initiatives. Get used to analysing which are drivers and which are effects – which is the horse and which is the cart – in each scenario.

Drivers and enablers for sustainable procurement

1.10   Tables 5.1 and 5.2 set out some of the key general external and internal drivers and enablers for sustainable procurement. (If you require further explanation or examples, refer back to Chapters 3 and 4, where external and internal factors were discussed in detail.)

Table 5.1 *General external drivers for sustainable procurement*

External drivers	External support factors
Political factors: government policy; targets and standards; incentives and penalties; government practice as a buyer/supplier and employer; transnational commitments (eg the Kyoto protocol)	*Political factors*: standards and best-practice sharing; incentives; government support for sustainability innovation
Economic factors: loss of market demand for unsustainable products/services; rising market demand for (and price premiums available on) sustainable products/services	*Economic factors*: availability of skilled labour; availability of sustainable resources; exchange rates (supporting local/global sourcing); interest rates (supporting borrowing)
Social/ethical factors: societal attitudes and values creating media, public, labour and consumer pressure for sustainable practices; emerging social justice and ethical issues (eg corporate governance, citizenship, corruption, trading ethics, fair trade, human and labour rights); industry/professional codes of ethical practice	*Social/ethical factors*: education/skilling for sustainability; global frameworks and initiatives for fair trade (eg Fair Trade, Ethical Trading Initiative); media, public, labour and consumer support for sustainable brands
Technological factors: competitor/market innovation and take-up of sustainable technologies (new products, materials, processes); exposure of unsustainable technologies (eg re resource usage, wastes); opportunities in new sustainable technology markets (eg alternative energy)	*Technological factors*: availability and improving affordability of new sustainable products, materials and processes
Legal factors: national and international legislation on sustainability (or threat thereof): waste, pollution, emissions, employment rights, health and safety, consumer rights, corporate governance, public sector procurement – etc	*Legal factors*: availability of legal guidance; frameworks and guidance for compliance (eg standards and codes of practice)
Environmental factors: resource depletion and costs (especially energy costs); issues of concern to key stakeholders (eg climate change, GHG emissions, deforestation, water management, conservation, biodiversity, pollution, waste reduction); national targets under international agreements	*Environmental factors*: availability of alternative ('green') products, materials, processes and energy sources; research, information and best-practice sharing; education of consumers in 'green' consumption
External stakeholder factors: interest and pressure in any or all of the above factors, creating threats and opportunities for the organisation in obtaining resources and collaboration (eg customers, labour, investors, pressure group activism, potential for cause-related marketing)	*External stakeholder factors*: stakeholder support for sustainable procurement initiatives (eg customer and investor support, pressure group partnership); stakeholder theory and concepts such as corporate citizenship and CSR (supporting attention to wider stakeholder interests)

Table 5.2 *General internal drivers for sustainable procurement*

Internal drivers	Internal support factors
Corporate mission, vision and objectives including sustainability values and aspirations	Strategic alignment, supporting flow-down of sustainability to procurement objectives
Existing CSR and/or corporate citizenship objectives/policies	Strategies, policies and procedures for sustainable procurement (NB may also be an effect.)
Senior management visionaries, champions and supporters of sustainability	Communication of sustainability vision to lower levels of management; 'buy in' to sustainability values and objectives
Business case arguments for sustainability: enhanced reputation, brand strength and sales revenue; cost/waste reduction (eco-efficiencies); growth potential (eg new markets); enhanced supply chain innovation and efficiency; reduced regulatory burden	Data in support of business case; acceptance of business case by management; positive added-value-seeking through sustainability; positive management attitudes and abilities in securing employee 'buy-in', initiative and commitment
Accountability mechanisms, which demonstrate seriousness, and make rewards contingent on sustainability progress/performance	Existing processes and procedures for risk identification and management; general risk aversion
Priority given to risk management; perception of business, reputational and supply risk from non-sustainability; PR crisis and reputational damage	Corporate governance, sourcing/trading and HR/people development policies which are sustainable and ethical – and which support employee skilling/motivation/empowerment for sustainability (NB may also be an effect.)
Internal stakeholder demand for sustainability (eg need to attract and retain quality managers, employees, investors and supply chain partners)	Availability of resources (labour, skills, finance), capacity and capabilities (eg in innovation, supply chain management, reverse logistics and recycling/re-use) to implement sustainable procurement

1.11 It should be obvious that some of these factors will be more immediately relevant and influential in some sectors and industries than others. We will look at some of these distinctions in later sections of this chapter – but you should also begin to apply the above 'checklists' to some specific examples, as you encounter them in your studies. Which issues will be particularly relevant for a specific organisation? Which factors will be particularly influential in the decision making of that organisation? (Or, as a procurement professional, which drivers might you most effectively use as 'leverage' to champion a sustainable procurement initiative?) Are the necessary support factors in place for that organisation? Can you cite examples of how particular drivers or support factors have contributed to the successful introduction of sustainable procurement in an organisation?

Drivers emerging and changing over time

1.12 It is worth noting that an organisation will not simply respond to a 'package' of drivers operating at a given time. External factors constantly emerge and shift in priority, with technological developments, social changes, new information and so on. Internal drivers will depend on the changing information and priorities of management. As we stated in Chapter 4, organisations will develop and readjust their sustainability priorities over time.

1.13 Senge (*The Necessary Revolution*) argues that organisations subject to the same environmental drivers may respond in different ways, at different paces and with different motives.

'As with every trend, for all the early adopters, there are the laggards who wait to see how the prevailing winds are blowing before jumping in. Many people wonder who is walking the talk and who is just paying lip service and avoiding the hard work of integrating sustainable practices into the fabric of their business. But you've got to start somewhere. Wal-Mart CEO Lee Scott openly admitted that the company's early conservation efforts were part of a campaign to clean up its sullied image. Once organisations make this commitment, however, customers and employees will hold them to it.'

1.14 Senge suggests that organisations start in one of five stages along the path to full integration of sustainability into their strategy and purpose, and that different sets of drivers may emerge to move them to each new stage: Figure 5.1.

Figure 5.1 *Five stages and emerging drivers (adapted from Senge)*

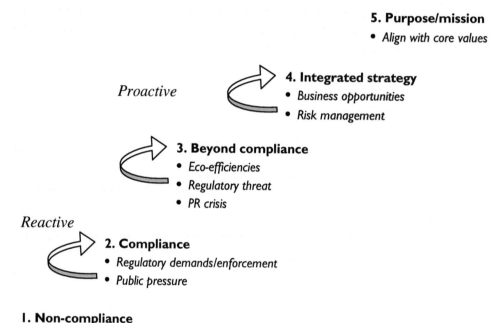

1.15 The key 'driver shifts' in this model can be outlined as follows.

- Organisations may get stuck in the non-compliance or compliance stage, where the drivers for sustainability often involve reacting to external pressures: NGO activism, or enforcement notices from a regulator or employment tribunal, say. 'As this is a very expensive way to change, executives often assume that making the leap beyond compliance will cost even more, and so they miss the benefits and substantial savings of a proactive approach.'

- Momentum for change starts to build when organisations see the cost-effectiveness of going beyond compliance with minimum legal requirements. 'This can become a self-reinforcing snowball, as the re-investment of initial savings leads to more and more gains including an improvement in reputation and brand value.'

- The move to Stage 4 often occurs when organisations discover that broader business opportunities are available – if the sustainability factors are integrated more thoroughly into business strategy, investment and decision-making processes. At this point, sustainability is driven increasingly by senior management, rather than the corporate communications or stakeholder management function. It 'directly impacts internal capital and budget allocations, supply chains, the pursuit of major new markets, core operations and R & D.'

- Some sustainability-leading organisations skip straight to Stage 5: either seeing the opportunities in sustainability from the outset (eg The Body Shop), or recognising the harm they have been doing and shifting direction (eg BP). The shift to Stage 5 can also occur as part of a natural progression from Stage 4, 'as leaders learn from their experience of launching new initiatives and getting positive feedback from their employees. They discover for themselves that enormous additional energy can be unleashed by taking steps to align their purpose and mission with the core values their people hold.'

1.16 Sustainability drivers thus operate via a kind of domino or snowball effect. 'As proactive companies make strategic moves in their industries and markets, customers, suppliers, investors and competitors sit up and take notice. These leaders change the game for everyone else by raising the expectations of customers, the public, NGOs and governments alike... Once companies enter Stage 4 or 5, they step into the role of influencing not just their own future but the futures of others in the larger systems in which they operate.'

2   The private sector

Characteristics and sustainability drivers

2.1   As you should be aware from your studies so far, the private sector is the sector of an economy which is controlled and financed by individuals, partnerships and corporations. The key characteristics of the private sector, as they relate to sustainable procurement and wider sustainability issues, are as follows.

2.2   Organisations are owned by their investors (owner/proprietors or shareholders), and controlled by directors or managers on their behalf. This places issues such as profitability, the creation and protection of shareholder value and corporate governance at the forefront of sustainability planning.

2.3   Private sector activity is funded by a combination of investment, revenue (from the sale of goods or services) and debt. This gives a priority to sustainability drivers such as the need to maintain profitability; the potential to show a return on investment from sustainability initiatives; the need to attract and retain sustainability-focused investors and lenders (and to reduce the cost of capital); the need for responsible borrowing and gearing (to protect business viability); and so on. It may also create barriers to investment in sustainable procurement (or pressure to show short-term efficiencies and cost savings) in the face of economic recession.

2.4   The primary purpose of private sector concerns is the achievement of commercial objectives: generally, maximising profits for their owners and/or for reinvestment in the business. Managerial decisions are assessed on the extent to which they contribute to organisational profit or shareholder value. This means that business case arguments for sustainable procurement, such as those discussed in Chapter 4, are likely to be their primary driver.

2.5   Competition is a key factor. Several, or many, firms may offer goods or services of a particular type, with consumers free to choose between their offerings. Key drivers for sustainability are thus likely to include: customer demand for sustainable (green or ethically sourced) products and product attributes; the need to keep pace with (if not pre-empt) competitor sustainability initiatives; the need to identify and differentiate product and corporate brands with sustainability values; the need to build core (distinctive, non-replicable, value-adding) competencies for sustainability; the need to develop process capability for sustainability (as demonstrated by standard certification, for example); and the need to build and defend corporate and brand reputation for sustainability.

2.6　The core 'constituency' served by firms is shareholders, customers and employees, all of whom are involved with the firm by choice. Firms must therefore be able to select and justify sustainability strategies in terms of their benefits to these priority stakeholders.

2.7　Private sector corporations (particularly large transnational corporations) are – or are perceived to be – major contributors to environmental exploitation (eg land use and resource depletion); economic exploitation (eg of labour and markets); over-consumption (and associated wastes); environmental damage (eg from GHG emissions and pollution); social inequity (eg the growing divide between rich and poor nations, the influence of major corporations over governments); and social costs (eg negative health impacts of products, pollution, traffic congestion, redundancies and so on). Now that society demands transparency and accountability for such impacts, and has become more vigilant (due to increasing global information and activism), sustainability is no longer 'optional' in the private sector.

2.8　One of the key roles of the public sector, in a mixed economy, is to regulate the private sector in the public interest.

- Private sector firms are subject to an increasing range of sustainability-related legislation and regulatory control, in areas such as corporate governance and financial reporting, employment, health and safety, consumer protection, environmental protection and so on – as we will see in Chapter 11.

- Privatised firms (such as British Telecom and British Gas), which used to be in public ownership but were sold into private hands, are subject to a regulatory regime in order to protect consumers in the absence of a genuinely competitive market. Bodies such as Ofcom (telecommunications) and Ofgem (energy supply) are mainly concerned with limiting price rises.

- While there has been a move towards deregulation and/or voluntary self-regulation by industries, governments generally recognise that some intervention in the private sector is desirable in order to protect consumer rights; promote competition; assist firms to prosper; and protect the national interest (eg by protecting domestic companies from unfair competition from imports)

2.9　The private sector, as a whole, is well-placed to contribute to the sustainability agenda, with the resources and market-honed competencies to drive: innovation and the diffusion of innovation; the education of sustainable/intelligent customers; networking and partnering to mobilise resources for sustainability; sustainable supply chain development; role-modelling/leadership within industries and supply chains; and so on.

2.10　The emergence of supply chain management (SCM) and world-class manufacturing techniques has raised the status and influence of procurement in the private sector, with the emphasis on added value, strategic procurement, lean and/or agile supply, relationship management, and support for quality and innovation. Procurement may therefore be well placed to act as change agent in support of sustainability, or to justify a sustainable procurement agenda in terms of business and shareholder value.

Focus on business benefits

2.11　The primary responsibility of business is business. The focus of private sector firms will be on what tangible financial benefits are likely to accrue from sustainability strategies. At the same time, as Senge argues: 'The issue always boils down to risk versus opportunity. While the short- and medium-term risks vary for each company and industry, the ultimate risks of ignoring sustainability issues are clear: If we continue to put more toxic waste into the environment and more CO2 into the atmosphere than can be naturally disposed of, or if we insist on extracting and wasting more natural resources than can be replaced, business in the traditional sense will cease to exist. You can't have a fishing industry if there are no fish, or a soft-drink company without clean water.'

2.12 Goldman Sachs recently researched the energy, mining, steel, food, beverages and media sectors, and found that those companies considered leaders in implementing environmental, social and governance policies have outperformed the general stock market by 25% since August 2005. Of these companies, 72% have outperformed their sector peers over the same period.

2.13 This is substantially due to the economic value added by corporate goodwill, reputation, credibility and brand strength, in relation to the environment and related social issues. In a sector in which consumer choice is king, a 2007 Ipsos MORI poll showed that significant numbers of consumers (over half the respondents in the survey) prefer to buy products and services from companies with good environmental reputations. 'Ethical consumerism' is reported to be on the rise in percentage and value terms in the UK, US and Europe. The sustainability of goods and services is becoming a high-profile, mainstream brand attribute, alongside value/price and quality. And, as Senge notes, 'once a corporate brand gains traction in this space, as with quality or innovation, the stakes and expectations remain high'.

2.14 Just as private sector corporations compete for customers, they also compete for investors, employees/skills, quality supply chain partners and business allies. A reputation and track record in sustainability is increasingly likely to be a component in their ability to compete in these markets. The same Ipsos MORI poll found that nearly eight out of ten people prefer to work for 'environmentally ethical' organisations, for example.

Example: Google

In late 2007, Google announced plans to set up an internal research group to develop cheaper renewable energy sources. Many industry and investment analysts believed the company had lost sight of its business focus and priorities.

However, Google currently has a very large carbon footprint, due to the enormous amount of power required to operate the computer servers which are at the heart of its search engine service. And its company motto is: 'Do no evil.'

Co-founders of the company, Larry Page and Sergey Brin, have been reported as saying that if Google succeeds in the renewable energy venture: 'The world will have the option to meet a substantial portion of electricity needs from renewable sources and significantly reduce carbon emissions... Alternative energy is also vital for economic development in many places where there is limited affordable energy of any kind. We expect this would be good business for us as well.' (Brad Stone, 'Google's next frontier', New York Times, November 28, 2007)

Besides funding its own internal research, Google is providing research grants to other companies, independent laboratories and academic institutions, in the belief that unexpected cross-fertilisation of ideas, synergies and innovation may be crucial to its own success. 'Google appreciates the audaciousness of its goal and recognises the need for partners in tackling problems that are much bigger than any one company can handle.' (Senge)

Small and medium-sized enterprises (SMEs)

2.15 From your own experience, you will have gathered that private sector organisations vary widely by size: from one-person operations to small businesses to vast global conglomerates. According to a 2005 European Union definition (used for grant-aid purposes) a small to medium enterprise has 10–249 employees and an annual turnover of less than €50 million.

2.16 Particular attention has been given to SMEs in recent years, because (a) they are a significant contributor to economic activity (by the above definition, some 99% of enterprises in the EU in 2005, providing around 65 million jobs), and (b) because they require financial and guidance support in order to overcome lack of economic strength in competition with larger players – in itself a sustainability issue.

2.17 Here are some particular drivers and support factors for sustainable procurement in SMEs.

- The sustainable procurement and CSR policies of larger private sector customers (derived demand for sustainable products and services)
- Sustainability criteria imposed on tenders by public sector customers (as part of their own sustainability targets)
- Increasing consumer demand for more specialised and customised sustainable products, to which small firms are better able to respond. SMEs may have an advantage over large firms in clearly defined, small markets: it would not be worth large firms entering markets where there is no scope for cost-effective mass production. Such an advantage may apply in a geographically localised market, say, where sustainability values include local sourcing.
- The entrepreneurial nature and speed of communication in small enterprises, making them particularly well suited to innovation, and giving them a potential advantage over larger, less flexible firms in fast-changing, high-technology markets
- Closeness to and dependence on local host communities for employment, investment and supplies – dictating pursuit of sustainable procurement through local sourcing and employment, and community involvement, say.

2.18 On the other hand, SMEs are at a disadvantage in areas such as: raising loan and share capital (because they are a greater risk); managing cashflow (being harder hard hit by late payment or non-payments); ability to take financial risks (including investment in research and development); dealing with bureaucratic requirements; and attracting and mobilising sustainable procurement and innovation expertise.

2.19 These factors may all create constraints on sustainability initiatives, and the UK government has attempted to mitigate them, with a range of initiatives designed to: encourage on-time payment of bills by PLCs and public sector bodies; relax rules and regulations applicable to SMEs; reduce the tax burden on small business; provide grants to assist SMEs in rural areas or areas of industrial decline (eg the EU SME Initiative and the Enterprise Fund, themselves supporting social and economic sustainability); and provide information, advice and support (eg through the Business Link network).

2.20 There is no sustainability standard at present that SMEs can realistically aspire to. Although BS 8555 was designed for SMEs, both it and the more comprehensive ISO 14001 standard for Environmental Management Systems (EMS) impose a heavy bureaucratic, time and cost burden.

3 The public sector

Characteristics and sustainability drivers

3.1 As you should know from your earlier studies, the public sector is the section of an economy which is controlled by central government, local authorities and publically-funded corporations, on behalf of the State (which represents the public). The key characteristics of the public sector, as they relate to sustainable procurement and wider sustainability issues, are as follows.

3.2 Public sector organisations are owned by the government on behalf of the State, which represents the public. This means that their primary mission, purpose and strategic driver should be the wellbeing and best interests of the public, both for present and future generations: by definition, 'sustainability'. In a democratic system, the satisfaction of the public's wants and expectations in key areas of sustainability (eg for law and order, economic prosperity, lifestyle amenities, equitable treatment, access to opportunity, and the conservation of valued natural resources, cultural heritage and environmental amenities) is an important determinant of votes and political legitimacy.

3.3 Public sector activity is financed by the state, mainly via taxation – as well as any revenue the organisation's activities may generate (eg from the sale of products or fees charged for services). This means that core drivers for sustainability will be the need for transparency and accountability in the use of public funds; and the potential for sustainability efficiencies and cost-savings.

3.4 The primary purpose of public sector activity is achieving defined service levels (rather than profitability): providing efficient and effective services to the public, often within defined budgetary constraints and sustainability strategies. Sustainability targets are therefore, to a far greater extent than in the private sector, integrated with the core objectives of the organisation. In a mixed economy, the State plays a key role in sustainability, by:

- Providing essential goods and services which might not be provided by the private sector, owing to 'market failure'
- Redistributing wealth, via taxation, in order to provide financial support for non-wage earners such as the sick, pensioners and the unemployed
- Regulating private sector activity in the public interest, eg in the case of bodies such as the Competition Commission or the Health and Safety Executive.

3.5 There has traditionally been little or no competition in the public sector, although, since the 1970s, successive UK governments have sought to introduce some market disciplines (eg competitive tendering and procurement efficiency targets). In the absence of consumer choice, sustainability values (along with value, quality and efficiency) are imposed by mechanisms such as regulation, customer charters, performance targets and competition for funding allocations.

3.6 The 'constituency' of concerned stakeholders is wider and more diverse than in the private sector, including government, taxpayers, funding bodies, private sector partners, those who consume products and services (broadly defined) – and society as a whole. There is a far greater need for accountability and stakeholder consultation in developing the strategies and policies of the organisation, and in defining sustainability, responsibility and the value to be derived from them.

3.7 The public sector includes both:

- Central government, which may participate in transnational consultation and agreements on sustainability issues (eg through the EU or UN) and commit to implementing sustainability targets on a national level (eg in relation to the Kyoto Agreement on climate change)
- Local government authorities, which have a key role in implementing national sustainability policies: (a) in their own procurement practices; (b) via oversight of local infrastructure development, land use and by-laws (eg in relation to recycling); and (c) via community education and promotion of the sustainable development agenda. The UN's Agenda 21 (discussed in Chapter 3) specifically envisages a key role in consultation, agenda-setting and implementation for local authorities.

Example: Procuring for Health and Sustainability 2012

Procuring for Health and Sustainability 2012 is the response of the health and social care sector (via the Department of Health) to the Sustainable Procurement Action Plan. The Executive Summary to the report runs as follows.

The overall aim of the Department of Health is to improve the health and wellbeing of the people of England. Sustainable development has an important role to play in this. When considering the balance of social, environmental and economic factors we realise that what we buy, and how we buy it, has such an important role to play...

This action plan is the health and social care sector response to the Sustainable Procurement Task Force report, and will be followed up with route map planning and supporting activities to take us on the journey to the final destination – good procurement that recognises sustainable development as an essential outcome...

Examining this in the context of the health budget, which includes the NHS accounts for £30.1 billion of the total £150 billion government procurement spend, we can understand that there could be significant dividends for the health service and the country at large. There is a clear business case for sustainable procurement, and now is the time for action.

This action plan sets out how, in the next five years, the health and social care sector in England will use sustainable procurement, not only of equipment and supplies, but also buildings, facilities and services, to achieve improved health and wellbeing for the people, the environment and the economy. The action plan sets the direction for NHS trusts, collaborative procurement organisations, Department of Health and its arms length bodies, including NHS Supply Chain and the NHS Purchasing and Supply Agency (NHS PASA). It also indicates our intentions to suppliers with whom we work, staff we employ and the patients to whom we provide services and care.

Key actions proposed include:

- committing NHS organisations to purchasing goods and services, as well as construction and refit activity, which will reduce the NHS carbon footprint (ie contribute to our carbon reduction goals)

- developing a best practice procurement framework that places sustainability and innovation at the heart of decision making processes, and is available for use across the health and social care sector

- developing British Research Establishment Environmental Assessment Method (BREEAM) for Healthcare as the accredited system of choice to promote excellence in sustainable construction in the NHS

- strengthening commissioning practices for health and wellbeing, and increasing involvement by the third sector and social enterprises

- creating a health suppliers sustainability award

- supply chain mapping to increase understanding of ethical and environmental impacts within the healthcare supply chain

- encouraging progress across the sector and by suppliers against the Sustainable Procurement Task Force's Flexible Framework for improved, more sustainable procurement practices.

The health sector will increasingly be asked what we are doing not only to improve health, but also to reduce carbon footprint, work with local communities and ensure that goods are ethically and sustainably sourced. This action plan sets out how greater health can be delivered through professional attention to the outcomes and consequences of health and social care procurement. It demonstrates that procurement's contribution to a sustainable society is far beyond financial.

The sustainable public procurement agenda

3.8   The massive buying power of the UK public sector is envisaged as a key driver of sustainable development in all sectors: 'setting an example both to business and consumers in the UK and to other countries', as well as 'making rapid progress toward its own goals on sustainable development' (National Action Plan).

3.9 A wide range of bodies has contributed to the strategy and implementation of the UK public sector agenda, including local government, professional organisations, the Audit Commission, IDeA (the Improvement and Development Agency for Local Government), the Environment Agency, procurement consortia, academics and representatives of the private and third sectors.

3.10 Environmental and sustainability strategies cascade down from central government to local authorities and purchasing agencies.

- The Stern Review focused attention on the economics of climate change.

- The Eco-Management and Audit Scheme (EMAS) commits public sector bodies: to implement initiatives, and to work in partnership with suppliers and contractors, to minimise the adverse environmental impact of the purchase and use of goods and services.

- The 2007 UK Government Sustainable Procurement Action Plan sets out a framework for 'action through policies, performance frameworks and procurement practice, working with the supply chain to provide innovative eco-technologies and solutions' (discussed further below).

- Meanwhile, on the economic dimension of sustainability, public sector procurement has been subject to a number of efficiency programmes over recent years. These have focused on attaining a more efficient, value-promoting and integrated procurement operation, eg via the introduction of e-procurement, consolidated buying and shared e-procurement platforms, compulsory competitive tendering (based primarily on economic criteria) and so on. Among the flow-on benefits for wider sustainability, however, are the promotion of transparency, diversity, equal access and fair treatment in tender procedures; and a more structured regime within which to introduce and integrate sustainable development targets.

The Sustainable Procurement National Action Plan

3.11 In June 2006 the Sustainable Procurement Task Force (SPTF) put forward its action plan to help buyers use the UK public sector's £150 billion spend to 'achieve value for money on a whole-life basis' while also incorporating environmental, social and economic sustainability criteria. The Sustainable Procurement National Action Plan (*Procuring the Future*) was issued to examine how to make more efficient use of public resources and to demonstrate that the public sector was serious about sustainability.

3.12 The action plan makes six key recommendations.

- Lead by example, with a clear commitment from the top of government through to permanent secretaries, local authority members and chief executives in all public bodies.

- Set clear priorities via a single integrated sustainable procurement framework.

- 'Raise the bar.' Existing minimum standards for central government should be properly enforced and extended to the rest of the public sector. Further standards should be developed in the priority spend areas of construction; energy; food; furniture; health and social care; consumables, office machinery and IT; pulp, paper and printing; uniforms, clothing and other textiles; transport; and waste.

- Build capacity by introducing a flexible framework to enable public sector organisations to benchmark their own capability. This is a five-stage implementation programme that allows bodies to assess their current position and plan an implementation route. Over time the ambition levels increase through Stage 1 (Foundation); Stage 2 (Embedded); Stage 3 (Practice); Stage 4 (Enhanced); to Stage 5 (Leadership). This framework is discussed in detail in Chapter 8.

- Remove barriers. Identified barriers include: lack of meaningful benchmarks; lack of capacity (managerial skills, knowledge and procurement expertise); lack of sustainability champions; budgetary/resource constraints; focus on cost reductions; the failure to implement whole-life costing; and uncertainty on how to account for non-monetary benefits. We will discuss these barriers – and solutions to overcome them – further in Chapter 14.

- Capture opportunities, through better engagement with suppliers to encourage innovative solutions. There is a particular emphasis on 'quick win' opportunities (eg through high-leverage waste and construction projects, and the purchase of environmental products): quick wins can be highly effective in engaging and motivating managers and staff.

3.13 Some specific recommendations of the Action Plan include: using the purchasing power of government authorities and agencies to promote sustainable procurement throughout supply chains; reducing the GHG emissions (carbon footprints) of government and its supply chains, in line with national targets; using outcome-based specifications to support innovative solutions; making greater use of whole-life costing (for a better evaluation of cradle-to-grave costs and eco-efficiencies); and including social criteria and environmental risk assessments as key non-economic criteria for purchase decisions.

National Procurement Strategy for Local Government

3.14 The National Procurement Strategy for Local Government sets out a number of key outcomes that the implementation process should seek to achieve.

- Corporate procurement strategy should be aligned to sustainable community strategy.
- Achieve community benefits.
- Improve supplier engagement.
- Establish agreements with the SME and third sectors.
- Encourage effective supply chain development.
- Assure equality and diversity.
- Evaluate whole-life costs.
- Stimulate markets.

Summary: sustainable procurement in the private and public sectors

3.15 A glance through the standard textbooks is enough to show that private sector organisations are regarded as the main sphere of procurement operations. Private and public sector organisations and environments are different in some key respects, as we have seen. The key implications for purchasing management have been catalogued by Gary Zenz, whose analysis forms the basis of Table 5.3, with our own points added.

3.16 The differences between public and private sector sustainable procurement should not be overemphasised, however. Differences in objectives, organisational constraints and so on may not necessarily lead to differences in sustainability values, key concerns or indeed procedures. In fact, the increasing recognition of wider stakeholder interests and sustainability responsibilities is a key source of convergence between the agendas of both private and public sectors – with potential for partnership, as we will see in later chapters.

Table 5.3 *Differences between public and private sector sustainable procurement*

Area of difference	Private sector	Public sector
Objectives	Usually, to increase profit or brand value or manage reputational risk	Usually, to achieve defined service levels and sustainability objectives
Responsibility	Buyers are responsible to directors, who in turn are responsible to shareholders	Buyers are responsible ultimately to the general public
Stakeholders	Purchasing has a defined group of stakeholders to take into account	Purchasing has to provide value to a wider range of stakeholders
Activity/process	Organisational capabilities and resources are used to produce more sustainable goods/services	Add value through supply of sustainable outsourced or purchased products/services
Legal restrictions	Activities are regulated by company law, employment law, environmental protection law, product liability law etc	Additional regulations, eg public sector procurement, corruption
Value for money	Maintain lowest cost for competitive strategy, customer value and profit maximisation	Maintain or improve service levels and sustainability within value/cost parameters
Diversity of items	Specialised stock list for defined product/service portfolio	Wide diversity of items/resources required to provide diverse services: need to prioritise spend areas
Budgetary limits	Investment is constrained only by availability of attractive opportunity	Investment is constrained by externally imposed spending limits
Information exchange	Private sector buyers do not exchange information, because of confidentiality and competition	Public sector buyers exchange notes, use shared e-purchasing platforms etc.
Supplier relationships	Emphasis on long-term partnership development where possible, to support sustainable value chain.	Compulsory competitive tendering: priority to cost minimisation and efficiency, at the expense of partnership development.

4 The third sector

Types of organisation in the NFP sector

4.1 The 'third sector' of an economy comprises non-governmental organisations (NGOs) which are operated on a not-for-profit (NFP) basis, generally reinvesting any 'surplus' from their activities to further social, environmental, cultural or other value-driven objectives. Such organisations include: charities, churches, political parties, museums, clubs and associations, co-operatives, interest/pressure/advocacy groups, trade unions and professional bodies such as CIPS.

4.2 Organisations in the third sector have typically been set up to achieve a defined objective (eg for a charitable, cultural or social purpose). They usually derive their income from donations, legacies (money left to the organisation in someone's will), sponsorships and government grants and subsidies, although they may also have a trading arm to generate revenue (as in the case of Oxfam shops, say). They may be owned by their members (as in a club or association) or by a trust (as in a charity), and managed by a board of trustees or directors.

Characteristics and sustainability drivers

4.3   Obviously, the range of third-sector organisations is very wide, and they may have a range of different purposes – many of which are likely to be directly relevant to sustainability concerns.

- Raising public awareness of a cause or issue (eg environmental or social pressure and interest groups)

- Political lobbying and advocacy on behalf of a cause, issue or group

- Raising funds to carry out activities (perhaps using commercial operations to generate profits, in addition to requesting grants, donations or subscriptions)

- Providing material aid and services to the public or specific beneficiaries (eg homeless or aged care charities, wildlife protection and conservation groups)

- Providing services to members (eg trade unions advocating employment rights, and professional bodies securing ethical and technical standards)

- Mobilising and involving members of the public in community projects, for mutual benefit (eg Volunteer Service Overseas).

4.4   You may like to browse the websites of some NGOs in areas that interest you – selecting some environmental and some social justice or welfare themes – and see how clearly articulated their sustainability or CSR values are, and how these flow down to procurement, sourcing, responsibility, ethics and employment policies.

4.5   As with public sector organisations, the range of a third-sector organisation's stakeholders can therefore be wide, including: contributors (staff, volunteers, members, donors); funding bodies (sponsors, funding authorities); beneficiaries of the services or activities; the media (since activities are often 'in the public interest'); and regulatory bodies (such as the Charities Commission). This means that there will be multiple influences on the organisation's definition of sustainability, determination of the value offered by sustainability, and related policy and decision-making.

4.6   Key drivers for sustainable procurement in third-sector organisations therefore include the following.

- The values of internal and external stakeholders (including founders, staff, voluntary workers, donors and supporters), which are often directly related to the mission and purpose of the organisation

- The management of reputation and reputational risk. Public relations crisis, caused by some internal failure of sustainability policy or implementation, is both more likely for third-sector organisations (because of the extent of scrutiny and high standards) and more significant in its impact (because of the dependence on volunteer labour, political support and discretionary funding – most of which will, in turn, be intentionally directed to the values for which the organisation purports to stand).

- The need to align sustainable procurement and sustainability initiatives with the core values, cause, issue or theme promoted by the organisation.

- The need for differentiation (in part on the basis of sustainability values), in order to compete for attention, volunteers and funding

- The need for transparency, accountability and stewardship in the management of funds. Third-sector buyers are spending money that has been derived not from the organisation's own trading efforts, but from someone else's donations or taxes. In fact, funding will often come from persons or organisations not themselves benefiting from the services provided. For this reason, purchasers in this sector are more closely regulated, with a strong emphasis on accountability and stewardship.

- The need for economic sustainability. The term 'non-profit' or 'not-for-profit' should not be interpreted as implying a disregard for commercial disciplines: on the contrary, such disciplines may be more important than in the private commercial sector, because of the scarcity of funds; pressure to devote as much as possible of their income to beneficiaries; or expenditure limits set by funding authorities or trustees.

- Regulation. As an example, the Charities Commission (the regulatory body for UK charities) aims to ensure that charities are run for public benefit and not for private advantage; that they are independent; and that there is no serious mismanagement or abuse by or within them.

Example: Oxfam GB

The following is an excerpt from Oxfam's published sustainability policy.

'An accepted definition of sustainable development is "achieving economic growth, environmental protection and social progress at the same time". Much of Oxfam GB's programme work seeks to achieve sustainable development for people living in poverty. But Oxfam also needs to be aware of the impact of all its activities on the environment and on communities...

'Oxfam's activities impact on the environment and communities through its:

- supply chains' employment conditions,

- direct and indirect use of non-renewable carbon fuels in its buildings and for passenger and freight transport via road and air,

- use of scarce/non-renewable raw materials in the supply chains of the items it purchases,

- use of harmful materials or high energy consuming processes in the production of the items it purchases,

- disposal of waste products,

- relationships with local communities where activities take place,

- welfare of staff, visitors, volunteers, neighbours and other stakeholders.

'Oxfam will follow the principles of Reduce, Re-use, Repair, Recycle in managing its environmental impact. Using the 4Rs will not only minimise environmental impacts, it also makes sound economic sense.'

---

5 Different industries and businesses

5.1 It is common to distinguish between three major industry sectors, according to the type of process they perform.

- *Primary industries* are concerned with extracting natural resources or producing raw materials. This sector includes oil and mineral extraction (mining), agriculture and forestry.

- *Secondary industries* are engaged in transforming raw materials into end components, assemblies or finished products. This sector includes the manufacturing, engineering and construction industries, for example.

- *Tertiary industries* are those engaged in the development and provision of services. This sector includes professional services, financial services, transport, hospitality and so on.

5.2 This classification is neither clear cut nor exhaustive. Agriculture these days has some of the features of secondary industry, for example, and is often classified as such. The retail, energy and IT sectors do not fit clearly into any one category and are sometimes regarded as sectors in their own right. Nor is it necessarily helpful to separate the three types of activity when thinking about supply chains. The procurement function in a manufacturing organisation, say, might have to buy across a number of categories: raw materials, manufactured goods (such as components, or computers, tools, machinery and office furniture) and services (such as IT consultancy, insurance and transport).

5.3   It should not be surprising, however, to find that procurement drivers, priorities and practices do differ from one sector to another. Clearly, the organisational characteristics, operational priorities and sustainability issues of an oil drilling company are likely to be very different from those of an airline, management consultancy, hospital or food retailer — and these differences are likely to be apparent at least to some extent in their approaches to sustainable procurement. We can only make some general comments here: start collecting and analysing your own examples — and pay close attention to the context and characteristics of case study organisations in the exam.

Sustainable procurement in a primary industry

5.4   In an extractive industry:

- Purchasing expenditure will be very high, because of the need for large, specialised heavy-duty machinery: this will place a strong priority on responsible capital investment decision-making.

- There will often be environmental sustainability concerns around issues such as: the over-extraction and consumption of non-renewable resources; environmental damage and degradation as a result of extraction activity (eg open cast mining); wastes, emissions and pollution (eg oil spills, dust and noise pollution, toxic waste disposal, slag); carbon emissions and other impacts of transport to and from remote locations; and ongoing environmental impacts from refining and use (eg burning of fossil fuels).

- There may also be social impacts on local communities, caused by the use of fly-in-fly-out workers, for example, and social sustainability/ethical issues arising from dangerous and difficult conditions for workers.

5.5   Each industry will be different. Agriculture, for example, has its own set of sustainability priorities: changing methods to protect and replenish natural resources such as water, soil and seed quality; maintaining or increasing productivity to feed growing populations (posing dilemmas around genetic modification, the use of pesticides and deforestation, say); growing consumer demand for organic and non-genetically modified produce; maintaining viability in the face of changing or difficult weather conditions, and supermarket buying power; and so on.

Sustainable procurement in a secondary industry

5.6   The essence of a manufacturing industry is to purchase raw materials and/or manufactured components, for conversion into finished goods.

- Because there is a continuous need for inputs to the production line, the priority may be to ensure that production teams have materials of the right quality available in the right place at the right time in the right quantity, achieving all this at the right price: the traditional 'five rights' of purchasing.

- There may also be a need for responsibility in managing long-term, high-value (capital) investment in plant and machinery.

- Because procurement is a relatively advanced function in many manufacturing companies, and its role may extend from new product development to customer delivery, there may be strong potential to drive sustainability from 'cradle to grave': early buyer/supplier involvement in sustainable design and development; value analysis and waste/energy reduction; supply chain management and development; logistics and reverse logistics management and so on.

- Capacity and capability to develop and produce innovative, distinctive and competitive new products, on the basis of sustainability features, is a strong driver in a manufacturing setting.

- Manufacturing processes may be particularly prone to unnecessarily high resource and energy consumption, waste products, pollution and emissions – as well as industrial accidents and the handling and storage of hazardous substances. Each of these areas will be high priority for sustainability measures, with potential for 'quick wins' and measurable economic benefits.

- Off-shored or globalised production (with outsourced, licensed or owned-and-managed facilities in overseas countries) may be prone to quality, safety, labour and environmental problems, especially in low-cost countries with less onerous regulatory regimes and standards.

5.7 Again, particular industries will raise specific environmental issues and reputational risks. We have already used the example of the automotive manufacturing industry, for example, and the challenge of CO_2 emissions and oil stock depletion. You should be able to draw on other examples, highlighting issues such as consumer health and safety (eg toy manufacture), environmental protection (eg chemicals and plastics), or employment ethics (eg clothing manufacture and textiles).

Sustainable procurement in the retail sector

5.8 In the retail sector, buyers are purchasing goods for sale onwards to customers – with little or no work done on them by the organisation itself. The main focus of procurement will therefore be on selecting products that will appeal to external customers. Increasingly, this will include Fair Trade brands (as in the case of Marks & Spencer's cotton garments, say, and the various coffee, tea and chocolate brands now available in supermarkets), and products differentiated and branded on the basis of sustainability features (eg safe, value for money and durable, 'green', ethically and/or locally sourced, reduced packaging, recyclable, energy-saving).

5.9 Additional sustainable procurement issues in the retail sector include the following.

- The use of plastic bags (or the sourcing of alternative cloth bags), the reduction in packaging, and the increase in recyclable packaging material, with the aim of reducing waste sent to landfill

- The reduction of transport emissions and impacts (eg through the use of local sourcing and regional distribution centres)

- Diversity and equal opportunity in retail staffing; ethical relationships with suppliers (particularly where the retailer has significant buying power)

- Prompt payment and fair terms of trade (eg not exploiting sale or return terms)

- Issues relevant to particular retail specialisms: the take-back of end-of-life electrical and electronic products, for example, or the potential for large supermarket chains to support or exploit small producers.

Sustainable procurement in the services sector

5.10 The major input of many service companies is staff time and expertise, generally sourced by the human resources (HR) function, rather than purchasing – although with the trend towards outsourcing of service functions, procurement may have a more important role. Service organisations also purchase office equipment and supplies, IT systems and support, motor vehicles, office maintenance services, advertising services and so on, but these sorts of items are often sourced by general managers or the users of the items: procurement may occupy a merely administrative or support role in the organisation – creating a barrier to the integrated development of sustainable procurement.

5.11 Physical supply may be more important in some circumstances, however: services may be based on the use of hard assets such as property (as in a hotel or fast food restaurant), vehicles (as in an airline or logistics company) or machinery (as in a computer bureau or printing factory).

Example: Sustainable Construction

The UK strategy for sustainable construction (*Building a Better Quality of Life*) suggests key themes for action by the construction industry (*Sustainable Construction Brief 2: BERR*, 2004).

- Design for minimum waste
- Lean construction to minimise waste
- Minimise energy in construction and use
- Do not pollute
- Preserve and enhance biodiversity
- Conserve water resources
- Respect people (including concern for construction site safety and the long-term health of construction workers) and local environments
- Monitor and report (ie use benchmarks)

'Construction has a huge contribution to make to everyone's quality of life and in enabling the positive impacts of its work to be achieved in a more sustainable manner. Construction outputs alter the nature, function and appearance of the towns and countryside in which we live. This infrastructure's construction, use, repair, maintenance and demolition consume resources and energy and generate waste'.

'Means' of sustainable construction (BERR 2008) include the following.

- Procurement: 'achieving whole life value through the promotion of best practice construction procurement and supply side integration… A successful procurement policy requires ethical sourcing, enables best value to be achieved and encourages the early involvement of the supply chain. An integrated project team works together to achieve the best possible solution in terms of design, buildability, environmental performance and sustainable development.'
- Design: 'to ensure that buildings, infrastructure, public spaces and places are buildable, fit for purpose, resource efficient, sustainable, resilient, adaptable and attractive'
- Innovation: 'to enhance the industry's capacity to innovate and increase the sustainability of both the construction process and its resultant assets'
- People: increasing commitment to training and health and safety

'Ends' of sustainable construction

- Climate change mitigation (new homes to be zero-carbon from 2016; new non-domestic buildings to be zero-carbon by 2019)
- Reduced water consumption
- Consideration of biodiversity conservation through all stages of development
- Reduction of construction, demolition and excavation waste sent to landfill
- Minimal environmental and social impact of materials.

5.12 Key issues for sustainable procurement in the services sector – depending on the nature of the service – may include the following.

- Ethical and sustainable staffing practices: equitable use of temporary and part-time staff, equal opportunity and diversity; training and involvement of staff in sustainability programmes and so on

- The careful assessment, contracting, management and ethical/environmental monitoring of outsourced service contractors, especially if they are located in low-cost countries with less onerous regulatory regimes and standards

- Ethical issues surrounding confidentiality and intellectual property, where staff have access to premises and information

- Health and safety (and related liability) issues surrounding temporary or unskilled staff, or staff working in client/customer or off-site premises; the use of hazardous substances and equipment (eg in catering, cleaning or transport) and so on

- Environmental issues in the delivery of services (eg energy use and emissions as a result of using equipment; waste electrical and electronic products arising from obsolescence in the IT services industry; unnecessary transport emissions in providing off-site services or managing off-site staff; high carbon footprints of particular service types such as travel services)

- Sustainability issues in the delivery of potentially damaging services such as gambling or fast food, and the need to mitigate such damage (eg by warnings, ethical guidelines, service modification and restriction)

- Potential to develop new products and markets for sustainability-oriented services (eg environmental impact auditing, sustainability consulting, chemical-free dry-cleaning, ethical investment advice)

Chapter summary

- There are both internal and external drivers for sustainable procurement. These are subject to change over time. Senge models a five-stage process towards full commitment to sustainable procurement.

- In the private sector, the adoption of sustainable procurement must usually be justified by a 'hard' business case. However, even if this is insufficient to convince managers, they may be constrained to adopt best practice by increasing regulation of the private sector.

- Traditionally, the public sector has been more ready to embrace sustainable procurement. Organisations in this sector are not dominated by a profit motive and often recognise a broader range of social and environmental responsibilities.

- Many organisations in the so-called third sector have specific aims related to adoption of sustainable procurement. Even where they don't, they often have to satisfy stakeholders with a high commitment to social and environmental values.

- Best practice in procurement stretches across all industry sectors. Despite this, the pressures towards sustainable procurement may differ from one sector to another.

Self-test questions

Numbers in brackets refer to the paragraphs above where your answers can be checked.

1   What is meant by forcefield analysis? (1.1, 1.2)

2   List some general enabling factors for sustainable procurement. (1.6)

3   What are the five stages in Senge's model of the adoption of sustainable procurement? (1.14)

4   In what ways are private sector firms regulated by the public sector? (2.8)

5   Why have SMEs attracted particular attention from governments in recent years? (2.16)

6   How does the State play a key role in sustainability? (3.4)

7   List as many recommendations as you can from the Sustainable Procurement National Action Plan. (3.12)

8   List as many differences as you can between private and public sectors in relation to sustainable procurement. (3.15 and Table 5.3)

9   List drivers for sustainable procurement in the third sector. (4.6)

10   Distinguish between primary, secondary and tertiary industries. (5.1)

11   List issues peculiar to the retail sector in relation to sustainable procurement. (5.9)

Further reading

From your 'Essential Reading' list, you might look at Blackburn (*The Sustainability Handbook*), Chapter 3: The Value of Sustainability: Why Bother? – if you haven't already done so. If you have extra time and interest, you might browse through:

- Chapter 13: Approach to Sustainability for NGOs

- Chapter 14: Approach to Sustainability for Governmental Organisations

– although some of the material will be more relevant to later areas of the syllabus, where we cover the development and implementation of sustainability policies and programmes.

CHAPTER 6

A Strategic Approach to Sustainable Procurement

Learning objectives and indicative content

2.1   Evaluate the area of sustainable procurement aligned with organisational strategy and the operational impact of its implementation across the procurement function and the other functions within the organisation.

- Incorporation of sustainable procurement principles into mission statements and core values
- 'Balanced scorecard' approach for consistency across the organisation: financial; customer; internal business; innovation and learning
- Corporate social responsibility (CSR) statement
- Implications for organisation structure and resources
- Common targets and objectives
- Realistic timescales
- Benefits and trade-offs for the business (eg reputation)

Chapter headings

1   Strategic alignment

2   Sustainable procurement from the top down

3   The balanced scorecard

4   Implications for the organisation

5   Implications for procurement

6   Implications for other functions

Introduction

In Chapter 4, on the internal influences on sustainable procurement in organisations, we introduced the idea of 'strategic alignment': the need for sustainability values, policies, objectives and plans to flow or cascade down from the top level of strategic intent (expressed in mission, vision and core value statements) to the lower-level strategic plans of business units and functions – and the need for these lower-level strategic plans to be consistent, coherent and co-ordinated (and therefore, hopefully, mutually reinforcing) across the organisation.

In this chapter, we look further at the need for sustainable procurement strategy to be aligned to corporate strategy, and at how this can be achieved. We also look at the broader strategic consequences of implementing sustainable procurement: its impact on organisational strategy, structure and processes; its implications for other functions within the organisation; and its impact on the procurement function itself.

In Chapter 7, we will go on look at the development of sustainable procurement policies – with a better understanding of how they 'fit' in the overall strategic and operational context of the organisation.

1 *Strategic alignment*

The need for strategic planning

1.1 The aim of top-down strategic planning is basically to establish the direction, purpose, scope and priorities of the organisation. This in turn provides decision guidelines for executives at all levels across the organisation. Will proposed strategies and plans 'fit' the organisation's identity and values? Will they further its core purposes? Do they reflect its priorities for the allocation of effort and resources? Do they reflect the needs and interests of its identified key stakeholders?

1.2 Strategic planning at the corporate level supports the integrated and coherent focus of attention and resources on identified high-priority objectives – which in turn improves the likelihood that they will be accomplished with the least expense of time, effort and money. 'If a company is committed to exploring the risks and opportunities associated with sustainability, then strategic planning is a critical tool for bringing focus to that effort.' (Blackburn, 2007)

1.3 Focus and 'fit' are important issues in sustainability management, because of the wide scope and range of sustainability issues. Any organisation might agree that support for a 'save the whales' campaign is in line with its CSR values, and would enhance its green/ethical credentials – but while such a strategy would 'fit' the mission of a company in the fishing industry, say, it would be 'off message' for a car manufacturer.

1.4 Prioritisation is also particularly important because, as we have already noted, an organisation will not be able to tackle all possible sustainability initiatives and improvements straight off, or all at once! It needs to start somewhere, and will often in the initial stages prioritise areas of key risk or opportunity, areas where 'quick wins' are possible (to build buy-in and momentum), or areas of 'leverage' (where a comparatively small investment of effort and resources offers comparatively significant results).

Strategic alignment

1.5 If an organisation is to achieve its corporate objectives, the plans set for each business unit and function – while specific to their own roles – must be co-ordinated with each other so that they contribute towards the overall objectives. As we saw in Chapter 4, this integration or alignment needs to happen in two directions.

- Vertical alignment is about ensuring that the goal of every activity contributes towards the overall or higher objectives of the business.
- Horizontal alignment is about ensuring that the plans of every unit in an organisation are co-ordinated with those of others, so that they work effectively together – and present a consistent, coherent face to the world.

1.6 Vertical alignment may be achieved in two ways.

- Bottom-up: with various functional specialists providing recommended objectives and goals in their areas (eg sustainable procurement)
- Top-down: with the CEO and senior management team laying out the broad direction for the business (ideally, incorporating specialists' recommendations as appropriate)

1.7 Sustainable procurement is an area in which functional specialists can offer valuable input to corporate strategy, because (a) procurement activities influence key inputs to business processes, and (b) procurement specialists act as the interface between internal and external stakeholders in the supply chain. Sustainable procurement objectives can thus drive or enable sustainable innovation, design, product development, operations and marketing (on the basis of sustainable brand attributes).

1.8 At the same time, sustainable procurement priorities will be driven, enabled and guided (or constrained) by corporate-level values, policies and resource allocations, as they cascade down to the functional level.

1.9 A sustainable procurement policy may therefore be:

- The procurement function's response to the organisation's overarching strategic plan and/or sustainability/CSR objectives: setting out how procurement will deliver against those objectives in its own areas of activity

- The procurement function's response to sustainability issues and drivers within its own areas of activity: potentially used to make a business case for wider sustainability initiatives and policies at the corporate level – or to dovetail with the sustainability policies of other functions to identify shared priorities and directions, as the basis of a corporate-level policy.

1.10 Horizontal alignment flows, to an extent, from vertical alignment, since different functions have the same over-arching objectives and guidelines. However, it also requires processes designed to initiate and maintain communication between functions (and between suppliers and customers in both internal and external supply chains):

- To establish a shared understanding of the issues or topics which fall within the scope of sustainability and corporate social responsibility policy, and to identify which are a priority or area of key risk/opportunity for each function or unit

- To co-ordinate or dovetail functional goals, objectives, policies and plans in areas of shared concern/priority – rather than allow them to duplicate, diverge or conflict. For example, an organisation-level steering group may work to validate functional policies and plans for consistency and co-ordination.

- To identify or allocate responsibility for driving policy or monitoring performance in each area, where appropriate

- To ensure the commonality or consistency of objectives, targets, performance indicators and measures across the organisation (as highlighted by the syllabus)

- To share information, good practice, feedback and learning on sustainability issues.

Aligning sustainability with corporate strategy

1.11 Senge (*The Necessary Revolution*) argues that it is crucial to link sustainability objectives to business case arguments based on shareholder value, in what he calls a Sustainable Value Framework (based on the work of Hart and Milstein). 'If managers and employees are apathetic about their organisation's sustainability efforts, it is most likely because they don't see how it ties in to business goals. As a result, efforts are generally piecemeal, reactive and poorly integrated into the company's core mission and business plans.'

1.12 The Sustainable Value Framework (Figure 6.1) links sustainable practices directly to an organisation's core strategies. (It also offers another way of categorising drivers for sustainability: add this to your repertoire from Chapter 5.)

- A first set of drivers relates to increasing industrialisation, and its side effects: material/resource consumption, pollution, waste and so on. Firms can create immediate value by reducing the level of these effects.

- A second set of forces concerns the increasing influence of external stakeholder groups concerned with monitoring and advocating social and environmental standards. NGOs, using the connecting power of the internet, create increasing pressure for transparency – and reputational and bottom-line benefits for organisations which are transparent and responsive to the public's desire for sustainability.

- Another set of drivers includes emerging 'disruptive' technologies that challenge the *status quo* – and could render energy- and material-intensive industries obsolete: biomimicry, nano-technology, ICT, renewable energy and so on. These represent significant threats to existing value – and significant opportunities for future value creation.

- A fourth set of drivers relates to global problems such as resource depletion, deteriorating ecosystems and climate change; poverty and inequity in developing countries; global security and development issues; and so on. 'Not only is responding to [these drivers] essential for the health of the planet: firms can also create value by pursuing sustainability-related opportunities that are rapidly emerging in all industries'.

Figure 6.1 *The Sustainable Value Framework*

	Internal	External	
Drivers: • Disruption • Clean technology • Footprint	**Strategy: Clean Technology** Develop sustainability competencies of the future *Payoff:* Innovation and repositioning	**Strategy: Sustainability Vision** Create a shared roadmap for meeting unmet needs *Payoff:* Sustainable growth trajectory	**Drivers:** • Climate change • Resource depletion • Poverty
Tomorrow			
Today	**Strategy: Pollution Prevention**	**Strategy: Product Stewardship**	
Drivers: • Pollution • Material consumption • Waste	Minimise waste and emissions from operations *Payoff:* Cost and risk reduction	Integrate stakeholder views into business process *Payoff:* Reputation and legitimacy	**Drivers:** • Civil society • Transparency • Connectivity

Adapted from Senge (who credits Hart & Milstein, 'Creating Sustainable Value')

1.13 Organisations may start with the lower left ('here and now') quadrant, for short-term wins and bottom-line benefits. Moving outward (engaging with stakeholders), or towards a future orientation (developing future competencies) – or both (seeking a genuinely sustainable path to growth) – are potentially transformative strategies.

Elements of a Sustainability Operating System

1.14 Senge's model highlights the link between drivers and strategic alignment. Blackburn (2007) similarly includes these as key elements in his model of a Sustainability Operating System, which may be a helpful framework for thinking about the development and implementation of sustainable procurement programmes: Figure 6.2.

Figure 6.2: *Basic elements in a Sustainability Operating System*

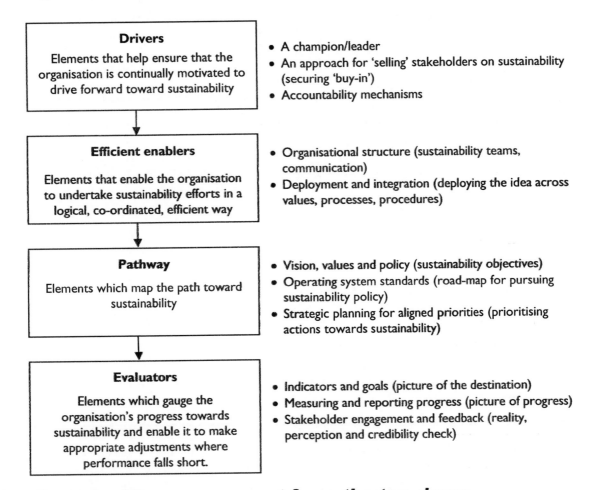

Drivers
Elements that help ensure that the organisation is continually motivated to drive forward toward sustainability

- A champion/leader
- An approach for 'selling' stakeholders on sustainability (securing 'buy-in')
- Accountability mechanisms

Efficient enablers
Elements that enable the organisation to undertake sustainability efforts in a logical, co-ordinated, efficient way

- Organisational structure (sustainability teams, communication)
- Deployment and integration (deploying the idea across values, processes, procedures)

Pathway
Elements which map the path toward sustainability

- Vision, values and policy (sustainability objectives)
- Operating system standards (road-map for pursuing sustainability policy)
- Strategic planning for aligned priorities (prioritising actions towards sustainability)

Evaluators
Elements which gauge the organisation's progress towards sustainability and enable it to make appropriate adjustments where performance falls short.

- Indicators and goals (picture of the destination)
- Measuring and reporting progress (picture of progress)
- Stakeholder engagement and feedback (reality, perception and credibility check)

2   Sustainable procurement from the top down

Cascading down sustainability values

2.1 We introduced the concept of the hierarchy (or 'cascading down') of strategic objectives in Chapter 5. Blackburn (2007) suggests that this will be reflected in a hierarchy of documents (Figure 6.3): written statements and plans, by which the road map for sustainability can be deployed at different levels.

Incorporating sustainability in mission and value statements

2.2 The first step in ensuring that sustainable procurement and other sustainability strategies are aligned with overall corporate strategy (and vice versa) is to check whether they are compatible with the corporate purpose, values, principles and aspirations set out in the existing corporate mission statement and any value, vision or business principles statements.

2.3   Blackburn argues that: 'linking sustainability into a company's existing core documents [such as mission and value statements] is a convenient way of helping employees build on the familiar past and thereby easing the transition to sustainability. On the other hand, if the existing statements have generally been ignored in the company or are too general to form the basis for action, then a separate sustainability policy should be considered.'

Figure 6.3: *Hierarchy of documents for leading an organisation towards sustainability*

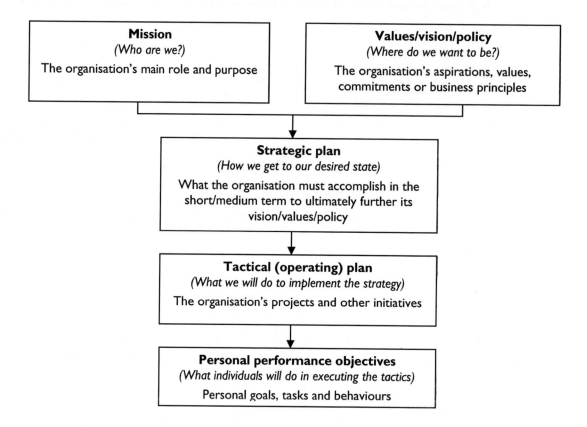

2.4   An organisation seeking to re-define or re-brand itself on the basis of sustainability may well need to revise its mission and/or values statements, or to introduce specific sustainability or CSR statements, in order to embed sustainability values at the heart of corporate culture, identity and performance objectives.

2.5   We gave a number of brief examples of mission statements in Chapter 4. Below, we give two more comprehensive examples (from Ben & Jerry's and the World Wildlife Fund), to give you a flavour of how sustainable procurement principles can be embedded at the level of organisational purpose and direction. You should be able to browse the websites of organisations that interest you for further examples: look for links to 'core values', 'who we are' or 'business principles', for example.

The corporate social responsibility (CSR) statement

2.6   For many organisations, the first specific formulation and publication of sustainability (and sustainable procurement) principles will take the form of a CSR statement: a concise statement drawing together the values, principles, commitments and policies of the organisation in regard to CSR issues. Since this will be tailored to the context, aspirations and operations of the organisation, it may have more direct relevance and appeal to its members than external published 'codes of practice'. It will also make the organisation's sustainability values and plans transparent to wider stakeholders.

2.7   A CSR statement may therefore have a multiple role as: a guide to decision-making and action; a tool of internal stakeholder buy-in; and a tool of sustainability marketing and reputation management, establishing the organisation's credentials and commitments in the area of sustainability. Because of the increasing importance of this last role, the statement will tend to emphasise whatever issues are of most concern to organisational stakeholders – and there is a common perception that this may represent 'lip service' to sustainability, without meaningful commitment or action.

Example 1: Ben & Jerry's

Ben & Jerry's is founded on and dedicated to a sustainable corporate concept of linked prosperity. Our mission consists of three interrelated parts.

Product Mission

To make, distribute and sell the finest quality all natural ice cream and euphoric concoctions with a continued commitment to incorporating wholesome, natural ingredients and promoting business practices that respect the Earth and the Environment.

Economic Mission

To operate the Company on a sustainable financial basis of profitable growth, increasing value for our stakeholders and expanding opportunities for development and career growth for our employees.

Social Mission

To operate the company in a way that actively recognises the central role that business plays in society by initiating innovative ways to improve the quality of life locally, nationally and internationally.

Central to the mission of Ben & Jerry's is the belief that all three parts must thrive equally in a manner that commands deep respect for individuals in and outside the company and supports the communities of which they are a part.

Leading with Progressive Values across our Business

We have a progressive, nonpartisan social mission that seeks to meet human needs and eliminate injustices in our local, national and international communities by integrating these concerns into our day-to-day business activities. Our focus is on children and families, the environment and sustainable agriculture on family farms.

Capitalism and the wealth it produces do not create opportunity for everyone equally. We recognise that the gap between rich and poor is wider than at any time since the 1920s. We strive to create economic opportunities for those who have been denied them and to advance new models of economic justice that are sustainable and replicable.

By definition, the manufacturing of products creates waste. We strive to minimise our negative impact on the environment.

The growing of food is overly reliant on the use of toxic chemicals and other methods that are unsustainable. We support sustainable and safe methods of food production that reduce environmental degradation, maintain the productivity of land over time, and support the economic viability of family farms and rural communities.

We seek to support nonviolent ways to achieve peace and justice. We believe government resources are more productively used in meeting human needs than in maintaining weapon systems.

We strive to show deep respect for human beings inside and outside our company and for the communities in which they live.

Example 2: World Wildlife Fund (WWF)

WWF's global mission

The mission of WWF is to stop the degradation of the planet's natural environment and to build a future in which humans live in harmony with nature, by:

- conserving the world's biological diversity

- ensuring that the use of renewable resources is sustainable, and

- promoting the reduction of pollution and wasteful consumption.

2.8 Even if it is seen primarily as a tool of corporate communication, however, a CSR statement may act as a driver or enabler of sustainable procurement.

- It provides a corporate-level statement of principle with which procurement principles can be aligned, and on the basis of which they can be justified.

- It supports stakeholder 'buy-in' by validating procurement's contribution to sustainability as a core organisational value.

- It acts as a guide to decision-making, prioritisation and implementation (or a 'code of practice') – especially insofar as it includes roadmaps for delivery, accountabilities, methods of monitoring and measuring progress and so on.

- It may also enhance the credibility of procurement, where it specifically addresses issues such as sustainable procurement, resource efficiency, reverse logistics or supplier management, to which the procurement function makes a significant contribution.

2.9 CSR statements are typically lengthy – and, of course, organisation-specific – so we will not attempt to reproduce one here. You should be able to find your own examples, from organisations that interest you: they are designed to be accessible to stakeholders, via published annual reports and websites (look for links to 'sustainability', 'corporate social responsibility', 'responsibility' and so on). You might like to start with some of the companies listed as: Brands with a Conscience (http://www.medinge.org) or Britain's Most Admired Companies (http://bmac.managementtoday.com/BMAC_2008.htm).

Sustainable procurement policy

2.10 A sustainable procurement policy will align with and support the organisation's commitment to procure all goods, services and works in a sustainable manner. The aims are to integrate sustainability into all procurement activities, to ensure systems are in place to support and develop the policy, and to develop mechanisms for measuring and reporting on performance.

2.11 The broad objectives of a sustainable procurement policy may include the following.

- To support and demonstrate an organisation-wide commitment to sustainability issues throughout the organisation

- To promote sustainability issues throughout the supply network

- To comply with environmental legislation and regulatory requirements

- To buy more environmentally friendly inputs, and to avoid adverse environmental impacts arising within the organisation and the supply chain

- To make more efficient use of resources

- To define the potential contribution of procurement to sustainable product innovation, development and production

- To ensure that sustainability factors are considered in making all purchasing decisions
- To define how procurement will support and comply with organisational CSR policies in its dealings and relationships with suppliers and other stakeholders.

Example: CapGemini consulting

To support our sustainability goals, we will be working on initiatives to:

- reduce our energy consumption
- reduce travel
- minimise packaging and returns
- use more recycled products or products with a high recycled content
- minimise logistics activity and wasted journeys
- optimise our end-to-end processes We will also ensure our supplier and product selection procedures take into account whole life costs including sustainability impacts.

We expect suppliers to:

- document and report on their sustainability performance
- where necessary, set performance targets for themselves and their downstream supply chain and work to meet them
- agree to identify and correct any activities of immediate concern or risk which fall below the principles set out in our sustainable procurement policy
- work with Capgemini in the spirit of continuous improvement
- commit to reviewing their compliance with the Capgemini sustainability requirements periodically while continuing to deliver robust goods and services. Suppliers must notify us immediately if there are any negative changes to their compliance with the requirements

---

3 *The balanced scorecard*

3.1 As we noted earlier, one of the key factors in achieving horizontal alignment of strategy is having common, and consistently applied, targets, objectives and progress/performance measures across the organisation.

3.2 A problem with traditional performance measurement techniques is that whilst any particular key performance indicator (KPI) can be aligned to an overall business objective, its achievement might very well be at the expense of another part of the business. For example, there might be an overall business objective to reduce costs, in pursuit of which procurement may source from low-cost suppliers: it has fulfilled its objective – but possibly at the expense of the quality, sustainability and reputation management objectives of other functions, or of the business as a whole.

3.3 The balanced scorecard model was developed in 1990 by Robert Kaplan and David Norton (*The Balanced Scorecard: Translating A Strategy into Action*). They argued that traditional financial objectives and measures are insufficient to control organisations effectively. Organisations need other parameters and perspectives, in order to avoid the problem of 'short-termism', which arises when managers are judged by criteria which do not measure the long-term, complex effects of their decisions.

3.4   Karlof & Lovingsson (*An A–Z of Management Concepts and Models*) suggest that: 'Few can withstand the simple and obvious logical underlying balanced scorecard: namely, that there are factors other than the financial which are important to control and follow up and that it can be a good idea to establish which factors these in fact are.' The main thrust of this argument is obviously strongly in tune with the concept of sustainability and the Triple Bottom Line (discussed in Chapter 1): the idea that organisations need to measure their performance not just on financial or economic criteria, but also on their environmental and social impacts and contributions.

Four key perspectives

3.5   Kaplan and Norton proposed four key perspectives for a balanced scorecard (sometimes called a balanced business scorecard or BBS): Figure 6.4.

- *Financial.* Are we creating value for our shareholders? (In relation to sustainable procurement, this might include cost savings, contribution to profit, shareholder value from reputational strength and so on.)

- *Customer.* Are we creating value for our customers? Who are our target customers, and what do they value? How are we doing on measures such as customer satisfaction, customer retention and market share? (In relation to sustainable procurement, customer value might be defined and measured by sustainable product, service and brand attributes.)

- *Internal business processes.* What must we excel at? What are the critical success factors (CSFs) for our business? How efficient and effective are our processes in achieving them? (In relation to sustainable procurement, this might most obviously include environmental management systems, and the management of both internal and external supply chains.)

- *Innovation and organisational learning.* How can we continue to improve and create value? What gaps are there between our aspirations and our current capabilities? What do we need to do better? How strong are our resources for innovation and improvement: skills, information systems, organisation structure and so on? (These questions can obviously be related directly to the development of sustainable procurement capability.)

Figure 6.4 *The balanced scorecard*

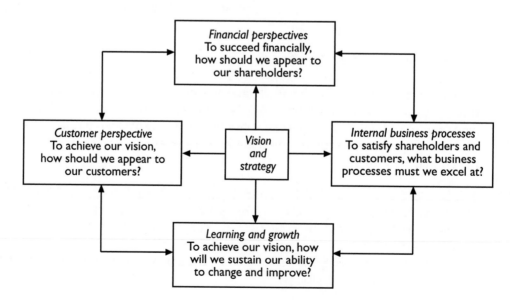

3.6   The scorecard has been designed to balance decision-making by focusing on the interrelationship between the differing competitive pressures facing the organisation and stimulating continuous improvement. The 'balance' of the balanced scorecard is thus between: financial and non-financial performance measures; short-term and long-term perspectives; and internal and external focus.

3.7   Working with a balanced scorecard requires describing, for each 'perspective':

- The organisation's long-term goals
- The success factors established to achieve those goals
- The key activities which must be carried out to achieve those success factors
- The key performance indicators which can be used to monitor progress.

3.8   Once the strategic-level scorecard has been developed, focusing on a dozen or so specific objectives, it must be cascaded through the organisation, in the form of business unit and functional plans. (The procurement function may extend this further, to develop joint scorecard measures for supplier and supply chain performance.)

Incorporating sustainability in scorecards

3.9   Some authors have argued that sustainability can be integrated within the balanced scorecard simply by adding a fifth box to Figure 6.4, labelled 'sustainability perspective'. However, this goes against the principle of the balanced scorecard in that it would make sustainability a separate issue, not allowing for integration across the four categories.

3.10   A more integrated approach to a balanced/sustainable scorecard embeds the balanced scorecard within the 'triple bottom line': Figure 6.5. For each of the three main areas of sustainability, there are four categories of indicators of organisational performance.

Figure 6.5 *Sustainability and the balanced scorecard*

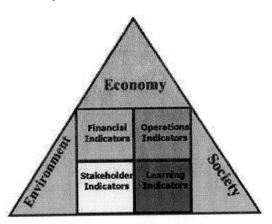

3.11   Blackburn (2007) has identified an alternative set of balanced scorecard measures specifically adapted for the area of sustainability, and built around key stakeholder groups.

- Employee objectives: build the best global team in our industry
- Financial (investor/lender) objectives: delivering significant shareholder return

- Supply chain (customer/supplier) objectives: create sustainable win-win supply chain relationships
- Citizenship (community/government) objectives: improve lives in local and global communities.

3.12 He proposes this as an 'alignment tool', as well as a more sustainability-focused approach to performance measurement, because: 'To the extent possible, each group proposing strategic sustainability objectives and goals should present their information in the same format and under the same overarching strategic categories used for the companywide strategic plan. This will help show how the sustainability initiatives align with the business objectives.'

3.13 You should be able to see how procurement-specific objectives could be set for each of the stakeholder objectives proposed in Blackburn's model. Here are some examples.

- *Employee*: attract, develop and retain procurement talent to achieve current and future results
- *Financial*: improve cost efficiency by achieving targets for inventory turns and costs of supplies
- *Supply chain*: consistently evaluate and meet agreed internal customer requirements; contribute to the development of innovative products and services to meet external customer needs; pursue policies for sustainable and ethical supply chain relationships and development
- *Citizenship*: contribute to the reduction of waste and achieve targeted improved efficiencies in energy and packaging use; gain certification for fair trading.

3.14 We will follow up on the idea of sustainability performance measurement in Chapter 13 of this text.

4 Implications for the organisation

4.1 The syllabus invites us, at this point, to consider the operational impacts of implementing a sustainable procurement strategy – on the organisation, procurement and other functions. We will confine ourselves to a fairly broad overview of the issues here, for several reasons.

4.2 Firstly, the impacts will depend on the content of the strategy (what measures it advocates, and whether these 'fit' existing structures, resources and capabilities) and the process by which it is developed and implemented (the extent of alignment, top-down championship, stakeholder consultation and buy-in and so on). The point is to be aware that there may be impacts and implications in certain areas: you will need to consider the specific details of an exam case study organisation, or an organisation of interest to you which you might use as an example in the exam.

4.3 Secondly, policy development and implementation issues have not yet been covered: they are introduced in the following learning objectives, and will be discussed in Chapters 7 and 8. Similarly, we have not yet tackled the detailed content of sustainable procurement policies and programmes: they are introduced still later in the learning objectives, and will be discussed in Chapters 9–12.

Benefits and trade-offs for the business

4.4 We have already discussed the business case arguments for sustainable procurement – the reputational, economic and operational benefits expected to accrue from its implementation – and will not repeat our coverage in detail here. You can recap the points made in Chapters 1 and 4, if you need to.

4.5 Senge (*The Necessary Revolution*) summarises some of the concrete benefits of sustainability programmes in a user-friendly way — and we have added some examples drawn specifically from sustainable procurement.

- There is significant money to be saved (eg through reducing waste and energy usage)
- There is significant money to be made (eg through re-use and recycling, and the development of sustainability products and services)
- You can provide your internal and external customers with a competitive edge (eg by offering products, services and consultancy for sustainability)
- Sustainability is a point of differentiation from competing brands
- You can shape the future of your industry (eg via effective voluntary self-regulation and best-practice and policy development)
- You can become a preferred supplier and/or customer (eg by offering and demanding higher social and environmental standards, and developing supportive, long-term supply chain partnerships in doing so)
- You can change your image and brand (eg by communicating and investing in stakeholder-valued sustainability initiatives).

4.6 At the same time, it is recognised that in some key areas there will be conflicts, compromises and trade-offs between business objectives (and the objectives of other functions) and sustainable procurement objectives. The last section of the syllabus explicitly raises some of these.

- Pressures for economic performance may conflict with social and environmental responsibility. One classic example would be procurement's desire to reduce sourcing costs by global sourcing from low-cost countries — which might at the same time damage domestic supply markets, risk the use of suppliers with lower labour standards, and increase GHG emissions through supply transport. Cost is generally perceived as an issue for sustainable procurement, particularly where targets require short-term cost reductions or maintenance (rather than long-term return on investment over the life of the purchase). Alternative energy, green and fair-trade products (conflict between lowest achievable price and ethical considerations) often cost more in the early stages of their market development. Sustainability policies on supplier diversity, small business and local sourcing may likewise impact adversely on cost performance in the short term.
- Pressures for quality and compliance (suggesting sourcing from developed countries) may conflict with cost and sustainable development considerations (suggesting sourcing from developing countries, which may lack standards and infrastructure, but offer low-cost labour).
- Common national and international standards for sustainability, quality and environmental management systems and corporate ethics are key enablers of sustainable procurement and supply — but at the same time, their effect is to lift general practice in an industry or sector: increasing competition and eroding the differentiating competitive edge available from sustainability leadership.
- A pre-occupation with sustainability objectives, in the initial phase of development and implementation, may represent a significant short-term investment in benefits which will take a long time to accrue (and deliver demonstrable shareholder value). It may also represent a disruption to business continuity, as processes and structures are realigned.

4.7 These issues will be discussed in detail in Chapters 14–16.

Implications for organisation structure and resources

4.8 A robust approach to sustainable procurement will have several implications for organisation structure, both as a whole and within the procurement function – depending, of course, on the specific approach adopted.

4.9 Processes may need to be aligned or re-aligned, creating a more 'horizontal' process flow in the interests of sustainability. CSR and sustainability explicitly cuts across 'vertical' barriers and the separation of functional specialisms (often called 'silos' in a vertical/compartmentalised structure), emphasising the flow of sustainable value through the value chain.

4.10 Organisation structures may need to be made more 'horizontal' to reflect business processes and the need for cross-functional co-operation on sustainability. Sustainable procurement experts, for example, may be appointed to cross-functional project teams. Multi-disciplinary sustainability teams may be formed to ensure consultation and collaboration in the development and implementation of sustainability policy. This may involve: a core team (acting as sustainable procurement champions and change agents); a deployment team (setting sustainable procurement objectives and measures, and reporting on progress); and a wider network of consultation, reporting and feedback teams (a bit like quality circles) which discuss sustainability improvements, share best practice and co-ordinate sustainability activities.

4.11 There are several advantages to the use of multi-disciplinary sustainability teams, which should be familiar from your studies in purchasing organisation.

- Sustainable procurement is, by nature, a multidisciplinary issue, requiring expertise in areas such as compliance, governance, procurement, operations, logistics, marketing and corporate communications.

- Including a range of internal stakeholders in discussion of sustainability issues encourages ownership and buy-in, embeds interest in sustainability across the organisation – and may encourage healthy 'competition' to drive the agenda.

- Including a range of internal stakeholders also ensures that sustainable procurement plans are thoroughly evaluated from multiple stakeholder perspectives (improving their quality and acceptability); and that conflicts and trade-offs are recognised and dealt with in a collaborative way.

4.12 The organisation may decide to centralise responsibility for sustainability, CSR or global citizenship, under a dedicated director or manager. This would create a visible presence, a 'hub' for sustainability information, a point of co-ordination and oversight for initiatives and so on. Whether this leadership role is full-time or part of another role (eg operations, stakeholder management or Environment Health and Safety) depends on the size and complexity of the organisation and its 'exposure' on sustainability issues.

4.13 A centralised function may be set up with line authority to execute and oversee sustainability programmes, or there may be a matrix-style support staff who work with or within the company's functional departments and business units (eg in a 'business partner', consultancy or Centre-Led Action Network model – similar to the ways in which procurement is commonly organised).

Example: Shell

'Shell initially established a separate sustainable development and planning function at the corporate level. It also had sustainability managers positioned at the division and local levels and assigned to major projects. Later, though, the company melded the corporate group with EHS (Environment Health and Safety), and reassigned some auxiliary sustainability roles to HR and communications. At the business (division) level, sustainability functions were merged with either EHS or strategy groups. Although the new organisation no longer has a dedicated corporate group, many of the reassigned sustainability people maintain their full-time sustainability roles. Their primary function continues to be integrating environmental and social considerations into decision-making and representing Shell externally on sustainability matters.

'BP and DuPont formed separate sustainability functions at the corporate level, focusing primarily on sustainability issues concerning products, services, and business planning, as well as external stakeholder matters. These corporate groups co-ordinate various multifunctional and cross-business teams to achieve company objectives. Other companies, like IBM, have no dedicated sustainability function but work through similar teams to report on sustainability and coordinate progress.'

(Blackburn)

4.14 It is unclear exactly what the syllabus means by 'implications for resources', and the guidance published by CIPS for this unit gives no clue. But clearly, sustainable procurement may have a number of general implications for organisational resource requirements, priorities and deployment. The implementation of sustainable procurement may:

- Require additional strategic resources (in the sense of competencies, capacity and capabilities)

- Require the investment or deployment of additional physical assets (such as plant and machinery), finance (or budget allocation), information (and information systems), and human resources (people and skills)

- Create or add value to intangible strategic resources such as brand strength/equity, corporate reputation and reputational capital

- Alter the organisation's pattern of resource consumption (eg by reducing energy/materials consumption, switching to renewable/green resources and so on).

4.15 If we get further clarification on this point, we will post additional notes on the CIPS student website.

The need for alignment

4.16 The syllabus specifically mentions 'common targets and objectives'. This is obviously an implementation issue, and will be discussed as such later. However, in the context of this learning objective, it draws attention to the need for strategic alignment, already discussed in Section 1 of this chapter. Procurement cannot 'go its own way' on sustainability: its targets and objectives must be (a) derived from and supportive of the corporate strategy (b) dovetailed with the targets and objectives of other functions, to avoid overlaps, gaps and unresolved conflicts.

The need for prioritisation and pace

4.17 The syllabus also specifically mentions 'realistic timescales'. Again, this is an implementation issue, and will be discussed later. In the context of this learning objective, however, it draws attention to the potential for disruption, frustration, poorly evaluated plans and hasty actions caused by unrealistic expectations for the pace of change. What, then, is a realistic timetable for change?

4.18 The introduction of sustainable procurement, as with any strategic change, will have significant impacts on an organisation, because change is inherently disruptive: changing process and skill requirements, structures and relationships; eroding security and raising resistance. Like any change programme, the implementation of sustainable procurement may be approached in one of two basic ways.

- *Incremental change* is often used as a proactive approach, building on the existing situation in small steps over a long period of time. This is the basis of business improvement strategies such as *kaizen* (continuous improvement) and total quality management. Because it requires only realistic, small operational improvements and elimination of wastes, it can be implemented substantially 'from the bottom up', involving employees through sustainability circles, suggestion schemes, departmental improvement and supplier development planning, and so on.

- *Transformational change* is often a more reactive approach, responding to 'disruptive' change, crisis or the need for a completely new paradigm and direction. It seeks to overthrow the *status quo* and introduce radical transformation in a relatively short period of time: the basis of business improvement strategies such as business process re-engineering (BPR). Because it requires discontinuous and sweeping change across organisational structures and systems, it can only be implemented 'from the top down'. Although it requires heavy investment, and some risk and upheaval, it can achieve transformative improvements.

4.19 Sustainable procurement may be implemented as part of a transformational sustainability or CSR programme, in the face of 'disruptive' triggers such as reputational crisis, resource depletion or industry regulation. As we saw in Chapter 5, companies such as Shell, Nike and McDonald's have radically re-organised, re-imagined and re-branded on the basis of sustainability, in response to strong negative media and consumer pressure. Even so, a realistic timetable for change will include adequate time for consultation and education; the mobilisation of resources and supportive changes to systems and structures; the unlearning of old ideas/methods; and a realistic, staged learning curve for adopting new ideas/methods, with periods for reinforcement and consolidation.

4.20 However, as we have already noted, sustainability is not an area in which you can 'do everything, all at once'. Organisations will have to prioritise areas of high risk exposure, high visibility, potential leverage (eg the public sector's 'priority spend areas'), momentum-building small wins and demonstrable value gains. Once basic policies are in place, there may a role for ongoing incremental change, which:

- Builds on existing skills, routines and beliefs: implementation is likely to be more efficient, less traumatic and more likely to win acceptance

- Allows more flexible response to environmental changes and stakeholder feedback: resources are not wasted on long-range plans which are undermined by uncertainty

- Allowing a continuous sense of progress, even through uncertainty and difficulty. Small changes may be easy to achieve (eg purchasing energy-saving light bulbs and recycled paper for the office) – and may trigger bigger changes (eg as a result of partnership with the green supplier). 'Big strategies can grow from little ideas' (Mintzberg).

- Empowering employees. Because big strategies can grow from little ideas, front-line employees can contribute significantly to sustainable procurement initiatives.

5 Implications for procurement

Strategic sourcing and procurement

5.1 In a sense, of course, this whole text is about the implications of sustainability for the procurement function. Many of the implications already discussed for the organisation as a whole (skilling, resources, pace/priority of change management and organisation structure) will apply equally to procurement. We will just draw together some aspects here, on which you should be able to elaborate if required.

5.2 As we have seen throughout this chapter, sustainable procurement is an explicitly strategic approach, involving top-down, organisation-wide strategic alignment. If the procurement function does not already occupy a strategic role and focus, it will probably need to move in this direction, in order to:

- Take a longer-term and more holistic view of value addition and contribution (rather than sub-optimal focus on short-term cost reductions, say)
- Take a strategic view of supply chain development and management for sustainability, in support of the organisation's long-term sustainability objectives
- Take a more proactive consultancy or business partner role in marketing, product development and organisational development strategies, as a meaningful contributor to 'green'/ethical branding, design and processes.

Organisation for sustainable procurement

5.3 As we saw in Section 4 above, sustainable procurement may have implications for organisation structure. Mechanisms may need to be developed or adjusted to facilitate:

- The allocation of clear responsibilities and accountabilities for sustainability within the procurement function
- The integration of sustainability responsibilities, objectives and targets within the current work of the procurement function where possible
- Liaison, cross-functional teamworking, consultancy or other forms of partnership between procurement and other functions on sustainability issues (or to integrate sustainable procurement perspectives into projects)
- The championship of sustainable procurement by representatives of the procurement function: that is, a change agency role.

Skills and resources for sustainable procurement

5.4 The deployment of sustainable procurement policy may require new knowledge, awareness and skills. Education may have to be provided on sustainability issues and policy frameworks. Awareness training may be required to change attitudes to sustainability issues (and particularly, say, their priority in relation to former priorities which may have focused on price/cost). Skills training may be required to utilise new systems, tools of analysis (eg lifecycle analysis or whole life costing), negotiating techniques and so on.

5.5 Knowledge, awareness, skills and principles will have to be supported with adequate resources: authority to carry out allocated responsibilities; information (eg on corporate social responsibility targets and performance feedback); budget allocation (to cover short-term investment in sustainability); and so on.

Implications for procurement processes and tasks

5.6 Chapters 7–13 specifically address the operational impacts of implementing sustainable procurement across core processes and tasks. Here are some examples.

- *Procurement objectives and performance measures*: the need to take a long-term, stakeholder value, TBL or balanced scorecard view, rather than a short-term view of cost reduction or best price

- *Market analysis*: the need to appraise supply markets with specific sustainability criteria in mind (eg supplier diversity, environmental management systems, sustainability risks and so on)

- *Sourcing policies*: the need to take into account sustainable access to contracts for local, small and diverse suppliers; social/environmental sustainability issues in using overseas (especially developing country) suppliers; and the sustainability of both overly wide (inefficient) and overly narrow/dependent (high supply risk) supply bases

- *Product and service specification*: the potential to incorporate sustainability criteria into specifications and product selection; the need to develop early buyer/supplier involvement in sustainable product/service development

- *Supplier selection and contracting*: incorporating sustainability criteria into the tender/selection process; incorporating sustainability-supporting clauses into contracts, service level agreements, partnership and continuous improvement agreements; and ensuring the responsible and ethical management of the process

- *Contract and relationship management*: monitoring and measuring suppliers' sustainability performance (and potential sources of compliance, supply and reputational risk); pursuing continuous improvements; managing relationships for sustainable collaboration (as an ethical and attractive customer).

- *Promoting social and environmental responsibility standards within the procurement function*: equality, diversity and respect; development of human potential (eg through staff empowerment); ethical conduct and good governance; reduced GHG emissions (eg through energy-saving practices, reduced use of transport).

6 *Implications for other functions*

6.1 Whether it is explicitly an organisation-wide policy (as part of a corporate sustainability or CSR strategy) or a procurement-driven initiative, the implementation of sustainable procurement will have operational impacts on other functions in the organisation.

- Sustainability will become a key decision-factor in the requisitioning, specification and selection of the inputs to their activities and processes. The business need for requisitioned purchases and unsustainable specifications may legitimately be challenged by procurement and/or sustainability specialists.

- Sustainability policy principles may impact on their processes, procedures and practices: eg to reduce the carbon footprint of transport operations and office working, or to re-engineer production operations, in order to minimise waste.

- There may be new operational requirements: eg for reverse logistics, disassembly or recycling.

- New materials, technologies and systems may need to be developed and/or incorporated in operations – and new skills learned to manage and utilise them.

- New performance measures, accountabilities and organisation structures (including cross-functional collaboration) may have to be developed.

- There may be new opportunities for strategy development and added value: new marketing strategies, say, or new research and development projects.

- There may be new risks (eg in innovation, transparency to stakeholders or new markets) – and a perceived lack of experience, competence or resources to manage them.

- There may be a need for increased cross-functional collaboration, consultation and information, in order to align sustainability decisions and activities.

- There may be a need for cultural change, in order to embed sustainable procurement principles and priorities in functional value systems, 'norms' of behaviour, reinforcement mechanisms (eg staff selection, training and reward) and so on.

6.2   Some more function-specific impacts are shown in Table 6.1.

6.3   There will be a strong need for the procurement function to articulate and 'sell' sustainable procurement principles and policies at the interface with all these functions – particularly if procurement is carried out within user departments, by 'part-time' buyers (not procurement specialists). We will address this issue in the following chapters.

Table 6.1: *Impacts of sustainable procurement on other functions*

Function	Examples of impacts
Marketing	• Strategic opportunities to develop sustainable products/services and brands • Need to research the market, to define customer value, competitive advantage and potential brand positioning in relation to sustainability • Need for close collaboration with design/development, procurement and product to specify products/services for market appeal • Need to provide market research data and customer feedback for continuous improvement planning • Role in internal corporate communications to 'sell' the sustainability policy • Need to promote sustainability in external corporate communications, in order to crystallise marketing/branding/reputational value • Sustainable procurement of own requirements (eg for IT, promotional materials and packaging, advertising services, office supplies, vehicles, print)
Research and development, design and engineering	• Need to develop sustainable designs, specifications and processes • Need to collaborate with procurement on materials specifications: may face challenge on sustainability and/or commercial grounds • Potential for new design/development projects: 'green' products etc • Potential for new research projects: eg renewable energy • Sustainable procurement of own requirements, if carried out by 'part-time' in-unit buyers
Manufacturing, production or operations (and other 'user departments')	• Need to collaborate with procurement on value analysis, inventory management and purchase requisition/specification • May have requisitions and specifications challenged on grounds of sustainability. Need for flexibility in considering more sustainable options: different suppliers, innovative solutions, standardisation etc • Need to accept trade-offs on some criteria (eg high-specification performance, bespoke items) to support sustainable sourcing • Need to develop sustainable processes, procedures and practices: ways of utilising environmentally-preferred materials, new technologies, energy-saving ways of working • Need to develop sustainable capabilities: eg disassembly, recycling, waste management • Sustainable procurement of own requirements, including capital plant and equipment, manufacturing facilities, transport fleets etc.
Transport/logistics (if not outsourced)	• Need to collaborate with procurement on demand management and delivery planning, to minimise transport miles, fuel use, carbon footprint etc • Need to develop fuel-efficient, low-emission transport fleets (eg hybrid) • Need to develop reverse-logistics capability (for recycling etc), return load planning etc
Finance	• Need to mobilise, allocate or re-allocate resources for sustainability projects and initiatives (including policy development and deployment) • Need to accept a TBL or balanced scorecard measure of performance – vs the primacy of profit (and targets such as short-term cost reductions) • Need to support other functions in sound governance procedures (eg financial and management reporting, budgetary control, internal controls) • Need to prepare financial information for stakeholder reporting (including a sound business case for sustainability, for internal stakeholders and investors) • Need for sustainable procurement of own requirements (eg IT, stationery, office furniture)

Chapter summary

- In strategic planning, plans must be aligned both vertically (with the overall objectives of the business) and horizontally (with the objectives of other functions). This applies to any organisation attempting to implement a sustainability strategy.

- A first step in a strategic plan for sustainability is to ensure that it is compatible with the corporate purpose, values, principles and aspirations. This will often mean that it is embodied in the mission statement and/or the company's CSR statement.

- The balanced business scorecard is a way of aligning key performance indicators for all areas of an organisation's activities. It adopts four perspectives: financial; internal business processes; learning and growth; and customer.

- Despite the many benefits of a sustainability policy (including 'hard' financial benefits), there are often trade-offs when it comes to implementation. These must be managed sensitively, often by use of multi-disciplinary teams.

- Adoption of a sustainability policy has important implications for procurement. In particular, the procurement function will become more strategic in focus.

- Equally, a sustainability approach will impact on other functions, such as marketing, R&D, manufacturing, logistics, and finance.

Self-test questions

Numbers in brackets refer to the paragraphs above where your answers can be checked.

1 Explain the top-down and bottom-up methods of achieving vertical alignment of organisational plans. (1.6)

2 List the four sets of drivers for sustainability from Senge's Sustainable Value Framework (1.12)

3 List the basic elements of Blackburn's Sustainability Operating System. (Figure 6.2)

4 Describe the multiple roles of an organisation's CSR statement. (2.7)

5 What are the broad objectives of a sustainable procurement policy? (2.11)

6 Describe the four perspectives of the balanced business scorecard. (3.5)

7 List Blackburn's alternative set of balanced scorecard measures. (3.11)

8 List benefits of sustainability programmes. (4.5)

9 Explain the trade-offs that will be needed as a result of sustainability initiatives. (4.6)

10 Distinguish between incremental change and transformational change. (4.18)

11 List implications of sustainability for procurement processes and tasks. (5.6)

12 List implications of sustainability for the manufacturing function. (Table 6.1)

Further reading

From your 'Essential Reading' list, you might look at Blackburn (*The Sustainability Handbook*):

- Chapter 4: Building an SOS: The Key Elements and Basic Structure

- Chapter 6: Strategic Planning for Focused Sustainability Improvement

CHAPTER 7

Developing a Sustainable Procurement Policy

2.2   Examine the stages in the development of a sustainable procurement policy and policy deployment guidelines.

- Obtaining commitment
- Communication to stakeholders
- Setting targets and objectives
- Clear responsibilities
- People development
- Implementation
- Ongoing management/review
- Flexible approach to respond to new or different drivers

Chapter headings

1   Developing a sustainable procurement policy

2   Stakeholder communication

3   Targets, objectives and responsibilities

4   Resourcing deployment and implementation

5   Ongoing management and review

Introduction

In Chapter 6, we emphasised the need for the procurement function to articulate its sustainability priorities, goals and plans to internal customers and stakeholders, including other functions likely to be impacted by changed processes and practices – and part-time purchasers who will have to implement sustainable procurement policies in user departments.

In this chapter, we look at ways of doing this: developing, communicating and securing buy-in to a sustainable procurement policy, and setting up guidelines and systems to manage and maintain it in action.

Although the syllabus mentions 'implementation' and 'ongoing management/review' at this point, it is worth being clear that this learning outcome deals with development of the policy and guidelines for deploying or implementing the policy: the issues of implementation itself are dealt with in the following learning outcome, and will be discussed in Chapter 8.

1 Developing a sustainable procurement policy

1.1 As we saw in Chapter 6, the development of a sustainable procurement policy does not take place in isolation, as a procurement-generated, procurement-specific process. It is part of a wider process of:

- Formulating corporate-level aspirations, values and commitments around CSR and sustainability

- Encouraging all business units and functions to identify their own key CSR/sustainability issues, priorities and potential contributions

- Formulating a process-focused view of CSR and sustainability, which crosses boundaries between design, engineering, procurement, operations, logistics and so on (so that 'sustainable procurement' is about the whole business process, not just procurement function activity)

- Creating a multi-disciplinary sustainability team or steering committee, to identify shared (organisation-wide) sustainability priorities for incorporation into corporate CSR/sustainability statements, and to integrate and align sustainability policies and plans

- Creating multi-disciplinary sustainability forums or networks to share best practice, information and ideas for ongoing issues identification, problem-solving and improvement/innovation planning

- Identifying and mobilising sustainability champions, drivers and enablers in the organisation, including policy development in functions with particular 'leverage' over sustainability issues – such as procurement, with its role at the interface with both external and internal supply chains, and its potential input across business processes.

1.2 Now, however, it is time to move beyond the wider context of sustainability management in the organisation, and to focus more specifically on sustainable procurement policy.

Benefits of formulating policy

1.3 Lysons and Farrington (*Purchasing & Supply Management*) argue that policies are helpful for a number of reasons.

- They provide guidelines to executives for formulating functional and operating strategies.

- They can be used to provide authority for a chosen course of action, based on principle and/or precedent. This supports employee initiative and empowerment, by eliminating the need for constant upward reference.

- They support managerial decision-making: providing a basis for managerial control (by measurement of performance against policy guidelines); reducing decision times; and providing guidelines for routine actions (so that reporting and new decisions are only required 'by exception')

- They support cross-functional co-ordination (by communicating shared goals and principles), alignment of procedures, and consistency in thought and action.

A framework for policy development

1.4 A simple general process for policy development may be outlined as follows.

- *Define the vision* for sustainable procurement, and its fit within corporate sustainability/CSR strategies (if any)

- *Identify and prioritise key issues/topics and core processes* as the initial focus of sustainable procurement policy, with reference to: the corporate mission, vision and strategies, critical success factors for the business (and procurement function), and existing and emerging sustainability issues and trends

- *Identify and define opportunities for improvement in priority areas*, on the basis of benchmarking and process analysis (including relevant national and international standards) and self assessment (gap analysis).

- *Assess available resources for improvement*, including information systems, management systems, budgetary constraints and the strengths, needs and capabilities of human resources (talent management review) to pursue sustainable procurement objectives.

- *Identify key principles* (if these have not already been articulated) of sustainable procurement, setting out the procurement function's key values and commitments in relation to economic, social and environmental sustainability in its own activities – and perhaps also its expectations of internal and external supply chain partners. These may be formulated in consultation with key internal and external stakeholders. They will also need to be reviewed for consistency with corporate sustainability/CSR statements.

- *Identify measurable objectives and targets* for achieving improvement in identified priority areas, with realistic time-scales and budget estimates, and built-in provisions for progress measurement and review. Objectives and targets will need to be reviewed for consistency with corporate sustainability and business strategies. Their feasibility will need to be assessed, in consultation with management representatives and other stakeholders responsible for their achievement. Budget proposals will need to be approved by fund holders.

- *Identify roles and responsibilities* in the communication, implementation, operation, monitoring and review of the policy.

- *Engage in consultation on the draft policy*, as required, and *gain authorisation* for a final version.

- *Resource the policy.* Staff/supplier training, communication, tools and resources, deployment and operation guidelines, procedure manuals, codes of practice and other measures may need to be planned and developed to support effective deployment of the policy.

- *Document, launch, deploy and integrate the policy.* At a certain point, the policy will 'go live' (or be 'rolled out') and adherence and ongoing management will become part of the responsibility of employees, suppliers and contractors.

- *Establish processes for ongoing management and review.*

The sustainable procurement policy document

1.5   A simple sustainable procurement policy document (whether in printed or digital form) may include the following documents.

- *Introduction* – definition of sustainable procurement; why it is needed; identified drivers and priority issues; its place within wider organisational CSR/sustainability objectives and strategy

- *Core/guiding principles* – what the strategy is trying to achieve; how it links with the values and mission of the organisation; beliefs, assumptions, values and commitments by which the organisation defines sustainable procurement; what the organisation expects from its suppliers, contractors and other supply partners, as part of their contribution to sustainable procurement

- *Objectives and targets* – how progress and performance will be defined and measured.

1.6   More detailed strategic, tactical and operational plans may then be drawn up, setting out: how the programme will be implemented, and action plans with timescales, milestones and targets for meeting specific objectives.

Example: Olympic Development Authority

The following case study is offered in the CIPS Knowledge Summary on Sustainability.

'Preparations for the 2012 Olympic Games and Paralympic Games provides a good case study to draw together sustainable procurement in practice. Sustainability is core to the two organisations at the centre of delivering the 2012 Games – LOCOG and the ODA. The sustainability policy identified five key themes to run throughout the three phases in the development of the project, covering planning and construction, staging the games and realising the legacy. The five overarching themes are:

*   Climate change

*   Waste

*   Biodiversity and ecology

*   Inclusion

*   Healthy living

The total budget for the Games is £9.345 billion. Of this, £1.7 billion has been allocated for infrastructure development and regeneration of the local vicinity.

With particular reference to sustainable procurement, it is a condition of supply that potential suppliers agree to support all sustainable procurement principles. The three most applicable to the procurement environment are climate change, waste and inclusion.

The ODA aims to minimise the carbon emissions associated with the Olympic Park and venues and achieve a 50% reduction for the built environment by 2013. As an example the ODA aims for all permanent Olympic Park venue structures to achieve a BREEAM 'excellent rating', and be 15% more energy efficient than the 2006 Part L Building Regulations. The carbon footprint will be reduced further by the use of Combined Cooling, Heating and Power Plants (CCHP) and the use of renewable energy.

Managing waste is closely aligned with the climate change agenda. The ODA have followed a well-established hierarchy for managing waste as follows: Eliminate; Reduce; Re-use; Recycle; Recover; and Dispose of waste.

Ninety percent of buildings demolished on site have been recycled. Purchasing and supply management professionals are engaging innovation within the supplier base to deliver products that will use forty percent less water than current industry practice.

An organisation's greatest assets are its employees. The ODA recognise that at its peak (between March 2010 and November 2010) there will be 18,000 workers per day on site. It is therefore important to engage the diverse supplier base. About 2,000 small-value contracts will be established.

1.7   We will now go on to look at the areas of this process highlighted by the syllabus.

2   *Stakeholder communication*

Consultation and involvement

2.1   A sustainable procurement policy must be robust, feasible and supported by key stakeholders in its implementation. This means that it must stand up to scrutiny from a wide range of interested parties and take account of their particular needs, viewpoints and contributions.

2.2 This is one of the strong arguments, raised in Chapter 6, for using a multi-disciplinary project team in the development of sustainable procurement policy. However, other mechanisms of consultation and involvement may also be used, such as: briefing and consultation meetings; circulation and presentation of draft policy documents and supporting information; one-to-one presentation of proposals to key stakeholders. Such mechanisms may be led by sustainability champions at the corporate level, but may also be driven by the procurement function.

2.3 Procurement will have a particularly important role in consulting with suppliers. In formulating the organisation's commitments to sustainable procurement, for example, it will be helpful to know: what kind of treatment and relationship suppliers define as ethical and sustainable from their point of view; whether commitments will be feasible using available suppliers (and at what cost); and whether key suppliers will be willing to continue to supply the organisation under those policy requirements. In formulating the organisation's expectations of suppliers, it will equally be helpful to know whether these are perceived as equitable, reasonable, feasible (and, ideally, beneficial and motivational) from the point of view of suppliers.

2.4 Key contributors to the policy development project may therefore include representatives of:

- Senior management
- Senior procurement professionals
- Major suppliers and contractors
- Internal customers and functions potentially affected by the proposals (which, as we saw in Chapter 6, can be quite a wide-ranging list!)
- Staff (in procurement and other departments) who will have to implement the policy
- Other relevant external stakeholders, where appropriate: eg key customers/clients, pressure/interest groups (who may act as advisers, certifiers or partners) or specialist consultants (eg in environmental risk management).

2.5 One of the key points about consultation at this stage is that, as we will see in Chapter 15, different stakeholder groups may well have divergent or conflicting objectives and interests. Internal departments and suppliers, in particular, may have a vested interest in the *status quo* — or in avoiding the costs and risks of change — which will create problems for subsequent buy-in and implementation if not openly addressed. Some suppliers who lack sustainable capabilities may lose out on contracts under the new policy — and this will be an important sustainability consideration in itself (eg if the policy penalises small, local or diverse suppliers).

2.6 In addition, stakeholders may have legitimate concerns on grounds of feasibility, which offer useful input to the decision-making process. They may also raise alternative priorities and ideas, which may helpfully change procurement's thinking on policy issues. Consultation and involvement can thus contribute to the quality of policy development decisions — as well as to their 'acceptability' and stakeholder buy-in.

Obtaining stakeholder engagement and commitment

2.7 A sustainable procurement policy will need to be supported and signed off at the highest level of management, in order to have legitimate authority over the activities and resource decisions of all relevant functions and business units. It will also need to have the 'buy in' — acceptance, ownership and commitment — of a range of internal and connected stakeholders (including suppliers) who will be affected by its deployment.

2.8 Blackburn pithily argues that: 'the organisation isn't going anywhere near sustainability unless someone explains why it should. Personnel, time and other resources are too valuable to waste on an initiative that has no merit. Someone must answer the question: 'Why?'

2.9 In earlier chapters, we have discussed the content of business case arguments for sustainable procurement. Some process guidelines for making such a case, whether to top management, other internal stakeholders or supply partners, are as follows (adapted from Blackburn).

- Reconfirm the corporate mission/vision – and indicate that sustainable procurement can help achieve that vision

- Offer a clear definition of sustainability and sustainable procurement

- Link the drive towards sustainable procurement with business objectives – showing how sustainable procurement principles tie to the top three of four identified business priorities (eg how waste/energy reduction supports cost reduction)

- Present the business case for a sustainable procurement policy, and supporting management system – giving concrete examples of business advantage and risk

- Create a sense of urgency for action – eg using a current public scandal, internal problem or critical incident, audit/consultancy report, customer/investor feedback or benchmarking information to highlight immediate reputational and business risks and opportunities

- Highlight some key sustainability issues and trends that are most relevant to the organisation's procurement, and identify the threats, challenges and opportunities they represent

- Use the language stakeholders will find most persuasive. For senior management, this will be the language of business: eg 'enterprise risk and opportunity assessment', 'protecting assets and investments', 'strengthening brands', 'building credibility with key constituents', 'return on investment'.

- Request that specific action be taken in response: eg comments on the draft sustainable procurement policy, or authorisation to draft one; a plan for further consultation or the formation of a cross-functional deployment team; or a target date for final approval.

2.10 We will discuss techniques for securing the compliance and commitment of suppliers in Chapter 8, since these are issues which will mainly be relevant to the implementation of specific sustainable procurement programmes.

Communicating the policy to secondary stakeholders

2.11 Once the policy has been finalised and deployed, it will need to be communicated to external stakeholders (including government, regulators, customers, investors, business allies, relevant NGOs and the public), in order to crystallise the value available from enhanced compliance, credibility, reputation and brand strength.

2.12 This will usually be the responsibility of the corporate communications or public relations function, using a range of communication tools such as: press relations; product/service and brand marketing; shareholder relations (including annual meetings and reports); the corporate website (including intranets and extranets); statutory reporting (eg on health and safety); trade/industry conferences, exhibitions and sustainability think-tanks; and so on. More formal attempts may also be made to gain recognition of the policy, eg as part of certification under national or international standards.

3   Targets, objectives and responsibilities

Prioritising sustainability issues and action areas

3.1   The first step in setting targets and objectives will be to prioritise sustainability issues, supply/spend categories and action areas. This may be done using techniques such as the following (which will be discussed further in Chapter 13).

- Review of legal/regulatory requirements
- Environmental, purchasing and/or sustainability audit: identifying current and emerging issues, resources and capabilities
- Spend analysis: identifying major spend categories (eg as a proportion of total spend, or over a certain threshold of value)
- Portfolio analysis: eg using the Kraljic matrix to categorise supplies according to their importance and supply risk
- Gap analysis: comparing current performance to plans and aspirations, to identify gaps or shortfalls
- Risk and impact assessments: analysing the likelihood and consequences of risk events related to sustainability
- SWOT analysis: assessing internal strengths and weaknesses, and external opportunities and threats
- Benchmarking exercises: assessment of the organisation's sustainable procurement policies and practices against sector/industry leaders, key competitors or national/international standards.

3.2   Issues will be high priority if:

- They are important to the organisation's business success, in terms of both risks and opportunities
- They are identified critical success factors for procurement
- They are identified as high priority by senior management and corporate CSR/sustainability policy
- They have high public visibility (creating strong external pressure on the organisation to address the issue, or high reputational risk)
- They indicate a significant shortfall in performance, capability or management processes, which might expose the organisation to significant risk
- They offer potential for 'leverage': being relatively easily and cost-effectively addressed, but offering relatively high benefits and returns.

Setting targets and objectives

3.3   Once the key areas of focus for the policy have been identified, the policy development team can articulate specific objectives and targets, expressing exactly what the policy is designed to achieve – and how progress and performance will be measured.

3.4   An *objective* is defined by ISO 14001 as a 'policy statement of intended action which may or may not be quantified' (for example: to develop reverse logistics, re-use and recycling capability through the supply chain). A *target* is 'a specific, measurable action to achieve the objective' (eg to increase the proportion of recycled materials used by 10% from the previous year). An *indicator* is 'a measure or other expression of information about performance,

performance influencers or conditions (eg proportion of recycled materials per unit of production).

3.5 The guidance published by CIPS for this unit appears to use slightly different terminology, offering the following examples.

- *Sustainable procurement objective*: communicating the organisation's performance, activities and policies on sustainability to suppliers and contractors

  Target: all suppliers to be conversant with the organisation's policies

  Measure: sustainability requirements included in all RFQs, tender documentation and contracts; sustainability an agenda item for all supplier conferences and business reviews; all new suppliers to submit company CSR policy.

- *Sustainable procurement objective*: considering fuel economy and alternative fuels in fleet procurements

  Target: no vehicle in company car fleet to perform at less than 50 mpg

  Measure: manufacturers' brochure or transportation department data.

3.6 Objectives and targets must be effectively formulated. A general framework for effective target-setting is provided by the mnemonic: 'SMART'.

- **S**pecific: not generalised statements such as 'achieving best practice', but, for example, specifying '5% reduction in measured GHG emissions' or 'zero waste to landfill by 2015'. This ensures that all parties know unambiguously whether and how far the objective has been achieved.

- **M**easurable: offering observable or assessable performance indicators or success criteria (using available or accessible monitoring methods and data) – for example: percentage/value of spend allocated to minority or women-owned vendors; percentage/value increase in procurement-influenced spend

- **A**greed: vertically and horizontally aligned, and jointly agreed by participant stakeholders – particularly where targets will form the basis of terms and conditions in supply contracts (eg number/percentage of suppliers certified under ISO 14001), or performance measurement processes (eg targets for percentage/number of budget holders trained in whole life costing or use of call-off contracts)

- **R**ealistic: challenging enough to motivate stakeholders and create a sense of urgency – but not so difficult as to set participants up for failure, causing frustration, corner-cutting or de-motivation. A series of staged targets allowing 'small/quick wins' is often advocated, as a way of building momentum, providing reinforcement and driving flexibility and continuous improvement. Examples might include review of all specifications for the introduction of Fair Trade brands; 5% savings in paper and/or energy use through the rationalisation of office equipment; or formation of a cross-functional sustainability deployment team within three months.

- **T**ime-bounded: with a date by which the objective is to be achieved.

3.7 A sustainable procurement policy should not set too many objectives, as this will dilute focus and spread resources too 'thin'. Ten to twelve key objectives (subject to periodic review) may be sufficient for any one strategic planning period.

Allocating responsibilities for sustainable procurement

3.8 The sustainability policy or related deployment guidelines should clearly allocate responsibilities (and accountabilities) for implementation – and for the ongoing management of the policy. Depending on the size and structure of the organisation, and how sustainability is 'set up' within it (as discussed in Chapter 6), specific areas of responsibility may be allocated to:

- A corporate-level sustainability leader, steering committee or team, with responsibility for the authorisation, review and co-ordination of functional sustainability policies, and for resource allocation and consultancy to sustainability initiatives and projects

- A senior sustainability 'champion' within the procurement function, with responsibility for developing and co-ordinating sustainability-related activity within the function; representing the function on sustainability issues (eg on sustainability committees or project teams); and acting as a hub for communication and reporting on sustainability issues. This role may include responsibility for supplier management, staff training, document development, performance monitoring and so on – or these responsibilities may be delegated to other individuals within the procurement team.

- The Chief Procurement Officer, Purchasing Manager or other head of the function, with responsibility to support the sustainability policy in various ways: allocating resources, authorising training, steering changes to systems and procedures, sponsoring implementation projects, and integrating sustainability measures into job specifications, recruitment/selection, team objectives, performance management and reward – and so on.

- Members of the procurement team, who may be appointed as sustainability representatives, supervisors, consultants or stakeholder managers, as the policy is cascaded down to procurement departments, part-time buyers in user departments, cross-functional project teams and supply networks. These roles may be generalist, or specialised on the basis of sustainability issues/topics (eg ethics, diversity, climate change or waste reduction), categories of spend or vendor groups.

3.9 Meanwhile, all members of the procurement team have the general responsibility of implementing and adhering to the sustainability policy in all areas of procurement activity: incorporating principles and practices into specifications, terms of trade, supplier contracts, contract reviews, supplier selection and appraisal criteria, supplier development programmes and so on (as discussed in later chapters).

3.10 The important thing is to ensure that there is clear allocation of responsibility of all key activities and issues, with no overlaps or gaps; matched to the capability and authority of the individuals or teams concerned; and without creating a separate 'layer' of responsibility or accountability which might frustrate or distract people. Sustainability may initially require 'special attention' – but the aim is to integrate as fully and swiftly as possible into 'business as usual' for the procurement function and its stakeholders.

4 *Resourcing deployment and implementation*

Policy deployment guidelines

4.1 Policy deployment means 'rolling out' or spreading a policy across an organisation. This is a crucial step for processes such as sustainable procurement which have wide-reaching impacts across business processes. Blackburn argues that many organisations fail to secure broad ownership and momentum in sustainability initiatives, 'because no one effectively deployed the initiative into the ranks of employees or integrated it into the company's existing tools, processes, procedures, programmes and values. Business teams often devote considerable effort to plan the development of some new programme, policy or tool but give little thought to the roll-out'.

Example: Nokia

Phone giant Nokia builds CSR into all phases of its supply chain relationships: supplier network management, supplier requirement statements, support through training, supplier assessment and industry collaboration.

'At Nokia we feel that sound environmental and social principles are an important part of sustaining a successful and responsible business. We expect the companies in our supplier network to take a similar ethical business approach. To ensure this we have developed a comprehensive set of global Nokia Supplier Requirements (NSR), which include specified environmental and social [health and safety, labour and ethics] requirements...

'We carry out regular supplier assessments as a tool to help promote good performance and also to monitor compliance. This is not, however, a policing activity. We see on-site assessments as an opportunity to raise awareness, identify potential risks and share best practices.

'If we find a supplier is not meeting Nokia's expectations, we compel them to commit to and implement corrective action. This is the best solution for the supplier, for Nokia, for the workers, and for the environment. In practice, our suppliers have generally reacted positively and seen this as a way to improve their business. However, if a supplier were to refuse to address any of these issues we would be prepared to reconsider our business relationship.'

4.2   It will be important for sustainability champions to give thought to how the sustainable procurement policy will be rolled out across the organisation. In addition to the policy itself, they may seek to develop guidelines for its deployment: resources for stakeholder communication and engagement (explanations, definitions, business case arguments and so on); allocated responsibilities for communication, education, training and coaching; objectives and timescales for various phases of roll-out; milestones for measuring progress; and so on. The elements of such guidelines have been covered in this chapter.

Deployment tools

4.3   A range of support tools may need to be developed or mobilised to support deployment, including:

- *Communication tools*: brochures, manuals and handbooks (and their web-based equivalents); employee notice boards (and their intranet equivalents); staff/supplier meetings and discussions; executive speeches; memos; letters; newsletters and bulletins; media releases; websites; sustainability 'circles'; posters; shareholder, employee and management reports; supplier conferences; supplier extranet

- *Education and training tools*: diagrams and process flowcharts; exhibits, models and samples; presentations; manuals and handbooks; online FAQs; training and train-the-trainer programmes; coaching and mentoring schemes

- *Motivation and engagement tools*: executive speeches; awards/celebrations; customer/supplier testimonials; symbolic activities (eg staff tree-planting or environmental clean-up days, charity fun-run); criteria for approved/preferred supplier status; site visits, supplier audits and appraisals; supplier penalties and incentives

- *Integration and administrative support tools*: audit, appraisal and self-appraisal checklists and guidance notes; supplier appraisal and vendor rating forms; model form purchase requisitions, specifications, contracts and other model documents (eg specimen personal performance objectives); supplier development programmes; and so on.

4.4   Consideration will need to be given to: identifying the target audiences for such tools (and the best information/influence hubs and routes through which to meet them); developing appropriate tools and materials (taking into account the range of groups or regions that may need to be targeted eg by using options, fill-in-the-blanks provisions, modular training, different versions tailored to different needs and so on); and finding efficient and effective ways of delivering those tools (eg via sustainability teams or consultants embedded in, or with access to, target audiences).

4.5   Flexibility is a key issue for deployment in multi-functional, multi-regional or trans-national organisations and supply chains. The procurement policy, and associated deployment tools, must be formulated in accessible language (or languages): avoiding technical jargon and culture-specific expressions, say. It must be fitted to the cultural values and norms of the target audience: authoritarian/participative style, assumptions and values around specific sustainability issues, legal/regulatory frameworks and so on.

Resource plans

4.6   Plans will be needed for the development or acquisition of deployment tools, as well as the information, skills, finance, equipment and other resources needed to implement the sustainable procurement policy on an ongoing basis. Budgets for deployment and implementation will need to be drawn up as part of the planning exercise.

People development

4.7   Of all the resources required for policy deployment and implementation, the syllabus highlights people development. The 'limiting factor' in sustainable procurement will often not be finance, but the human resource: the awareness, skills, competencies, motivation and educated/intentional behaviours required to deploy, implement and support sustainability.

4.8   As we saw in Chapter 5, people development policies are a key internal influence on the success of sustainable procurement. A 'Talent Management Review' may be an important early step in policy development. This involves a review of:

- The existing skills, competencies, experience, attitudes and performance levels of staff in areas relevant to sustainable procurement
- Training and development needs of staff in order to further sustainable procurement
- The career paths and potentials of staff, and existing succession plans, in order to ensure continuity and development of staff in key sustainable procurement roles.

4.9   Such a review may be carried out in collaboration with the human resources department, perhaps as part of the existing cycle of performance reviews and learning needs analysis. Identified gaps or shortfalls in skills, attitudes or succession will have to be met, either by strengthening HR capabilities (eg through recruiting, training, counselling or redeploying staff) – or by adjusting the objectives until the necessary resources can be recruited, mobilised or developed.

4.10   Sustainability values will be reinforced by embedding them in the HR systems of the organisation. Procurement may help to draw up sustainability-related performance criteria and attributes for use in: recruitment and selection (job descriptions, recruitment advertisements and person specifications); appraisal, reward and training/development planning (performance and competence measures); retention and succession planning and so on.

4.11 Blackburn suggests that it will be helpful to determine specific criteria to guide discussion on individual and team performance and development needs, in such contexts, in order to avoid lack of focus, politics, bias, blaming, judgement and so on. He suggests success criteria for sustainable management (Table 7.1) – although you may wish to add more specifically procurement-oriented criteria such as supplier engagement, ethical negotiation, commercial acumen and cross-functional teamworking to the mix.

Table 7.1 *Success criteria for sustainable management (for use in talent review)*

Respect	Results	Responsiveness
Integrity, ethics	Leadership	Value creation
Communications	Innovation	Customer satisfaction
Listening, empathy	Courage and tenacity	Managing expectations
Teamwork	Ability to make tough decisions	Personal initiative
Conflict resolution	Business acumen	Ability to prioritise
Constructive attitude	Planning	Continuous improvement
Objectivity	Execution on commitments	
Developing the talent of others	Ability to manage projects/programmes	

4.12 Identified weaknesses or potential will then be the focus of further planning: individual development/learning plans (for coaching, training, work experience and so on); performance management for persistent underperformers (including, where necessary, reassignment, counselling or disciplinary measures); reinforcement of high performance and potential through praise, reward and/or opportunities for greater responsibility.

5 Ongoing management and review

Ongoing management of the policy

5.1 The syllabus mentions 'ongoing management and review' at this point. Within the context of this learning objective, this should refer specifically to management and review of the sustainable procurement policy – rather than ongoing monitoring, review and adjustment of procurement and supplier performance (which is covered later in the syllabus, and discussed in Chapter 13).

5.2 The following learning objective, which deals with the implementation of sustainable procurement programmes, addresses issues such as 'maintaining commitment' and 'planning for continuous improvement' – but again, this isn't quite the same thing.

5.3 Looking at the syllabus as a whole, we interpret ongoing management and review of a sustainable procurement policy to imply planned mechanisms for processes such as:

- Reviewing and reporting on the extent to which the policy has been successfully communicated, understood and 'bought into' by key stakeholders
- Monitoring and reporting on compliance with the policy
- Monitoring and reporting on the extent to which the implemented policy fulfils its objectives (minimises risks, exploits opportunities), and furthers wider corporate objectives
- Compiling and reporting on the feasibility, costs and benefits of the policy, in order to justify continued investment in it (since its return on investment should also be periodically reviewed at the corporate level)

- Measuring progress and performance periodically against identified targets, milestones and detailed performance metrics
- Identifying new or different sustainability issues/drivers, or changes in priority, and adjusting the policy (if required) to take them into account
- Feedback-gathering, problem-solving and adjustment (ie managerial control)
- Identifying next-stage learning/improvement needs and opportunities (eg via progress review, benchmarking and gap analysis): continuous improvement planning
- Maintaining communication with key stakeholders, to aid the identification of emerging issues; pre-plan and co-ordinate responses to issues, emergencies and crises; gather feedback on the workability and impact of the policy; gaining commitment to continuous improvement; and so on
- Drawing out and documenting learning from policy development, deployment and review processes – to support future change programmes.

Progress and performance management

5.4 Progress and performance – in regard to the deployment and implementation of the policy, as well as the attainment of policy objectives and targets – should be regularly monitored, reviewed and measured against identified milestones, objectives, targets, performance measures and key performance indicators. This may involve a range of performance measurement and management techniques: stakeholder feedback surveys, supplier questionnaires, vendor rating, procurement audits, sustainability audits and so on.

5.5 You might recognise the basic elements of any process improvement, learning or planning and control cycle, such as the Deming Cycle ('Plan, Do, Check, Act'). A plan is formulated and implemented; feedback on progress/performance is compared to the plan (using associated targets and performance indicators); and where there is a deviation or shortfall, the decision is made either to correct performance or to adjust the plan; thus creating a new plan – in a continuous cycle.

5.6 The frequency of review will be determined by organisational reporting conventions; the level of risk/visibility of sustainability issues; the pace of change in the environment, in regard to sustainability issues and trends; and constraints on the time and resources required.

- Policy review at a corporate level may be carried out annually, with a view to adjusting targets for the following year – although this may be supported by half-yearly or quarterly milestone reports and exception reporting.
- At the level of the procurement function, sustainability policy targets, issues and progress may be reviewed during monthly management reviews.
- At the project level, they may be included in weekly team meetings, end-stage assessments and reports, gate/milestone reviews – and post-completion audits.

Policy reviews

5.7 The policy itself will have to be periodically reviewed, to ensure that it is still up-to-date (with emerging sustainability issues), relevant (to current strategic objectives), realistic/feasible (given current resources and constraints), challenging (with new targets being set as old ones are achieved), acceptable to stakeholders – and, in fact, being implemented.

5.8 Stakeholder feedback and attitude surveys may also be used to test the credibility and acceptance of the policy – and to indicate areas which may need adjustment to secure greater stakeholder engagement and commitment. The credibility of a sustainable procurement plan depends on factors such as the following.

- The relevance of objectives to procurement, business and stakeholder interests
- SMART, well-communicated, achievable and clearly understood objectives, targets, measures and road maps for implementation
- Focus and priority: leveraging the 'vital few' measures to secure quick wins and avoid the proliferation of issues and dilution of effort
- Appropriately designed, meaningful but not overly onerous mechanisms for review
- Flexibility: the ability to adapt, adjust and refocus policy where required by differing or changing needs, drivers and issues.

Responding flexibly to emerging drivers and priorities

5.9 In Chapter 3, we emphasised the need for continuous environmental scanning or monitoring, because factors in the purchasing environment are subject to constant change: new sustainability issues (or information about them) emerge; particular issues become 'hot', visible or critical on the public agenda, while others subside; sustainability 'trends', by definition, show movement over time; and there is always the risk of unforeseen contingencies presenting a one-off sustainability challenge, issue or crisis – in the form of technological breakthroughs, competitor initiatives, critical incidents and other 'disruptive' changes.

5.10 There will therefore be a continuous need to scan for new issues, risks and opportunities; to incorporate them into the sustainability policy where required; and to adjust priorities and objectives as conditions change.

5.11 In addition, the drivers, enablers and constraints which shape procurement policy may be shifting. Management changes may rob the organisation of a sustainability champion. A financial crisis and recessionary forces may (as at the time of writing) place a new constraint on investment in sustainable procurement, and a higher priority on economic survival. A natural disaster in a key supply market may create new drivers for economic and social responsibility (eg supporting the recovery of supply partners, to ensure the continuity of supply). A critical incident (such as supplier strikes or an environmental disaster) may raise the profile of an issue. The attention of activist/advocacy groups or the media may focus on the organisation – or move on.

5.12 Meanwhile, various forms of benchmarking, gap analysis and continuous improvement planning may be used periodically to explore next-step areas for target-setting and improvement. Sustainable procurement is potentially so vast in its scope – with so many issues to be addressed – that an organisation can never 'rest on its laurels'. Decisions will have to be made as to whether to pursue higher levels of performance in the objectives already identified by the policy – or to broaden its scope to take on new or different objectives.

5.13 In all these cases, attention must be given to:

- The openness and flexibility of the sustainable procurement policy to new or different information, issues and drivers (eg through regular policy reviews, the use of non-prescriptive guidelines and principles, and relatively short-range plans)
- Mechanisms to progress new proposals and policy amendments through consultation and approval at the corporate level, where required – to maintain strategic alignment and integration
- The availability of mechanisms to communicate approved changes in policy or priority to key stakeholders

- Mechanisms to alter the documentation of the sustainable procurement policy, in such a way as to maintain the up-to-dateness and consistency of versions in circulation (eg via version numbering, centralised version control, and posting of updated master versions on internet/intranet/extranet sites)
- The flexibility of resource plans, to allow the deployment of resources to new priorities where required (including 'contingency' sums, where possible, to respond to unexpected threats).

Example: Herman Miller

Herman Miller is a manufacturer of office furniture, renowned for its innovation. In the UK, its Herman Miller for Government division is an OGC 'buying solutions framework holder': that is, a preferred supplier to public sector organisations under a framework agreement.

Its environmental policy begins as follows.

2020 environment goals

In 2004 we established the 'Perfect Vision' programme. The initiative established a target date of 2020 to meet a precise and challenging list of sustainable goals.

- Zero VOC (volatile organic compounds) emissions to air

- Zero hazardous waste

- Zero solid waste to landfill

- Zero process water consumption

- 100% renewable electrical energy use

- 100% of sales from DfE (Design for Environment) approved products

- 100% of owned or leased company buildings achieve USGBC (United States Green Building Code) LEED (Leadership in Energy and Environmental Design) silver certification

We are committed to being 80% of this objective by 2010 and have already achieved target in some areas.

With continuing improvements in technology and a strong commitment among Herman Miller employees, we fully intend to reach these goals. And to make sure we're on track, we measure our performance against these targets and the process is managed by an in-house environmental specialist.

In order to help meet our 2020 vision, Herman Miller has a documented Environmental Management System (EMS) that satisfies requirements of ISO 14001:2004. The EMS is fully integrated within the company's overall management system and we comply with statutory duties, relevant legislation, regulations and other applicable requirements concerning the environment. We have a procedure to identify the environmental impact of our activities, products and services. It includes emissions to air, releases to water and land, use of raw materials and natural resources.

We are one of the founder members of the 'Furniture Industry Sustainability Programme', launched in 2006 in the UK by the Furniture Industry Research Association (FIRA) and Office Furniture and Filing Manufacturers' Association (OFFMA). It is a focus for the development of new industry standards and has become established as the trade's premier forum on environmental and quality matters.'

Chapter summary

- The development of a sustainable procurement policy does not take place in isolation. It is part of a much wider company-wide process.

- When developed, the sustainable procurement policy is usually embedded in a formal document containing introduction, core principles, and objectives and targets.

- A sustainable procurement policy must be supported by stakeholders. This is one reason why it is often developed by a multi-disciplinary team.

- It is important to communicate the policy to external stakeholders so as to crystallise its value.

- A first step in setting targets is to prioritise sustainability issues, supply/spend categories, and action areas.

- Objectives should be SMART: specific; measurable; agreed; realistic; time-bounded

- Sustainability champions must think carefully about how to roll out the sustainability programme across the organisation.

- People development is often a critical factor in implementing a sustainability programme.

- Progress and performance management in relation to the sustainability programme must be systematically monitored over time. Systematic environmental scanning is also essential.

Self-test questions

Numbers in brackets refer to the paragraphs above where your answers can be checked.

1　List benefits of formulating defined organisational policies. (1.3)

2　List stages in a process for developing a policy on sustainable procurement. (1.4)

3　Who are the main contributors to development of a sustainability policy? (2.4)

4　List steps that can be taken to make a business case for a sustainability policy. (2.9)

5　In what circumstances may sustainability issues be a particular priority? (3.2)

6　Explain what is meant by SMART objectives. (3.6)

7　Which individuals or groups bear particular responsibilities for sustainable procurement? (3.8)

8　What tools can be used to support deployment of a sustainability policy? (4.3)

9　List steps to be taken in a 'Talent Management Review'. (4.8)

10　List as many of Blackburn's success criteria for sustainable management as you can remember. (4.11)

11　Explain the Deming PDCA cycle. (5.5)

Further reading

If you have time, you might look at Blackburn (*The Sustainability Handbook*):

- Chapter 4: Building an SOS: The Key Elements and Basic Structure (if you haven't already done so)
- Chapter 7: Selecting Goals and Indicators
- Chapter 8: Bringing Sustainability to the Front Line.

CHAPTER 8

Implementing a Sustainable Procurement Programme

2.3   Explain how to implement the practical steps for introducing a sustainable procurement programme

- Key stages in the development of an implementation plan
- The 'flexible framework' approach
- Procurement professionals as agents for change within the organisation
- Procurement professionals as 'key players' in the interface with the external environment
- Management of stakeholders and getting buy-in
- Maintaining commitment to sustainable procurement principles
- Planning for continuous improvement

Chapter headings

1   The implementation plan

2   The 'flexible framework' approach

3   The role of procurement professionals

4   Gaining and maintaining commitment

5   Planning for continuous improvement

Introduction

In Chapter 7, we covered the development, deployment and implementation of a sustainable procurement policy.

We are not sure how useful the distinction between the deployment of a sustainable procurement policy (learning objective 2.2) and the implementation of a sustainable procurement programme (learning objective 2.3) is – or how seriously the examiner might take it. Many of the issues, principles and steps will be similar.

However, the syllabus does make the distinction, and it may be helpful to distinguish between the development and deployment of strategic policy (corporate-level commitments, principles, objectives and guidelines) and the planning and implementation of a tactical or operational programme.

1   The implementation plan

1.1   As far as we are aware, there is no standard model or framework for developing an implementation plan in this area, so you should be free to advocate any appropriate sequence of steps or stages. We will offer a few alternative models.

Steps in strategy implementation

1.2   Below is a standard nine-step model for the implementation of strategic plans, drawn from Lysons & Farrington (*Purchasing and Supply Chain Management*), which may be adapted to programme implementation as follows: Table 8.1.

Table 8.1 *Process for the implementation of strategic plans*

	Stage/step	Sample actions
1	Communicate the programme/plan to those who have not been involved in its formulation	• Briefing meetings, supplier conferences • Circulation of plans, guidelines etc. • Meetings with key stakeholders • Posting on internet/extranet/intranet
2	Obtain commitment from those concerned	• Vision articulation and business case • Accountability mechanisms, penalties/incentives • Performance feedback • Reinforce via HR and supplier management
3	Ensure that framing policies and procedures are in place to support implementation	• Highlight programme's contribution to sustainable procurement policy • Adjust or develop policies to reinforce programme values (eg capital purchases, sourcing, supply relationships, e-procurement or HR)
4	Set operational targets and objectives, aligned to corporate objectives	• Formulate SMART objectives (as discussed in Chapter 7), milestones and progress measures for the programme
5	Assign responsibilities and commensurate authority to individuals and teams for the achievement of objectives	• Assign special responsibilities for implementation, oversight, consultancy, liaison etc • Generally, embed implementation within existing responsibilities: 'different approach to business as usual' – not 'new tasks'
6	Change organisation structures, where necessary	• Develop cross-functional sustainability teams or matrix structures • Re-align business processes • Create leadership/accountability/liaison positions
7	Allocate resources and agree budgets	• Allocate deployment resources, staff (where required for 'additional' tasks) • Budget for extra costs (where relevant)
8	Provide employees with required training	• Train-the-trainers (if required) • Education, training, coaching, e-learning
9	Constantly monitor progress/performance and make required revisions	• Monitor progress/performance against milestones and targets • Adjust performance/resources where required by shortfall • Adjust programme plans where required by change

Source: adapted from Lysons & Farrington

The Sustainable Procurement National Action Plan

1.3   In Chapter 5, we introduced the Sustainable Procurement National Action Plan. The Action Plan offers the following process for integrating sustainability into procurement: Figure 8.1.

Figure 8.1 *Process for integrating sustainability into procurement*

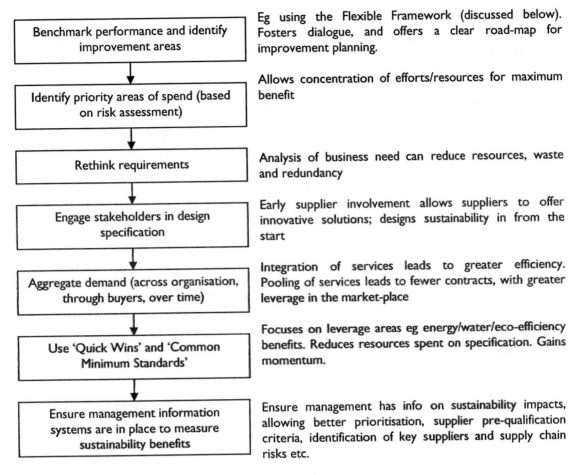

Benchmark performance and identify improvement areas	Eg using the Flexible Framework (discussed below). Fosters dialogue, and offers a clear road-map for improvement planning.
Identify priority areas of spend (based on risk assessment)	Allows concentration of efforts/resources for maximum benefit
Rethink requirements	Analysis of business need can reduce resources, waste and redundancy
Engage stakeholders in design specification	Early supplier involvement allows suppliers to offer innovative solutions; designs sustainability in from the start
Aggregate demand (across organisation, through buyers, over time)	Integration of services leads to greater efficiency. Pooling of services leads to fewer contracts, with greater leverage in the market-place
Use 'Quick Wins' and 'Common Minimum Standards'	Focuses on leverage areas eg energy/water/eco-efficiency benefits. Reduces resources spent on specification. Gains momentum.
Ensure management information systems are in place to measure sustainability benefits	Ensure management has info on sustainability impacts, allowing better prioritisation, supplier pre-qualification criteria, identification of key suppliers and supply chain risks etc.

1.4 In terms of behavioural change management, the process is envisaged as follows: Table 8.2. (We have generalised some of the terms, in order to show how the process may be applied to any sector or organisation.)

Table 8.2 *Four Es of behavioural change management for sustainable procurement*

Enable	Leadership commitment to sustainable procurement Clarify ownership Set clear policy priorities within a streamlined framework Develop capabilities to deliver sustainable procurement Ensure budgetary mechanisms support sustainable procurement Put in place a delivery team to support change
Engage	Engage organisations through benchmarking (Flexible Framework) Support a 'forward commitment' approach to stimulate innovation Build long-term supplier relations through dialogue with key markets and early supplier involvement
Encourage	Incentive systems to reflect sustainable procurement Internal rewards linked to performance Showcase and recognise 'best practice'
Enforce	Scrutiny through audits and accountability systems Sanctions for not meeting mandatory standards and targets

Checklist for deployment and integration

1.5 Blackburn offers the following checklist of action steps towards the deployment of a sustainability policy, which can be adapted to the implementation of a programme or procedure.

- Define what is being implemented
- Draw up an implementation plan, defining the objective and scope of the exercise
- Check that the implementation plan will result in vertical/horizontal alignment
- Encourage the integration of sustainability-related considerations in personal performance objectives and bonus or other reward criteria
- Ensure that the implementation plan includes the integration of programme elements into existing policies, procedures, practices and tools (job descriptions, standard operating procedures, supplier selection criteria, product/service development criteria and specifications, team success factors, planning procedures, audit checklists, agenda for staff meetings and so on)
- Prepare flexible, culturally appropriate deployment (training and awareness) materials and tools
- Identify internal expert who can respond to questions
- Identify and train trainers; develop methods and tools for evaluating training effectiveness; pilot and implement training activities, as required
- Be prepared to respond to questions, challenges, resistance and so on.

Ten practical steps to a sustainable procurement programme

1.6 At an entirely practical level, the *Supply Management Sustainable Procurement Supplement* offered the following helpful checklist for setting up a sustainable procurement programme (Ambridge, 'Power to change', 21 June 2007, p 42).

Now

- Find out if there's any support from the top to implement sustainability – will there be budget, time and resources allocated to it?
- Think about what you can measure before you start and map what you currently do, so you have a baseline (eg what percentage of your materials budget goes on environmentally friendly products?)

Next week

- Study your company's objectives to see what procurement can do to support them regarding CSR, and begin writing a business plan

Next month

- Break down how procurement could make a difference in each of the three areas: social, economic and environmental
- Start communicating with internal customers and suppliers to help them understand what you're trying to do and why – and seek their ideas
- Tackle small environmental projects, such as recycling paper

Next three months

- Work out what you want suppliers to do and communicate this to them
- Devise a tool to measure progress against your objectives

Next year

- Measure again after a year to see what progress you have made. This will encourage you to improve and to realise what you have learned so far.

Example: Virgin Group

In Chapter 4, we noted the particular sustainability challenges of travel and airline businesses, due to their inevitable promotion of high carbon footprints. The Virgin Group makes an interesting (and typically accessible) case study in CSR and sustainability in this context, with a focus on what Virgin call 'People and Planet'. For example:

Virgin's people and planet promise: tourism

Virgin will work towards offering holiday destinations where tourists and locals benefit today and tomorrow in a lower carbon and sustainable way.

What we think we should focus on:

- Ensuring the adoption of appropriate certification for hotel procurement and hotel operations, editing out all non-certified hotels
- Engaging with our peers to understand what we can do to protect against the overdevelopment of key commercial destinations
- Having active involvement in the plethora of sustainability and tourism debates and promoting these key issues to our customers and opinion formers

Some of our plans to achieve this are:

- Endeavouring to procure from hotels that are appropriately certified on sustainability criteria
- Increasing the number of responsible tourism products in our holiday ranges
- Working collaboratively with other tour operators and bodies – taking a significant role in contributing to the development of sustainable tourism in key destinations
- Encouraging, rewarding and supporting our suppliers to be more sustainable

---

2   The 'flexible framework' approach

2.1   Among the key recommendations of the Sustainable Procurement National Action Plan was the building of capacity by introducing a 'flexible framework' to enable public sector organisations:

- To undertake a detailed review and appraisal of their procurement capabilities, against clear benchmarks
- To identify priority areas for change
- To plan improvements
- To measure ongoing progress, using a five-stage monitoring tool
- To 'locate' all organisations within a benchmark standard: encouraging lower-end organisations to get started – while still challenging those at the higher end.

2.2 The framework identifies five key themes, presenting the key behavioural and operational change programmes that need to be delivered for sustainable procurement.

- People
- Policy, strategy and communication
- Procurement process
- Engaging suppliers
- Measurement and results

2.3 It defines five levels of performance in each of these themes, against which organisations can review and appraise their procurement capabilities, and plan an improvement route against recommended time-frames.

- Stage 1   Foundation
- Stage 2   Embedded
- Stage 3   Practice
- Stage 4   Enhanced
- Stage 5   Leadership

2.4 We hope you would be unlikely to need to know the benchmark descriptors in detail, but we have thought it wise to give them just in case: Table 8.3. The Sustainable Procurement Taskforce set targets for all public sector organisations in the UK to get to at least Level 3 by 2009, and to Level 5 in at least one area.

2.5 You may like to carry out an informal 'benchmarking' exercise, by locating your own organisation (or one of interest to you as a potential exam example) on the Flexible Framework, and identifying the next step for improvement in each area.

Example: The Welsh Procurement Initiative

The Welsh Procurement Initiative has established a Sustainable Procurement Programme which aims to:

- Present the economic case for sustainable procurement and gain buy-in to the benefits of sustainable development and the role of sustainable procurement from both senior level executives and procurement professionals

- Increase the use of whole-life costing and provide practical steps to take in the first 12 months

- Demonstrate how a sustainable procurement strategy can be made meaningful and able to deliver benefits

- Provide technical information, tools and case studies and help on specific contract issues

- Show how to gain benefits through early supplier involvement and dialogue.

---

3   *The role of procurement professionals*

Procurement professionals as internal change agents

3.1 Change agents are individuals or teams who are appointed or empowered to drive a change programme: they may be change programme or project managers, external change management consultants, or functional managers pursuing change objectives.

Table 8.3 *The Flexible Framework summary (www.defra.gov.uk)*

	Level 1: Foundation	Level 2: Embed	Level 3: Practice	Level 4: Enhance	Level 5: Lead
People	SP champion identified. Key procurement staff have received basic training in SP principles. SP is included in key staff induction programmes.	All procurement staff have received basic training in SP principles. Key staff have received advanced training in SP principles.	Target refresher training on latest SP principles. Performance objectives and appraisal include SP factors. Simple incentive programmes in place.	SP included in competencies and selection criteria. Sustainable procurement included as part of employee induction programme.	Achievements publicised, used to attract proc. professionals. Internal/ external awards. Focus on benefits achieved. Good practice shared with other organisations.
Policy, strategy and communication	Agree overarching sustainability objectives. Simple SP policy in place, endorsed by CEO. Communicate to staff and key suppliers.	Review and enhance SP policy: consider supplier engagement. Check alignment. Communicate to staff, suppliers and key stakeholders.	Augment SP policy > strategy covering risk, process integration, marketing, supplier engagement, measurement and review process. CEO endorsed.	Review and enhance SP strategy: recognise potential of new technologies. Try to link strategy to EMS and include in overall corporate strategy.	Strategy reviewed regularly, external scrutiny, linked to EMS. SP strategy recognised by leaders, communicated widely. Detailed review undertaken to determine future priorities.
Procurement process	Expenditure analysis undertaken, key sust. impacts identified. Key contracts start to include general sust. criteria. Contracts awarded on the basis of VFM, not lowest price.	Detailed expenditure analysis undertaken, key sustainability risks assessed and used for prioritisation. Sustainability considered at early stage in procurement of most contracts. Whole life cost analysis adopted.	All contracts assessed for general sustainability risks and management actions identified. Risks managed through all stages of procurement process. Target to improve sustainability agreed with key suppliers.	Detailed sustainability risks assessed for high impact contracts. Project/contract sustainability governance in place. A lifecycle approach to cost/impact assessment applied.	Lifecycle analysis undertaken for key commodity areas. KPIs agreed with key suppliers. Progress rewarded/penalised. Barriers removed. Best practice shared with other organisations.
Engaging suppliers	Key supplier spend analysis undertaken and high impact suppliers identified. Key suppliers targeted for engagement and views on procurement policy sought.	Detailed supplier spend analysis undertaken. General programme of supplier engagement initiatives, with senior management involvement.	Targeted supplier engagement programme in place, for continual improvement. Two-way communication between procurer and supplier, with incentives. Supply chains mapped for key spend areas.	Key suppliers targeted for intensive development. Sustainability audits, supply chain improvement progs in place. Achievements recorded. CEO involved in supplier engagement prog.	Suppliers recognised as essential to delivery of SP strategy. CEO engages with suppliers. Best practice shared. Suppliers recognise they must continually improve sustainability profile.
Measurement and results	Key sustainability impacts of procurement activity have been identified.	Detailed appraisal of sustainability impacts undertaken. Measures implemented to manage identified high risk impact areas.	Sustainability measures refined from general departmental measures to include individual procurers. Linked to development objectives.	Measures integrated into a balanced scorecard approach. Comparison made with peer organisations. Benefit statements produced.	Measures used to drive strategy direction. Progress formally benchmarked. Benefits from SP clearly evidenced. Independent audit reports in public domain.

3.2   Huczynski & Buchanan (*An Introduction to Organisational Behaviour*) point out that change agency is becoming increasingly dispersed, involving change teams whose membership is drawn from all levels of the organisation. They argue further that a change agent can be 'any member of an organisation seeking to promote, further, support, sponsor, initiate, implement or deliver change. Change agents are not necessarily senior managers and do not necessarily hold formal "change management" job titles and positions'.

3.3   Johnson & Scholes (*Exploring Corporate Strategy*) similarly suggest that there is a range of ways in which leaders and influencers can manage change in an organisation. Adapted to the context of sustainable procurement, these approaches may be described as follows.

- Where leaders have a strategic role (as procurement may have in relation to sustainable procurement), they can take direct responsibility for articulating mission and values, scanning the environment and formulating plans: that is, championing and developing sustainable procurement strategies and policies.

- They can develop people: creating the knowledge, skills and competencies required to implement sustainable procurement strategies at the operational level.

- They can control performance, ensuring the efficiency of processes and the predictability of outputs: eg by developing and communicating procedures, performance measures and control, and monitoring performance against them.

3.4   Procurement professionals therefore may be in a particularly strong position to take the role of change agent in the development and implementation of sustainable procurement because:

- They have direct responsibility for implementing sustainable procurement principles and policies throughout their work, at an operational level: thereby 'delivering' change

- They have expertise which may be valued (and therefore influential) as supporting internal customers in pursuing their CSR/sustainability objectives: knowledge of the supply market, contacts with suppliers, awareness of commercial and legal aspects of procurement, input to value analysis and whole-life costing and so on

- They are in a position to generate sustainable materials, sourcing and standardisation options, to improve the quality of sustainable design and specification at an early stage, with demonstrable added value benefits

- They may be able to generate eco-efficiencies and cost savings, which can be used to bolster the business case for sustainable procurement

- They may be in a position to enforce sustainable procurement policies in various ways: eg through the preparation of approved supplier lists, standard minimum specifications, framework agreements or call-off contracts and so on — to which buyers in user departments must adhere

- Functioning increasingly in cross-functional roles (eg on project teams or in business partnering structures), they have established networks, circles of influences, and processes which can be used to facilitate sustainable procurement.

- They may be strongly motivated to support and further change, in order to enhance their strategic role, contribution and status — and to promote the policy position and standards of their profession on sustainability.

Procurement as the interface with the external environment

3.5   Another crucial source of procurement's potential influence as a change agent for sustainable procurement is its role at the interface with the external supply market. (The marketing and corporate communications functions are in a similar position in relation to the product market and wider stakeholder audiences.) This makes it a 'key player', as the syllabus puts it, because of its role in:

- Monitoring, assessing and managing key sources of business, supply and sustainability risk, arising from the supply market, supply chain and supplier relationships

- Scanning and engaging the supply market to identify innovations, new technologies, processes and materials to support the organisation's sustainability objectives

- Selecting, contracting and managing suppliers, and developing and managing supply chains, whose capabilities and performance are critical for the organisation's own success in delivering customer and shareholder value, and sustainability

- Mediating communication, relationships and co-ordinated activity between the internal and external supply chain members: that is, maintaining the 'linkages' in the supply/value/quality/sustainability chain. Procurement may facilitate early supplier involvement, for example, as well as being the gatekeeper for ongoing vendor communication, contract management and continuous improvement programmes

3.6   In this role, procurement professionals will be responsible for:

- Communicating sustainable procurement policies, targets and supplier standards to the supply market and supply chain

- Monitoring, measuring, motivating, feeding back, managing and improving supplier performance in relation to sustainability policies, objectives and standards

- Ensuring that the organisation's purchasing and supply management policies and practices are ethical and sustainable in their selection and treatment of suppliers

- Identifying emerging sustainability issues and risks, for incorporation in sustainable procurement planning, policy modification and continuous improvement.

4   *Gaining and maintaining commitment*

Stakeholder management

4.1   We have already highlighted the importance of internal and external stakeholders, as influences on the agenda for – and successful implementation of – sustainable procurement. In Chapter 7, we considered some basic tools of stakeholder consultation and communication for the development and deployment of policy. However, the syllabus includes 'stakeholder management' for the first time at this point. You should be familiar with the concept from your studies in other modules, but we will recap briefly.

4.2   Stakeholders have a legitimate interest or 'stake' in sustainable procurement, for various reasons. They may have invested money in the organisation and want to protect the return on their investment (as in the case of shareholders). They may be impacted by the implementation of the sustainable procurement policy (as with procurement staff, other internal functions such as production and marketing, suppliers – and, less directly, customers). They may have contributed to sustainability policy, and have an interest in its successful implementation (as with policy champions and steering committees). They may have an interest in corporate sustainability activity by virtue of being its advocates (as for government and NGOs) or its beneficiaries (as for communities and the general public as a whole).

4.3   At the same time, stakeholder groups can apply pressure to influence the organisation's sustainability policy and performance, in different ways and to different degrees. Managers exercise direct influence over planning, organisation and control. Staff members influence implementation. Investors, employees, suppliers and customers all control key organisational resources. All these influences may impact on the organisation's policy decisions on sustainability. (A key principle of sustainability, however, is that the rights and interests of 'secondary' stakeholders – including those who are relatively voiceless or powerless, such as poor workers, flora and fauna and future generations – must also be protected.)

4.4 Stakeholder management recognises the need to take stakeholders into account when formulating strategies and plans. For a procurement manager, seeking to implement a sustainable procurement programme, stakeholder management is likely to be helpful in several ways. It enables you to gain expert input from stakeholders at the planning stage of the programme, to improve the quality of your decisions. Stakeholders are more likely to 'own' and support plans to which they have had input: this will make ongoing collaboration easier. Gaining the support of powerful stakeholders may, in turn, mobilise power and resources within the organisation in support of the programme. And at the very least, sources of resistance to the programme (from stakeholders whose goals or priorities are different from or incompatible with yours) can be anticipated and planned for.

4.5 A systematic approach to managing stakeholders is as follows: Figure 8.2.

Figure 8.2 *Managing stakeholders*

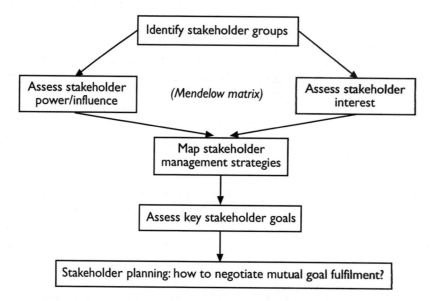

4.6 Mendelow's power/interest matrix (referred to in Figure 8.2) is a useful tool for mapping stakeholders according to their power to influence purchasing activity and the likelihood of their showing an interest in it: Figure 8.3. Take a blank matrix and, for any given situation, write each stakeholder group into the quadrant which best describes their power/interest level.

Figure 8.3: *Mendelow's power/interest matrix*

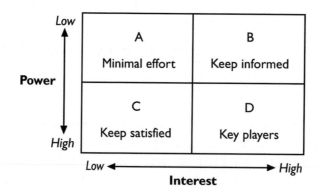

4.7   Working through each of the segments:

- Stakeholders who have neither interest nor influence in the sustainable procurement programme (Segment A) are a low-priority group: resources will not be wasted taking their goals into account, and they are likely simply to accept changes.

- Stakeholders in Segment B are important because of their high interest: they may have low direct influence, but unless they are kept 'in the loop' and understand the need for the programme, they may seek additional power by lobbying or banding together against it. (Employee or small supplier groups may be in this category.) The recommended strategy is to keep them informed of strategies and outcomes, through stakeholder marketing and communication.

- Stakeholders in Segment C are important because of their high influence: they currently have low interest, but if dissatisfied or concerned, their interest may be aroused. (A large institutional shareholder may be in this category.) The recommended strategy is to keep these stakeholders satisfied.

- Stakeholders in Segment D are known as 'key players': they have influence and are motivated to use it in their own interests. (Major customers and key suppliers may be in this category.) Such stakeholders can be major drivers – or opponents – of sustainable procurement. The recommended strategy is one of early involvement and participation, so that stakeholder goals can be integrated with organisational goals as far as possible.

4.8   Blackburn suggests a range of stakeholder engagement techniques for: informing stakeholders (using a range of corporate communication tools); gathering stakeholder feedback (eg from surveys, feedback cards, complaint hotlines to focus group meetings, public meetings and supplier conferences, to more extensive dialogue through vendor managers and community liaison officers); and collaborative identification of issues and design of solutions (using working groups, design/procurement teams, supplier development, business partnership/consultancy and so on).

Getting stakeholder 'buy-in'

4.9   One of the key consequences of the strategic alignment concept is that the vision and objectives for any strategic or policy change must be 'sold' downward to contributing units and individuals, in order to secure co-operation or buy-in. Conversely, the vision and proposals of a procurement manager or sustainability champion may need to be 'sold' upward to gain the support of senior management. And, of course, the same applies to internal stakeholders (other functions) and external stakeholders (suppliers).

4.10   We have already suggested some ways of 'selling' the business case and vision for sustainable procurement to stakeholders, in Chapter 7.

4.11   A number of other widely recognised strategies for managing change also address this issue of securing stakeholder buy-in. Johnson & Scholes (*Exploring Corporate Strategy*) suggest five basic approaches.

- *Education and communication.*

    This strategy relies on the belief that communication about the need for change, and its benefits, can be used to persuade stakeholders to accept the programme. Education and communication approaches are likely to be based on promoting and justifying the compelling reasons for, and benefits of, sustainable procurement (to the stakeholders themselves, where possible). This is one reason why it is helpful to emphasise sustainability risks and critical incidents: stakeholders can more readily grasp the need for and urgency of action.

In addition, education and communication equip stakeholders to contribute, giving the information they need to implement sustainable procurement policy. Johnson & Scholes also emphasise that communication is a two-way process: 'Feedback on communication is important, particularly if the changes to be introduced are difficult to understand, or threatening, or if it is critically important to get the changes right.'

- *Participation and involvement*

Stakeholders are considered more likely to support sustainable procurement policies if they are encouraged to own them through having participated in the development and decision-making process. Quite apart from the advantages of enhanced commitment to change, participation may allow better quality decision-making by taking advantage of people's expertise and knowledge in relevant areas.

- *Facilitation and support*

Facilitation involves assisting stakeholders to implement changes (eg with training, coaching, resources, policy guidelines, or supplier development programmes). Support involves helping stakeholders to come to terms with the disruption and uncertainty aroused by change (eg through staff counselling, supplier reassurance). It is important that any reassurances given are followed through – otherwise it will be perceived as attempted manipulation.

- *Negotiation and agreement*

A negotiation strategy may be required where potential resistance groups have significant power: in interdependent buyer-supplier partnerships, for example. Opposing interests bargain towards an agreement based on compromise. Penalties and incentives may be used to mobilise stakeholder self-interest on behalf of the programme. The main advantage of such an approach is that it (ideally) allows conflicts of interest to be acknowledged and taken into account in a systematic fashion. Compliance can be insisted on, on the basis of a negotiated agreement – and if a genuine win-win outcome is reached through the process, it may encourage positive commitment and enhanced morale.

- *Manipulation and coercion*

It is important to remember that change leaders may have the option of simply applying various forms of power to implement whatever they perceive is required, and to enforce compliance. The advantage of such an approach is that decisions can be made and implemented swiftly, and in the face of opposition, when necessary. The disadvantages are that coercive changes may (at best) secure mere compliance, where commitment has greater power to harness the positive energies and efforts of stakeholders in support of sustainability initiatives.

Obtaining supplier commitment

4.12 It may be comparatively easy to secure the compliance of suppliers with sustainability policies – unless they have significant bargaining power in the buyer-supplier relationship – through mechanisms such as: information (widely disseminating the policy via contract managers, the corporate website or extranet, in contract terms and conditions, at supplier conferences and meetings, and so on); the use of contract incentives, penalties and sanctions in regard to adherence to the policy; and making continued business (or approved/preferred supplier status) contingent on adherence to the policy.

4.13 If the buying organisation wants the extra benefits of commitment, flexibility, innovation, proactive problem-solving, continuous improvement and co-operation – over and above what is expressly required by the policy, and contracts under it – they will have to make it worth the supplier's while. A range of incentives may be used.

- Contingency payments (eg part of the payment is linked to sustainability measures)
- Sustainability key performance indicators (KPIs) or improvement targets linked to recognition and rewards: extension of the contract or the promise of further business; inclusion on the approved or preferred supplier list; publicised supplier awards and endorsements; financial bonuses (eg for extra units of productivity); and so on.
- Revenue, profit or gain sharing (eg allocating the supplier an agreed percentage or flat fee bonus for cost savings arising for reduced resource usage). Where supplier improvements create added value, revenue or profit for the buyer, the 'gain' is shared: a 'win-win' outcome.
- The promise of long-term business agreements, increased business, or guaranteed or fixed order levels, allowing the planning of investments and improvements by the supplier
- Opportunities for innovation: the contract gives the provider the chance to implement or devise new solutions that will develop their business and reputation
- The offer of development support (eg training or technology sharing).

Maintaining commitment to sustainable procurement principles

4.14 Maintaining commitment to sustainable procurement principles will be difficult at the best of times. The aim is, after all, to ensure that sustainability eventually becomes part and parcel of 'business as usual', being thoroughly integrated into procurement and supplier procedures and practices. However, this also means that it is no longer new, exciting or 'front of awareness' for participants and other stakeholders. Critical incidents recede into the past, issues 'go off the boil', risks fail to materialise, public and NGO attention moves elsewhere...

4.15 In the current economic climate, there is the further issue that, while social and environmental sustainability are widely recognised as necessary or desirable, they may cease to be the top priority in the face of recessionary pressure: strategic priorities may switch to corporate survival, shorter time-frames for return on investment, the need for cost reductions and so on.

4.16 Here are some strategies for maintaining momentum and commitment to sustainable procurement principles.

- Keeping sustainability at 'front of awareness' through ongoing communication (eg via newsletters, bulletins, progress updates, agenda items for supplier reviews and staff meetings)
- Maintaining top-level championship, demonstrating the continuing importance of the issues and the seriousness with which they are regarded (eg in executive speeches, annual reports)
- Implementing rolling reviews and improvement targets, tied to accountabilities, so that participants cannot become complacent about performance
- Implementing periodic learning needs analysis, refresher training and so on, to continually upgrade skills and awareness
- Maintaining risk and environmental reporting, so that key issues and drivers are continually refreshed

- Setting targets for quick/small wins, to create the momentum of success and reported impacts/benefits
- Creating opportunities for symbolic action to re-energise the vision (eg staff involvement with charity fund-raisers, participation in 'Earth Hour')
- Offering incentives for improvements and initiative (eg supplier awards, employee suggestion schemes, performance-related rewards)
- Tying continuing improvement to staff and supplier performance appraisals
- Maintaining accountabilities, penalties and sanctions for non-compliance
- Continually documenting, disseminating and acknowledging sustainability results, impacts and benefits, to reinforce the sense of achievement, contribution, 'feel good factor' – and business case.

Example: Wal-Mart

'Self-reinforcing spirals [momentum for sustainability] are crated when new business imperatives move through supply chains. There is no bigger example of this today than what's been happening at Wal-Mart, the world's largest retailer, which announced a new goal in 2008: to work with suppliers to make many of the products it sells 25% more energy-efficient within three years. Noah Horowitz, a senior scientist at the Natural Resources Defence Council, says: "When Wal-Mart asks, suppliers jump... There are positive ripple effects throughout the supply chain." As suppliers work to improve their products, a snowball effect occurs, and innovations will spread to other products, industries and customers.' (Senge, *The Necessary Revolution*)

Wal-Mart's CEO Lee Scott has openly admitted that the company's early conservation efforts were part of a campaign to clean up its sullied image – but it now has an integrated sustainability strategy.

'At Wal-Mart, we see sustainability as one of the most important opportunities for both the future of our business and the future of our world. Our opportunity is to become a better company by looking at every facet of our business – from the products we offer to the energy we use – through the lens of sustainability.'

Wal-Mart is introducing Fair Trade banana and coffee products; implementing sustainable seafood procurement, in partnership with conservation organisations; and developing 'high efficiency' pilot stores (sustainable building practices, energy-efficiency, use of geo-thermal energy etc).

Meanwhile, it has traditionally had a poor reputation for social sustainability, particularly in using its size and buying power to squeeze out small, local and specialist retailers. It has striven to counteract this perception, by emphasising 'economic opportunity' benefits:

'Wal-Mart's overall impact on the retail industry and beyond has changed the way business is conducted globally, and increased consumer benefits – regardless of where they shop. From raising tax revenues and lowering overall pricing on goods, to boosting customer traffic at surrounding stores and creating new jobs, Wal-Mart takes every opportunity to be a good neighbour and to provide economic advancements in communities it serves throughout the world.'

---

5 *Planning for continuous improvement*

5.1 Sustainable procurement – like quality management and other process improvement techniques – involves the ongoing and continual examination and improvement of existing processes: 'getting it more right, next time'. This process is sometimes referred to by its Japanese name of *kaizen*: 'a Japanese concept of quality management based on continual evolutionary change with considerable responsibility given to employees within certain fixed boundaries' (Mullins: *Management and Organisational Behaviour*).

5.2 *Kaizen* looks for uninterrupted, ongoing incremental change: there is always room for improvement, for example by eliminating further wastes (non value-adding activities) or making small adjustments to equipment, materials or team behaviour.

5.3   In Chapter 7, we briefly mentioned the 'Plan, Do, Check, Act' (PDCA) cycle popularised by quality guru W Edwards Deming (though developed by Dr Shewhart, a colleague of Deming's). PDCA is designed as a 'universal improvement methodology': an approach to process improvement – but also to problem solving and change management in general. It is about learning and ongoing improvement: learning what works and what does not in a systematic way, in a continuous cycle.

- **P**lan what is needed
- **D**o it
- **C**heck that it works (or what worked and what didn't) by measuring results and comparing them with the plan
- **A**ct to correct any problems or improve the process.

5.4   Planning for continuous improvement is one way of ensuring, as we noted above, that there is continuing commitment to sustainable procurement principles. There are various ways in which this can be done in practice.

- Periodically benchmarking organisational, supplier or supply chain performance against peer organisations, industry/sector leaders, key competitors, national/international standards or (in the public sector) the flexible framework – as a way of identifying potential for improvement
- Best-practice sharing (eg through professional knowledge networks, supplier networks or trade/industry conferences) – as a way of identifying potential for improvement
- Gathering feedback from key stakeholders (including internal and external customers and suppliers, and NGO partners/consultants), highlighting risks and areas for improvement
- Implementing rolling performance reviews, objectives and targets, so that the 'bar' is continually set higher as each milestone is reached
- Negotiating continuous improvement agreements as part of supplier contracts – with incentives (eg bonuses or gain-sharing) built in for progressive sustainability innovations, improvements and cost savings
- Setting up staff and supplier suggestion schemes, with rewards for implemented suggestions for improvement (including small ones – to reinforce the perception that incremental change is valued)
- Performance-related appraisal, awards or bonuses, tying staff and supplier rewards directly to measurable sustainability improvement targets. (An element of inter-team – as well as inter-supplier – competition may be added to maintain motivation.)
- Making progress indicators and reports, and year on year improvements, highly visible (eg on the corporate website), to maintain accountability and motivation.

Chapter summary

- It is worth learning the nine-step model for implementation of strategic plans, particularly as regards sustainability programmes. Equally, it is worth studying the checklists provided by Blackburn and *Supply Management*.

- The flexible framework is an approach by which public sector organisations can review their procurement capabilities against clear benchmarks.

- To manage change – eg in implementing a sustainability programme – it is important to use effective change agents. Purchasing professionals are well placed to take this role.

- Stakeholders must be effectively managed when formulating strategies and plans, in particular in relation to sustainability. Mendelow's power/interest matrix is a useful tool in this regard.

- Johnson & Scholes suggest five approaches to securing stakeholder buy-in: education and communication; participation and involvement; facilitation and support; negotiation and agreement; manipulation and coercion.

- Purchasing professionals have an important role to play in securing supplier commitment to sustainability.

- Sustainable procurement involves ongoing and continual examination and improvement of existing processes.

Self-test questions

Numbers in brackets refer to the paragraphs above where your answers can be checked.

1   List the stages in the SPNAP process for integrating sustainability into procurement. (1.3)

2   List Blackburn's action steps for deployment of a sustainability policy. (1.5)

3   What are the five key themes in the 'flexible framework'? (2.2)

4   A change agent is always necessarily a senior manager. True or false? (3.2)

5   Why are procurement professionals particularly well placed to act as change agents for sustainability? (3.4)

6   Explain the four segments in Mendelow's power/interest matrix. (4.7)

7   Explain the five approaches suggested by Johnson & Scholes for securing stakeholder buy-in. (4.11)

8   What kind of incentives might a buyer offer to suppliers to secure their commitment to sustainability? (4.13)

9   List ways by which we can monitor continuing commitment to sustainability. (5.4)

Further reading

If you have time, you might look at Blackburn (*The Sustainability Handbook*):

- Chapter 8: Bringing Sustainability to the Front Line (if you haven't already done so)

- Chapter 11: Stakeholder Engagement

As before, you should bear in mind that Blackburn addresses corporate-level sustainability programmes, rather than their specific implications for sustainable procurement – and in much more detail than (we hope) you would require in the exam. Browse – and take what you can use...

CHAPTER 9

Sustainable Purchase Specification

Learning objectives and indicative content

3.1 Explain and analyse the process of developing and applying sustainable procurement to purchase specifications for products and services in the context of different organisations and sectors

- Sustainability of customer requirements
- Classification of materials, components and services using the Kraljic model
- Innovation and sustainable design
- Sustainable materials and processes
- Service level agreements
- Impact of the end product or service

Chapter headings

1 The sustainability of customer requirements

2 Classifying requirements

3 Specifying requirements

4 Service level agreements

5 Innovation and sustainable design

6 Whole-life sustainability

Introduction

In this and the following four chapters, we turn to the operational implementation of a sustainable procurement approach, exploring sustainability issues in purchase specifications, sourcing, contract management and supplier management and development.

One of the key steps in the purchasing cycle, as we will see in Chapter 10, is 'description of the need': that is, various ways of specifying purchase requirements.

There are a number of significant sustainability issues in specification: the extent to which customer requirements can be steered in the direction of sustainability; the extent to which specifications offer inclusion or exclusion of certain supplier groups; the extent to which sustainability can be 'designed' in to products and services at the development and specification stage; and the extent to which the process of specification promotes efficient resource usage and adds economic value.

1   *The sustainability of customer requirements*

Procurement and the customer

1.1   When the syllabus talks about 'customers', this may mean:

- The customers of the focal organisation in the external supply chain: downstream producers and processors (eg manufacturers, assemblers or finishers), distribution intermediaries (distributors, agents, wholesalers, retailers), and consumers or end users of the product or service

- The customers of the procurement function in the internal supply chain: other business units (divisions, branches, work sites and facilities) and functions (eg R&D, design, engineering, operations/manufacturing and facilities management) requiring purchased inputs or purchasing services or advice

- The organisation as a customer for and consumer of products and services, with the procurement function (and/or part-time buyers in user departments) as the primary supplier-facing customer.

The sustainability of external customer requirements

1.2   The primary focus of sustainable procurement activity in relation to consumer markets may be to anticipate and meet consumer demand for sustainable goods, services and processes – ideally, more swiftly, effectively and efficiently than competitors. This demand is generally on the rise, forming a key driver for sustainability initiatives (as discussed in Chapter 5), but the organisation will need to monitor consumer priorities and sustainable consumption trends and 'fashions'. Issues such as GHG emissions, energy consumption, animal testing and Fair Trade brands are currently front-of-awareness for many consumers, and the specification of products and services in these areas will, to a large extent, be led by market demand and risk.

1.3   At the same time, as we will discuss further below, corporations may need to leverage and crystallise value from their innovation and sustainability capabilities by stimulating consumer demand for sustainable products: initiating the wave, rather than riding it. This may involve publicising issues and risks, engaging in cause-related marketing (eg partnering with NGOs), informing and educating consumers, co-opting consumers to sustainability agendas (eg Marks & Spencer's Plan A 'pledges') – while offering product/service/brands which embody solutions to the highlighted problems.

1.4   The anticipation or stimulation of demand is primarily a marketing function, but procurement has a key role in the design and delivery of sustainable consumption solutions and offerings – which in turn help shift consumer norms and expectations.

The sustainability of internal customer requirements

1.5   The internal customer concept implies that any unit of the organisation whose task contributes to the task of other units (whether as part of a process, or in an advisory, support or service relationship) can be regarded as a supplier: each link in the value chain is a customer of the one before. This is a constructive way of looking at internal relationships, because it helps to integrate the objectives of different units throughout the value chain; it focuses on the process of adding value for the ultimate customer (rather than the separate goals and methods of each unit or function); and it makes each unit look carefully at what added value it is able to offer.

1.6 For procurement, internal customer service most obviously involves fulfilling purchase requisitions and specifications drawn up by designers and users. However, a sustainable procurement orientation argues that buyers also need to partner with internal customers to support them in achieving corporate sustainability objectives. This may mean re-examining and challenging customer definitions of requirement — which may, or may not, be shaped by sustainability policies and priorities.

1.7 We will discuss the priorities of various internal stakeholders in product/service specification — and how they can be managed for enhanced sustainability — later in the chapter. However, the formulation or review of purchase specifications is an ideal opportunity for demand review, asking:

- Does this item comply with or further the environmental, social and economic targets stated in the organisation's sustainable procurement policy?

- Is there a genuine operational need for this item (or this quantity of it)? Are demand forecasting methods accurate?

- Can the need be met from substitute items in stock, or by renting, leasing, sharing or refurbishing, rather than purchase?

- Could a lower specification (less resource-intensive) or a generic item be used without compromising functionality or performance?

- Could the item be used more efficiently?

The procurement function as customer

1.8 In addition to shaping the requirements of customers in the direction of sustainability, the procurement function will have to pursue sustainability in its own role as customer, in specification of requirements, sourcing decisions and dealings with suppliers. As a customer, the procurement function (and part-time buyers in user departments) will have to ensure that requirements are sustainable; that they are defined and specified in a way that clearly communicates sustainability demands and expectations to suppliers; that specification, tendering and contract negotiation and development processes are administered in ethical and sustainable ways; and that the whole process is conducted so as to fulfil business requirements effectively and efficiently.

The intelligent customer

1.9 The term 'intelligent customer' is given to an internal or external customer who has strong capabilities for effective and efficient procurement. Intelligent customer qualities include: product knowledge; supply market and supplier knowledge; ability to translate internal customer requirements into specifications which enable suppliers to provide effective solutions; and procurement expertise and efficiency.

1.10 We might extend this concept to a 'sustainable customer', with strong capabilities for sustainable procurement, including: an understanding of sustainability issues; commitment to sustainability policy and targets; use of whole-life product/service costing and relationship management; ability to specify clearly and flexibly for sustainability; and so on. We have argued that the procurement function must seek to be an intelligent/sustainable customer — but also to educate and support its own internal customers in being intelligent/sustainable customers.

> **Example: University of Edinburgh Procurement Office**
>
> The University of Edinburgh Procurement Office makes an interesting case study in sustainable procurement.
>
> As an example of managing the sustainability of internal customer requirements, the Procurement Office runs an 'Equipment Exchange'.
>
> The Procurement Office is co-ordinating this facility which should allow redundant equipment to be advertised, and sold between departments, within the University of Edinburgh.
>
> The aims of this facility are as follows:
>
> - To reduce the deterioration of capital equipment through lying in disuse
>
> - To reduce the amount of waste created through redundant equipment being discarded
>
> - To enable departments to recover some of their outlay on equipment that is no longer needed
>
> - To reduce the necessity for money and resources to be expended on buying new items which may already be available within the University
>
> - To comply with the Waste Electrical and Electronic Equipment (WEEE) Regulations

2 Classifying requirements

2.1 As we saw in Chapter 7, one of the key early processes in sustainable procurement is the prioritisation of areas of purchase or spend, so that sustainability efforts can be focused where they have the greatest leverage, impact and return on investment. There are various ways of categorising and prioritising an organisation's purchase requirements or 'portfolio', using risk analysis, Pareto analysis and other tools. However, we will highlight two common methods: spend analysis and procurement positioning.

Spend analysis

2.2 Spend analysis identifies high-priority categories, purchases and suppliers by examining factors such as:

- Level of spend (per item/category, per supplier, per internal business unit)
- Level of contract renewal activity
- Key suppliers by type and location
- Level of risk against each sustainability objective
- Year on year trends.

2.3 The Sustainable Procurement Action Plan for the UK public sector, for example, identifies a number of 'priority spend areas' on which sustainability targets are focused: construction; energy; food; furniture; health and social care; consumables, office machinery and IT; pulp, paper and printing; uniforms, clothing and other textiles; transport; and waste.

Procurement positioning (the Kraljic matrix)

2.4 Peter Kraljic drew up a matrix model to help organisations classify their purchase portfolios according to two dimensions: supply risk (including factors such as sourcing difficulty, and buyer vulnerability to supply or supplier failure) and purchase value (including factors such as the profit potential of the item, and the importance of the purchase to the business). This is particularly relevant for sustainable supply, for which supply risk is a key driver: Kraljic highlighted threats such as resource depletion and raw materials scarcity, political turbulence, government intervention in supply markets, intensified competition and accelerating technology change – all of which are sustainability issues.

2.5 Rating supply risk and purchase value as either high or low, the Kraljic matrix offers four quadrants: Figure 9.1.

Figure 9.1 *The Kraljic purchasing portfolio matrix*

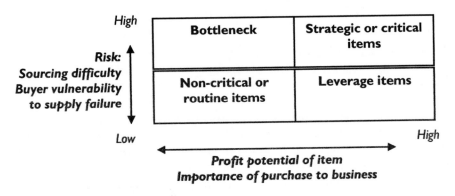

2.6 Taking the quadrants one by one:

- For *non-critical or routine items* (such as common stationery supplies), the focus will be on reducing transaction costs. Arm's length approaches such as blanket ordering and e-procurement solutions will provide routine efficiency. Quick wins on environmental and social sustainability may be available at relatively low cost, eg through stipulating green, recycled, low-energy consumption or Fair Trade items. (The National Procurement Action Plan, for example, features a list of such quick wins.)

- For *bottleneck items* (such as proprietary spare parts or specialised consultancy services, which could cause operational delays if unavailable), the buyer's priority will be ensuring control over the continuity and security of supply. This may suggest approaches such as negotiating medium- or long-term contracts with suppliers, which may also be an opportunity to secure cost and other sustainability improvements.

- For *leverage items* (such as local produce bought by a major supermarket), the buyer's priority will be to use its dominance to secure best prices and terms, on a transactional basis. This may mean taking advantage of competitive pricing; standardising specifications to make supplier switching easier; and using competitive bidding and/or buying consortia to secure the best deals. However, attention will still have to be paid to sustainability issues such as fair/ethical trading and whole-life costs of purchases.

- For *strategic items* (such as key subassemblies bought by a car manufacturer, or Intel processors bought by laptop manufacturers), there is likely to be mutual dependency and investment, and the focus will be on the total cost, security and competitiveness of supply. There will therefore be a need to develop long-term, mutually beneficial strategic relationships – with opportunities for supplier development, co-investment and innovation for sustainability.

3 Specifying requirements

The role of specification

3.1 A specification can be simply defined as a statement of the requirements to be satisfied in the supply of a product or service.

3.2   As part of the purchase cycle, the role of a specification is to:

- Define the requirement – encouraging all relevant stakeholders (including the purchasers and users of the supplied items) to consider what they really need, and whether what they think they need is the only, most cost-effective or most value-adding solution

- Communicate the requirement clearly to suppliers, so that they can plan to conform – and perhaps also use their expertise to come up with innovative or lower-cost solutions to the requirement 'problem': in other words, so that you get what you need!

- Provide a means of evaluating the quality or conformance of the goods or services supplied, for acceptance (if conforming to specification) or rejection (if non-conforming).

3.3   Specification is particularly important for sustainable procurement in the public sector. EU public procurement directives provide that environmental and social considerations should be built into the earliest stages of the procurement process – and opportunities to do this are limited, under competitive tendering rules, at the supplier selection and contract award stage (because of the definition of 'best value'). Design and specification thus offers the best opportunity to incorporate sustainable procurement criteria.

Effective purchase specification for sustainability

3.4   An effective specification for sustainability is one that is:

- Clear and unambiguous as to what is required

- Concise (not overly detailed: the shorter the specification, the less time/cost it takes to prepare) but

- Comprehensive (covering all points of the requirement. As Lysons & Farrington note: 'If something is not specified, it is unlikely to be provided' – and suppliers will normally charge requirements added later as 'extras'.)

- Compliant with all relevant national or international standards; health, safety and environmental laws and regulations; and the buying organisation's own sustainability policies and guidelines

- Up-to-date (with current sustainable design solutions and supply market developments)

- Expressed in terms which can be understood by all key stakeholders (ie not too technical for suppliers or purchasers or users)

- Value-analysed: every additional requirement increases the price (and possibly also the usage of physical resources), so sustainable specifications specify only requirements that positively add value – challenging customer 'requirements' where necessary

- Integrated in its approach to sustainability: that is, incorporating sustainability principles in all elements of the specification – not just adding a separate sustainability criterion to an existing specification.

3.5   Some of procurement's key objectives for sustainable specification may be:

- To seek cost-effective (and where necessary, innovative) alternatives to environmentally or socially unsustainable materials, products and processes

- To minimise waste, including packaging, waste produced by the product (or service), and waste generated by the eventual disposal of the product

- To maximise the re-use and recycling of materials

- To ensure ethical and socially responsible trading and employment practices at all tiers of the supply chain

- To maximise access to contracts for small, diverse, local suppliers
- To maximise resource and cost efficiency in sourcing, supply and production processes.

3.6 The consequences of ineffective specification processes are potentially costly for the organisation, and may, in particular, pose a number of sustainability risks.

- There may be misunderstandings with suppliers over requirements and expectations (eg if the specification was vague, inaccurate or overly technical), leading to rejection of deliveries (waste), lost production time, legal disputes and damaged supplier relationships.

- There are more likely to be quality defects, or performance/conformance shortfalls (eg on sustainability attributes) in the goods supplied. These are costly in terms of lost time, scrapped goods, rework, additional inspections and controls, penalties for non-compliance and so on. If non-conforming outputs reach the customer, there may be additional serious consequences of lost customer loyalty, lost business, the adjustment of complaints, reputational damage, social/environmental impacts and so on.

- Goods and services may be over-specified: related to some 'ideal' standard, without reference to users' actual needs, the cost of higher standards, or the added value actually contributed by higher standards.

- Goods and services may be specified on the basis of existing documentation, precedent or internal customer request – without taking the opportunity to re-think the business need or sustainability impacts, consider potential for variety reduction or innovation, investigate more sustainable alternatives and so on.

- Specifications may be too prescriptive, creating the risk of over-specification, stifling potential for supplier innovation or more sustainable options, and unnecessarily excluding some suppliers (which may itself be a sustainability issue).

Conformance and performance specifications

3.7 Two main categories of specification are conformance specifications (or design specifications) and performance specifications (or functional specification).

- With a *conformance specification*, the buyer details exactly what the required product, part or material must consist of. This may take the form of an engineering drawing or blueprint, a chemical formula or 'recipe' of ingredients, a brand name and model number, a market grade or standard specification, or a sample of the product to be duplicated. Suppliers may not know in detail, or even at all, what function the product will play in the buyer's manufacturing. It is their task simply to conform to the description provided by the buyer.

- With a *performance specification*, the buyer aims to describe what he expects the part or material to be able to achieve, in terms of the functions it will perform and the level of performance it should reach. It is then up to the supplier to furnish a product which will satisfy these requirements: the buyer specifies the 'ends', and the supplier has relative flexibility as to 'means' of achieving those ends (materials, designs and processes).

3.8 A technical conformance specification would typically include aspects such as the following.

- The scope of the specification (its objectives and content)
- Definitions: explanation of any technical or specialised terms used
- The purpose of the equipment or material that is the subject of the specification
- Reference to related documents (such as quality, safety, environmental and social performance standards or legislation)

- Materials requirements (including materials approved or excluded on grounds of sustainability), properties (eg dimensions, strength, recyclability or biodegradability), tolerances and permissible variability

- Appearance, texture and finish requirements of the finished product, including identification marks, safety instructions and so on (which may also contribute to sustainability in areas such as safe use, take-back, recycling and disposal)

- Drawings, samples or models of the required product (where available)

- Conditions in which the item is to be installed, used, manufactured or stored (taking into account whole-life sustainability issues)

- Maintenance and reliability requirements

- Specification of packaging and protection, including any special conditions in transit (an opportunity to specify reduced and recyclable packaging)

- Information to be provided by the supplier for users, such as instructions, or advice on installation, operation and maintenance.

3.9 A performance specification would typically include the following.

- The functionality, performance or capabilities to be achieved, within specified tolerances (an opportunity to define key sustainability parameters, such as disassembly for re-use and recyclability, energy efficiency, or extended useful life)

- Key process inputs which will contribute to performance, including available utilities (electricity, solar power, water and so on: an opportunity to specify resource efficiency)

- The operating environment and conditions in which the performance is to be achieved (and extreme or unusual conditions in which it is not expected)

- How the product is required to interface with other elements of a process

- Required quality levels (including relevant standards)

- Required safety levels and controls (including relevant standards)

- Required environmental and social performance levels and controls (including relevant standards such as ISO 14001 and SA 8000, discussed in Chapter 11)

- Criteria and methods to be used to measure whether the desired functionality/sustainability has been achieved.

3.10 Conformance specifications may be perceived as less supportive of sustainable procurement than performance specifications, for a number of reasons.

- Performance specifications are easier and cheaper to draft, compared to a more detailed, prescriptive (conformance) approach.

- With conformance specifications, the buyer bears the risk of the design not performing to the required standard of sustainability.

- Conformance specifications may restrict the potential supplier base. A tight specification may be capable of fulfilment only by a small number of suppliers: in effect, the capabilities of other potential suppliers have been 'specified away'.

- The prescriptive nature of a conformance specification may restrict innovation and the range of solutions to problems. This is a particular problem if the specification details the means by which the supplied items should be manufactured: the buyer potentially closes himself off from manufacturing developments of which he may be unaware – especially in supply markets where sustainable technology is developing quickly. With performance specifications, suppliers can use their full expertise, technologies and innovative capacity to develop sustainable solutions.

3.11 According to Lysons & Farrington (*Purchasing & Supply Management*), it may be appropriate to use performance specifications in circumstances such as the following.

- Suppliers have greater technical and manufacturing expertise for sustainability than the buyer – so that the best knowledge is being used and leveraged. (It should also be noted that the buyer will be more reliant on the supplier's expertise: this puts pressure on supplier selection and evaluation, which are discussed in Chapter 10.)

- Sustainability technology is changing rapidly in the supplying industry – so that the buyer is not in a position of specifying yesterday's methodologies, but gets the best out of suppliers' innovation capacity and technological development.

- There are clear criteria for evaluating alternative solutions put forward by suppliers competing for the contract. These should be clearly communicated to potential suppliers, who may invest considerable time and resources in coming up with proposals, and will want to be assured that the selection process is fair.

- The buyer has sufficient time and expertise to assess the potential functionality and sustainability of suppliers' proposals and competing alternatives (particularly where the technology is unfamiliar). The complexity of the evaluation process is the major disadvantage of the performance specification approach.

3.12 Sustainability generally involves issues and risks across business processes and supply chains, however, so specifications will increasingly set standards or requirements (if not prescriptions) for issues such as the following.

- Materials to be used in manufacture of purchased components, subassemblies or finished items: preferred sustainable materials and/or excluded unsustainable materials – or sustainability standards, attributes or functionality to be attained by materials (compliance with national/international standards, recyclability, biodegradability, renewable, sustainably managed, low-GHG emission, non-toxic)

- Processes and standards to be used in manufacture: eg ethical product testing, certified environmental management systems (eg ISO 14001), quality management systems (eg ISO 9000), GHG emissions control, health and safety and labour standards

- Sourcing and supply chain management processes: eg ethically sourced materials or products, Fair Trade certification, ethical/environmental supplier monitoring and management (to avoid risks arising from lower tiers of the supply chain)

- Logistics, transport and delivery requirements: eg transport planning and fleet management/maintenance for reduced fuel use and emissions; warehouse health and safety; location of distribution hubs to minimise community/environmental impacts and so on.

3.13 These issues may, alternatively, be set out in the broader definition of requirements (eg in tender documentation, requests for quotation, pre-qualification checklists and contract negotiations), to which product/service specifications are appended.

Cross-functional contributions to specification

3.14 In most cases, the lead role in specification development is taken by users of the product or service. After all, they may be most familiar with the requirement, and most technically 'savvy' about what is required. But this is not always the case.

- For some purchases, the process is relatively simple: a suitable and sustainable product may be widely available on the market. In such cases, it would be normal to leave the 'specification' (ordering) to the purchasing department.

- Procurement may also have a free hand in cases of purchases for internal use, rather than resale or incorporation into production: eg furniture, stationery or uniforms.

- Purchasing departments may also take a lead role where purchasing staff are technically expert in the product or category specified (eg knowledgeable about grades, standards and so on).

In less straightforward cases, however, the preparation of a specification may require cross-functional input, so that technical considerations are balanced with commercial ones.

3.15 Design or engineering departments will be well placed to contribute technical specifications. However, they may:

- Focus on features that maximise functional excellence (product orientation), or production efficiency (production orientation) – but contribute little or nothing to sales potential or customer satisfaction (marketing orientation) or sustainability (stakeholder orientation)

- Over-specify, with unnecessarily tight tolerances or non-value-adding functions, in pursuit of quality or engineering excellence – but at unnecessary cost

- Specify bespoke or custom-built items, when acceptable standard or generic items are available – again causing waste

- Specify for each new requirement, even where existing items could be used or adapted to the purpose – creating multiple stock items where one would do, and thus incurring unnecessary inventory, ordering costs and materials handling costs

- Write 'narrow' or 'closed' specifications, not permitting variations or alternatives, which may tie the buyer to a small supplier base, or one supplier – or which may be very difficult to source.

3.16 The marketing department may be able to contribute an important customer focus to the specification: seeking unique product features which will satisfy customer demands and perceptions in regard to sustainability and therefore crystallise sustainability benefits in terms of competitive differentiation, premium pricing and reputational/brand strength. However, marketing suggestions may not meet technical and cost criteria: customer-satisfying and customised features may be difficult to engineer and/or costly.

3.17 Reconciling these differences requires skilled management! Dobler and Burt (*Purchasing & Supply Management*) identify four major items that have to be brought into harmony.

- Design considerations of function
- Marketing considerations of consumer acceptance and satisfaction
- Manufacturing considerations of economical production
- Procurement considerations of markets, materials availability, supplier capability and cost.

The overarching concern of sustainability could be added to this list – since each discipline's definition of sustainability, and its costs and benefits, will need to be harmonised and integrated.

3.18 Procurement professionals are in a good position to contribute:

- *Supply market awareness:* the availability of standard/generic items (for variety reduction), the availability of suppliers with sustainability/innovation capability, the possibility of alternative suppliers and sustainable solutions (especially if expensive or otherwise unsustainable brands are requisitioned), market prices and supply market risk factors

- *Supplier contacts*, to discuss potential sustainable solutions in advance of specification, or to introduce pre-qualified suppliers to the design team (early supplier involvement), which may contribute to more sustainable design

- *Awareness of legal aspects* of sustainable procurement, eg the need to comply with national and international standards, and regulations on health and safety, environmental protection and (in the public sector) procurement methods.

- *Purchasing disciplines*, for variety reduction, value analysis, cost reduction, whole-life costing and so on. The buyer should be ready to discuss the real needs of the user, and to question desired performance levels or tolerances, to pursue sustainability gains in these areas. The greatest scope for cost reduction is at the design and specification stage.

Specifying sustainable materials and processes

3.19 As we noted earlier, specification or definition of requirement is an ideal opportunity to ask questions relevant to sustainability.

- Does the item further the environmental, social and economic targets stated in the organisation's sustainable procurement policy?

- Is the item really needed (or needed in this quantity)? Is a buy or re-buy needed, or are usable items in stock? The sustainable option is to use and purchase less.

- Could a lower (less resource-intensive) specification be used without compromising functionality or performance? Could a generic commercial item be used instead of a bespoke item?

- Does the item as requisitioned or specified comply with relevant environmental criteria? Is it classed as an 'environmentally preferred product': one which has a lesser or reduced effect on human health and the environment when compared with competing products or services that fulfil the same function? (Is it, for example, made of re-used, recycled or renewable materials? Does it minimise waste, pollution and GHG emissions, and/or conserve energy or water? Is it effectively but minimally packaged?)

- Can the item be sourced from local, small or diverse suppliers – or does the specification unnecessarily exclude them?

- What is the 'whole-life cost' of the item? What are its running costs, taking into account energy/resource efficiency, consumables, maintenance, spares and usable life span? What costs may be incurred in staff training, health and safety and so on?

- Will the product require special disposal arrangements, or cause environmental impacts on disposal (eg paints, solvents and oils)? Can the product be re-used or recycled once it is obsolete? Is it biodegradable in land-fill?

- If a brand or supplier is specified, how sustainable are the supplier's processes (environmental management, labour and supply chain management and so on)?

3.20 The principles of the UK waste hierarchy (Reduce; Re-use; Recycle; Rethink) may offer a useful framework for discussion with internal customers: Table 9.1.

Table 9.1 *The UK waste hierarchy*

Reduce	• Ensure products are definitely needed
	• Ensure products are fit for purpose to avoid wasteful mistakes
	• Ensure products are durable and covered by a long warranty
	• Ensure packaging is the minimum necessary for protection
	• Avoid disposable products designed for single use
Re-use	• Check for redundant equipment that could be redeployed
	• Specify goods that are repairable and easily upgraded
	• Specify goods with clear and comprehensive maintenance, repair and operating instructions, supported with guaranteed stocks of parts
	• Give preference to suppliers that operate take-back schemes for end of life equipment and packaging
Recycle	• Specify products made from recovered or recyclable materials
	• Purchase products on which the materials are identified for ease of recycling
	• Minimise mixed-material products which are more difficult to recycle
Rethink	• Re-evaluate precedents and assumptions
	• Consider and evaluate options and alternatives
	• Consider consortium buying, if required, to gain sufficient buying power to promote sustainable performance among suppliers.

3.21 Note that sustainability issues may not be immediately obvious from the visible attributes of the product, or from supplier marketing messages. Paper production, for example, requires high consumption of energy, water and wood – and the use of chemicals (potential toxic pollutants). Forests may or may not be sustainably managed, to minimise deforestation, loss of topsoil and biodiversity and so on – while any paper that contains over 55% recycled content may be marketed as 'recycled'. The independent Forest Stewardship Council (FSC) promotes environmentally, socially and economically beneficial forest management, and the FSC logo identifies that paper products are sourced from sustainably managed forests.

An example of a performance specification for sustainable paper purchase might be: 'Copier paper, 80gsm, suitable for printing on fax, laser printers and photocopiers, with a minimum 75% content of recycled post-consumer waste' (www.solace.org.uk).

Sustainable specification across sectors and industries

3.22 You should be able to identify some of the key sustainable specification criteria for different types of materials and products – and therefore priority areas for different industries and organisations. For example:

- Vehicles: fuel efficiency
- Paper: recycled, chlorine-free, sustainable forestry management
- Office equipment: energy efficient, clean manufacturing processes, safety, end-of-life take-back
- Energy: renewable
- Food and beverage: organic, fresh/seasonal, hygienic processes, minimised packaging, sustainable water management.

3.23 In terms of the sustainable specification priorities of different sectors and industries, you should be able to apply our coverage of differing drivers, priorities and issues in Chapter 5.

Quick wins

3.24 'Quick wins' were established as part of the toolkit for sustainable procurement in the public sector, as part of the Sustainable Procurement National Action Plan. They are a set of published sustainable specifications for a range of commonly-purchased products, such as IT equipment, white goods, paper (including tissue) and so on, in each of the priority spend areas. The products specified were chosen for their environmental and financial impact, scope for environmental improvement and 'political or example-setting function'.

3.25 'Buy Sustainable – Quick Wins are comprised of both a set of mandatory minimum standards at the market average level and best practice specifications. These best practice specifications are more stretching than the mandatory minimum. They are voluntary for those procurers that wish to purchase the "best in class" products in certain areas. These are likely to become the minimum over different time periods depending on the product or product group.' (www.defra.gov.uk/sustainable/government)

Example: Quick Wins

The following is the basic 'Quick Wins' specification for buying furniture.

FURNITURE

Purchase of furniture produced from recycled materials and/or renewable materials. Reduces VOC emissions and avoids certain hazardous substances in materials production and surface treatment.

Minimum specification(s)

Timber must be purchased in accordance with UK timber procurement policy [link to policy]

Only timber and timber products originating either from independently verified legal and sustainable sources or from a licensed Forest Law Enforcement Governance and Trade (FLEGT) partner can be purchased.

NB From April 2015, only sustainably produced timber will be purchased

Best practice specification(s)

Same as the minimum specification and complies with the EU green Public Procurement comprehensive criteria [Link to criteria]

If you have an interest in particular procurement categories – transport, construction, office equipment, paper and so on – it would be worth browsing some of the other Quick Win specifications. See: http://www.defra.gov.uk/sustainable/government/what/priority/consumption-production/quickWins/index.htm

---

4 Service level agreements

4.1 So far, when we have discussed the sourcing requirements of organisations, we have lumped together products and services. But the fact is that, in many ways, they are not the same. A service may be defined as 'any activity or benefit that one party can offer to another that is essentially intangible and does not result in ownership of anything' (Kotler). Some obvious examples include travel, call-centre, cleaning, transport/logistics and IT services: something is 'done for you', but there is no transfer of ownership of anything as part of the service transaction. (It is also worth remembering that some form of service is part of the 'bundle of benefits' you acquire when you purchase materials and goods: sales service, customer service, delivery, after-sales care, warranties and so on.)

Challenges of specifying services

4.2   Services (and service elements) present buyers with problems additional to those that arise in purchasing materials or manufactured goods, when it comes to specifying requirements.

- Goods are tangible: they can be inspected, measured, weighed and tested to check quality and compliance with specification. Services are intangible: specifying service levels – and subsequently checking whether or how far they have been achieved – is therefore fraught with difficulty.

- Goods emerging from a manufacturing process generally have a high degree of uniformity, which also simplifies their evaluation. Services are variable: every separate instance of service provision is unique, because the personnel and circumstances are different. It is hard to standardise requirements.

- Goods can be produced, purchased and stored in advance of need, for later consumption. Services are inseparable and perishable, provided in 'real time': they can't be provided first and consumed later. Transport, accommodation and catering services, for example, are only relevant when they are needed. Specifications therefore need to include the time of provision, so that the supplier can schedule provision accordingly.

- The exact purpose for which a tangible good is used will usually be known, and its suitability can therefore be assessed objectively. It is harder to assess the many factors involved in providing a service: what weight should be placed on the environmental friendliness of chemicals used by a cleaning service, say, compared with the efficiency with which they get the job done?

4.3   It is harder to draft accurate specifications for services than for goods, because of their intangible nature – and yet this makes it even more important, otherwise buyer and supplier (and other stakeholders) could argue interminably as to whether the service was exactly what was asked for, or of an adequate standard.

Service level agreements

4.4   Service level agreements (SLAs) are formal statements of performance requirements, specifying the exact nature and level of service to be provided by a service supplier, as part of a service specification. The purpose of a service level specification and agreement is to define the customer's service level needs and to secure the commitment of the supplier to meeting those needs: this can then be used as a yardstick against which to measure the supplier's subsequent performance, conformance (meeting standards) and compliance (fulfilling agreed terms).

4.5   The main objective of an SLA is to quantify (state in specific, measurable terms) the minimum quality of service which will meet the customer's business needs, as a basis for the monitoring and maintenance of service levels.

4.6   The benefits of effective SLAs, summarised by Lysons & Farrington, are as follows.

- The clear identification of customers and providers, in relation to specific services
- The focusing of attention on what services actually involve and achieve
- Identification of the real service requirements of the customer, and potential for costs to be reduced by cutting services or levels of service that (a) are unnecessary and (b) do not add value
- Better customer awareness of what services they receive, what they are entitled to expect, and what additional services or levels of service a provider can offer (including more sustainable options)

- Support for the ongoing monitoring and periodic review of services and service levels, for ongoing quality and sustainability improvements.

- Support for problem solving and improvement planning, by facilitating customers in reporting failure to meet service levels

- The fostering of better understanding and trust between providers and customers.

4.7 Note our emphasis on ascertaining what services and levels of service are actually required, and on examining what they actually achieve and whether they add value. It is important not to over-specify requirements – for services as for goods. Specifying unnecessarily high standards or frequency of service, tight response times or grade of staff adds cost without necessarily adding value. (This is a point worth making in a season of global recession – where resource and cost efficiency is a key sustainability issue.)

Contents of a service level agreement

4.8 The basic elements of an SLA are as follows.

- What services are included (and not included, or included only on request and at additional cost)

- Standards or levels of service (such as response times, speed and attributes of quality service, such as conservation of resources or the use of sustainable materials) and other expectations of the supplier (such as its equal opportunity and employment standards)

- The allocation of responsibility for activities, risks and costs

- How services and service levels will be monitored and reviewed, what measures of evaluation will be used (including sustainability reports, for example), and how problems (if any) will be addressed

- How complaints and disputes will be managed

- When and how the agreement will be reviewed and revised. (Service specifications may need to change as requirements, circumstances or sustainability priorities change.)

4.9 Of course, these elements will be adapted to the specific nature of the service contract – a point worth remembering if you are asked to draft a sustainable SLA for a particular type of contract in the exam. As an example, suppose a company decides to outsource its cleaning services. The basic service level issues for agreement – including relevant sustainability standards – will include the following.

- How often is the service to be provided?

- During what hours will the service be carried out, and will there be any disruption to office activities?

- How many staff will be involved in providing the service (and, if relevant, with what skills, qualifications or experience levels)?

- How far will the service extend (eg does it include cleaning of computer monitors and desktop areas? Does it exclude washing up left in the staff kitchen?)

- What speed of response is expected from the supplier when the customer makes a non-routine service request?

- What environmental sustainability guidelines and standards will the supplier be required to adopt? (Preferred or excluded chemicals, energy usage of equipment, responsibility for switching off lights and appliances, sorting of rubbish for recycling and so on.)

- What diversity, equal opportunity, health and safety and other employment policies must the supplier adhere to, in hiring, training and managing its staff? How will performance in these areas be reported or monitored?

- What rates will the supplier pay its staff? (If these appear to be below average, there may be a sustainability issue – as well as a potential impact on the quality of service likely to be delivered.)

- How will cleaners report completion of their work and any issues or problems that arose? How will customers monitor and feed back their evaluation of the work? How will customer complaints be dealt with?

5 Innovation and sustainable design

Environmentally sensitive design

5.1 Design issues have traditionally concerned themselves with aesthetics, function and profitability. However, decisions made during the design phase have a direct impact on the materials and energy used during manufacture, the energy consumed and pollution/emissions produced during the product's lifetime, and the environmental impact of end-of-life disposal.

5.2 Environmentally sensitive design has three aspects: design for environmental manufacturing, design for environmental packaging and design for disassembly and disposal.

5.3 *Design for environmental manufacturing* aims to minimise energy consumption, emissions and waste. For the operations manager this means a new set of considerations relating to process design (reducing energy consumption and minimising waste) and material design (to minimise waste and pollution during product manufacture and disposal). However, potential cost savings, reputational risk management, public pressure and legislation are strong drivers towards environmentally sustainable manufacturing.

5.4 *Design for environmental packaging* centres around four main areas, in line with European legislation on waste reduction.

- Minimising the use of packaging materials: increasingly enforced by making the manufacturer liable for disposal costs

- Encouraging the use of re-usable pallets, totes and packaging: made possible by adopting unitised sizes throughout an industry, coupled with a returns capability

- Encouraging the use of biodegradable and recyclable packaging materials.

5.5 *Design for disassembly* facilitates the reclaiming, re-use and recycling of materials. Beitz ('Designing for ease of recycling', *Journal of Engineering Design*, 1993) argues that when a product reaches the end of its life it should be able to be dealt with in such a way that it has future use. This may mean:

- Designing for ease of disassembly, to enable removal of parts without damage

- Designing for ease of purifying, to ensure that the purifying process does not damage the environment

- Design for ease of testing and classifying, to make it clear as to the condition of parts which can be re-used and to enable easy classification of parts through proper marking

- Designing for ease of reconditioning – this supports the reprocessing of parts by providing additional material as well as gripping and adjusting features

- Designing for ease of re-assembly, to provide easy assembly for reconditioned and new parts.

> **Example: BMW**
>
> The 1991 BMW Z1 Roadster was conceived and designed for disassembly and recycling. The side and other panels are designed to come apart. The use of glues was limited and replaced with fasteners to enable areas such as the bumpers and the dashboard to be removed and disassembled more easily. At design, the portion of the car to be recycled was 80 per cent. BMW now aims for 95 per cent.

Early buyer involvement in design

5.6 As we saw earlier, there are significant benefits to involving purchasers at the specification stage – and potential problems if procurement input is not taken into account. The term early buyer involvement (EBI) is used to describe a process whereby purchasing specialists are involved in defining specifications – rather than merely turning specifications, prepared by users, into purchase orders. Where this is not the case, the purchasing function may need to 'promote' its expertise and potential contribution, in order to obtain greater input.

5.7 Where EBI is implemented, purchasing specialists may act in an advisory or liaison capacity to product development teams, or may be integrated into the project team on a full-time basis. Purchasing experts may provide the design/specification team with the following contributions.

- Input to make/do or buy decisions: which technologies should be kept/developed in-house and which should be outsourced
- Policy formulation for supplier involvement and internal purchasing
- Pre-selection of suppliers for involvement in a sustainable design project
- Supplier relationship management
- Ordering and expediting of samples and prototypes from suppliers
- Information on sustainable products and technologies already available or being developed
- Suggestion of alternative suppliers, products or technologies that could yield greater value and sustainability benefits
- Evaluation of sustainable designs in terms of materials availability, manufacturability, lead time, quality and costs
- Promotion of standardisation, variety reduction and simplification

Early supplier/contractor involvement in design

5.8 The concept of early supplier involvement (ESI) is that organisations should involve suppliers at an early stage in the product or service development/innovation process: ideally, as early as the conceptual design stage, although this is not always practical. This contrasts with the traditional approach, whereby the supplier merely provides feedback on a completed product design specification.

5.9 The main purpose of ESI is to enable a pre-qualified supplier (with proven supply and technical abilities) to contribute technical expertise which the buying organisation may lack, by making proactive suggestions to improve product or service design, or to reduce the costs of production. There are numerous ways in which suppliers can contribute to the product development process. For example, they can provide constructive criticism of designs, and suggest alternative materials or manufacturing methods at a time when engineering changes are still possible.

5.10 In service contracting, it is common for the potential service provider to collaboratively develop and negotiate service specifications and service level agreements as part of a cross-functional team with users and purchasers.

5.11 The benefits to be gained from ESI have mainly focused on relatively short-term organisational gains via more accurate and achievable technical specifications, improved product quality and sustainability performance, reduction in development time, and reduction in development and product costs. However, there may also be some long-term benefits. ESI can, for example, be a catalyst for long-term, partnership relationships with excellent, sustainability-promoting suppliers. It can also improve the buyer's understanding about technological developments in the supply market, with potential for further exploitation.

5.12 As with most approaches, practitioners also need to be aware of potential drawbacks. The product or service may be designed around the supplier's capabilities, which (a) may be limiting, and (b) may lock the buyer into a supply relationship. This may become a problem if the supplier becomes complacent and ceases to deliver the quality, sustainability or innovation it once did – or if market developments present better alternatives. In addition, ESI may pose confidentiality and security issues (eg the risk of leakage of product plans to competitors).

Supporting design and supply innovation

5.13 Sustainable innovation may be defined as 'the successful exploitation of new ideas which further social, environmental or economic sustainability objectives'. As we saw in Chapter 2, innovative solutions in product design, production processes and supply chain management are being demanded to meet sustainability challenges (such as resource depletion, climate change and entrenched poverty).

5.14 It is important to realise that innovation in design, procurement practices and supply markets does not necessarily involve 'brand new' ideas. Innovative supply solutions for one organisation may already be well established in another. Innovation is about the development, integration, diffusion, adoption and commercialisation of ideas – not just 'invention'.

5.15 Many best-practice procurement techniques are intended actively to stimulate innovation in the supply chain: early supplier involvement; partnering; supplier development and best-practice sharing; innovation councils (cross-functional innovation steering groups); Forward Commitment Procurement (FCP) and so on. We looked at some of the challenges of driving and maintaining supply chain innovation in Chapter 2, as one of the key trends in sustainable procurement.

6 *Whole-life sustainability*

Whole-life impacts of purchases

6.1 Fiskel defines Design for the Environment (DFE) as 'the systematic consideration of design issues related to environmental and human health over the lifecycle of a product'.

6.2 It should be clear from our discussion in this chapter that sustainable purchase specification is not just about building sustainability into the sourcing or purchase cycle (ending with delivery or installation of specified items or services) – but into the on-going impacts of those items throughout their lifecycle within the organisation. The sustainability values built into purchase specifications will influence the sustainability of their:

- Handling and storage
- Consumption or use
- Maintenance and repair
- Running costs and energy/resource usage
- Contribution to wastes, pollution and emissions

- Training requirements
- Health and safety implications
- Impact on the built/work environment and quality of working life
- Value for money, useful life and potential for upgrade or refurbishment
- End-of-life disposal
- Whole-life costs.

6.3   In later chapters of this text, we will explore lifecycle analysis, whole-life costing and whole-life contract management in detail.

Impact of the end product or service

6.4   In addition, organisations must recognise that their design and procurement policies (among others) have 'flow-on' consequences for their customers and consumers, the natural and social environment, once products and services have been produced and delivered. For example:

- If an organisation fails to source recyclable materials or components, its end product may be non-recyclable, or difficult to recycle (eg difficult to separate recyclable from non-recyclable elements)

- End products incorporating hazardous or toxic materials, or manufactured/ assembled to poor quality standards, may pose a risk to consumer health or safety at some point in their lifecycle

- End products with built-in obsolescence contribute to over-consumption, exploitation of developing markets (through the 'dumping' of excess production) and waste products ending up in landfill

- End products which are difficult to use, or lack user-friendly documentation and labelling, may impose health and safety risks, unnecessary training costs, or failure and repair costs, on users.

6.5   So, for example, a car manufacturer needs to think not just about supplier diversity and ethical monitoring, employee safety at work, and reducing resource consumption, pollution and the carbon footprint of its manufacturing processes. It also needs to think about road safety, support for responsible driving and driver/passenger safety; the fuel efficiency and emissions of the car; its running and maintenance costs; contribution to traffic congestion and ease of parking; the potential for disassembly and recycling of parts; the environmental impacts of end-of-life disposal; and so on.

6.6   In other words, even at the design and specification stage, it's not just about inputs: it's about outputs and their impacts as well.

End of life issues

6.7   European legislation is placing considerable emphasis on environmental issues surrounding the product lifecycle and this is being enacted into English law. For example, the EC Directive on Waste Electrical and Electronic Equipment (WEEE Directive) places responsibilities on both manufacturers and users in relation to design, recycling and disposal. The UK Waste Electrical and Electronic Equipment (WEEE) Regulations 2006 have been progressively rolled out to include measures such as the requirement to mark EEE products with a producer identifier and crossed-out wheelie bin ('do not recycle').

6.8 Other environmental legislation concerns packaging and waste (EC Packaging and Waste Directive 94/62/EC), covering identification of the 'waste stream' and all aspects of waste, recycling and disposal.

6.9 A further example is end of life vehicles (ELVs) legislation covering the composition of vehicles going on to the market, the amount of waste produced from ELVs, and the levels to which usable materials should be recovered and recycled.

The Integrated Product Policy (IPP)

6.10 In 2003, the European Commission published an Integrated Product Policy (IPP), outlining its strategy for reducing the environmental impact caused by products throughout their lifecycle. The IPP is based on five key principles.

- *Lifecycle thinking*: aims to reduce a product's environmental impact from the cradle to the grave. In doing so it also aims to prevent individual parts of the lifecycle from being addressed in a way that results in the environmental burden being shifted to another part.

- *Working with the market*: establishing incentives in order that the market moves in a more sustainable direction and rewarding companies that are innovative, forward-thinking and committed to sustainable development

- *Stakeholder involvement*: aims to encourage all those who come into contact with the product (industry, consumers and the government) to act across their sphere of influence and encourage the purchase of more environmentally aware products and how they can better use and dispose of them

- *Continuous improvement*: the IPP seeks to encourage improvements that can be made to decrease a product's environmental impacts across its lifecycle.

- *Policy instruments*: the IPP approach requires a number of different initiatives and regulations to be enacted. The initial emphasis will be placed on voluntary initiatives although mandatory measures may be required.

6.11 Meanwhile, the Eco-Management and Audit Scheme (EMAS) will be made more product-focused, and organisations will be encouraged to adopt the systemised and recognised approach embedded within it.

Chapter summary

- For external customers, we need to anticipate their demand for sustainable products. For internal customers, we need to partner with them to achieve sustainability objectives.

- In establishing sustainability priorities, two important tools are spend analysis and procurement positioning (the Kraljic matrix).

- Purchase specifications have a central role to play in achieving sustainability objectives. Ineffective specification poses risks for sustainability.

- With a conformance specification, the buyer details what the required product must consist of. With a performance specification he details what it must be able to do.

- It is common to adopt a cross-functional approach in drawing up specifications.

- Specifying services involves problems additional to those of specifying tangible products. A written service level agreement is an essential tool in this respect.

- There are three aspects to environmentally sensitive design: environmental manufacturing, environmental packaging and environmental disassembly and disposal.

- Sustainability objectives are more likely to be achieved if both buyers and suppliers are involved early in the design process.

- Sustainability is a whole-life issue: we must concern ourselves with environmental impacts over the whole life of a product.

Self-test questions

Numbers in brackets refer to the paragraphs above where your answers can be checked.

1. What is the primary focus of sustainable procurement in relation to consumer markets? (1.2)

2. What is meant by the term 'intelligent customer'? (1.9)

3. Explain the four quadrants in the Kraljic matrix. (2.6)

4. List purchasing objectives for sustainable procurement. (3.5)

5. Distinguish between conformance and performance specifications. (3.7)

6. In what circumstances may performance specifications be particularly appropriate (Lysons & Farrington)? (3.11)

7. What are the four principles in the UK waste hierarchy? (3.20)

8. Explain reasons why it is more difficult to specify for services than for tangible products. (4.2)

9. List benefits of a service level agreement. (4.6)

10. What are the three aspects of environmentally sensitive design? (5.2)

11. What contributions can purchasers make to the design stage? (5.7)

12. What are the five principles of the Integrated Product Policy? (6.10)

Further reading

If you have time, this would be a helpful point at which to read through:

*   *The Sustainable Procurement National Procurement Action Plan*, downloadable (free of charge) from:

http://www.defra.gov.uk/sustainable/government/documents

*   The CIPS Knowledge Summary on Sustainable Procurement
*   The CIPS Practice Guide on Corporate Social Responsibility

    http://www.cips.org/documents

CHAPTER 10

Sustainable Sourcing

Learning objectives and indicative content

3.2 Using a purchasing and supply management model, identify and evaluate the main considerations for sustainable sourcing at each stage of the sourcing process for different organisations and sectors

- A review of the stages in the sourcing process including: identification of requirement, sourcing plan, marketplace analysis, pre-qualification, evaluation and shortlisting of suppliers, preparation of enquiry/tender document, receiving and evaluation of offers, supplier selection and creation of contract or relationship
- Models: Office of Government Commerce (OGC) procurement process, CIPS procurement cycle, Ministry of Defence acquisition operating framework (AOF), the supply chain operations reference (SCOR)
- Economic considerations: financial, operational, technological
- Social and ethical considerations: CSR, skills base, workforce practices
- Environmental considerations: location, impact on the environment

Chapter headings

1 The sourcing process

2 Purchasing and supply management models

3 Sustainability considerations in defining requirements

4 Sustainability considerations in sourcing the market

5 Sustainability considerations in supplier selection and contract award

6 Key considerations for different organisations and sectors

Introduction

In Chapter 9, we covered the definition and specification of requirements, exploring a broad set of economic, social and environmental sustainability considerations applied mainly to the design and functionality of purchased materials, products and services. Purchase specification, as we have seen, is one major discipline in which the procurement function can contribute significantly to sustainable procurement by an organisation.

Another such discipline is sustainable sourcing. Sourcing, as you should be aware from earlier studies, is that part of the procurement process that is concerned with 'how and where services or products are obtained' (CIPS), embracing processes such as requirement definition, sourcing the market, tendering (or evaluation of quotations and offers), supplier selection and contract development. While definition requirement focuses mainly on the sustainability of the items to be purchased, sourcing raises a wider range of issues to do with ethical process and supply risk management.

The syllabus draws attention to the three key dimensions of sustainability: economic, environmental and social. Rather than cover each of these sets of considerations in turn, we have followed the process focus of the learning outcome by identifying and discussing them as they are most relevant to each stage of the sourcing process.

The syllabus also draws attention to a wide range of standards and legislation that may impact on various stages of the sourcing process. While we will 'flag' these impacts in this chapter, detailed discussion is reserved for Chapter 11, where we draw together various syllabus references to law, regulation and standardisation.

1 The sourcing process

1.1 Lysons & Farrington (*Purchasing & Supply Chain Management*) define sourcing as 'the process of identifying, selecting and developing suppliers'. They emphasise that this can be carried out at two basic levels: tactical/operational and strategic.

1.2 Tactical and operational sourcing processes are concerned with:

- Lower-level decisions relating to high-profit, low-risk and routine items – identified as 'leverage' and 'non-critical' items in the Kraljic matrix (discussed in Chapter 9)

- The formulation of short-range decisions as to how specific supply requirements are to be met, in response to changing or temporary conditions in the organisation or supply market (eg supplier failure or fluctuations in demand)

- Clearly defined requirements and specifications, and transactional sourcing decisions based mainly on open bidding and purchase price (as suits leverage and non-critical items).

1.3 Strategic sourcing processes are concerned with:

- Top-level, longer-term decisions relating to high-profit, high supply risk items (identified as 'strategic' items in the Kraljic matrix) and low-profit, high-supply risk ('bottleneck') items

- The formulation of long-range decisions about procurement policies, the supplier base, supply chain relationships, the purchase of capital equipment and ethical and sustainability issues

- Developing a deep understanding of requirements (eg using value analysis) and of the supply market and individual supplier drivers and capabilities (as suits strategic and bottleneck items).

1.4 Lysons & Farrington argue that 'the status and importance purchasing now has requires a transition from thinking of it as a purely tactical activity to seeing it as a strategic activity.' We therefore focus on strategic sourcing in this chapter.

1.5 CIPS defines strategic sourcing as: 'satisfying business needs from markets via the proactive and planned analysis of supply markets and the selection of suppliers with the objective of delivering solutions to meet predetermined and agreed business needs'.

The strategic sourcing process

1.6 Strategic sourcing is a complex process, involving a number of staged, interrelated tasks. A number of models have been developed to map and describe this process, and in the following section of this chapter we will outline the ones specified in the syllabus. (An exam question might ask you to identify sustainability considerations at each stage of the strategic sourcing process using a model of your choice – but in theory may also specify the model to be used.)

1.7 Meanwhile, the syllabus also offers a basic nine-step process, apparently synthesised from various more specific models.

- *Identification of the requirement*

  This may take the form of purchase requisition from a user department, a stock-replenishment requisition from inventory control, or a more complex process of requirement definition via early buyer/supplier involvement in a design and development project. This process may also, as we saw in Chapter 9, include re-evaluation of needs, and the definition of requirements in product and service specifications.

- *Sourcing plan*

  Make/do or buy decisions, and identification of the type of purchase (straight re-buy, modified re-buy or new buy), together with sourcing policies, will feed into a sourcing plan: the process and methodologies to be used to source the market and select suppliers. A contract may be awarded to an approved or preferred supplier, on the basis of a framework agreement, for example; or requests for quotation (RFQs) may be sent to pre-qualified suppliers; or the contract may be put up to open tender (competitive bidding); for example.

- *Market analysis*

  Purchasing research into product and supply markets will be used: to forecast long-term demand for the product (of which bought-out materials/components are a part); to gauge market prices and forecast price trends of bought-out items and materials; to identify a range of potential supply sources; to assess the security/risk of various supply sources; and to evaluate PESTLE factors impacting on sourcing decisions. An important part of this process will be the identification of potential suppliers.

- *Pre-qualification*

  This involves establishing key criteria for supplier suitability, and pre-screening potential suppliers to identify those who can meet the organisation's demands and standards. This is an important opportunity to apply sustainability criteria as a pre-qualifier, 'weeding out' suppliers who lack necessary values and capabilities (so that later evaluation and selection processes can focus on more easily comparable price/value criteria).

- *Evaluation and shortlisting of suppliers*

  Pre-qualified suppliers are evaluated and assessed on various criteria, and a shortlist drawn up for invitation to tender or quote on a contract – unless open tendering is used, in which case the tender is more widely advertised.

- *Preparation of enquiry/tender documents*

  Tender documents or requests for quotation (RFQs), accompanied by relevant information such as purchase/service specifications, are prepared and issued to shortlisted suppliers.

- *Receiving and evaluation of offers*

  Tenders/offers and quotations are received, sorted, clarified (where necessary) and evaluated against relevant specifications and criteria. This is done primarily on a best price/value basis, to ensure transparency and fairness of comparison and competition.

- *Supplier selection*

  The 'winning' supplier is selected for the contract. Best practice suggests that unsuccessful bidders be treated fairly and given supportive feedback, in order to maintain business relationships for future contracts.

- *Creation of contract or relationship*

  A purchase order, contract, framework agreement or other form of legal relationship is formulated, to define the terms of sale/purchase or engagement. This may take the form of a one-off purchase; an ongoing contract for the supply of goods, works or services; or a partnership agreement, say.

1.8   Of course, this is really only the beginning of contract management and fulfilment, and potentially ongoing relationship development. Further processes include the delivery of the product or performance of the service; post-purchase performance evaluation; post-contract 'lessons management'; and whole-life contract management (which will be discussed in Chapter 12).

1.9   We will use these broad stages in our stage-by-stage evaluation of sustainability considerations. However, first we will outline the other process models which you might choose (or be asked) to use in your own analysis.

2   *Purchasing and supply management models*

The CIPS procurement cycle

2.1   We have been unable to find any official CIPS definition of the procurement cycle, and the guidance published by CIPS for this unit is not much help in this respect, offering only a model distinguishing between e-sourcing and e-procurement. Different CIPS exam syllabuses use different models of a sourcing/procurement/purchasing cycle, but putting their various stages together, we might come up with a basic cycle such as the following: Figure 10.1.

2.2   The more extensive CIPS Purchasing and Supply Management Model (a complete diagram of which can be downloaded from the CIPS website) includes several major elements, including:

- Acquisition: pre-contract (corresponding most closely to our procurement cycle):
    1.   Identification of need
    2.   Procurement plan
    3.   Marketplace solicitation/development
    4.   Evaluate/select suppliers
    5.   Receive/evaluate offers
    6.   Create the contract/relationship
- Acquisition: post-contract: contract/relationship management; receipt of product/ service; asset management; and post-contract 'lessons' management. (These aspects will be explored in Chapter 13.)
- Renew contract and/or relationship OR end contract and/or relationship.

Figure 10.1 *A basic procurement cycle*

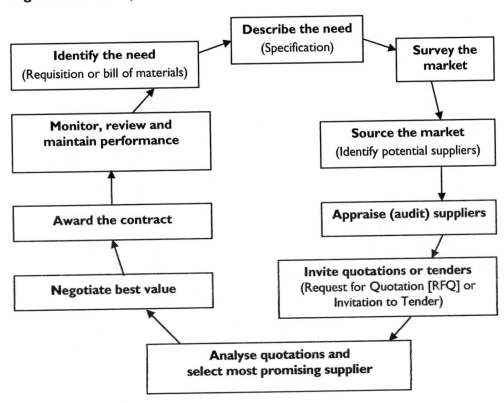

The Office of Government Commerce (OGC) procurement process

2.3 The Office of Government Commerce (OGC) is an independent office of HM Treasury, established to help central government departments and other public sector organisations to deliver best value from Treasury spend; to improve the sustainability of the government's estate and operations (with policies in areas such as reducing carbon emissions, promoting equality and supporting SMEs); and driving capability improvements in procurement, project and programme management.

2.4 OGC provides policy standards and guidance on best practice in procurement; promotes and fosters collaborative procurement across the public sector to deliver better value for money and better public services; and provides innovative ways to develop Government's commercial and procurement capability, including leadership of the Government Procurement Service.

2.5 Again, the OGC has published different versions of a model public procurement process. A comprehensive 15-stage process is depicted on the OGC website as in Figure 10.2.

2.6 The OGC document *Introduction to Public Procurement* sets out three phases.

- Pre-procurement: planning (including consultation with stakeholders, and establishment of governance arrangements and resource plans); developing specifications; business case and investment appraisal; market engagement; and procurement strategy (contracting process, length and type of contract required, funding/partnership options)
- Tender process and contract award: tendering (using processes prescribed by the EU Public Procurement Directives, discussed later in this chapter); and evaluation of tenders against criteria set out in the tender advertisement and documentation
- Contract and supplier management: service delivery management; relationship management; and contract administration and change management.

Figure 10.2 *OGC Procurement Process*

2.7 Meanwhile, the version of the model cited in the guidance for this unit published by CIPS has ten basic stages.

- *Before procurement:* business case; establish need; develop need; procurement strategy; pre-qualification
- *During procurement:* tender preparation; selection and award; implementation
- *After procurement:* manage contract, evaluation.

2.8 If you are interested in using this model, for public sector case studies or examples, you would be well advised to download some of the user-friendly guidance published by OGC – including analysis of social sustainability issues at each stage of the process (*Social Issues in Public Procurement*).

The Ministry of Defence Acquisition Operating Framework (AOF)

2.9 In 2008, the AOF replaced the old Acquisition Management System (AMS) as the primary source of information, guidance and instruction for the acquisition community. It is designed to support the Defence Values for Acquisition (DVfA) and establish strong professional guidelines for sustainable and ethical procurement and compliant advertising, tendering and contract award processes.

2.10 The AOF (set out at http://www.aof.mod.uk) has three 'layers'.

- A Strategic layer, defining acquisition and how it works.
- An Operational layer, with information on the MOD's organisation structure, people development and conduct of acquisition business
- A Tactical layer, with detailed guidance and instruction.

We were unable to find any specific process model that would be useful to you in an exam: broadly, the mandated procurement process follows the EU Procurement Directives on tendering, which will be discussed later in the chapter.

Example: Ministry of Defence

The MOD's website provides an interesting public sector case study, setting out its sustainability commitments (in the areas of climate change, heritage, biodiversity, land contamination and waste), and its key objectives for sustainable procurement, including:

- Achievement of Level 3 of the Flexible Framework with one section of Level 5 complete by 2009

- Undertake environmental risk assessments for all procurement activities

- For all procurement activities demonstrate sustainable procurement considerations throughout project development, specifications, decision making and delivery

- Demonstrate a whole life cost approach

- Comply with Government minimum standards (e.g. Quick Wins).

The Supply Chain Operations Reference model (SCOR)

2.11 The Supply Chain Council is an independent not-for-profit corporation formed in the US in 1996 as a grassroots initiative to develop a supply chain implementation model. Sixty-nine founding companies included Bayer, Compaq, Procter & Gamble, Lockheed Martin, Nortel and 3M – and there are currently around 750 member companies worldwide.

2.12 The SCOR model was developed by the SCC, as a cross-industry standard diagnostic tool for supply chain management, covering process modelling, performance measurement and best practice. The process model sets out five basic management processes: planning, sourcing, making, delivering and returning (reverse logistics). Planning includes a process labelled 'Assess supply resources'. Sourcing includes the processes: obtain; receive; inspect; hold; issue; and authorise for payment. (You might think of this more as a purchase-to-pay or P2P cycle than a genuine sourcing cycle.)

2.13 The latest version of the model (SCOR version 9.0) has been updated to address environmental sustainability efforts, incorporating GreenSCOR (previously a stand alone reference model). GreenSCOR includes:

- Industry best practices for making the supply chain more environmentally friendly, such as collaborating with partners on environmental issues, reducing fuel and energy consumption and minimising and re-using packaging materials.

- Metrics to measure the effects of 'greening', including carbon and environmental footprint, emissions cost per unit, energy costs as a percentage of production costs, waste produced as a percentage of product produced, and returned products disposed of versus re-manufactured.

- Processes to address waste management, eg how to collect and manage waste produced during production and testing (including scrap metal and non-conforming product).

2.14 If you want to follow up the model in detail, see: http://www.supply-chain.org.

3 Sustainability considerations in defining requirements

Identification of requirement

3.1 We have already looked in detail at the key sustainability considerations in identification and specification of need, in Chapter 9. Requisitions, stock replenishment orders and bills of materials will typically be formulated by user departments or inventory managers. However, procurement professionals may have input to requirement identification, definition and specification as part of an early buyer involvement policy, co-opting their commercial and supply market knowledge to design and development processes. They may also refer requisitions back to the originator: for clarification, or to challenge over-specification or unnecessary variation, or to suggest alternatives that will offer better sustainability benefits (including better quality or lower price) than the item requisitioned.

3.2   The need definition and specification stage offers the strongest opportunity to embed sustainability principles proactively throughout the sourcing process. This may be approached prescriptively by the buying organisation: eg specifying sustainability requirements for products and services. Or it may be approached more flexibly, by communicating the organisation's sustainability objectives and targets, and inviting suppliers to suggest potentially innovative solutions.

3.3   The key considerations at the need identification and specification stage, as discussed in Chapter 9, can be summarised as follows.

- *Economic considerations:* is there a genuine business need for the product/service (ie does it add value, as determined by value analysis or value engineering)? Can the need be met with less cost, resource use or variety (eg through standardisation and variety reduction)? Can the need be met in a way that promotes greater operational efficiency? Can the need be met in a way that leverages available or emerging technology more effectively? Will the item, as specified, support or enhance customer satisfaction with and demand for the end product/service; brand and reputational strength; or increased profitability (eg through premium pricing)?

- *Social and ethical considerations:* does the specification unfairly exclude small or diverse suppliers? Does the specification embody ethical and fair trade practices – and promote them in the supply chain? Does it require minimum standards for human rights, labour standards and worker health and safety (including compliance with relevant law and standards) in the supply chain? Will the item, as specified, contribute to or detract from the social responsibility of the end product/service, in terms of its production and consumption/use? Can the need be met in an alternative way that promotes any or all of these aims more effectively?

- *Environmental considerations:* does the specification require specific minimum standards of environmental performance in items/services specified (including compliance with relevant law and standards)? Does it promote the development of environmental management systems, capabilities and skills in the supply chain? Have the whole-life impacts of the end product/service (eg end-of-life issues) been considered in the specification?

- Can the specification be developed (eg in consultation with stakeholders) and formulated in such a way as to maximise support for sustainable procurement principles and the potential for innovative solutions, which benefit society and the environment without compromising functionality and commercial objectives?

3.4   Specifications will often refer to relevant legislation and standards, as a kind of 'short-hand' for expressing minimum acceptable process controls and performance levels. A range of law and standards is now applicable to environmental and social sustainability issues, in particular: these will be surveyed in Chapter 11.

Sourcing/procurement plan

3.5   A second main opportunity for embedding sustainability principles is offered by the formulation of a sourcing/procurement plan for the item. This may raise a range of sustainability considerations.

3.6 Make/do or buy decisions will primarily be based on economic criteria: whether the organisation can viably (sustainably) deploy or develop resources to produce the item or deliver the service in-house, or whether it would be more economically advantageous to outsource production/provision or buy-in goods/services.

3.7 Such decisions also relate to the core competencies of the organisation. Does it have the capabilities (capacity, resources, processes, knowledge/skill base) to produce the item more sustainably in-house, or can greater value be added – on economic, social or environmental criteria – by harnessing the technology, resources and competencies of external suppliers or contractors? What value might be added, for example, by co-opting suppliers with special capability in 'green' production or ethical branding? A focus on core competencies may itself be an issue of economic sustainability for the organisation, as defined in its corporate sustainability objectives (and the identified mission and purpose of the organisation).

3.8 The nature of the purchase will also raise a number of issues.

- For straight re-buys or inventory replenishment, will time and budget be allocated to re-evaluate specifications and supply sources? What would be the best time to re-examine such purchases for potential sustainability gains?

- For repeat or modified purchases, what arrangements are already in place, in relation to preferred or approved suppliers, framework agreements or call-off contracts, or informal long-standing supplier relationships? Sourcing sustainability demands that such arrangements be handled ethically, in such a way as to maintain supply chain relationships. How can economic, environmental or social sustainability gains be obtained within existing arrangements? When and how might they be renegotiated to include sustainability criteria, targets and continuous improvement criteria? Might additional suppliers be sought and developed, to improve the diversity or sustainability of the supply base?

- For new products or services, there will be more freedom to apply a range of sustainability criteria both to the requirement and to the sources of supply. What will be the organisation's sustainability priorities? (Increasing the diversity of the supply base? Using open tender to encourage competitive innovation and sustainable solutions?) What criteria will be used to pre-qualify suppliers? What kind of supply relationship will best secure sustainable supply? (Transactional, for efficiency? Partnership for continuity, development and sharing of complementary competencies? Some form of public-private sector partnership, for co-funding?)

- How can the sourcing process itself be handled most equitably, ethically and sustainably (maximising added value, while preserving future relationships and sources of supply)? What information will existing and potential suppliers require? What support may be given to unsuccessful bidders, or suppliers whose contracts are not being renewed?

4 Sustainability considerations in sourcing the market

Marketplace analysis

4.1 Purchasing research is 'the systematic study of all relevant factors which may affect the acquisition of goods and services, for the purpose of securing current and future requirements in such a way that the competitive position of the company is enhanced' (van Weele). This may include various forms of strategic information gathering and analysis, including:

- Environmental audits, PESTLE factor analysis and Strengths, Weaknesses, Opportunities and Threats (SWOT) analysis – which we will cover in Chapter 13.

- Industry analysis (the structure of the industry, its key players, and the nature and intensity of competition in the industry), competitor analysis (the actions, strengths and weaknesses of key competitors), and critical success factor analysis (what objectives must be achieved in order to secure competitive advantage)

- Supply, demand and capacity forecasting (eg using statistical analysis or expert opinion gathering) to estimate future sourcing requirements

- Vendor analysis: evaluating the performance of current suppliers, and potential suppliers not currently being used

- Market analysis: appraising general supply conditions in the market. What is the likely availability of each material, and are any shortages possible or probable? What is the prevailing price of each material, and what fluctuations (if any) are likely?

4.2 This research is conducted, on an ongoing or project basis, with the aim of providing information on the basis of which the organisation can plan to adapt to changes in the supply environment (ideally, earlier and better than its competitors) – to take advantage of new opportunities and/or to take defensive action in the light of perceived threats. It is thus potentially a key contributor to sustainability, in identifying, and shaping the organisation's response to, sustainability-related opportunities and threats.

4.3 In relation to a particular sourcing plan or cycle, the focus may be on vendor and market analysis. How many suppliers are there in the supply market? Where are they based? Of what type/size are they? What new products, processes and technologies are developing in the market? What sustainability-supporting capabilities are available or emerging? What are the sustainability commitments, objectives, performance, track-record and reputation of current vendors and potential suppliers in the market? What position does the buying organisation occupy in a supplier preferencing model, in relation to key suppliers?

4.4 The initial sustainability consideration will thus be: what sustainability issues will be built into the research and analysis project? Will the procurement function be 'looking for' financial stability and continuity of supply; supplier diversity and workforce practices; environmental management systems, performance and reputation?

4.5 The next consideration will be: what key sustainability 'issues' and trends are revealed by the analysis? What risks and opportunities arise from them? Are suppliers vulnerable to failure because of unsustainable sourcing practices by large buyers in the market? Is the buyer vulnerable to supply risk, owing to its lack of power or attractiveness in relationship to suppliers on whom it is dependent? Are resources increasingly scarce (and costly) in the supply market? Are the carbon footprints of suppliers a source of reputational risk to the downstream value chain? Do new technologies offer potential for more sustainable supply?

Pre-qualification

4.6 'Pre-qualification' in its broadest sense is the definition and assessment of criteria for supplier 'suitability', so that only pre-screened suppliers with certain minimum standards of capability, capacity and compatibility are invited or considered for participation in a given sourcing process. This may be carried out across a range of requirements: to prepare an approved supplier list, for example. Or it may be carried out on a procurement-specific basis, to pre-screen suppliers to receive an invitation to tender or to quote for a contract.

4.7 Pre-qualification avoids wasted resource and effort in supplier selection, by 'weeding out' suppliers who do not pre-qualify. It is also an important opportunity to embed social and environmental criteria in the supplier selection process – without compromising clarity, fairness, competition and economic value in the final selection decision (which can be made primarily on the basis of value). This is a particularly important consideration in the mandatory procedures for tendering in the public sector, for example.

4.8 Pre-qualification involves two basic processes. The first is the development of objective evaluation criteria by which potential suppliers' sustainability will be screened (and later evaluated in detail). The second is the screening of potential suppliers: for example, using a pre-qualification questionnaire (PQQ) or request for information (RFI) including sustainability criteria − or a supplier questionnaire specifically focused on sustainability (such as that developed by Oxfam).

Example: Johnson & Johnson

Johnson & Johnson has long been one of the world's most admired and ethical corporate brands. It also has a history of partnership with inventors, academics and suppliers, and a strong sustainable procurement policy ('Our Credo').

Johnson & Johnson follows a procurement approach that is based on Our Credo: to obtain the highest-quality products and services at a cost that represents the best possible value, while maintaining the highest ethical standards, and taking our social and environmental responsibilities seriously.

The Johnson & Johnson Family of Companies is committed to the ongoing identification of small and diverse suppliers that can add value to our businesses and help us achieve our long-term growth objectives. Small and diverse businesses not only provide economic and social vitality to the communities in which we live and work, but they add value to our companies, and help us enhance our role as a health care leader. In keeping with this commitment, our Supplier Diversity Program is designed to provide opportunities for qualified small and diverse businesses. Included in our program are:

- Certified minority-owned businesses, small and large

- Certified woman-owned businesses, small and large

- Certified Small Disadvantaged Businesses

- Small veteran-owned and service disabled veteran-owned businesses.

It is our policy to identify and include qualified businesses of these types when we buy the goods and services we need to serve the parents, patients and customers who purchase our products.

4.9 A range of sustainability criteria may be developed for general supplier pre-qualification or approval, although particular criteria may apply for specific purchases. Here are some examples.

- *Economic criteria*: financial stability, cost transparency and whole life costing, process capability, management expertise, sound governance structures, risk management processes, innovation capability, willingness to commit to continuous improvement

- *Environmental criteria*: location in relation to the buyer and lower tiers of supply (with implications for transport impacts); reverse logistics and recycling capability; environmental management systems and/or certification under ISO 14001 environmental standards, the Eco-Management and Audit Scheme (EMAS), or equivalent; compliance with environmental protection and emissions law/regulation

- *Social/ethical criteria*: CSR/sustainability policies; location in relation to the buyer (support for local suppliers/communities); evidence of responsible and ethical labour practices (including terms and conditions, health and safety, equality, diversity, compliance with International Labour Organisation standards); evidence of ethical trading practices (eg compliance with Fair Trade standards); commitment to transparency (eg willingness to undergo monitoring and evaluation); and so on.

5 Sustainability considerations in supplier selection and contract award

Evaluation and shortlisting of suppliers

5.1 At this stage of the sourcing process, the buying organisation evaluates the capability, compatibility and performance of potential (pre-qualified) suppliers in relation to specified requirements for a particular contract or procurement project, and draws up a shortlist of suppliers who will be invited to quote or tender, or to enter into contract negotiation (eg if a preferred supplier is being considered for sole supplier status or a partnership agreement).

- Sustainability criteria may be used as a basis for shortlisting suppliers.

- Where an open tender approach is used – or mandated, as in some public sector contexts – a shortlist will not be used. In such a case, tender advertisements should indicate clearly which social and environmental criteria will be used in evaluating tenders.

5.2 You should be aware from your studies in other modules of some general frameworks for pre-contract evaluation of suppliers, or 'supplier appraisal'. Some common examples are shown in Table 10.1. Note that each of the criteria mentioned can be seen as a contribution to economic, social and/or environmental sustainability – over and above the explicit 'CSR' or 'Environmental/ethical' criteria which are included.

Table 10.1 *Models for supplier appraisal criteria/perspectives*

FACE 2 FACE (Dawn Dadds)	8 Cs (Ray Carter)
Fixed assets: physical resources to meet buyer needs	*Competence* of the supplier to fulfil the contract
Ability to deliver the goods: production capacity and reliability of delivery/quality/service	*Capacity* of the supplier to meet the purchaser's current and future needs
Cost: competitive total acquisition costs	*Cost* and value for money over the life of the purchase
Efficiency: use of resources, minimisation of waste	*Control* systems in place for monitoring and managing resources and risks
Financial stability: for sustainability of supply	*Cash* resources for financial stability
Ability to work with the buyer: compatibility of culture, contacts, willingness to co-operate	*Consistency* in delivering and improving levels of quality and service
Commitment to quality: reliability of quality systems, pursuit of continuous improvement	*Commitment* of the supplier to quality, service, cost management, sustainability
Environmental/ethical factors: policies, systems and practices in regard to CSR/sustainability	*Clean and compliant* performance, in terms of environmental and CSR objectives

5.3 Some of the sustainability criteria that might be drawn up for supplier appraisal (and/or for incorporation in invitations to tender or evaluation of quotations), using the headings suggested by the syllabus are shown in Table 10.2.

Table 10.2 *Evaluation criteria for supplier appraisal, quotations or tenders*

Economic	Social/ethical	Environmental
Financial:	**CSR:**	**Location:**
Competitive whole-life cost	CSR/sustainability policies	Distance from customer
Financial stability	Ethical codes/practices	Distance from sub-suppliers
Fixed asset backing	Corporate governance	**Environmental impacts:**
Resource efficiency	Compliance with law/regulation	
Cost transparency/fair pricing	Reputational risk management	Environmental policies
Operational:	**Skills base:**	Environment management systems (ISO 14001)
Production capacity	Skills base for sustainability	Impacts of materials, products, packaging and processes
Process capability	HR development/succession	Green design/production and innovation capability
Quality management systems	Supply chain skills base	Transport energy/emissions
Managerial expertise	Learning capability/culture	Design for disassembly
Risk management	**Workforce practices:**	Reverse logistics, re-use and recycling
Supply chain management	Ethical HR policies	Environmental risk management
Technological:	Compliance on human/labour rights, equality/diversity	Willingness to 'green'
R & D/innovation capability	Health and safety	
Technology leverage	Supplier management	
Integrated information systems		

5.4 Information on these matters may be acquired by various means: pre-qualification or appraisal questionnaires completed by suppliers (although at this stage, the buyer will need to verify the truth and accuracy of information); perusal of the supplier's financial statements and reports; checking the supplier's certifications, accreditations, policy statements and so on; arranging to get references from existing customers; and checking product samples or portfolios of work.

5.5 Once a shortlist of potential suppliers has been identified, the buyer may use a supplier audit, site visit or capability survey: visits to the supplier's premises by a cross-functional appraisal team (eg with experts on purchasing, quality, engineering and sustainability) which shares responsibility for the decision to approve or reject the supplier.

Preparation of tender documents/request for quotation

5.6 The requirement can be signalled to pre-qualified or approved suppliers in various ways, depending on the type of purchase and company policy.

5.7 The organisation may already have negotiated a framework agreement or standing contract with a supplier, to meet a requirement of a certain type. In such a case, the requirement will simply be notified by purchase or call-off order, on the pre-agreed terms. Sustainability criteria will have to be built into the original agreement or subsequent contract reviews and renewals.

5.8 There may be only one available supplier, or the organisation may have negotiated a preferred supplier or sole supplier agreement with a dependable supply partner. In such a case, the buyer may simply negotiate a contract with the preferred or designated supplier: sustainability criteria will be negotiated into the contract.

5.9 The organisation may send an 'enquiry' to one or more shortlisted suppliers, also called a request for quotation (RFQ). The RFQ will set out the details of the requirement, including: the quantity and description of goods/services required (incorporating sustainability criteria), the required place and date of delivery, and the buyer's standard terms and conditions of business. Suppliers will be invited to submit a proposal and/or price for the job, which will be evaluated on a competitive basis.

5.10 A full competitive bidding or tendering process may be required for contracts over a certain value threshold – and is compulsory in the public sector on this basis. Lyson & Farrington define tendering as 'a purchasing procedure whereby potential suppliers are invited to make a firm and unequivocal offer of the price and terms on which they will supply specified goods or services which, on acceptance, shall be the basis of the subsequent contract'. There are two basic approaches to tendering. In selective or restricted tendering, potential suppliers are pre-qualified and 3–10 suppliers are shortlisted for invitation to tender. In open tendering, the invitation to tender is widely advertised and open to any potential bidder.

5.11 The purpose of open, direct competition on the basis of best economic value, as enshrined in public sector procurement regulations on tendering, is both (a) to ensure best value and (b) to ensure a fair and transparent process. While this supports sustainability objectives in general, it restricts the extent to which sustainability criteria can be applied in the evaluation of tenders: different tenders may propose different sustainability values and solutions, which are not directly comparable. The Canny Buyer website for Scottish government procurement notes that: 'Generally speaking, the earlier in the tender process you place environmental considerations, the more is possible.'

5.12 Regardless of sector, a best-practice tender procedure would have the following steps. (Note that the fair and ethical administration of tenders is itself an issue of economic and social sustainability.)

- Preparation of detailed specifications and draft contract documents by the purchasing department. Once the tender procedure is in motion, there is little room for re-negotiation and adjustment of specifications. Attention must be given to accurate specification of the requirement, including sustainability criteria, so that the buyer's task will be simply to (a) check that tenders received comply with the requirements, and (b) choose the lowest price (or best value) bid.

- Determination of a realistic timetable for the tender process, allowing reasonable time for responses at each stage

- Issue of invitations to tender. In the case of selective tendering, this would be by means of an invitation to bid or request for quotation (RFQ) sent to shortlisted suppliers. In the case of open tendering, it would be by means of a public advertisement, with invitations to bid issued to suppliers who respond to the advertisement within the stated time frame. Specifications (including all sustainability criteria) should be issued to each potential supplier in identical terms and by the same date. It should also be made clear to all tenderers that they are to comply strictly with the timetable for submission.

- Submission of completed tenders or bids by potential suppliers.

- Opening of tenders on the appointed date. Tenders received after this date should be returned un-opened. The tenders received should be logged, with the main details of each listed on an analysis sheet for ease of comparison.

- Analysis of each tender, according to stated criteria, with a view to selecting the best offer. This will usually be on a lowest-price or best value basis. Non-economic criteria (such as environmental or social sustainability or innovation) must be clearly notified in the invitation to tender, together with the weightings to be allocated to those criteria.

- Post-tender clarification, verification of supplier information, and/or negotiation, where required. Again, the invitation to tender must state clearly that the buyer will not be bound to accept the lowest price quoted, and that post-tender negotiation may be entered into, if necessary to qualify or clarify tenders, or to discuss potential improvements or adjustments to suppliers' offers.

- Award of the contract.

- The giving of feedback, on request, to unsuccessful tenderers.

Receipt and evaluation of quotes or offers

5.13 Tenders should be evaluated against the specific, objective award criteria set out in the initial invitation to tender (particularly if the contract is subject to statutory control). Normally, the successful tender will be the one with the lowest price, or representing the best economic value over the lifetime of the purchase.

5.14 However, as we have seen, there may need to be further discussion and analysis among the evaluation team, to decide whether and how effectively each bid meets the requirements. Even amongst tenders that do meet the basic requirement, there may be considerable variety in the product and total solution 'package' being offered. One solution may be more attractive than another (innovative, environmentally friendly, risk-reducing, showing potential for sustainable business development) – even if price tells against it. Non-price criteria will have to be reviewed with particular care (and more details sought, if required), if suppliers have not been pre-qualified for sustainability.

Supplier selection

5.15 Whatever process is used, at some point the buying organisation will have to select what it considers the optimal offer or preferred supplier.

5.16 Sustainable best practice (and, in the public sector, tender regulations) dictate that unsuccessful bidders or applicants be offered feedback on why they did not win the contract. This enhances the transparency and fairness of the process: ensuring that decisions are justifiable. It also supports sustainability by facilitating learning, improvement and capability/skill development, and enhancing the ability of small, local and diverse suppliers to compete more effectively for contracts.

Example: Orange

Global telecommunications provider Orange publishes the following Ethical Sourcing Policy.

In our ethical sourcing policy we commit to:

- Understanding our supply chains, including health and safety, environmental, labour and human rights issues
- Expecting responsible behaviour, as well as quality and value
- Working with suppliers to make improvements, where their practices fall short of our expectations
- Withdrawing from contracts where improvement is impossible
- Respecting suppliers' confidential information and running fair selection processes
- Making payments in accordance with our contractual commitments

Under the ethical, social and environmental criteria, suppliers are assessed, among other things, on:

- Compliance with relevant legislation and regulations
- Use of energy and other natural resources
- Respect for confidentiality
- Whether they have a civic and responsible attitude
- Whether they have principles for action defining their commitments and priorities
- Whether they have an environment policy.

These assessments are reviewed jointly with our suppliers and lead to an improvement plan being drawn up if necessary.

Creation of contract or relationship

5.17 A variety of sustainability considerations will be built into contract negotiation and development, or the creation or deepening of a sourcing relationship.

5.18 For example, the sourcing process may have been leading up to a one-off purchase order; a framework agreement, call-off contract or rolling contract to fulfil requirements over a period of time; or a partnership or joint-venture agreement to pursue shared objectives and areas of interest (such as the development of 'green' brands or technologies). The type and duration of the supply relationship will depend to an extent on sustainability considerations.

- As the Kraljic matrix indicates, the type of relationship sought will depend in part on supply risk. Economically sustainable supply may dictate arms' length systems contracts, for example, for routine and leverage items – and long-term relationships or partnership for bottleneck and critical/strategic items.

- Social and environmental sustainability may best be managed in the context of collaborative, long-term supplier relationships, because of the need for trust, continuous improvement, capability development and innovation.

- Economic and environmental sustainability may best be managed in the context of the whole life of the purchase: including issues such as whole-life costs, maintenance and repair, upgrade, warranty, running costs, resource/energy consumption and end-of-life issues such as take-back and disposal.

5.19 The development of contract terms will crystallise the commitments, responsibilities and rights of both parties in regard to the full range of sustainability issues; the apportionment and transfer of costs and risks; legislation and standards that will be adhered to; how performance will be monitored and measured; what commitments are made in relation to continuous improvement; how disputes will be managed; and so on. Sustainability aspects may be built into the purchase order; standard terms and conditions of purchase; supply contracts; service level agreements; partnership agreements – and any schedules and appendices added to these documents in regard to sustainability criteria and commitments.

5.20 The detail of contract terms and sustainability-related clauses should be beyond the scope of this syllabus, but you should be able to draw on your studies for other modules focused on law and contract. Some general examples are given in Table 10.3.

6 *Considerations for different organisations and sectors*

Sustainable sourcing in different sectors

6.1 In Chapter 5, we looked at the key sustainable procurement issues and drivers for different sectors, industries and organisation types. We will not duplicate that material here. You should be able to review the material and relate specific issues/drivers to their implications for the sourcing cycle.

6.2 It is worth highlighting some major differences between the public sector and the private and third sectors, in relation to the sourcing and procurement process.

- As you can see from the examples of the OGC and Ministry of Defence procurement frameworks (discussed earlier in the chapter), public sector procurement is subject to highly centralised regulations, strategies, policies and procedures. In contrast, private and third sector organisations are free to develop their own approaches to sourcing, constrained mainly by issues of supply risk and relationship, governance regulations (in relation to financial controls and reporting), and market/reputational pressures for CSR and ethical sourcing.

- The public sector procurement process explicitly includes phases for stakeholder consultation and value definition, market engagement and the exploration of funding structures (including various forms of public-private sector co-investment, which we will discuss in Chapter 12).

- Although private and third sector organisations may choose to use similar tender processes, as an embodiment of good practice, public sector procurement is subject to specific EU directives, which have been enacted into UK law.

Table 10.3 *Examples of standard contract terms supporting sustainability*

Term/clause	Sustainable procurement considerations
Commercial provisions	Rights and obligations of the supplier and of the purchaser. Standard terms of purchase, for example, might include: • *Inspection/testing*: the allowance of reasonable time to inspect incoming goods (eg for specified materials, eco-labelling) • *Packing*: stipulating that this should be in accordance with instructions (eg re reduced or recyclable materials) • *Assignment*: eg that no part of the order shall be subcontracted to a third party without the buyer's written agreement (avoiding risk of subcontractors not approved on sustainability criteria) • *Payment terms* (since on-time payment is a sustainability/ethical issue)
Secondary commercial provisions	• *Confidentiality and intellectual* property protection (to prevent unauthorised exploitation of IP assets) • *Indemnity*: supplier will make good any loss suffered by the buyer as a result of product defects, environmental damage, non-compliance • *Guarantee clause*: supplier guarantees to make good any defects/non-conformance in the items supplied, given reasonable notice. • *Termination*: eg when and how the contract will be discharged (responsibly and sustainably)
Standard clauses	• *Force majeure*: exclusion of liability if a 'major force' outside the control of the parties (eg an act of God, war, flood etc) prevents or delays the performance of the contract (preventing unsustainably harsh liabilities).

EU public procurement directives

6.3   The EU Public Sector Procurement Directive was implemented into UK law by the Public Contracts Regulations 2006, which apply to purchasing by public bodies (above certain financial thresholds: about €200,000 for supplies and services purchased by non-central government bodies).

6.4   The purposes of the EU procurement directives are broadly supportive of economically sustainable development.

- To open up the choice of potential suppliers for public sector organisations and utilities, in order to stimulate competition and reduce costs

- To open up new, non-discriminatory and competitive markets for suppliers

- To ensure the free movement of goods and services within the European Union

- To ensure that public sector purchasing decisions are based on value for money (via competition) and that public sector bodies award contracts efficiently and without discrimination.

6.5 The main provisions of the regulations are summarised in Table 10.4.

Table 10.4 *Public Contracts Regulations (Public Procurement Directive)*

Advertising	Subject to certain exceptions, public bodies must use open tendering procedures: advertise invitation to tender according to rules designed to secure maximum publicity across the EU.
Contract award procedures	• *Open procedure*: no requirement for pre-qualification of suppliers. Suppliers have 52 days (minimum) to submit bids. • *Restricted procedure*: suppliers may be pre-qualified, but there must be a pre-stated range of suppliers (5–20) to whom invitations will be sent. Prospective bidders have 47 days to register interest and 40 days (minimum) to submit bids. • *Negotiated procedure*: with advertisement or without (eg in the case of urgency, exclusivity agreements, or no tenders being received under other procedures). Not less than three parties must be selected to negotiate. • *Competitive dialogue (for complex contracts):* a process conducted in successive stages to identify potential solutions and gradually reduce the number of tenders to be negotiated.
Award criteria	• Contracts should be let on the basis of objective award criteria, ensuring transparency, non-discrimination, equal treatment and competition. • Buyers are generally obliged to award contracts on the basis of *lowest price* OR *most economically advantageous tender* • All tenderers must have reasonable, equal and timely information about criteria and the weighting or ranking of non-price criteria (which may include environmental and social sustainability) • The buyer may exclude bidders if they fail to meet certain defined criteria in regard to suitability, financial standing and technical competence
Right to feedback (debrief)	• The results of the tender must be notified to the Official • Unsuccessful bidders have the right to a de-brief within 48 days of request. The focus should be on the weaknesses that led to rejection of the bid, as well as strengths. The de-brief should *not* be used to justify the award of the contract to the successful tenderer (and, in particular, confidential information about the successful bid should *not* be disclosed).
Other provisions	Contracting authorities may use: • Framework agreements (agreeing terms governing 'standing' contracts for defined periods of up to four years) • Electronic purchasing and tendering/auction systems: completely computerised systems for quotation submission, evaluation and contract award.

6.6 In relation to sustainability:

- Public bodies can specify sustainable options, provided that doing so does not unreasonably distort competition or discriminate against products or suppliers from any EU member state. It is possible, for example, to specify recycled paper or energy-efficient IT equipment. Fair trade options can be 'welcomed' – and an authority might require caterers to supply fair trade coffee or tea products, for example, as this would not affect competition between caterers.

- In relation to contract award, only two criteria are allowable: lowest price or best value – 'most economically advantageous tender', defined as the optimum combination of whole-life costs and quality to meet the user's requirement. Resource consumption and disposal costs, for example, may be taken into account. Social and environmental sustainability criteria must be directly related to the performance of the contract, and appropriately weighted.

- EU rules do not permit preference being given to any sector of suppliers such as local suppliers, social enterprises or SMEs (except for 'supported businesses' where particular rules apply). It is permissible, however, to remove any obstacles that might be preventing such groups from competing for public business. This might be done by, for example, ensuring they are aware of where opportunities will be advertised and making tendering documentation and procedure as simple as possible for all suppliers.

Sustainable sourcing in different industries and businesses

6.7 As we noted earlier, you should be able to apply the issues/drivers discussed in Chapter 5 to differentiate between the sustainable sourcing priorities of different industries and business types. Here are some examples.

- In the retail sector, sourcing decisions may be dictated substantially by consumer preferences for particular branded goods. This removes the emphasis of sourcing from supplier selection to purchase negotiation, and enables the definition of requirement simply by brand/model. Social and environmental value and criteria will be defined by consumer demand.

- In the extractive and manufacturing sectors, a high proportion of spend may be allocated to capital purchases, placing the emphasis in sourcing on investment appraisal and whole-life costs and management issues.

- Manufacturers have to consider the impacts of end products/services in sourcing materials and components. Some products will pose higher sustainability risks than others: examples include toys (health and safety issues), consumer electronics (waste products issues), cars (pollution, emissions and fossil fuels issues) and so on.

Chapter summary

- Sourcing processes can be analysed as either tactical/operational or strategic. In relation to sustainable procurement, strategic considerations are paramount.

- The strategic sourcing process may be divided into nine stages: identification of need; sourcing plan; market analysis; pre-qualification; evaluation and shortlisting of suppliers; preparation of enquiry; receiving and evaluating offers; supplier selection; creation of contract or relationship.

- There are many models of the purchasing and supply management process (eg those of the OGC and MOD).

- In identifying the requirement, the key sustainability considerations are economic, social and ethical, and 'green'.

- An opportunity for embedding sustainability principles is offered by the formulation of a sourcing plan.

- Purchasing research will investigate how many suppliers there are in the market, where they are based, what their sustainability credentials are like, etc.

- Sustainability factors must be built into the process of pre-qualifying suppliers.

- Various models exist to assist in supplier appraisal, eg FACE 2 FACE and Carter's 8Cs.

- Buyers can assess potential interest among suppliers by using tender documents or requests for quotation.

- There is variety in the extent of adoption of sustainability across different sectors. The public sector is usually regarded as leading the way.

Self-test questions

Numbers in brackets refer to the paragraphs above where your answers can be checked.

1   Distinguish between tactical/operational processes and strategic processes in sourcing. (1.2, 1.3)

2   List nine stages in a strategic sourcing process. (1.7)

3   Describe the SCOR model of strategic sourcing. (2.11–2.13)

4   What sustainability considerations arise when identifying the requirement for a purchase? (3.3)

5   Define 'purchasing research'. (4.1)

6   What sustainability criteria might be included in the process of supplier pre-qualification? (4.9)

7   List the supplier appraisal considerations in the FACE 2 FACE and 8C models. (Table 10.1)

8   List steps in a best practice tendering exercise. (5.12)

9   What are the purposes of the EU procurement directives? (6.4)

10   Explain differences in approach to sustainable sourcing in different industry sectors. (6.7)

Further reading

If you want more background to sourcing/procurement procedures, and you have access to the book from your studies in other modules, you could look at Lysons & Farrington (*Purchasing & Supply Chain Management*): Chapter 11 (*Sourcing and the management of suppliers*); Chapter 13 (*Contrasting approaches to supply*); and Chapter 17 (sections 17.9–17.14 on ethical and environmental aspects of purchasing).

CHAPTER 11

Sustainability Standards and Legislation

Learning objectives and indicative content

1.3 Evaluate the external factors influencing sustainable procurement and apply the PESTLE model in the context of different organisations and sectors, including the public, private, and third sectors and their tiers.

- International and local influences on sustainable procurement

    - Legislative (eg environmental laws, workforce legislation)

- Standards (eg labelling ISO 14023/25, environmental management systems ISO 14001, social accountability AS 8000)

3.2 Using a purchasing and supply management model, identify and evaluate the main considerations for sustainable sourcing at each stage of the sourcing process for different organisations and sectors

- Standards and legislation

    - Kyoto Protocol
    - International Labour Organisation (ILO) standards
    - EU Directives 2004/17/EC and 2004/18/EC on public procurement
    - ISO14001 environmental standards
    - ISO 15686 whole-life costing standards
    - Finance and tax laws (eg Sarbanes Oxley)
    - 'Fair Trade' standards

Chapter headings

1   Law and standards

2   General sustainability and sustainable development

3   Environmental sustainability

4   Social sustainability and ethics

5   Economic sustainability and governance

Introduction

As you will see from the learning objectives listed above, legislation and standards appear several times across the syllabus. So far, we have highlighted the need for compliance with legislation and standards (a) as a key aspect of the external environment of sustainable procurement (Chapter 3) and (b) as they impact on specific issues and stages of the sourcing cycle (Chapter 10).

Rather than complicate – and lengthen – our coverage of the main thrust of those learning objectives, we have chosen to survey relevant legislation and standards here, in a separate chapter. (This follows the approach taken by the CIPS guidance for this unit and by Blackburn, in your essential reading textbook.) You should be able to select and apply specific laws, regulations and standards as relevant to any given sustainability issue or operating procedure covered elsewhere – or raised in the exam.

1 Law and standards

Legislation

1.1 Legislation enacted at the national and transnational (eg EU) level covers a range of areas relevant to sustainability, including the following.

- *Human rights law*, which broadly covers issues such as the right to privacy; freedom from servitude (eg forced and child labour) and discrimination; working conditions and wages; freedom of association, expression, conscience and religion; and so on. In the UK, the Human Rights Act 1998 makes it unlawful for any public body to act in a way that is incompatible with the European Convention on Human Rights. The UK is also a signatory to the UN Convention on the Rights of the Child (CRC) which stipulates the rights of children to be protected from economic exploitation and from harmful labour.

- *Employment law,* which broadly covers issues such as discrimination and equal opportunity, health and safety, employment protection, employment rights, industrial democracy, employee relations and so on. In recent decades, there have been increasing legislative constraints on managerial decision-making in these areas. The social policy of the European Union has added momentum to this trend: European Directives are still being enacted into the law of member states.

- *Corporate, finance and tax law*, which broadly covers issues to do with the formation of companies, corporate governance, financial reporting and tax. UK legislation in this area includes the Companies Acts and Finance Acts. In the USA, corporate governance is legislated under the Sarbanes-Oxley Act, while the UK has voluntary regulation under the Stock Exchange Combined Code.

- *Anti-corruption law*, which broadly covers issues to do with bribery and inducements (eg the Public Bodies Corrupt Practices Act 1989, Prevention of Corruption Act 1916) and money laundering: obtaining, concealing or investing funds or property known or suspected to be the proceeds of criminal conduct or terrorist funding (Terrorism Act 2000, Proceeds of Crime Act 2002, Money Laundering Regulations 2007).

- *Competition law*, which broadly covers issues to do with the protection of competition: prevention of agreements between corporations (eg cartels) that would prevent, restrict or distort competition; and the control of monopolies, mergers which would result in monopolies, and the abuse of dominant market position. UK legislation in this area includes the Competition Act 1998, Fair Trading Act 1973 and Enterprise Act 2002 and similar provisions apply in European Law (Articles 81 and 82 of the Treaty of Rome).

- *Data protection and freedom of information*, which broadly covers the rights of individuals to access and control information held and used about them by organisations (eg Data Protection Act 1998); and the public right to access information held by public authorities, where this supports the public interest (eg Freedom of Information Act 2000)

- *Environmental law*, which covers an increasing body of issues including: air and water quality, climate change and GHG emissions, agriculture, biodiversity and species protection, pesticides and hazardous chemicals, waste management, remediation of environmental impacts, impact review, and conservation of public lands and natural resources. UK legislation includes: the Environmental Protection Act 1990, the Environment Act 1995, the Climate Change and Sustainable Energy Act 2006, the Climate Change Act 2008, the Energy Act 2008 and the Environmental Damage (Prevention and Remediation) Regulations 2009 (implementing the Environmental Liability Directive 2004/35/CE).

Standards and standardisation

1.2 As we mentioned in Chapter 3, in addition to legislation or statute, various international and governmental agencies, NGOs and commercial organisations have developed a range of voluntary regulatory codes of practice, and benchmark standards.

1.3 The British Standards Institution (BSI) describes a standard as 'a published specification that establishes a common language, and contains a technical specification or other precise criteria, and is designed to be used, consistently, as a rule, a guideline, or a definition'. Standardisation is a voluntary process, based on consensus among different stakeholders such as:

- National and international standardisation organisations, led globally by the International Standards Organisation (ISO)
- National public authorities
- Industry and business associations, including representatives of SMEs
- Non-governmental organisations (NGOs)
- Scientific and academic organisations.

1.4 Since the mid 1980s the European Union has made increasing use of standards in support of its sustainability policies and legislation, through organisations such as CEN (European Committee for Standardisation). Standardisation and legislation are in effect two tools that allow different options to address sustainability issues but can also be complementary processes as standardisation can support the regulatory approach.

1.5 A wide range of voluntary codes, statements of principle and industry/national/ international standards is now available in areas such as:

- *General sustainability:* eg the UN Global Compact and the Earth Charter
- *Environment:* eg the ISO 14001 Environmental Management System Standard; the European Eco-Management and Audit Scheme; Publicly Available Specification 2050 (British Standards Institution)
- *Human rights, labour standards and fair trading:* eg the Ethical Trading Initiative base code; International Labour Organisation standards on human rights; and Social Accountability 8000 standard
- *Governance:* eg the UK Stock Exchange Combined Code.

1.6 We will look briefly at both legislation and standards in some key areas highlighted by the syllabus and CIPS guidance.

2 *General sustainability and sustainable development*

The UN Global Compact

2.1 The Global Compact was launched in 2000, setting out ten principles for business, derived from the Universal Declaration of Human Rights; the International Labour Organisation (ILO) Declaration on Fundamental Principles and Rights to Work; and the Rio Declaration on Environment and Development.

2.2 The ten principles include: support for human rights (freedom of association and collective bargaining, and elimination of forced and child labour); labour rights (elimination of labour discrimination); environmental responsibility (embracing a precautionary approach, and developing and sharing environmentally-friendly technologies); and anti-corruption measures (working against bribery and extortion).

2.3 This is said to be the largest and most prestigious of all global sustainability codes: adopted by thousands of corporations and dozens of international NGOs and labour federations. However, criticisms focus on the lack of a system for transparent assessment and reporting on what endorsing companies have actually done to implement the principles.

2.4 For more detail, if you are interested, see: http://www.unglobalcompact.org.

The Earth Charter

2.5 The Earth Charter emerged from the 1987 UN Commission on Environment and Development, and was approved in 2000. The charter comprises sixteen principles of sustainable development, on four dimensions.

- *Respect and care for the community of life*: including the protection of human dignity, and consideration of the needs of future generations
- *Ecological integrity*: including sustainable development; sustainable resource consumption; and a precautionary approach (avoiding negative impacts)
- *Social and economic justice*: including the equitable distribution of wealth; rights to clean water/air/soil and food security; universal access to education, health care and economic opportunity; and the elimination of discrimination
- *Democracy, non-violence and peace: including transparency and accountability in governance*; stakeholder education for sustainable living; elimination of corruption, warfare and cruelty to animals; and cultural tolerance.

2.6 The Charter has been adopted by over 2,000 organisations worldwide. For more detail, if you are interested, see: http://www.earthcharter.org.

ISO 26000 Social Responsibility

2.7 The International Standards Organisation is currently working on the development of an International Standard providing guidelines for social responsibility (SR). The guidance standard will be published in 2010 as ISO 26000 and will be voluntary to use: it will not include requirements and will thus not be a certification standard. It will be designed to be usable by non-specialists and organisations of all sizes, in countries at every stage of development. (Watch the CIPS student website for details – or keep an eye on: http://www.iso.org/sr.)

BS 8900: 2006 Guidance for managing sustainable development

2.8 Meanwhile, in 2006 the British Standards Institution launched the BS 8900 Guidelines, designed to help organisations to develop an approach to sustainable development. The guidelines are applicable to all types and sizes of organisation, and are designed to:

- Provide a structured approach to sustainable development by considering the social, environmental and economic impacts of organisational activities

- Help organisations to connect existing technical, social and environmental standards, both formal (eg ISO 14000) and informal (eg Global Reporting Initiative)

- Provide organisations' stakeholders with a useful tool to assess and engage in improving organisational performance

- Contribute to dialogue towards the forthcoming international standard on social responsibility (mentioned above).

3 *Environmental sustainability*

Environmental legislation

3.1 The CIPS Practice Guide on CSR highlights the fact that 'the law is a floor': it represents minimum acceptable standards – not good practice. 'There are in most cases few or no globally-accepted norms on environmental behaviour, and so suppliers, often at several tiers' remove, may be operating perfectly legally but with environmental impacts that would be unacceptable if our representative organisations or companies were creating them.' Nevertheless, there are legal obligations on organisations in several areas, and it will be important for procurement professionals to be aware of them in order to minimise compliance and reputational risk.

3.2 For detailed up-to-date information on UK environment policy, and relevant legislation, you could browse: http://www.defra.gov.uk/environment/policy/index.htm. We will just highlight a few key points here.

- The Environmental Protection Act 1990 (EPA) is the principal legislation controlling waste management in England and Wales. It defines the steps required to ensure that waste is appropriately disposed of; establishes controls on 'nuisance' due to poor air quality, dust, litter, noise or odour; and imposes individual liability for pollution events.

- There are EU Directives (and Regulations implementing them into UK law) around a range of environmental issues: emissions standards for all new road vehicles; the disposal of waste electrical and electronic products (WEEE Regulations 2006); the control of landfill use and waste incineration; the protection of water quality, freshwater fish, and bathing waters; the control of agricultural chemicals; the reduction or elimination of pollution; the protection of habitats; the control of the discharge of dangerous substances; and the safe disposal of batteries.

- The Climate Change Act 2008 gives statutory force to the UK government's targets for cutting GHG emissions by 60% by 2050, and 26–32% by 2020 (on a 1990 baseline), with five year carbon budget periods, in line with its commitments under the Kyoto Protocol.

- The Energy Bill 2008 drills down into some of the detail of the Climate Change Act, with the roll-out of a regulatory framework for carbon capture and storage (CCS) projects; incentives for private sector investment into gas and electricity supply security; and targets for generation of energy requirements from renewable resources.

- The Environmental Damage (Prevention and Remediation) Regulations 2009, implementing the Environmental Liability Directive 2004/35/CE): implementing the 'polluter pays' principle, by holding corporate operators whose activities have caused environmental damage financially liable for remedying the damage – with the broader aim of encouraging prevention and precaution. 'Environmental damage' is defined as damage to protected species, natural habitats and sites of special scientific interest; damage to water; and land damage. Operators are required to take immediate steps to prevent further damage, and to notify the enforcing authorities.

3.3 The Environment Agency in the UK has the responsibility of regulating business and industry: implementing EU directives, issuing permits, monitoring compliance and carrying out risk assessments. There are five basic approaches to regulation.

- Direct regulation: enforcing legislation, and issuing permits, which typically set limits and targets, and require operators to carry out management processes

- Environmental (or 'polluter pays') taxes, such as the Landfill Tax or Climate Change Levy

- Offset or trading schemes, such as the EU Emissions Trading Scheme (for greenhouse gases) and the Landfill Allowances Trading Scheme. Participants can choose either to operate within their allowance (eg by reducing emissions or resource use), or buy extra allowances in the market to offset any excess: they can also sell surplus allowances if they perform better than expected.

- Voluntary or negotiated agreements, jointly agreed by businesses (usually to avoid the threat of legislation or compulsory regulation). The motor industry, for example, has a voluntary agreement with the EU on emission reduction targets, and other agreements are in force in the chemical industry and agricultural sector (on the use of pesticides).

- Education and advice: the promotion of regulatory requirements, risk assessment consultancy, and showcasing emerging issues and successful initiatives.

The Kyoto Protocol

3.4 The Kyoto Protocol is an international agreement linked to the United Nations Framework Convention on Climate Change. The major feature of the Kyoto Protocol is that it sets binding targets for 37 industrialised countries and the European community for reducing greenhouse gas (GHG) emissions.

3.5 Recognizing that developed countries are principally responsible for the current high levels of GHG emissions in the atmosphere as a result of more than 150 years of industrial activity, the Protocol places a heavier burden on developed nations under the principle of 'common but differentiated responsibilities' – although initiatives to co-opt countries like China and India to the climate change agenda are ongoing.

3.6 Under the treaty, signatory countries must meet their targets primarily through national measures. However, the Kyoto Protocol offers them an additional means of meeting their targets by way of three market-based mechanisms for 'offsetting' emission: emissions trading ('the carbon market'); the clean development mechanism (CDM), supporting emissions reduction programmes in developing countries; and joint implementation (JI), supportive programmes for collaborative emissions reduction and removal.

3.7 The Kyoto Protocol is generally seen as an important first step towards a truly global emission reduction regime that will stabilise GHG emissions, and provides the essential architecture for any future international agreement on climate change. It pursues emissions cuts in a wide range of economic sectors. The Protocol encourages governments to cooperate with one another, improve energy efficiency, reform the energy and transportation sectors, promote renewable forms of energy, phase out inappropriate fiscal measures and market imperfections, limit methane emissions from waste management and energy systems, and protect forests and other carbon 'sinks'.

3.8   The USA is the only developed country not to ratify the Kyoto treaty, but debate continues to rage about the usefulness of the protocol and the impact of reducing emissions on national economies and employment.

ISO 14001 environmental management system standard

3.9   Launched in 1996, ISO 14000 is a series of international standards on the design, implementation and control of environmental management systems (EMS). An EMS gives an organisation a systematic approach for assessing and managing its impact on the environment: the environmental consequences of its operations. The standard is designed to provide a framework for developing such a system, as well as a supporting audit and review programme.

3.10   The major requirements for an EMS under ISO 14001 include the following.

- An environmental policy statement which includes commitments to: prevention of pollution; continual improvement of the EMS leading to improvements in overall environmental performance; and compliance with all relevant legal and regulatory requirements
- Identification of all aspects of the organisation's activities, products and services that could have a significant impact on the environment (whether or not regulated): focusing on environmental aspects that are within the organisation's control or ability to influence
- Establishing performance objectives and targets for the EMS, taking into account legal requirements and organisational policy commitments and information about significant environmental protection issues
- Implementing an EMS to meet these objectives and targets, including: training of employees, establishing work instructions and practices, establishing performance metrics and so on
- Establishing a programme for periodic auditing and review of environmental performance against the environmental policy and legal/regulatory framework
- Taking corrective and preventive actions when deviations from the EMS are identified
- Undertaking periodic reviews of the EMS by top management to ensure its continuing performance and adequacy in the face of changing environmental information.

3.11   An organisation can make a self-assessment and self-declaration, or be audited and certified by a third party, if desired, to demonstrate compliance to customers, clients and regulatory bodies. Benefits claimed for an EMS based on ISO 14001 by various Environmental Protection Agencies include:

- Improvements in compliance and reduced costs of non-compliance; improvements in overall environmental performance
- Enhanced predictability and consistency in managing environmental obligations
- Increased efficiency and potential cost savings when managing environmental obligations
- Enhanced reputation and relationship with internal and external stakeholders.

ISO 14023/25 eco-labelling standards

3.12   The ISO 14020+ standard provides principles and protocols for third party labelling based on environmental criteria. Different categories of eco-labels are required to meet different criteria.

- Type 1 eco-labels ('seal of approval') must have third party certification on multiple criteria (with lifecycle consideration), awarded to the best environmental performers. As an example, the European Union 'flower' is a label that aims to encourage businesses to market greener products in order to increase their market share. This voluntary program helps public and private consumers identify officially approved green products across the EU.

- Type 2 eco-labels are self-declared by suppliers (eg 'made of x% recycled material'). The standard provides guidance on the terminology, symbols, testing and verification methodologies.

- Type 3 eco-labels embody environmental claims giving quantified product information based on a full lifecycle analysis. The standard requires third party certification, quantitative information and multiple attributes with lifecycle consideration. Car companies such as BMW and Volvo are currently leading the way in this area.

3.13   For more information on ISO 14001, and environmental management in general, if you are interested, you might like to browse:

- http://www.environment-agency.gov.uk   The UK Environment Agency
- http:/www.eea.europa.eu   The European Environment Agency

The European Eco-Management and Audit Scheme (EMAS)

3.14   The European Eco-Management and Audit Scheme (EMAS) is a voluntary EMS certification process created under European Community regulations. Certification under EMAS can be obtained by an organisation or site which has an ISO 14001 certification and, in addition:

- Issues a public, externally verified report on its environmental performance
- Has a verified environmental audit programme in place
- Has no apparent failures of regulatory compliance.

PAS 2050

3.15   Publicly Available Specification (PAS) 2050 was launched in 2008 by the British Standards Institution (BSI). It builds on existing methods established through ISO 14040/14044, by specifying requirements for the assessment of greenhouse gas (GHG) emissions arising from products across their lifecycle, from initial sourcing of raw materials through manufacture, transport, use and ultimately recycling or waste.

3.16   The standard is designed to help organisations and consumers to understand the 'carbon footprint' of goods and services, and may also be used for a variety of processes for analysing, improving, comparing and communicating the emissions carbon footprint performance of products and services. For organisations, PS 2050:

- Supports internal assessment of the life cycle GHG emissions of their goods and services
- Facilitates the evaluation of alternative product designs, sourcing and manufacturing methods, raw material choices and supplier selection, on the basis of GHG emissions

- Provides a benchmark for programmes aimed at reducing GHG emissions
- Allows for comparison of goods or services on the basis of GHG emissions
- Supports reporting (and promotion) on corporate social and environmental responsibility.

3.17 If you are interested, you can download a copy of PAS 2050 from the Carbon Trust, Defra or the BSI:

- http://www.bsigroup.com/en/Standards-and-Publications/Industry-Sectors/Energy/PAS-2050

4 Social sustainability and ethics

4.1 You should encounter a range of workforce or employment legislation in your studies for *Management in the Purchasing Function*. Some of the key statutes in the UK are highlighted here. Bear in mind that sustainable procurement means not only contributing to compliant policies and practices in one's own organisation – but assessing, supporting and enforcing compliance throughout the supply chain, in the interests of reputational and compliance risk management (as well as ethical principle).

Equal opportunity law

4.2 A range of legislation is in force (and being constantly amended and updated) in the area of equal opportunity and discrimination. 'Equal opportunity' in an employment context means that everyone has a fair chance of getting a job, accessing training and benefits and competing for promotion, regardless of individual differences or minority status. It is, effectively, non- or anti-discrimination. Key legislation on discrimination covers:

- Equal pay (Equal Pay Act1970 and Amendment Regulations 1984, implementing the EU Equal Pay Directive): the right of women to claim equal pay and conditions as men, for work of equal value (as determined by job evaluation).
- Equal opportunity, outlawing direct and indirect discrimination and harassment on grounds of: sex (including marital status), race (race, colour, national or ethnic origins), religion and belief, sexual orientation, disability – and, most recently, age. The main provisions are found in the Sex Discrimination Acts, Racial Discrimination Acts, the Disability Discrimination Act, and various Equality in Employment Regulations. The Equality Act 2006 created a new Commission for Equality and Human Rights (CEHR) to promote equality and tackle discrimination in all areas.

Health and safety law

4.3 Another heavily legislated area is health and safety at work. You should be aware of employers' obligations under the following regulations.

- The Health and Safety at Work Act 1974, under which every employer has a general duty to ensure the health, safety and welfare at work of all employees, so far as is reasonably practicable. This includes provisions for: safe systems and work practices; providing a safe and healthy work environment; maintaining plant and equipment to a necessary standard of safety; supporting safe working practices with information, instruction, training and supervision; consulting with safety representatives appointed by a recognised trade union; and communicating safety policy and measures to all staff, clearly and in writing.

- A range of specific regulations implementing EU directives on health and safety, including: the Workplace (Health, Safety and Welfare) Regulations 1992; the Control of Substances Hazardous to Health (COSHH) Regulations 1994; and the Management of Health and Safety at Work Regulations 1999 (which provides for health and safety risk assessment and management).

4.4 Other regulations cover particular safety and health risks in the workplace, and in particular industries: guidelines are available from the Health and Safety Executive.

Employment rights law

4.5 There is a wide-ranging body of law implementing EU Directives on issues such as: employment protection (protection from unfair dismissal, redundancy and change of terms on transfer of undertaking); working hours and rights to request flexible working arrangements (for parents and carers); procedures for the resolution of workplace disputes; equal treatment of fixed-contract and part-time workers; rights to maternal/parental leave and benefits; and worker rights to information, consultation and structures for industrial democracy (eg European Works Councils in transnational firms).

4.6 We would hope that the detail of such legislation (Employment Act 2002, TUPE Regulations 2006, various Employment Rights Acts) is beyond the scope of this syllabus — but watch the CIPS student website for updates, as further exam questions are set on this area.

International Labour Organisation (ILO) standards

4.7 The ILO is the UN's specialised agency promoting human, civil and labour rights. It develops consensus documents (Conventions), and less formal codes of conduct, resolutions and declarations (Recommendations). These have included the *Declaration of Principles Concerning Multinational Enterprises and Social Policy* ('The MNE Declaration'), on the contribution of multinational enterprises to economic and social progress, and how to minimise and resolve problems arising from their actions. The ILO has also issued *Guidelines on Occupational Health and Safety Management Systems*, among other matters.

4.8 The MNE declaration makes recommendations for: general sustainable development and compliance policies; employment (increasing employment opportunities and standards, building links with local supply chains, and promoting equal opportunity, employment security and fair treatment); training (encouraging skill development); work/life conditions (providing equitable and competitive remuneration, benefits and conditions, recognising the need for work/life balance, respecting minimum employment ages, and maintaining high standards of health and safety); and industrial relations (respecting freedom of association, collective bargaining and representation, and allowing for consultation and fair grievance/dispute procedures).

4.9 The general aims and objectives of the ILO illustrate their sustainability concerns: Table 11.1. If you are interested, you can find out more at http:/www.ilo.org.

Social Accountability (SA) 8000 Standard

4.10 SA 8000 (administered by Social Accountability International) is both:

- A management system standard for addressing workplace conditions and independently verifying factory compliance (based on ISO standards) and
- A code of conduct for workplace conditions and labour rights (based on various ILO and UN documents).

4.11 It addresses management and reporting requirements on areas such as: child labour, forced labour, health and safety, freedom of association, collective bargaining rights, discrimination, working hours and compensation, and discipline and grievance procedures. Companies endorsing the standard, and/or seeking certification under it, must select suppliers and contractors based on their ability to meet the SA 8000 standards, and require by contract that they do so. Hundreds of facilities have been certified under the scheme so far, mainly in the clothing, textile and chemical industries in China, India, Brazil and Vietnam (Blackburn).

Table 11.1 *Objectives of the ILO*

Objective	Comment
Decent work for all	Decent work considers the aspirations of people in their working lives, such as their aspirations for opportunity and income; rights, voice and recognition; family stability and personal development; and fairness and gender equality
Employment creation	The ILO identifies policies that help create and maintain decent work and income. These policies are formulated in a comprehensive Global Employment Agenda
Fair globalisation	Globalisation has its supporters and detractors. On one hand it enables global economic growth while on the other it can be said to exploit some of the poorest in society. This lack of consensus makes it harder to develop policies at national and international levels. The ILO seeks ways of ensuring that the benefits of globalisation reach more people
Rights at work	The ILO identifies four fundamental principles relating to workers' rights: freedom of association; elimination of forced labour; elimination of discrimination; and elimination of child labour
Social dialogue	The ILO defines social dialogue to include all types of negotiation, consultation and exchange of information between, or among, representatives of governments, employers and workers on issues of common interest
Social protection	Access to an adequate level of social protection in the form of medical cover, social security payments etc, is recognised by international labour standards and the UN as a basic right of all individuals. It is also widely considered to be instrumental in promoting human welfare and social consensus on a broad scale, and to be conducive to and indispensable for social peace and thus improved economic growth and performance
Working out of poverty	People should have the ability to improve their situation not only in terms of income but also in terms of respect, dignity and communication. Improvements in these areas will lead to economic, social and political empowerment

Fair Trade standards

4.12 The International Fair Trade Association (IFAT) prescribes standards that Fair Trade organisations must follow in their day-to-day work and carries out continuous monitoring to ensure these standards are upheld: Table 11.2.

Table 11.2 *IFA Fair Trade standards*

Standard	Comment
Creating opportunities for economically disadvantaged producers	Fair Trade is seen as a strategy for poverty alleviation and sustainable development. Its purpose is to create opportunities for producers who have been economically disadvantaged or marginalised by the conventional trading system
Integrity	Transparency and accountability in dealings with trading partners
Capacity building	To develop producers' independence by providing continuity, during which producers and their marketing organisations can improve their skills and access new markets
Promotion	Promoting Fair Trade using honest adverting and marketing techniques
Fair payment	Pay a fair price which covers not only the cost of production but enables production that is just and sound and takes into account the principle of equal pay for equal work by men and women
Gender equity	Women are appropriately paid for their labour and are empowered in their organisations
Working conditions	Provision of a safe and healthy working environment for producers
Children's rights	Fair Trade Organisations respect the UN Convention on the Rights of the Child as well as local laws and social norms
The environment	Fair Trade actively encourages better environmental practices and the application of responsible methods of production
Trade relations	Trading with concern for ongoing social, economic and environmental wellbeing.

The Ethical Trading Initiative (ETI)

4.13 The ETI is an alliance of companies, NGOs and trade union organisations committed to working together to identify and promote internationally-agreed principles of ethical trade and employment, and to monitor and independently verify the observance of ethics code provisions.

4.14 The ETI publishes a code of labour practice (the 'base code') giving guidance on fundamental principles of ethical labour practices, based on international standards. These principles should by now be familiar.

1   Employment is freely chosen
2   Freedom of association and the right to collective bargaining are respected
3   Working conditions are safe and hygienic
4   Child labour shall not be used
5   Living wages are paid
6   Working hours are not excessive
7   No discrimination is practised
8   Regular employment is provided
9   No harsh or inhumane treatment is allowed.

4.15 CIPS affirms that 'ethical supply chain management is one of the greatest challenges facing organisations. It is becoming unacceptable for organisations to be unaware of how the workers involved in making their products or supplying their services are treated. The global nature of trade often leads to complexity within the supply chain; this alone can make ethical trading a daunting task in itself' (Practice Guide on CSR).

5 *Economic sustainability and governance*

EU public procurement directives 2004/17/EC and 2004/18/EC

5.1 Public procurement contracts constitute a significant percentage of the EU's gross domestic product (16 %).

- Directive 2004/17/EC covers the procurement procedures of entities operating in the water, energy, transport and postal services sector.

- Directive 2004/18/EC (the Consolidated Directive) covers procedures for the award of public works contracts, public supply contracts, and public service contracts, bringing together three previous directives on public sector procurement (supplies, works and services).

5.2 The directives were enacted into UK law in the Public Contracts Regulations 2006. We have covered their main provisions – including specific implications for sustainable procurement – in Chapter 10.

The corporate governance framework

5.3 Corporate governance is 'the system by which organisations are directed and controlled' (*Cadbury Report*). It provides a framework for an organisation to pursue its strategies in an ethical and effective way from the perspective of all key stakeholder groups, and particularly addresses the need to ensure that directors use their power in the interests of shareholders, as agents appointed to run the business on their behalf. The CIPS Practice Guide on CSR highlights the fact that: 'Good corporate governance – in essence, the integrity with which a company is managed – is a central component of a robust CSR management programme.'

5.4 In the UK:

- The Cadbury Committee made recommendations and created a Code of Best Practice, based on openness, integrity and accountability, in a number of areas, including: the role of the board of directors; division of responsibilities at the head of a company; the role of independent non-executive directors; and remuneration of executive directors.

- The Greenbury Committee considered the issue of rewarding executive directors, and made recommendations to improve transparency and performance, including: a remuneration committee of non-executive directors; reporting on remuneration policy in annual accounts; and performance-related incentive schemes which balance the interests of directors and shareholders.

- The recommendations of Cadbury and Greenbury were merged into a Combined Code in 1998, with which companies listed on the London Stock Exchange are required to comply.

5.5 In the USA, a number of damaging corporate scandals (eg Enron and Worldcom) prompted legislation on financial and accounting disclosures, in the form of the Sarbanes-Oxley Act 2002 (SOX). The Act imposes provisions on all US public company boards, management and public accounting firms – but it also carries weight outside the USA as a model code in this area.

5.6   SOX contains extensive requirements aimed at preventing conflicts of interest, assuring the integrity of internal controls, and enhancing transparency in regard to corporate financial matters.

*   Internal controls must assure that any information material to financial performance is made known to the CEO and CFO, who must in turn certify to investors that the controls meet statutory criteria and that the financial reports fairly represent the company's position. An independent auditor approved by an audit committee of independent directors must attest to these statements.

*   The audit committee is also required to oversee controls, and establish financial risk management and assessment policies (including sustainability-related risks), in order to protect economic performance and sustainability.

5.7   The CIPS Knowledge Works document *Sarbanes-Oxley Act 2002* argues that SOX may affect procurement professionals dealing with US suppliers or subsidiaries, or seconded to US jurisdictions, or associated with non-US companies who are listed on US markets such as the New York Stock Exchange or NASDAQ. The document draws purchasers' attention to:

*   Section 401 concerning periodic disclosure of all transactions, arrangements, obligations and relationships which may affect financial conditions, revenues or expenses

*   Section 404, which requires annual reports to state the responsibility of management for establishing and maintaining an adequate internal control structure and procedures for financial reporting, and to contain an assessment of their effectiveness.

ISO 15686 Service life planning (whole-life costing) standards

5.8   ISO 15686 (2008) is a standard that addresses 'service life planning' of buildings and constructed assets (such as buildings and tunnels). Service life planning 'addresses the design of a structure or building with a view to its operation through its whole life. It means looking at long-term performance and overall operating stage and earlier, enabling the design to be tailored to meet client's long-term needs'.

5.9   Service life assessment is the consideration of service life at all stages of the construction process, from development of the client brief, through the design and construction phases, into operation of the asset itself. It represents:

*   A structured, traceable method to manage the risks in construction procurement

*   A mechanism for information management allowing the parties involved to learn from best practice and poor performance

*   A system to demonstrate value for money in construction procurement

*   A method to assess the implications of variations during a project and mitigate the impact of such variations.

5.10   The standard represents the first international standard for building lifecycle costing. It is anticipated that it will impact on two particular areas.

*   The design of new buildings, as builders and clients look to set the right budgets and optimise their lifecycle costs from both a whole life costing and sustainable development perspective

*   Major construction projects: in particular those involving high investment such as the Private Finance Initiative (PFI) and Public-Private Partnership.

It will primarily be used by purchasers of buildings and constructions, designers, construction companies and their suppliers, and facility operators.

5.11 Whole-life costing (lifecycle costing or through-life costing) is one form of analysis that can be used for determining whether a project meets stated performance requirements. It is defined in the standard as 'economic assessment considering all agreed projected significant and relevant cost flows over a period of analysis, expressed in monetary value. The projected costs are those needed to achieve defined levels of performance, including reliability, safety and availability'.

5.12 Beyond the specific requirements of the standard, whole life costing is recognised as a valuable approach to the sustainable procurement of capital assets with a long usage life.

- The buyer makes assumptions about the level of costs that will arise in each year of the asset's useful life, including the initial purchase price – but also the costs of delivery, installation and commissioning; routine maintenance and periodic overhaul; energy, labour, consumables and other running costs; time lost for breakdowns; disposal costs (which may be negative, if the asset has resale value at the end of its life) and so on.

- At the same time, the buyer attempts to quantify the benefits that will arise from the ownership of the asset – and to allocate them to each year of the asset's useful life.

- Discounted cashflow calculations are used to express costs and benefits, and therefore total costs, in today's values. (Annual costs, in today's values, can also be calculated to allow comparison of assets or proposed asset purchases, even if they have different life spans.)

5.13 The point of calculating whole-life costs is to identify options that cost least (economic sustainability) over the long term – which may not be apparent from the purchase price! It enables realistic budgeting over the life of the asset; highlights, at an early stage, risks associated with the purchase; promotes cross-functional communication on economic sustainability issues; and supports the optimisation of value for money.

Chapter summary

- Legislation relevant to sustainability covers areas such as human rights, employment, corporate and finance law, anti-corruption, competition law, data protection, and the environment.

- In addition to legislation, this area is affected by regulatory codes of practice and benchmark standards.

- In relation to sustainable development, the key regulatory frameworks include the UN Global Compact, the Earth Charter, ISO 26000 on social responsibility, and BS 8900 on managing sustainable development.

- In relation to environmental sustainability, the key regulatory frameworks include national legislation, the Kyoto Protocol, ISO 14001 on environmental management systems, ISO 14023/25 on eco-labelling, EMAS, and PAS 2050.

- In relation to social sustainability and ethics, the key regulatory frameworks include national legislation on equal opportunities, health and safety, and employment rights, ILO standards, SA 8000 on social accountability, the Fair Trade standards, and the Ethical Trading Initiative.

- In relation to economic sustainability and governance, the key regulatory frameworks include the EU public procurement directives, rules on corporate governance such as the London Stock Exchange Combined Code and Sarbanes-Oxley, and ISO 15686 on service life planning.

Self-test questions

Numbers in brackets refer to the paragraphs above where your answers can be checked.

1   Give examples of UK legislation relating to human rights, competition, and the environment. (1.1)

2   Give examples of voluntary codes relating to sustainability. (1.5)

3   What is the UN Global Compact? (2.1)

4   What are the four dimensions covered by the Earth Charter? (2.5)

5   What is the main principle of the UK Environmental Damage Regulations 2009? (3.2)

6   What is the main principle of the Kyoto Protocol? (3.4)

7   What are the major requirements for an EMS under ISO 14001? (3.10)

8   What is the main principle of the UK Health and Safety at Work Act 1974? (4.3)

9   What are the main objectives of the International Labour Organisation? (4.9)

10   What standards are laid down by the International Fair Trade Organisation? (4.12)

11   What are the main requirements of the Sarbanes-Oxley Act? (5.6)

12   What is meant by service life assessment? (5.9)

Further reading

From your 'Essential Reading' list, you might look at Blackburn (*The Sustainability Handbook*):

- Appendix 2: Sustainability-related codes of organisational behaviour

- Appendix 3: Sustainability-related management system standards

CHAPTER 12

Sustainable Contract and Relationship Management

3.3 Evaluate the benefits and risks of sustainable whole-life contract management for purchasing and supply contracts

- A review of contract management factors including: objectives and delivery plans, ongoing contract and relationship management, receipt of products and services, asset management and post-contract 'lessons' management
- Allowing for new sustainable procurement developments and targets within contract and relationship management
- Linking the benefits to organisational performance and success (eg whole-life costing and return on investment)
- The benefits of continuous improvement in sustainable contract management for the supply chain
- The risks and contingencies associated with a sustainable procurement approach to whole-life contract management: long-term supplier relationships; 'preferred' suppliers; public private partnerships (PPPs); private finance initiatives (PFIs)

3.5 Identify and apply appropriate supplier development tools and processes in order to both introduce and improve sustainable procurement within local and global supply chain

- Prioritisation of suppliers and products
- Clear sustainability objectives, targets and requirements
- Gap analysis
- Problem-solving and escalation
- Supply chain communication and co-operation
- Achievable deadlines
- Monitoring improvements

Chapter headings

1   Whole-life contract management

2   Benefits and risks of whole-life-contract management

3   Relationships for sustainable procurement

4   Developing sustainable supply chains

Introduction

In Chapter 9, we looked at the definition and specification of requirements to support sustainable procurement. In Chapter 10, we looked at the 'Acquisition pre-contract' stage of the CIPS Purchasing and Supply Management model: the sourcing cycle from identification of need to creation of contract or relationship, and how sustainability considerations could be built in at each stage.

In this chapter, we go on to look at the next stage of the CIPS model: 'Acquisition post-contract' – that is, everything that happens after the creation of a contract or relationship, through the life of that contract or relationship, up to its termination (or renewal). This has two key aspects: how supplier relationships can be sustainably managed (since this is itself a sustainability issue); and how supplier relationships can be managed and leveraged in support of the organisation's sustainable procurement objectives. In other words, contract and relationship management should both be sustainable and promote sustainability.

We have chosen to group two learning objectives together here, because their subject matter is closely linked. Supplier development tools and processes to introduce and improve sustainable procurement (learning objective 3.5) can be seen as a logical extension, or part of, the process of whole-life contract and relationship management (learning objective 3.6).

While the monitoring and assessment of sustainable procurement capability/performance (learning objective 3.4) may precede a supplier development programme – in order to ascertain what development activity is required – it will also be used in retrospective evaluation (in order to gauge the effectiveness of development activity, and plan ongoing improvements) in an ongoing cycle. We will therefore discuss monitoring and measurement tools in Chapter 13.

1 Whole-life contract management

1.1 The concept of 'whole-life contract management' should not be confused with 'whole-life costing' – although they are related.   Whole-life contract management means that the management of a purchase extends over the whole life of the contract – not just to the end of the purchase-to-pay cycle. The CIPS Purchasing and Supply Management Model emphasises this in its 'Acquisition: post-contract' phase, incorporating:

- Contract and relationship management
- Receipt of product/service
- Asset management and
- Post-contract 'lessons' management.

We will review these stages, as suggested by the syllabus, in the light of sustainable procurement issues.

1.2 In the context of capital asset purchases and ongoing service or outsourcing contracts, however, whole-life contract management assumes more radical dimensions.

- The management of a purchase extends over the whole life of the contract – and in the cradle-to-grave orientation of sustainable procurement, this will often mean 'over the whole life of the asset'.

- A supply contract may therefore cover life-time requirements for the management of the asset: including services such as ongoing maintenance, repair, upgrade, take-back and end-of-life disposal. (Note also that these services are directly contributory to the sustainability of the asset.)

- Such contracts imply a long-term relationship with the contracted supplier, within which there will need to be ongoing supplier management and development, and collaborative, continuous innovation-, improvement- and efficiency-seeking activity over time.

1.3 We will look at the benefits and risks of such a thorough-going approach to sustainable contract management in Section 2 of this chapter. First, let's review the phases of post-contract acquisition management for any type or duration of contract.

Objectives and delivery plans

1.4 Contract management is, initially, concerned with ensuring that a given contract is performed to the required standard, meeting the specifications, terms and conditions agreed between the buyer and the supplier. For a simple purchase contract, this may take the form of expediting: taking planned steps to ensure that suppliers are able and on schedule to deliver as agreed in the supply contract.

1.5 The first requirement for this process is therefore to have a clear idea of what the buyer is expecting, against which to measure the supplier's progress and performance. These expectations should be clearly set out in:

- A purchase order or supply contract, which will include terms and conditions of purchase, and should also refer to relevant specifications, service level agreements and any other schedules and appendices defining exactly what is to be undertaken or provided by the supplier – including all environmental and social sustainability criteria (as discussed in Chapters 9 and 10)
- A delivery plan, based on these documents, setting out time-phased expectations for what will be delivered (including key conformance criteria), where and when. This schedule will be used as the basis of expediting, goods inwards planning, inspection/testing and acceptance of the delivery, user/customer information – and subsequent evaluation of supplier performance.

Ongoing contract and relationship management

1.6 Contracts for the supply of goods or services may be much more complex, and longer in duration, than a simple purchase order. Once contracts are signed, therefore, it is not as simple as saying: 'The supplier will now do that'. There will be obligations to be followed up on either side. If contingencies arise, the contract may (or may not) lay down what happens next. If the supplier's performance falls short in any way, there will be a variety of options for pursuing the matter. Circumstances and requirements may change (for example, as new sustainability issues emerge, or as continuous improvements are sought), and contract terms may have to be adjusted accordingly. This is an ongoing process through the life of the contract – which is where contract management comes in.

1.7 Contract management is the process designed to ensure that both parties to a contract meet their obligations, and that the intended outcomes of a contract are delivered. It also involves building and maintaining a good working relationship between the buyer and supplier, continuing through the life of a contract. The term 'contract management' suggests that the focus of attention is on the performance of particular contracts: the term 'relationship management' is often used to describe the management of an ongoing relationship with a supplier, beyond the performance of individual transactions.

1.8 Key aspects of contract management are shown in Table 12.1.

Allowing for new developments and targets

1.9 It is worth highlighting the need for flexibility in the purchase contract or relationship agreement, to allow for new developments in sustainable procurement, and ongoing targets for improvement, to be incorporated over time.

Table 12.1 *Key activities in contract management*

Contract development	Contract negotiation should support ongoing contract management by: • Clearly identifying both parties' rights and obligations, and working methods • Recognising the need for flexibility to absorb changes to the contract over the contract/relationship period (eg as new sustainability issues emerge, or new improvement commitments are set). It should be clearly indicated (eg in a changes, alterations and variations clause), how these will be agreed, incorporated and communicated.
Contract communication	Copies of contract document and delivery plans (and notification of any changes, as they are incorporated) should be distributed to those involved with managing them on a day-to-day basis.
Contract administration	Implementing procedures to ensure that contract obligations are fulfilled. This may include procedures for: • Contract maintenance, updating and change control: ensuring that changes to the contract are agreed, authorised, accurately documented and implemented by both parties, and ensuring that all versions and related documents (such as budgets and service level agreements) are consistent • Budgeting and costs/charges monitoring • Purchase-to-pay procedures • Management reporting • Management of contract disputes
Managing contract performance	• *Risk management*: collaborating with users and suppliers to identify potential risks or barriers to performance, so that they can be managed or mitigated • *Performance monitoring and measurement.* SLAs and KPIs including social and environmental measures may be used to express the desired outputs from the contract. These documents will form an operational tool (usually more flexible than the contract itself) with which buyer- and supplier-side contract managers can monitor performance on a day-to-day basis. • *Continuous improvement planning.* Buyer and supplier may work collaboratively over the life of the contract to set year-on-year improvement targets, solve performance issues, identify emerging opportunities and so on. The contract may need to be revised to reflect new targets and agreements – or may make a general provision for improvement planning. • *Supplier motivation*: incentives and rewards for performance, added value, suggestions or improvements on sustainability. These may take the form of contract extension, preferred supplier status, supplier awards or gain-sharing, for example. Sanctions and penalties may also be used for non-compliance, and will form part of a performance management process. • *Performance management*: problem-solving and corrective action in the event of progress or performance shortfalls; pursuing dispute resolution procedures (as set out in the contract); pursuing remedies to mitigate loss/damage as a result of breach of contract or non-compliance.
Contract review	Buyer- and supplier-side contract managers should meet periodically to review performance and delivery of contract outputs. There may be regular issues to discuss (eg customer feedback, a complaints log or risk analysis), while other agenda items will relate to performance and sustainability issues arising during the review period.

Relationship management	Developing the working relationship between the purchaser and supplier, through regular contacts, communication and information sharing; developing and applying supplier incentives; managing and resolving conflicts; developing approaches to collaboration and mutual support (including supplier assistance or development); and moving towards deeper and more strategic relationships (eg preferred/sole supplier or partnership) where appropriate.

1.10 New sustainability issues, risks or opportunities may emerge, which buyer or supplier (or both) may wish to take account of in the supply contract or relationship. For example, one or both parties may introduce or revise CSR or sustainability policies. New technologies or alternative resources may be developed, offering solutions to sustainability challenges – or opportunities for green product development and marketing. Provisions for periodic contract review and the negotiation of adjusted terms should be built into contracts and service level agreements. The willingness of a supplier to agree to such flexibility may be an important consideration in contract award.

1.11 The buyer or supplier (or both) may wish to establish commitments and targets for continuous improvement – and related supplier development – in sustainability performance, within defined planning and review periods (eg year on year).

- Specific year-on-year improvement targets may be agreed at the contract stage: eg annual percentage reductions in carbon emissions or waste to landfill, or attainment of ISO 14001 over a defined period.

- Alternatively, commitment to continuous improvement may be embedded in the initial contract. Details of moving targets (and the commitment of resources to support them) can then be negotiated and formulated in separate continuous improvement agreements for each planning period. This approach may respond more flexibly to emerging sustainability issues, the pace of innovation, resource availability and so on.

1.12 Another key issue is that, acknowledging that sustainability issues and targets will change, the buyer will need to take into account the supplier's potential for future development, innovation and improvement (in terms of capacity, and learning, innovation and change management capabilities), when selecting suppliers for long-term contracts or relationships. The ability to fulfil today's requirements is less important, in a sustainable procurement orientation, than the ability to fulfil tomorrow's requirements.

Receipt of products or services

1.13 The focus of sustainable procurement in relation to the delivery of products, or performance of services, under the contract will mainly be the assurance of conformance with requirement – since sustainability factors will have been built into specifications and service level agreements.

1.14 The trend towards quality assurance and total quality management has shifted the responsibility for quality management up-stream: buying organisations generally require their suppliers to have quality management systems in place, (perhaps certified under the ISO 9000 quality management standards), so that delivered products have already been process-controlled and inspected for conformance. However, products may still be inspected or tested by the buyer on delivery (on a random sample basis), to ensure conformance with key specified criteria (including high-risk sustainability attributes). Similarly, products and services will be monitored and evaluated by users on consumption, so that non-conformance can be identified, rectified or fed back to the supplier for improvement, on an ongoing basis if necessary.

1.15 If conformance issues are not immediately identified and dealt with, sustainability problems may escalate, in terms of disruption to production; non-conforming items reaching end customers (with attendant commercial, financial and reputational damage); non-conforming items causing environmental damage or health and safety concerns; supplier complacency on future conformance issues; and the 'failure costs' of all these problems (lost sales, refunds, compensation claims, rectification costs, reputational damage and so on). High profile examples include Mattel's massive product recall of toys manufactured under contract in China, which were found to contain toxic lead paint (expressly excluded by their product specifications), responsible for incidents of ill-health in children.

1.16 Delivery schedules are also relevant to sustainable procurement for several reasons. Firstly, economic sustainability is promoted by eliminating the need for expediting ('delivery chasing'), which is a non-value-adding waste activity. Realistic lead times and deadlines should be built into the contract, and supplier delivery performance and planning systems should be assured. Sustainability in supplier relationships (and therefore potentially in the security of supply) is also promoted by realistic scheduling and an avoidance of micro-management and adversarial expediting: the buyer should be aiming to attain or maintain attractive customer status with suppliers. However, late delivery by a supplier may impact on service to the end customer, creating business and reputational risk, and measures must be put in place for delivery assurance and control.

Asset management

1.17 The cradle-to-grave orientation of sustainable procurement argues that provision should be made for the ongoing management of capital assets, once sourced and acquired, for the duration of their lifecycle. Such assets may include buildings, plant and equipment, IT systems and vehicles. Once acquired, they may require installation, set-up and commissioning; maintenance, repair and servicing; periodic overhaul, upgrading or modification; the supply of consumables; documentation and user training; and end-of-life de-commissioning and disposal.

1.18 While the organisation may apportion these tasks to a variety of suppliers, as part of an asset management plan, a number of them may be built into purchase specifications and contracts with the supplier of the asset, ensuring continuity of supply (eg of spare parts and consumables); continuity of expertise and development; compatible upgrades and modifications (eg of computer software); and protection of co-investment (eg in public-private partnerships to manage major infrastructure assets). We will discuss the benefits and risks of such an approach later in this chapter.

1.19 A particular impetus has been given to whole-life contracting by end-of-life issues, and the need to dispose of assets responsibly at the end of their useful lives. Provisions should be made in the purchase specification and contract for supplier contribution in areas such as: instructions and labelling on safe disposal (eg the marking of recyclable materials); design for disassembly, and recycling; and take-back for disposal. The onus is placed on suppliers in such areas as the automotive industry (by the European End of Life Vehicles Directive) and the electronics industry (by the Waste Electrical and Electronic Equipment Directive).

Exit strategy

1.20 As part of the risk assessment of a contract, it is important to identify where early contract exit or termination may be required, and how this will be managed. This is not mentioned by the syllabus, but it is an issue relevant to ethical contract management – and to economic sustainability, because the buying organisation cannot afford to get 'trapped' in contracts or long-term relationships with under-performing or incompatible suppliers.

1.21 There should be a clear understanding of the circumstances in which a contract can be terminated (other than those mandated by contract law, such as breach or frustration of contract), what processes should be followed, and what notice given. Ideally, there should also be provision for review, feedback and learning from the 'failure' of the contract – and for keeping the door open to future relations, where possible (eg with clear parameters for the changes and improvements required).

1.22 In a sustainable procurement context, particular consideration will have to be given to the social and economic impacts of termination of contract on dependent suppliers, and their workforces and communities. CSR policies may address areas such as the discouragement of supplier dependency, phased withdrawal and performance management procedures and options to be explored prior to termination.

Post-contract 'lessons' management

1.23 As we saw in Chapter 8, sustainable procurement programmes should contain provision for review and the planning of continuous improvement. There is an important opportunity for this activity in the immediate post-contract period, or post-completion review phase of a procurement project.

1.24 The contract management and/or sustainability team (or a multi-disciplinary review team comprising both) should intentionally review the contract's history and outcomes, and gather feedback from a range of contract/sustainability stakeholders on what went right and what went wrong in the life and performance of the contract; how things could have been done more effectively or efficiently; and what new knowledge or lessons have emerged from the contract and should be carried forward to future contracts and contracting processes.

1.25 A post-completion audit is often used as a formal review of a procurement, outsourcing or sustainability project, in order to assess its impact and ensure that any lessons arising from it are acknowledged and learned. Such an audit may be carried out using a survey questionnaire of all project team members and key stakeholders, or meetings to discuss what went well and what didn't. The focus will be on assessing:

- Whether and how far the project outcomes met the expectations of the sponsor and other stakeholders: were the deliverables up to standard, were sustainability objectives achieved, and were they on time and within budget?

- The effectiveness of the management of the process: the plans and structures set up for the project (eg sustainability improvement task forces); the performance of individuals and teams; what problems (communication lapses, conflicts etc) might affect similar projects in future – and how they can be avoided.

- What ongoing risks, challenges, conflicts, trade-offs and barriers to sustainable procurement emerged during the project, and what solutions, improvements, steps forward or potential future opportunities (if any) could be identified.

2 Benefits and risks of whole-life contract management

2.1 The *CIPS Knowledge Works Guide to Contract Management* links contract management and sustainability: 'Organisations in both the public and private sectors are facing increasing pressure to reduce costs and improve financial and operational performance. New regulatory requirements, globalisation, increases in contract volumes and complexity have resulted in an increasing recognition of the importance and benefits of effective contract management'.

2.2   The benefits of effective contract management in general are as follows.

- Better control by the buyer over the execution of a contract.
- Maintaining communication with the supplier during the course of the contract, and helping to achieve better performance of the contract by the supplier.
- Possibly, improvements in cost and quality, thereby adding value.
- The ability to anticipate and foresee problems early, and deal with them before they become serious.

2.3   There are particular benefits, however, to applying a whole-life approach to contract management – particularly in regard to long-lived capital assets and ongoing service contracts – in the way described earlier. The syllabus only mentions three specific benefits, but we will briefly evaluate a range of potential value-adding gains which might be cited as part of a business case.

Risk management

2.4   Defining requirements over the whole life of an asset, and integrating those requirements into a whole-life supply contract, helps to identify and manage key sources of risk. For example:

- The supplier may guarantee the ongoing availability of proprietary spare parts and consumables over the life of the asset
- The contract will offer continuity of expertise, knowledge, learning and improvement in the servicing, maintenance and upgrading of the asset. The benefits of familiarity, learning and development might otherwise be lost, if other suppliers are contracted to perform these services
- The supplier is more likely to ensure the compatibility of upgrades and modifications with earlier versions and existing systems (eg in the case of IT hardware or software), minimising technology risk from incompatibility
- Familiarity, relationship development and a performance track-record over time build trust, which reduces the effort and resources required for continual risk assessment – and supports flexibility, goodwill and resilience if and when contingencies happen
- The reliable, planned servicing and maintenance of plant, machinery and vehicles minimises technology, operational and compliance risks associated with failure. It may also help to avoid economic, environmental and social impacts, including early failure/replacement, energy wastage, pollution/emissions/leakages and accidents.

Economic/cost benefits

2.5   There are considerable economic and cost-related benefits available from whole-life contract management, which can support financial performance and shareholder value. For example:

- An integrated whole-life supply contract reduces supplier selection, tendering and transaction costs over the life of the asset. Learning curve factors should also mean that long-term supply relationships are more cost effective over time, as familiarity and learning increase supplier productivity. The integration of systems may also be possible (eg using EDI or collaborative planning), offering further efficiencies and reductions in transaction costs.
- Running, maintenance, disposal and other lifecycle costs can be accurately forecast, with the help of the supplier, in support of whole-life costing. This will be discussed further below, but as we saw in Chapter 11, whole-life costing enables sound investment appraisal/comparison and risk assessment, taking into account total costs of acquisition and ownership.

- Whole-life asset management and lifecycle extension (eg by maintenance and upgrading) enable the organisation to secure better asset performance – and therefore a better return on investment. Especially in times of recessionary pressure, it is important that capital assets perform to their potential in terms of productivity, useful life, re-sale value and so on: managed maintenance, repair, upgrade and disposal support this enhanced performance.

Relationship leverage

2.6 Whole-life contract management leverages the value-adding potential of supply relationships. We will discuss the benefits and risks of long-term relationships in the next section of this chapter, but here are some examples.

- The lifetime value of a whole-life contract to a supplier may act as an incentive to commit to value-adding offerings: extended warranties, continuous improvement, integration of systems (eg investment in EDI or collaborative demand and capacity planning), upgrades and so on.

- The development of trust and information-sharing over time often leads to synergistic gains: best-practice sharing, collaborative improvements or cost reduction programmes, co-investment in business development and so on.

- The buying organisation may benefit increasingly, with relationship development, from the knowledge, expertise, technology, resources and goodwill of the supplier in areas contributing to sustainability objectives: innovation, early supplier involvement in product development, flexibility in the face of contingencies, and so on.

- The buying organisation may gain reputational benefit from long-term association with a supplier with a strong sustainability/CSR reputation and brand.

- The buyer may be able to secure competitive advantage by establishing preferential or sole supply arrangements with long-term contracted suppliers who have core (value-adding, distinctive, hard to replicate) sustainability competencies and resources.

- Whole-life costing and contract management may also add value to relationships within the organisation, by encouraging cross-functional collaboration in appraisal of requirements, issues, risks and costs – rather than sub-optimal decisions by procurement, operations, maintenance, finance and so on.

Continuous improvement

2.7 Whole-life contract management may contribute to continuous improvement by virtue of increased mutual commitment, familiarity with each other's capabilities and requirements, and year-on-year learning and adaptation. However, it also lends itself to a more intentional, contracted commitment to continuous improvement targets – as already discussed. Contractual commitment may, in fact, be necessary in a long-term relationship, because of the potential for complacency: the supplier already has the business for the life of the asset, so he need not stay competitive.

2.8 The benefits of continuous improvement for the organisation should be obvious. It prevents supplier (and buyer) complacency, maintains competitiveness and ensures that year-on-year value gains can be demonstrated. Sustainable procurement and production may require substantial changes, so it will be a prudent (and sustainable) approach to set realistic incremental progress targets over time: avoiding unrealistic (unsustainable) demands on suppliers, and corporate 'indigestion' as a result of unconsolidated change. Continuous improvement enables emerging sustainability issues and priorities to be taken into account, because it sets up a framework for the re-negotiation of priorities and targets. Continuous improvements may be aimed at specific areas such as cost reduction, process efficiencies, standards accreditation, defect reduction or customer satisfaction, which would bring their own reputational, operational and commercial benefits.

2.9 The syllabus, however, appears to focus on the benefits of continuous improvement 'for the supply chain'. These may be summarised as follows.

- Incentives for the development of capacity and capability, which may improve suppliers' competitiveness and access to other contracts

- Disincentives to complacency, which may result in a reduction of customer loyalty, contract disputes and reputational damage

- Co-investment by the buyer in supplier and supply chain development (which will be discussed in a later section of this chapter): resources, information and support for process or performance improvements

- Financial incentives, built into the contract, for attaining continuous improvement targets. These may take the form of guaranteed or fixed levels of capacity, say, or preferential consideration for further contracts, or direct revenue or gain sharing (a share of the value added by the improvements)

- Opportunity for innovation: implementing or devising new solutions that may be commercially exploited with other customers, or enhance the supplier's reputation

- Opportunity for accreditation (eg on quality, social or environmental management standards), enhancing suppliers' value, standing and opportunities

Whole-life costing

2.10 It has long been recognised that purchase price is just one element in the total costs attributable to bought out materials. Procurement professionals are urged to look beyond their own targets for cost management and reduction, and to focus collaboratively on the potential to add value across the whole organisation – or indeed the whole supply chain.

2.11 We have looked at the idea of whole-life costing mainly in the context of capital assets, which have a long usage and investment life. However, as you will know from your wider purchasing studies, materials purchases also incur not just the costs of purchase, but costs associated with stock holding (and stockouts), quality management, usage, waste disposal and so on.

2.12 Malcolm Saunders (*Strategic Purchasing and Supply Chain Management*) distinguishes between costs of acquiring a product, costs of possessing it and costs of sustaining it.

- Costs of acquiring a product of course include purchase price, but also costs of specification, sourcing, negotiation, expediting, receiving and inspection.

- Costs of possessing a product include internal and external failure costs associated with faulty products, the costs of holding stocks of the item and handling and transportation costs.

- Costs of sustaining a product are related to ensuring conformance to requirements into the future. They include the costs of supplier audits and certification, and the costs of preventive measures with regard to supplier education and development.

2.13 Whole-life costing is the systematic consideration of all relevant costs and revenues associated with the ownership of an asset, with a view to supporting decision-making in areas such as: investment appraisal and risk management; product/asset comparison; asset management planning; and 'make or buy' decisions (determining long-term best-value options). Its essence is that decisions involving significant value and risks should take account of a range of cost and sustainability factors, not just price (*CIPS Knowledge Works Guide to Whole-life Costing*).

2.14 We outlined the general methodology of whole-life costing briefly in Chapter 11 – and it is difficult to see how more detail could be required in the exam, given the context in which the technique is mentioned in the syllabus. For the purposes of sustainable procurement, the key points are as follows.

- Whole-life costing supports the realistic assessment of costs and investment risks over the life of acquisitions, enabling decisions to be made about best value and economic sustainability. It may, in particular, support the business case for sustainable procurement initiatives: a 'green' desktop printer or photocopier, or energy-saving light bulbs, for example, may come at a higher purchase price – but represent savings on lifetime costs of consumables, energy bills and replacement.

- Whole-life costing may encourage cross-functional dialogue about requirements, priorities, value and cost: encouraging a healthy orientation towards overarching objectives, long planning horizon), stakeholder interests, the need for risk management, the potential for added value, – and perhaps the strategic contribution of the procurement function. All these are potentially supportive of sustainable procurement.

Risks and contingencies in whole-life contract management

2.15 The risks and costs of whole-life contract management mainly arise where it implies a need to commit to long-term contracts and relationships with suppliers, and to use a single supplier for the range of product and service purchases relevant to the lifecycle of an asset. We will discuss this in more detail in the following section of the chapter, but here are some examples.

- There is an opportunity cost in long-term contracts, because it limits the organisation's ability to buy opportunistically, adversarially or on a competitive basis, to secure the best available 'deal' for a given requirement.

- There is a risk of being locked into a long-term relationship with an under-performing or incompatible supplier or partner – especially in joint ventures, say, or Private-Public Partnerships (where the interests, objectives and operating styles of the partners may be quite divergent).

- There is a risk of a long-term contracted supplier growing complacent and ceasing to be competitive (on performance, cost or sustainability criteria).

- There is a reputational risk of strong association with a supplier, who may be (or become, over time) vulnerable to compliance, sustainability or reputational risk.

- There is supply risk attached to narrowing the supply base by using a single preferred supplier or small group of preferred suppliers, on whom the buyer becomes highly dependent. In the case of supplier failure or defection, or supply disruption (due to transport or technology failure, labour strikes, political instability, weather, natural disasters and other environmental contingencies), the buyer may be unable swiftly to identify and mobilise alternative sources of supply – or to command sufficient goodwill and motivation among 'emergency' suppliers, where it is known that ongoing business is already tied up.

- There is the risk of increasing dependency on suppliers, in the form of asset specificity or relationship-specific investments and adaptations (even in small matters such as the use of proprietary – rather than generic – spare parts). Again, this may cause significant cost and disruption in the event of supplier failure or defection.

Public-private partnerships

2.16 One special form of contractual relationship, which reflects a whole-life contract approach, is a partnership between a public sector organisation and a commercial private sector firm, known as a Public Private Partnership (PPP), with a view to designing, building and operating major capital and infrastructure assets. Such structured partnerships have been – and are being – used to create national infrastructure such as the Channel Tunnel, the QEII bridge across the Thames at Dartford, and the North Birmingham Relief Road, as well as smaller projects such as hospitals, schools and barracks.

2.17 Public-private partnerships (PPP) and Private Finance Initiatives (PFI) are schemes in which private sector firms and public authorities share capital and expertise, in various structured ways. A private developer may be asked to obtain capital, and/or to design and build a facility – and/or to operate the facility or to charge a fee for its use, for a period designed to recoup the firm's investment plus a reasonable return. Full involvement of this kind is known as a Design, Build, Finance and Operate or DBFO project.

2.18 PPP projects may take various forms.

- A *Design-Build contract* means that the private partner designs and builds a facility, which the public authority (eg a council or NHS Trust) will operate once it is completed.

- A *Build-Operate contract* means that the private partner builds the facility (eg a toll road) and operates it for a period, in order to recoup its investment, then transfers ownership to the public sector body.

- A *Turnkey Operation* is where the public sector provides funding and retains ownership of the facility, but the private partner designs and builds it, and also operates it for a period.

- An *Operation and Maintenance contract* means that a private partner is simply contracted, on a tender basis, to operate and maintain a public facility (eg a prison or a waste disposal facility).

- A *Private Finance Initiative* typically means that a private consortium raises the capital finance to design and build a public sector project. It is also contracted to maintain the buildings while a public authority uses them: eg providing cleaning, catering and security services. Once construction is complete, the public authority begins to pay back the private consortium for the cost of the buildings and their maintenance, plus interest. The contracts typically last for 30 years, after which time the buildings belong to the public authority.

2.19 One advantage of such schemes is that the public sector can tap into the expertise of a private partner. This can provide value for money, especially if the private partner has already invested in the required technology. It can also enable a public sector body to complete projects, upgrade facilities and improve public services much faster than would otherwise be possible, and without having to cover capital costs from tax revenue. According to healthcare think tank the Kings Fund, for example, the physical condition of most hospitals is now 'vastly improved' thanks to major PFI schemes.

2.20 But there are drawbacks also.

- Critics of PPP argue that the public sector may be surrendering control of the project, with the risk of lower levels of service, public accountability and consideration of environmental and social sustainability objectives.

- PFI contracts can represent poor value for money and saddle the public sector with unsustainable financial commitments for decades to come: some NHS trusts have found it too expensive to pay the annual charges to PFI contractors for building and servicing new hospitals, for example.

- The scheme may be unsustainably inflexible, because it ties public services into 20–30 year contracts – despite the fact that it is difficult to plan for changes in demand and service provision over such a long planning horizon.

- Trade unions such as Unison have claimed that PFI leads to poorer services, because private companies maintain the buildings as cheaply as possible.

- The pay and conditions of cleaners, catering and security staff in PFI buildings is typically worse than their counterparts in the public sector.

2.21   From the private sector partner's point of view, the arrangement will only be successful to the extent that it gains a reasonable return on its investment (and perhaps also enhanced political influence). Some PFI consortia have seen profits soar: Octagon, the private consortium that financed and built the Norfolk and Norwich hospital, refinanced the PFI deal so that the partners could take early profits, for example. But other firms, such as engineering firm Amey (with PFI contracts in education and road building) have been plunged into financial crisis.

3   *Relationships for sustainable procurement*

3.1   In exploring the benefits and risks of whole-life contract management, we raised the following points.

- Long-term, close and co-operative relationships with suppliers support sustainability, because they: help to manage risks to the continuity of supply; enable closer control over supplier's sustainability policies and performance; allow contract flexibility and reduced transaction costs; enable collaboration on innovation and continuous improvement over time; and reflect a non-exploitative, gain-sharing orientation to supply relationships which may itself be regarded as economically and socially sustainable.

- Long-term, close and co-operative relationships with suppliers create risks to sustainability, because they may: encourage buyer over-dependency on single sources of supply; allow supplier complacency; 'lock' buyers into relationships with incompatible or underperforming suppliers; or pose reputational risks by close association with suppliers exposed to social, environmental or compliance risk.

3.2   So what is the 'best' or most strategically advantageous type of supply chain relationship for sustainable procurement? Essentially, there is no one answer. It all depends...

Prioritising relationship investment

3.3   As we saw in Chapter 9, not all purchase items or categories of spend will be worth investment in long-term relationship development. For some categories – such as leverage and routine items – the aims of sustainability will best be served by arm's length, transactional or even adversarial buying, aimed at securing best price/value and transaction efficiency. For bottleneck and strategic/critical items, however, the aims of sustainability will best be served by securing long-term supply and developing collaborative value: in other words, by closer and longer-term relationships. (If these ideas don't ring a bell, recap our coverage of the Kraljic matrix in Chapter 9.)

3.4   A buying organisation may seek to develop closer relationships with:

- Suppliers who offer most potential for best-practice sharing, capacity-building, ongoing development and added value in the area of sustainability (and therefore offer a good return on relationship investment)

- Suppliers who present a potential risk to the organisation in the area of sustainability (which can be managed and minimised by closer relationship).

Securing complementary competencies for sustainability

3.5   An organisation may rely to a greater or lesser extent on its suppliers for access to core competencies which give it competitive advantage in its market. Core competencies are skills, capabilities and resources that are distinctive, non-replicable (not easily copied by competitors) and value-adding. An organisation may possess these competencies itself, or may access them via suppliers: the basis of make/do or buy/outsource decisions. According to Cox's 'relational competence' model, the greater a firm's reliance on its suppliers for core competencies, the greater the depth and commitment of the supply relationship will need to be.

3.6   Ramsay ('Purchasing's strategic relevance', *European Journal of Purchasing and Supply*) suggests a number of specific ways in which an organisation can use its supply chain to develop distinctive and non-replicable competencies for competitive advantage.

- Identify and develop unknown suppliers with sustainability/innovation capability, which competitors are unlikely to be able to access.

- 'Enclose' a supplier (eg by exclusive supply agreements or confidentiality agreements) in order to secure sole access to its expertise and resources for sustainability

- Apply procurement tactics which are hard for competitors to imitate eg exploiting high bargaining power or 'special relationships' with suppliers (based on personal contacts, information-sharing or systems integration, say) to gain access to supplier resources on exclusive or preferential terms.

Example: Volkswagen

'As a part of our supplier training courses, Volkswagen has been working with its business partners since the mid-nineties to optimise environmental protection in supply chains. The dialogue with our suppliers combines several elements: the exchange of environmental data, certificates and reports, seminars, workshops, symposiums and an award for green innovations in products and at plants. In recent years, solutions for new sustainability issues have been developed in collaboration with our partners. Environmental aspects like material recommendations and bans are incorporated in product-related specifications for components and modules, as quality standards for all parts. In addition, there are VW-specific and industry-specific environmental norms.

Together with our partners, Volkswagen is taking another step towards sustainability with the introduction of global environmental and social standards. Using the concept "Sustainability in Supplier Relations", the group has set the aim of moving forward the process of the partnership development for production and plant-related environmental and social standards: an environmentally aware and socially engaged supplier is also an economically good and reliable partner. Methods for early recognition, and requirements for environmental and social standards, as well as intensive communication with suppliers, are important elements of this sustainability concept. In the future, a team effort in regard to sustainability is expected from everyone, without exceptions, along the whole supply chain.

The production processes and working conditions at suppliers of Volkswagen should be oriented at global minimum standards. The standards which are used by Volkswagen itself also represent the measure for our suppliers.

Volkswagen orients its requirements to first-tier suppliers with whom we have direct contractual relationships. Efficient sustainability management for a carmaker like Volkswagen demands that the requirements of the OEM (Original Equipment Manufacturer) are passed along the whole chain.

The relationship spectrum

3.7 You should be familiar, from your other studies, with the fact that supplier relationships may vary widely in the extent of their intensity, mutuality, trust and commitment – in other words, their 'closeness'. This is often expressed as a relationship 'spectrum' or 'continuum' extending from one-off arm's length transactions at one end to long-term collaborative partnerships at the other. Cox's 'stepladder of contractual relationships', for example, describes a spectrum including (in order of increasing closeness and mutual dependency):

- *Adversarial leverage:* multi-sourcing and hard-negotiated short-term contracts for routine purchases, where no unique competence is required of suppliers. This may support sustainability by maximising value and cost efficiency.

- *Preferred suppliers:* smaller list of potential suppliers on the basis of vendor rating and accreditation, for more important purchases where some special competence is required of suppliers. This may support sustainability via pre-qualification eg on environmental or labour management standards.

- *Single sourcing:* purchasing strategic supplies from a single quality supplier who can offer distinctive, important competencies. This may support sustainability by enhancing potential for capability-sharing and ongoing development.

- *Network sourcing and partnerships:* partnerships between the main buyer and a first-tier supplier, which develops partnerships with second-tier suppliers, to integrate and control the wider supply chain. This may support sustainability by enhancing potential for ongoing development and collaboration, and by managing sustainability risks throughout the supply chain.

- *Strategic supplier alliances or joint ventures:* formation of a jointly-owned separate firm to produce the supplied product/service, where the buyer and supplier's competencies are complementary and of equal importance. This may support sustainability by leveraging both parties' sustainability capability and brand strength.

3.8 The most appropriate relationship type for a given purchasing situation may therefore depend on factors such as the following.

- The nature, importance, risk and sustainability issues of the items purchased
- The competence, capability, co-operation and performance of the supplier
- Geographical distance: close relationships may be more difficult to establish and maintain with overseas suppliers
- The compatibility of the supply partners (eg in relation to sustainability values)
- Supply market conditions: if supply is subject to risk, the buyer may wish to multi-source; if prices are fluctuating, he may wish to use opportunistic spot-buying – or to lock in advantageous prices through fixed contracts; if the market is fast-changing and innovative, he may avoid being locked into long-term supply agreements; if there are few quality/capable/high profile suppliers, he may wish to enter partnership with them – and so on.

3.9 The advantages and disadvantages of collaborative or partnership relationships for sustainable procurement are summarised in Table 12.2.

Table 12.2 *Advantages and disadvantages of partnering for sustainable procurement*

Advantages	Disadvantages
Greater stability of supply and supply prices	Risk of supplier complacency over time
Sharing of risk and investment	Less flexibility to change suppliers at need
Better supplier motivation and responsiveness, arising from mutual commitment and reciprocity	May be locked into relationship with an incompatible, inflexible, under-performing or compliance-vulnerable supplier
Cost savings from reduced supplier base, collaborative cost-reduction	May be locked into relationship, despite supply market changes and opportunities
Access to supplier's technology/expertise for sustainability	Costs of relationship management and supplier development
Joint planning and information sharing, supporting capacity planning and efficiency	Mutual dependency may create loss of flexibility and control
Ability to plan long-term improvements	Loss of price/cost gains from opportunistic buying

3.10   In the end, an organisation may need to develop a portfolio of relationships, appropriate to each supply situation. An 'adversarial-collaborative' approach, for example, might allow it to work co-operatively with a supplier on ethical/environmental monitoring, product development or continuous improvements – and to negotiate hard in order to secure the best possible share of the resulting value gains. In other words, collaboration 'enlarges the pie' – of which competition seeks to gain a bigger slice.

Supply chain management

3.11   Supply chain management (SCM) is a holistic and strategic approach to supply chain relationships. It may be defined as: 'the management of relations and integrated business processes across the supply chain that produces products, services and information that add value for the end customer... Use of the SCM concept entails that the links in the supply chain plan and co-ordinate their processes and relationships by weighing the overall efficiency and competitive power [and sustainability] of the supply chain' (Jespersen & Skjött-Larsen, *Supply Chain Management in Theory and Practice*).

3.12   SCM consists primarily of building collaborative relationships across the supply chain, so that the whole chain works together to add value for the end customer in a profitable and sustainable way. Christopher et al (*Relationship Marketing*) argue that, these days:

'The real competitive struggle is not between individual companies, but between their supply chains or networks... What makes a supply chain or network unique is the way the relationships and interfaces in the chain or network are managed. In this sense, a major source of differentiation comes from the quality of relationships that one business enjoys, compared to its competitors.'

3.13   Here are some benefits of an SCM approach to sustainable procurement.

- Reduced costs, by eliminating waste activities and implementing cost reduction programmes throughout the supply chain. ('Often there are many activities that do not create value involved in trade between two companies. Jointly locating and eliminating these activities, as well as developing co-operative goals and guidelines for the future, can focus resources on real improvements and development possibilities': Jespersen & Skjött-Larsen)

- Improved responsiveness to sustainability issues and drivers (by focusing the whole business process on customer sustainability in an integrated way)

- Access to complementary resources and capabilities (eg joint investment in research and development, technology- and ideas-sharing and so on)

- Enhanced sustainability performance (eg through collaborative sustainability management, increased supply chain communication, continuous improvement programmes and improved supplier motivation)

- Faster lead times for product development and delivery (so that new and modified products can be offered in response to changing customer demand and sustainability-related opportunities)

- Better control over sustainability performance and risks at lower tiers of the supply chain (since reputational risk may arise from suppliers' suppliers).

3.14 However, it is important (in exams, as in real life) to be realistic about the benefits claimed for SCM – and to analyse whether it is relevant, possible or beneficial for a particular organisation. It is not for everyone! For one thing, it requires considerable investment, internal support and supplier willingness – any or all of which may not be available. It also involves focusing on closer relationships with a smaller number of suppliers, and this may be risky (if the relationships don't work out, for example, or if the firm becomes dependent on a supplier which later has sustainability problems).

Drilling down through the supply chain

3.15 In *Supply Management's* special issue on embedding sustainable procurement (27 August 2009), the chair of the Commission for a Sustainable London 2012, Shaun McCarthy, notes that the most asked question on sustainable procurement is: 'How far down the supply chain should we go?'

3.16 The key factor in deciding how far down the supply chain you need to investigate will be exposure to risk.

Example: the sportswear industry

'The sportswear industry has suffered badly with international news coverage of poor labour conditions and excessive profiteering, which affected the sales and stock values of global brands [such as Adidas and Nike] significantly.

A major sportswear manufacturer told me: "We know where every garment we sell is manufactured and under what labour conditions. We know where every metre of fabric that goes into every garment is made and under what conditions. We don't yet know where every fibre comes from to make up the material – but we are working on it."

The issue of fibres is mostly about cotton. This product accounts for 25% of the world's pesticides and has a significant impact on ground and air pollution. In some countries, cotton is picked by forced labour. Man-made fibres have their own problems related to the energy intensity of manufacture, safety and toxic waste. Put these factors together and you have a major reputation risk for the industry, so it becomes necessary to trace every fibre. Organisations with less risk related to clothing may only choose to go back to the point of manufacture; others may not address the issue at all. A robust risk analysis is needed to develop the right solution.'

Shaun McCarthy, 'Source of concern', Supply Management, 27 August 2009

4 Developing sustainable supply chains

Supplier development

4.1 Supplier development may be defined as: 'Any activity that a buyer undertakes to improve a supplier's performance and/or capabilities to meet the buyer's short- or long-term supply needs' (Handfield & Nichols)

4.2 Hartley & Choi identify two overall objectives for organisations engaging in supply development programmes.

- Raising supplier competence to a specified level (eg in terms of reduced costs, or improved environmental performance). *Results-oriented* development programmes therefore focus on solving specific performance or sustainability issues: the buyer supports the supplier in making step-by-step technical changes, to achieve pre-determined improvements.

- Supporting suppliers in self-sustaining required performance standards, through a process of continuous improvement. *Process-oriented* development programmes therefore focus on increasing the supplier's ability to make their own process and performance improvements, without ongoing direct intervention by the buyer: the buyer supports the supplier in learning and using problem-solving and change management techniques. The process of *kaizen* or continuous improvement (discussed in Chapter 8) is an important aspect of this kind of supplier development.

Structuring supplier development

4.3 Supplier development programmes will often involve cross-functional representatives from both buyer and supplier organisations, perhaps working in a project team or sustainability task force. In addition, there will probably be multiple contact points in both organisations, for ongoing monitoring and management. Another common practice is the temporary transfer of staff: supplier staff may be seconded to the buyer organisation to learn, or buyer staff may be seconded to the supplier to advise or train, say.

A supplier development programme

4.4 A nine-stage approach to implementing a supplier development programme is suggested by Lysons & Farrington (*Purchasing and Supply Chain Management*) and appears to be the basis for the syllabus content: Figure 12.1.

4.5 Many of these steps will already be familiar from your studies in other modules – and to an extent, they should be self-explanatory. (They also overlap substantially with the learning objectives dealing with the implementation of sustainable procurement within an organisation, as the same basic process of planning and control.) However, we will draw out some points in relation to sustainable procurement, as suggested by the syllabus.

Prioritisation of suppliers and products

4.6 As we saw earlier, investment in relationship and supplier development is not worthwhile or sustainable for every supplier or category of purchase. Priority for development may be given to:

- Bottleneck and strategic items within the buyer's procurement portfolio (as defined by the Kraljic matrix)

- Suppliers with potential to improve and sustain improvements
- Suppliers with the capability and capacity to meet the future needs of the buying organisation (and therefore worth long-term investment)
- Suppliers who will show a reasonable return on development investment (otherwise, it may be better simply to select alternative suppliers)
- Suppliers with a high exposure to sustainability risk: the risk of supplier failure, supply disruption, reputational damage (eg due to labour or environmental practices) or environmental damage.

Figure 12.1 *The stages in a supplier development programme*

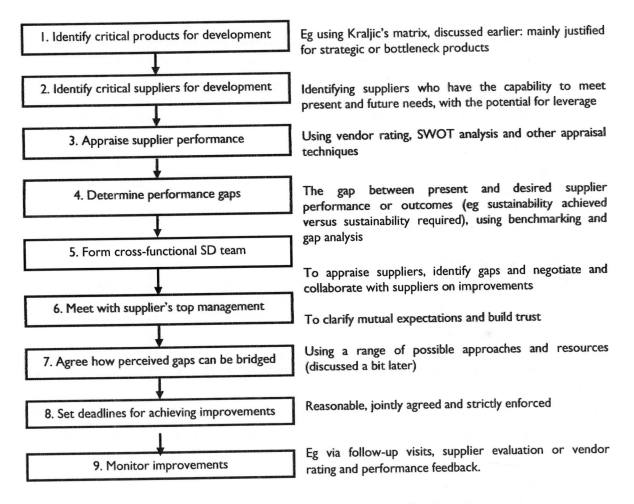

1. Identify critical products for development	Eg using Kraljic's matrix, discussed earlier: mainly justified for strategic or bottleneck products
2. Identify critical suppliers for development	Identifying suppliers who have the capability to meet present and future needs, with the potential for leverage
3. Appraise supplier performance	Using vendor rating, SWOT analysis and other appraisal techniques
4. Determine performance gaps	The gap between present and desired supplier performance or outcomes (eg sustainability achieved versus sustainability required), using benchmarking and gap analysis
5. Form cross-functional SD team	To appraise suppliers, identify gaps and negotiate and collaborate with suppliers on improvements
6. Meet with supplier's top management	To clarify mutual expectations and build trust
7. Agree how perceived gaps can be bridged	Using a range of possible approaches and resources (discussed a bit later)
8. Set deadlines for achieving improvements	Reasonable, jointly agreed and strictly enforced
9. Monitor improvements	Eg via follow-up visits, supplier evaluation or vendor rating and performance feedback.

Clear sustainability objectives, targets and requirements

4.7   As we have already seen in relation to the development and implementation of sustainable procurement policies within an organisation, it will be important to set SMART objectives, targets and requirements for supply chain partners, in order to:

- Clarify expectations, and the standards and measures that will be used to pre-qualify and select suppliers, award contracts and appraise supplier performance
- Motivate suppliers to improve, with a clear idea of how progress and performance will be measured
- Ensure that contract award and management, dispute handling and supplier rewards and incentives are handled transparently and equitably (and therefore sustainably, in terms of the potential for ongoing constructive relationships), on well understood criteria

- Ensure that supplier sustainability measures are properly aligned with the sustainability objectives of the buying organisation (and ideally also with procurement's functional objectives).

4.8 Similarly, the syllabus highlights the need for achievable or realistic deadlines for putting sustainability measures in place, or achieving targeted improvements – although this is already an integral part of SMART objective-setting. We will discuss specific KPIs for sustainability performance in Chapter 13.

Supplier performance evaluation

4.9 Performance measurement is an important part of supplier development, because both parties will want to:

- Select the right partners to work with: as we saw above, buyers will undertake development activities only with suppliers capable of improvement and leverage
- Measure the 'gap' between current and desired performance and outcomes: the process of gap analysis, discussed further below
- Measure the gains from the cost and effort put in. Both parties will want a 'before and after' picture of performance to reassure themselves that the activities were effective and justified.

4.10 There is a wide range of feedback mechanisms for gathering data on supplier sustainability performance, and comparing them against relevant performance measures. Examples include:

- The gathering of feedback from internal and external customers and other stakeholders, using market and customer research, focus groups, complaint procedures, survey questionnaires and project reviews
- The gathering of performance information through observation (eg on site visits), testing (eg inspections), and analysis of documentation, transaction records and management reports (eg inspection reports, complaint/dispute records, accident report forms and so on)
- Formal performance reviews or vendor rating exercises: reviewing performance against benchmark standards, KPIs and/or service levels, and feeding back the information for learning needs analysis and improvement planning
- Contract management, continually monitoring compliance with contract terms
- Regular meetings between buyer and supplier representatives (or project or account managers) to review general progress or specific issues
- The use of third-party consultants to monitor compliance with sustainability standards and benchmarks (eg monitoring overseas suppliers' workforce practices or environmental performance).

4.11 We will discuss performance monitoring and measurement tools in more detail in Chapter 13.

Gap analysis

4.12 Gap analysis involves identifying the difference between the current and desired situation or outcomes: between where we are now and where we would like to be in relation to sustainability objectives. Lysons & Farrington argue that for the purposes of planning supplier and supply chain development, gaps should be considered from the supplier side, as well as from the buyer side.

- From the buyer's side, for example, there may be gaps between: suppliers' current cost/price/value performance and the buyer's needs or expectations; suppliers' current environmental or CSR performance and the buyer's policy objectives (or the requirements of benchmark standards); suppliers' current capabilities and systems for innovation – and the buyer's future needs.

- From the supplier's side, there may be gaps between: the information required from buyers (eg re specifications or sustainability targets) and the information supplied; the level of profitability required from a contract and the level of profitability allowed by the buyer.

- From either side, there may be gaps between the level of collaboration, gain-sharing or relationship development desired/expected by both parties, and what is actually being delivered.

4.13 Gap analysis involves a systematic process of: defining the critical success factors in sustainable performance; defining key performance indicators which define desired levels of performance in those factors; measuring current performance on those indicators; and comparing the current and desired measures. The 'difference' between the two is the 'gap' to be closed, ideally by collaborative improvement and development planning.

4.14 Undertaking a GAP analysis is a key part of attaining environmental accreditations such as ISO 14001. It enables the organisation to work through a checklist of critical success factors such as: the existence of a clear environmental policy with top management support; adequate resources to implement and maintain an environmental management system; systems in place for compliance monitoring, identification of environmental impacts, identification of learning needs; and so on. Are these elements in place? If not, what needs to be done to put them in place?

4.15 Once gaps have been identified, targets and plans can be put in place to close them – whether in a single project or initiative, or in a series of incremental steps for continuous improvement.

Bridging performance/relationship gaps

4.16 A wide variety of approaches may be used to bridge perceived performance or relationship gaps, and to support sustainability. Here are some examples.

- Enhancing working relationships (eg by improved communication systems)

- Clarifying or increasing performance goals and measures (eg KPIs for improvements in waste reduction or workforce health and safety), and associated incentives and penalties to motivate improvements

- Seconding purchaser's staff to the supplier (or *vice versa*) for training, coaching, consultancy, support or liaison

- Providing capital (eg to help finance a new development project or the acquisition of greener, safer or more efficient plant and equipment)

- Providing progress payments during the development of a project or product, to support the supplier's cashflow

- Loaning machinery, equipment or IT hardware. (CIPS guidance cites some practical examples including: a buyer paying for a supplier's manufacturing processes to be updated, in return for discounted supplies in future; and a buyer giving an outsource supplier the machinery previously used to perform the activity in-house.)

- Granting suppliers access to IT and ICT systems and information (eg extranets and databases, computer aided design capability and so on)

- Offering training for the supplier's staff in relevant areas (eg technical aspects of requirements, or best practice in environmental management)
- Providing help or consultancy on value analysis (waste reduction) programmes, environmental procurement or other areas of expertise
- Encouraging the formation of supplier forums or a Supplier Association (Kyoryoku Kai in Japanese). These bring key suppliers together on a regular basis to share information, expertise and best practice, and to encourage joint problem-solving and improvement planning.

Example: Epson

Imaging company Epson – along with Hewlett Packard (HP), L'Oréal, Volkswagen and Titan – is a contributor to the CSR Europe web portal, which aims to share experiences of responsible supply chain management.

It has also developed strong policies for helping suppliers to meet CSR standards.

'Our position is unique because we purchase a lot from our own Epson facilities in Asia. In Europe, we expect suppliers to meet our standards, not just on the environment, but in areas like social fairness and community involvement. We are also on the look-out for the use of cheap or illegal labour.'

On issues such as the use of chemicals, Epson goes beyond EU law on hazardous substances and bans over 30 more. Suppliers need to comply with this. 'Our scrutiny goes down to the level of a small carton to put a product in. A supplier gives it to us assembled, but we check the glue, paper and ink used to ensure their origins comply with our standards.

The company conducts periodic supply audits and asks for data specifications to ensure suppliers are conforming to requirements. The size of supplier does not affect Epson's expectations, but [the company] admits smaller ones may need more support. 'Sometimes they need our help because they do not have our clout. For example, we work with a small supplier of plastic strapping to tie products together, and we asked about the origins of the printing on the banding. We asked what the ink was made of, and they went to their ink supplier who said the information was confidential. So we went back with the small supplier, and the ink manufacturer was then willing to comply.'

If there are gaps in what suppliers can provide, in many cases Epson works with them, but not always. 'Sometimes we stop working with them if they are not willing to change. We have good stories of people willing to take time out and come back with better ideas.'

Adrienne Margolis, 'A Global Revolution', Supply Management, 27 August 2009

Problem-solving, dispute management and escalation

4.17 Conflict can be constructive for supplier development and sustainability (including the sustainability of supply relationships), when its effect is to clarify 'gaps', issues and power relationships; focus attention on the need for improvement and problem-solving; avoid the risk of 'groupthink' and complacency by encouraging the testing and challenging of assumptions; and highlight the need for better communication. However, conflict can also be destructive, where it creates barriers to communication and collaboration; absorbs people's attention and energy; or escalates into hostility and/or legal disputes which may permanently damage a relationship.

4.18 The purpose of supplier and contract management is to facilitate communication, secure co-operation and minimise the risk of relationship problems and contract disputes. However, it is a sound principle of sustainable procurement to plan ahead for the risk of conflict and dispute.

4.19 There are many approaches to the management of conflict, and the suitability and sustainability of any given approach must be judged according to its relevance to a particular situation. There is no 'right way'. In some situations, the best outcome may be achieved by compromise; in others, imposition of a win-lose solution may be required; in others, the process of seeking a win-win solution, whatever the eventual outcome, may be helpful – particularly where the parties want to preserve ongoing working relations (a key sustainability issue).

4.20 There may be formal mechanisms for consultation and negotiation with suppliers to resolve problems or disputes around sustainability performance.

- *Consultation* is a form of 'issues' management, in which potential causes of conflict are discussed, and both parties have an opportunity to give their input, before the problem arises (or as soon as possible, once it has arisen). Less formal consultation and problem-solving may take place in sustainability project teams, supplier conferences and regular contract management communication.

- *Negotiation* is a useful approach to conflict resolution at any level. As an official mechanism, it is often used in supplier relations, to formulate agreements on contract terms, supplier development and continuous improvement plans and so on. Informal negotiation may also be used as a communication/management style, to reach mutually acceptable solutions to problems.

4.21 Supply contracts and performance agreements will often set out the methods that will be used to settle disputes, and when and how they will be 'escalated' (taken further or to a higher level) if necessary. If suppliers persistently under-perform or fail to meet agreed improvement targets, for example, the supplier development or sustainability team may refer the matter upwards to more senior management. There may be mechanisms for penalties to be applied (including, if necessary, early termination of a contract), or for formal dispute resolution. In all cases, sustainability will be a key consideration: problems and disputes should be handled as ethically and constructively as possible, leaving the door open to future dealings.

Supply chain communication and co-operation

4.22 In order to implement and manage sustainability programmes in the supply chain, there will need to be strong mechanisms for supplier communication and co-operation. This may include:

- Maintaining positive, relationship-building contacts and communications with suppliers – and perhaps also building on inter-personal co-operation and loyalty, through the use of dedicated contacts such as account managers

- Integrating (or sharing access to) relevant information systems, where possible, to facilitate collaborative issues identification, planning, performance monitoring and problem-solving

- Sharing sustainability knowledge and best practice throughout the supply chain, perhaps through staff secondments and collaborative training

- Supplier motivation and performance management: using supplier incentives (for good performance) and penalties (for poor performance), based on clear, jointly agreed expectations, expressed in contracts, specifications, KPIs and/or service level agreements

- Securing the commitment and sponsorship of senior managers in both organisations, providing influential support for co-operation within the supplier organisation

- Ethical, constructive, collaborative and, where possible, 'win-win' negotiation to resolve relationship and performance problems (in itself promoting the sustainability of relationships), as discussed above

- Being an attractive customer, by maintaining a sufficient volume of business to justify suppliers' investment in co-operation, and by maintaining ethical, co-operative, efficient, professional and congenial dealings with suppliers

- Engaging suppliers in co-investment and co-development for sustainability: collaborative product development, planning and training; systems integration; gain sharing; and so on – so that sustainability improvements are a 'win' for the supplier as well as the buyer.

Monitoring improvements and learning lessons

4.23 Monitoring improvements, progress and results for the purpose of control should be a familiar concept by now, as should the need to review processes in order to derive lessons for the future. We discussed 'ongoing management and review' of sustainable procurement policies in Chapter 7; 'planning for continuous improvement' in Chapter 8; and 'post contract lessons management' earlier in this chapter. We will not repeat ourselves here: recap the material if you need to.

Costs and benefits of supplier development for sustainability

4.24 Bearing in mind the expense and effort that may be involved in supplier development, buyers will expect to make significant gains from sharing in the specialist knowledge of the supplier and/or improving supplier and supply chain performance to achieve sustainability objectives (and their business benefits). Like other forms of collaborative relationship, however, the aim is for benefits to accrue to both sides: Table 12.3.

Table 12.3 *Costs and benefits of supplier development for sustainability*

Buyer's perspective	
Costs	*Benefits*
Cost of management time in researching, identifying and negotiating opportunities	Improved economic sustainability in the supply chain: reduced supply risk
Cost of development activities: risk of over-investment in a relationship which may not last or prove compatible	Improved sustainability performance by suppliers (and supply chains): reduced sustainability, compliance and reputational risk
Costs of ongoing relationship management (where required)	Streamlining systems and processes: reduced waste, process efficiencies, cost reduction
Risks of sharing information, intellectual property	Support for sustainable outsourcing
Supplier's perspective	
Costs	*Benefits*
Cost of management time in researching, identifying and negotiating opportunities	Support for eco-efficiencies, leading to greater profitability
Risk of over-investment and -dependence, if customer is demanding or unprofitable	Improvements in customer satisfaction, leading to retained/increased business
Costs of ongoing relationship management (where required)	Improved capability for sustainability, leading to additional sales to other customers
Risks of sharing information and intellectual property	Direct gains in knowledge and resources provided by the customer
Cost of discounts or exclusivity agreements given as *quid pro quo*	Enhanced learning and flexibility: skills for problem-solving and continuous improvement

Chapter summary

- The management of a capital purchase extends over the whole life of the purchase contract, which will often mean the whole life of the asset.

- Contract management is designed to ensure that both parties meet their obligations and that the intended outcomes of a contract are delivered.

- Key activities involved in contract management include contract development, contract communication, contract administration, managing performance, contract review, and relationship management.

- There are many advantages of effective contract management. One key advantage is the ability to identify and manage sources of risk. Another is the ability to leverage the value-adding potential of long-term supply relationships.

- Whole-life contract management contributes to continuous improvement throughout the supply chain.

- There is a spectrum of supply relationships, ranging from short-term transactional relationships at one end to more strategic long-term partnership at the other. Buyers must choose an appropriate relationship with each supplier.

- It is supply chains that compete, not individual organisations. This suggests that sustainable procurement is best achieved by working closely with other organisations along the chain.

- Buyers have an interest in developing their suppliers so as to raise supplier performance. However, this will probably apply only to 'strategic' supply relationships.

- Supplier performance evaluation is an important part of supplier development. Gaps between current performance and desired performance must be bridged in order to improve sustainability.

- Communication along the supply chain – including problem-solving, dispute management and escalation – is also critical to sustainability.

Self-test questions

Numbers in brackets refer to the paragraphs above where your answers can be checked.

1   List key activities involved in contract management. (Table 12.1)

2   Why are delivery schedules relevant to sustainable procurement? (1.16)

3   What issues will be addressed in a post-completion review of a purchase contract? (1.25)

4   List benefits of effective contract management. (2.2)

5   List benefits of long-term supply relationships. (2.6)

6   What are the benefits of continuous improvement for the supply chain? (2.9)

7   List different forms of public-private partnerships. (2.18)

8   Describe some of the relationships along the relationship spectrum. (3.7)

9   List advantages and disadvantages of partnership relations for sustainable procurement. (Table 12.2)

10   List nine stages in a supplier development programme (Lysons & Farrington). (Figure 12.1)

11   List feedback mechanisms for gathering data on supplier sustainability performance. (4.10)

12   List mechanisms for supplier communication and co-operation. (4.22)

Further reading

If you are in need of further review of the whole sourcing and contract management cycle, it might be worth your downloading the CIPS Knowledge Works 'Knowledge Insight' (KI) Guide to Contract Management, which surveys the whole spectrum of procedures and activities from pre-contract planning to post-contract management.

Of more general usefulness, we can highly recommend the CSR Europe Portal for Responsible Supply Chain Management, which offers extensive and accessible resources and tools for buyers, including an overview of 'How to Implement A Responsible Supply Chain Programme', with six steps: Understanding and Responsibilities; Communication; Strategy; Analysing Risks and Opportunities; Monitoring and Compliance; and Continuous Improvement.

Browse the many interesting resources via: http://www.csr-supplychain.org

CHAPTER 13

Measuring, Monitoring and Managing Sustainability Performance

Learning objectives and indicative content

3.4   Apply effective tools for the implementation, measurement and monitoring of sustainable procurement within an organisation and evaluate the similarities and differences compared to other organisations and sectors

- Supplier and supply chain audit, assessment and evaluation (eg green audit, Oxfam supplier questionnaire)
- Key performance indicators (KPIs)
- Total cost of ownership
- Cost management
- Product lifecycle analysis
- Stakeholder mapping and communication
- Source planning
- Supply chain mapping

Chapter headings

1   Monitoring and managing sustainability performance

2   Audit, assessment and evaluation tools

3   Key performance indicators for sustainability

4   Cost and whole-life sustainability tools

5   Stakeholder and supply chain management tools

6   Sustainability reporting

Introduction

A picturesque summary of this topic is given by Blackburn. 'Anyone familiar with agriculture knows that planting and harvesting are the two seasons of intense activity, but there's also work to be done in the interim. Weeds must be removed; pests must be controlled. In some places, irrigation is needed. Steps must be taken to assure the objective of a rich bounty is fulfilled. This is also true about [sustainable procurement]. Progress in growing [sustainable procurement] within an organisation must be monitored so adjustments can be made if the growth doesn't meet expectations.'

In this chapter, we explore a number of tools that may be used for monitoring, measuring and managing the progress of sustainable procurement – and the performance of the organisation, the procurement department and the supply chain. In some areas this overlaps with topics already covered, such as the implementation of sustainable procurement programmes (Chapter 8) and the implementation and improvement of sustainable procurement in the supply chain (Chapter 12). However, in this chapter, we focus on planning, monitoring and control mechanisms and tools.

1 *Monitoring and managing sustainability performance*

1.1　One of the key principles of sustainability is the need to satisfy the needs and interests of an extended group of organisational stakeholders, and this in turn implies the need to control performance. There is an old saying: 'what gets measured, gets managed', and in earlier chapters, we have emphasised the importance of setting clear goals and targets for sustainable procurement – and then monitoring, measuring, evaluating and reviewing progress and performance. This ensures that:

- Deviations or shortfalls can be corrected, and problems identified and solved
- Potential for improvement can be identified and lessons learned for future rounds of planning
- Individuals and teams can be motivated by clear objectives and targets, and the rewards of having demonstrably and measurably achieved them (or made progress towards them)
- Executives responsible to stakeholders can give an accurate account of progress and performance and the discharge of their responsibilities
- The expense of resources can be justified by the results, and the business case for sustainable procurement confirmed (hopefully, garnering support and resource allocation for a further round of improvements).

Yardsticks for measurement

1.2　The first key element of any performance management system (or control cycle) is the setting of indicators against which measured or assessed progress and performance can be compared: that is, measures or 'yardsticks' that will indicate (a) the targets and standards to which effort and resources will be directed; and (b) whether actual results are on track, going according to plan, or reaching the required or expected standard.

1.3　Such measures may be formulated as objectives, targets or key performance indicators, for example – which in turn may be formulated as a result of processes such as critical success factor analysis, the use of national or international standards, or benchmarking processes. We will discuss some of these approaches later.

Monitoring and measurement

1.4　The term 'monitoring' is used broadly to include the measurement of performance against goals and targets, as well as other means of periodic oversight, review and evaluation. Monitoring methods include self-reporting, audits, inspections or observations, interviews and surveys, and measurements. The focus, criteria and methodology of monitoring may be either quantitative or qualitative.

- *Quantitative:* based on numerical/statistical measurement. Examples in sustainability monitoring may include: cost-savings; the tracking of air pollution concentrations or the quantity of carbon emissions; the percentage of purchased products made of recycled materials; or the number of discrimination complaints, employee accidents or locally-sourced products.

- *Qualitative:* based on informed (though inevitably subjective) judgement, and focusing on qualitative aspects of sustainable procurement such as equity, teamwork, communication or stakeholder satisfaction.

1.5 Blackburn highlights a number of difficulties with monitoring in general.

- Qualitative monitoring, being subjective, can lead to doubt and conflict, potentially eroding support for sustainability initiatives.

- Quantitative measurements are not always easy to make, and there may be problems with data integrity: different definitions of items to be measured (eg 'hazardous waste'); untrained observers or analysts; or bugs in reporting software.

- Monitoring systems may not gather or manage information frequently enough, with a view to regular reporting, feedback, problem identification and tracking, lesson learning and improvement planning.

- Where computerised data systems are used, there is a risk of ineffectiveness due to poor system design; irrelevance to the organisation's specific sustainability issues and management systems; data build up, overload and obsolescence; lack of user training ('rubbish in, rubbish out'); and waste of resources.

1.6 It may be useful to note that 'measurement' and 'assessment' ('what is being achieved?') are not the same as 'evaluation' – which implies value judgements about whether the measured or assessed level of progress or performance is good or bad, adequate or inadequate, to be continued and encouraged or corrected.

Performance correction, adjustment and improvement planning

1.7 The third phase of the performance management cycle is the management and adjustment of performance to bring it back 'on course': solving problems, identifying and implementing improvements, and adjusting targets downwards (to be more realistic) or upwards (to set fresh challenges) where required. This process is covered in a range of contexts throughout this Course Book: implementation of sustainable procurement measures, seeking continuous improvement, developing the supply chain and so on. (Chapters 14 and 15 will deal more specifically with the handling of barriers, problems and conflicts.)

1.8 We will now examine the various monitoring, measurement and management tools mentioned in the syllabus.

2 Audit, assessment and evaluation tools

2.1 One major way in which sustainability monitoring may be accomplished is by appointing auditors to perform a systematic review of an operation, site or function: collecting, assessing and reporting on resources, processes, performance, risks and opportunities. This may be done as part of a portfolio of reviews: periodic reporting, checklist inspections, stakeholder surveys and so on.

Types of audit

2.2   Blackburn identifies several different types of audit relevant to sustainability monitoring.

- *Compliance audits*: assessing conformance to law and regulations (eg health and safety regulations), and requirements for government permits and licences (eg waste disposal licences)

- *Internal standards audits*: assessing how well the organisation meets requirements it has developed for itself (such as sustainable procurement principles)

- *External standards audits*: assessing conformance with an outside standard to which the organisation subscribes (eg the ILO standards, Earth Charter, Fair Trade standards or ETI Base Code)

- A *management systems audit*: assessing the organisation's adherence to processes described in an internal management standard (eg a sustainable procurement policy) or an external one (eg ISO 14001 or SA 8000). This is a type of process audit: more generally, for example, an audit may look at the implementation, effectiveness and efficiency of performance management or procurement processes.

- *Risk or best practice assessments*: assessing potential liabilities and risks, or seeking high-standard approaches that can be shared with others (which may be the focus of a purchasing audit, for example)

- *Productivity assessments*: assessing opportunities to improve efficiency (eg via energy conservation, waste reduction, material substitution or process change). Tools such as Six Sigma, which you may have encountered elsewhere in your studies, can be used to identify and develop such opportunities. A similar approach might be a value for money audit or cost-benefit audit.

2.3   We should add some more specific categories, highlighted by the syllabus.

- *Supplier and supply chain audits* focus on the capabilities, capacity, resources, skills, systems, processes, management and performance of suppliers.

- *Environmental (or 'green') audits* focus on an organisation's capabilities, resources, skills, systems, processes and management in support of environmental objectives; the environmental impacts of operations; and areas of environmental (and related compliance and reputational) risk

- *Statutory audits* are a legal requirement. Private sector companies above a certain size must appoint an independent external auditor to review their financial systems, accounts and records and must report to shareholders on whether the accounts show a true and fair view. Similar audits are conducted on public sector bodies by the Audit Commission and the National Audit Office.

2.4   *Internal audits* are conducted by the organisation's own staff, in the form of self-assessments (reviews of an operation conducted by its own personnel) or independent internal assessments (undertaken by a separate internal auditing group, outside the operation being reviewed). This approach is relatively inexpensive, encourages internal 'ownership' of compliance issues, and has the advantage of the assessors' familiarity with the activities, personnel and organisational context. However, it may be subject to influence from the operation's management, or limited in its perspectives. Self-assessment auditors, in particular, may lack technical skills or training for the task.

2.5   *External audits* are conducted by consultants or other independent entities outside the organisation. This approach is more expensive, potentially disruptive and subject to suspicion and resistance from subjects. However, it is useful for adding objectivity, fresh viewpoints, cross-functional and best practice perspectives and credibility (due to perceived independence). Specially qualified external auditors are usually required for formal certifications eg under ISO, EMAS and certain Fair Trade standards.

Benefits and drawbacks of the audit approach

2.6   Blackburn argues that a systematic audit process may be beneficial in various ways.

- Providing a new, fresh assessment of gaps in compliance, risk control or efficiency – which regular internal monitoring may not allow
- Adding credibility to a performance report – or to the presentation of a business case for sustainable procurement
- Certifying conformance to an ISO or other recognised standard (particularly if the audit is carried out by independent third-party assessors)
- Improving the quality of other review processes
- Demonstrating transparency in the face of suspected impropriety, reducing the risk of escalating legal and reputational cost later.

2.7   However, there are some drawbacks of auditing.

- The risk of serious legal and moral compromise, if compliance issues or threats to people (or the environment) are identified by the audit, and management does nothing
- The risk of 'analysis paralysis': gathering more performance information as a substitute for managing performance
- Potential damage to morale and motivation, due to a perceived lack of trust or a disincentive to initiative and action
- Over-reliance on auditing, fostering a compliance mentality (only doing what the audit recommends) and a bias for inaction ('no point doing anything now, in case the auditors tell us it's wrong'), and eroding the capacity for critical self-analysis and initiative for improvement.

2.8   'On balance,' says Blackburn, 'auditing by qualified experts done at frequencies based on risk can be a good thing for a company, providing an honest understanding of problems and prompting constructive change. This kind of auditing should be an important part of any sustainability program.'

Purchasing management audit

2.9   A purchasing management audit is 'a comprehensive, systematic, independent and periodic examination of a company's purchasing environment, objectives and tactics to identify problems and opportunities and to facilitate the development of appropriate action plans' (Scheuing, *Purchasing Management*).

- Comprehensive: the audit should cover every aspect of purchasing
- Systematic: a standard set of questions should be developed and used
- Independent: purchasing personnel should not evaluate themselves
- Periodic audits: the greatest value is achieved if the audit is performed periodically (eg annually), as this facilitates comparisons, checks and balances and monitors progress

2.10   Purchasing management audits have four main purposes.

- To verify the extent to which purchasing policies (including sustainable procurement) are being adhered to
- To ensure that procedures and methods conform to best working practice

- To monitor and measure the extent to which resources are used efficiently and effectively
- To assist in the detection of fraud.

Supplier and supply chain audit

2.11 The scope of a supplier audit or capability survey (eg for the purpose of supplier appraisal, approval or ongoing vendor rating) generally includes: a capability assessment, a review of the supplier's management systems, assessment of how they assure quality or sustainability, and how compatible they are with the buyer's systems and working practices. More focused sustainability audits may focus on the supplier's labour, environmental and ethical management standards, processes and performance – ideally enabling drilling down to the suppliers' supply chain.

2.12 Qualified independent auditors will usually be required to conduct supplier certifications under external quality, environmental and social responsibility management standards. Buyers may have to rely on external certifications, or on audit assessments provided by suppliers themselves. However, where suppliers have agreed to comply with the buyer's sustainable procurement principles or other standards, the buyer should be able to agree to conduct periodic site visits, audits and assessments. Again, these may involve the use of third-party assessors where appropriate (eg in the auditing of overseas suppliers or contractors). In the interests of relationship sustainability, however, audits should not be excessively frequent, onerous or disruptive.

2.13 Supplier audits may be carried out initially via self-administered supplier questionnaires, but these are generally supplemented with visits to supplier premises on a regular cycle (for high priority or high risk suppliers or purchases, for which the cost can be justified). The idea of site visits is to look at the supplier's operations – in this context, with a particular focus on sustainability issues – and discuss any shortcomings that are identified, with a view to achieving improvements by the time of the next visit. Operations can be observed, outputs sampled, and key personnel interviewed.

2.14 Site visits are an important source of information on such matters as: equipment, operations, working practices and processes, production capacity, human resources, management/technical capabilities, working conditions and so on. Multi-functional site visit teams are often used to provide the expertise required for a broad-ranging assessment.

2.15 In order to maximise the value of site visits, many assessments are based on information provided in a self-administered supplier questionnaire. General supplier questionnaires will include information on the organisation's history and current standing, its key management personnel, products and markets, attitudes to quality/sustainability issues, CSR/sustainability policies and so on.

Environmental (green) and sustainability audits

2.16 An environmental audit is the inspection of a company to assess the environmental impact of its activities, or of a particular product or process, as the basis for managerial decision-making. For example, the audit of a manufactured product may look at the impact of production (including energy use and the extraction of raw materials used in manufacture), usage (which may cause pollution and other hazards), and disposal (potential for recycling, and whether waste causes pollution).

2.17 An environmental review would normally start with the identification of areas of a site to be assessed: external areas (such as vehicle access, waste storage and drainage areas) and internal areas (offices, process areas). A checklist of environmental issues (wastes, emissions, hazardous substances, energy consumption) can then be assessed for each area, using observation, interviews and review of documentation and records: waste management documentation, Integrated Pollution Control (IPC) authorisations, discharge consents from water companies and/or the Environment Agency and so on. An assessment report will be communicated to key stakeholders, and a register of impacts drawn up, as the focus for problem-solving, risk assessment and management, and ongoing improvement planning.

Example: Oxfam GB supplier questionnaire

Oxfam GB's Ethical Purchasing Policy 'recognises that the globalisation of trade means that more and more of the goods and services we buy are at risk of being produced by workers in unregulated environments'. It states that Oxfam will 'strive to purchase goods and services which are produced and delivered under conditions that do not involve the abuse or exploitation of any persons and that have the least negative impact on the environment'.

'When we assess new suppliers we first ask them to complete a Supplier Questionnaire, which is risk-rated as high, medium or low ethical risk. Then depending on where production is carried out, we will also ask for an ethical audit report on the factory to be used. We make clear to suppliers that we are not looking for complete compliance with all standards at the outset; but we do expect a commitment to the standards in the code at director level, we expect continuous improvement towards the standards where necessary, and we expect risks in the supply chain to be assessed and managed.'

The Supplier Questionnaire contains four sections.

- Business details: locations, contact details, number of employees, main products/services, turnover

- Operational standards: governance/ethics contact; proportion of women employed; use of home-workers; quality/social/environmental policies; trade union recognition; communication of human and labour rights; wages and working hours; minimum age; health and safety; and operational/management standards achieved

- Sourcing from sub-suppliers: assessment of social and environmental risk; sourcing policy and criteria; location and type of subcontractors

- Continuous improvement: actual and planned, own and sub-supplier improvements in quality, labour, environment and health and safety

---

2.18 The Envirowise agency, a government-funded business consultancy focusing on environmental sustainability, recommends audit tools similar to those used in supplier audits: an audit checklist (to structure the audit and ensure completeness); self-administered questionnaires (to cover matters of fact); interviews (to test staff awareness of issues and policies); discussion (for briefing, consultation and clarification); and reporting on findings, highlighting areas for decision-making and action.

2.19 Environmental audits may be general eg in the case of supplier appraisal or vendor rating, or as a first step in developing an environmental management system – or in gaining accreditation for such a system, under standards such as ISO 14001 and EMAS (discussed in Chapter 11). Alternatively, they may focus on particular areas.

- A *waste audit*, for example, is concerned with waste production and handling – as the first step in waste minimisation programmes. The focus will be on safe, environmentally-friendly and cost-efficient handling, storage and disposal (including transport and disposal by contractors). Quantities and origins of waste will be identified with a view to reduction. Waste management record-keeping processes, and documentation compliance (eg waste management licences) should also be checked.

- A *water audit* is concerned with water use and waste water production. A 'mass balance' can be derived, identifying inward and outward water volumes: discrepancies may indicate leakage, for example. Areas of high water usage or wastage can be investigated for reduction.

SWOT analysis

2.20 Audit information can be used for strategic planning. One useful tool in this respect is Strengths, Weaknesses, Opportunities and Threats (SWOT) analysis. SWOT analysis is a strategic planning technique, used to assess the internal resources and capabilities of a supplier (or indeed the buying organisation or the purchasing function) to cope with and/or capitalise on factors in its external environment.

- In the present context, strengths and weaknesses are internal aspects of the supplier (or other subject) that enhance or limit its ability to perform sustainably. Internal appraisal may cover physical and financial resources; the product/service portfolio; human resources; the efficiency and effectiveness of functions, operations and systems; organisation structure; and distinctive competencies.

- Opportunities and threats are sustainability issues and factors in the external environment that may emerge to impact on the business. What potential do they offer to either enhance or erode competitive advantage or profitability?

2.21 Internal and external factors can be mapped in a SWOT grid: Figure 13.1.

Figure 13.1: *SWOT analysis*

Internal	**Strengths** New technology Environmental management system Stable, high-quality staff Strong brand reputation	**Weaknesses** Low capability for design and innovation Poor financial and governance controls High use of non-renewable resources
External	**Opportunities** E-procurement Green consumer preferences Tax breaks for regional development	**Threats** Non-renewable resource issues Risk of scrutiny re governance Pressure to innovate

2.22 SWOT is used to identify areas where there may be sustainability-related risks and/or potential for mitigation and development. The buyer may need to:

- Plan to build on strengths and/or minimise weaknesses – in order to be able to capitalise on the identified opportunities (or create new ones) and to cope better with the identified threats.

- Plan to convert threats into opportunities – by developing the strengths (and contingency plans) to counter threats more effectively than competitors, and by being prepared to learn from them.

3 Key performance indicators for sustainability

3.1 Key performance indicators (or KPIs) are agreed, specific measures of the performance of a unit or organisation, against which progress and performance can be evaluated.

3.2   The process of developing KPIs can be summarised as in Figure 13.2.

Figure 13.2 *Developing key performance indicators*

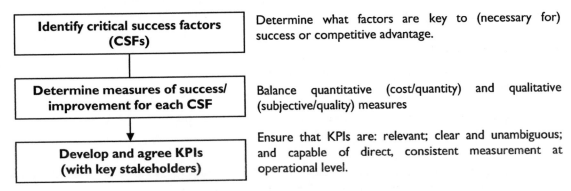

Advantages and disadvantages of using sustainability KPIs

3.3   Here are some benefits of developing KPIs as performance measures for sustainability.

- Increased and improved (results-focused) communication on sustainability performance and issues
- Motivation to achieve or better the specified performance level (particularly with KPI-linked incentives, rewards or penalties). Motivation is in any case stronger where there are clear targets to aim for.
- Support for collaborative buyer-supplier relations, by enabling integrated or two-way performance measurement (with KPIs on both sides of the relationship)
- The ability directly to compare year on year performance, to identify improvement or deterioration trends
- Focus on key results areas (critical success factors) such as cost management, reputational protection and environmental compliance
- Clearly defined shared goals, facilitating cross-functional and cross-organisational teamwork and relationships.

3.4   Setting KPIs for supplier sustainability performance, in particular, may be beneficial in the following ways.

- Setting clear performance criteria and expectations for compliance and improvement
- Managing sustainability-related risk
- Supporting contract management and supplier motivation
- Identifying high-performing suppliers for inclusion on approved/preferred supplier lists (which in turn supports efficient buying by user departments)
- Identifying high-performing suppliers with potential for closer partnership relations
- Providing feedback for learning and continuous improvement in the buyer-supplier relationship – both for the supplier, and for the purchasing department.

3.5   It is worth noting that KPIs can have some disadvantages as well. The pursuit of individual KPIs can lead to some dysfunctional or sub-optimal behaviour: cutting corners on quality or service to achieve efficiency targets, say, or units focusing on their own targets at the expense of cross-functional collaboration and co-ordination. Targets will have to be carefully set with these potential problems in mind. KPIs should be limited in number; focused on critical success factors, to maximise their relevance and leverage potential; and vertically and horizontally aligned.

Sample KPIs for sustainability

3.6   Suggesting KPIs for sustainable procurement is potentially a fertile area for exam questions. Table 13.1 offers some sample suggestions for KPIs in each of the Triple Bottom Line areas. Bear in mind that these are generic: more specific KPIs may be appropriate in particular industry sectors and business types, according to their sustainability priorities and current levels of performance.

Benchmarking

3.7   A useful definition of benchmarking is: 'Measuring your performance against that of best-in-class companies, determining how the best-in-class achieve these performance levels and using the information as a basis for your own company's targets, strategies and implementation' (Pryor). The aim is to learn both where performance needs to be improved and how it can be improved, by comparison with excellent practitioners.

3.8   Benchmarking can be used to analyse any aspect of organisational performance, including environmental and social sustainability, or sustainability management. Benchmarked performance targets and quality standards are likely to be realistic (since other organisations have achieved them), yet challenging (since the benchmarking organisation hasn't yet achieved them). This is the most effective combination for maintaining motivation! At the same time, benchmarking helpfully stimulates more research and feedback-seeking into customer needs and wants, and generates new ideas and insights outside the box of the organisation's accustomed ways of thinking and doing things.

3.9   Bendell, Boulter & Kelly distinguish four types of benchmarking, which can be applied to sustainability benchmarking.

- *Internal benchmarking*: comparison with high-performing units in the same organisation. For example, a divisional purchasing function might be benchmarked against a sustainability 'centre of excellence' in another division.

- *Competitor benchmarking*: comparison with high-performing competitors for whom sustainability is a source of competitive advantage.

- *Functional benchmarking*: comparison with another, high-performing organisation. For example, an electronics manufacturer might benchmark its procurement against that of a construction company known for excellent waste management.

- *Generic benchmarking*: comparison of business processes across functional and industry boundaries. The benchmark may be set by the example of CSR/sustainability leaders (as featured in sustainability rankings and awards), or may be formalised in sustainability standards (such as those discussed in Chapter 11).

Table 13.1 *Example KPIs for sustainability*

	Example procurement KPIs	**Example supplier KPIs**
Economic performance	• Cost (eg procurement costs as a percentage of spend) or cost savings (annual cost savings as a percentage of spend) • Productivity (eg cost per procurement cycle, time taken per procurement cycle) • Supplier leverage (eg percentage of suppliers providing 80% or more of annual spend) • Customer satisfaction (eg percentage of deliveries received on time in full)	• Price (eg basic purchase price, value/percentage of cost reductions) • Quality/conformance (eg reject, error or wastage rates) • Delivery (eg or percentage of on time in full deliveries) • Service/relationship (eg promptness in dealing with enquiries/problems) • Innovation capability (eg number of innovations proposed/implemented) • Overall performance (eg benchmarking against other suppliers)
Environmental performance	• Percentage reduction in energy, water purchase • Percentage reduction in supplier (or logistics or procurement) GHG emissions • Percentage reduction in supplier water and energy usage • Percentage purchase of recycled materials • Percentage of vehicle fleet which is hybrid • Volume of waste to landfill (buyer and supplier) • Percentage of spend with suppliers who report on environmental impacts, or operate EMS.	• Percentage reduction in energy, water and other resource use • Percentage reduction in waste to landfill, pollution, GHG emissions etc • Percentage recycled materials used • Progress towards accreditation of EMS (under ISO 14001) • Attainment of environmental benchmark standards • Green innovations proposed/implemented • Sustainable management of land and practices (eg forestry, agriculture) • Reporting on environmental impact
Social/ ethical performance	• Diversity and equal opportunity among procurement staff • Training/development opportunities (and percentage of take-up) • Compliance with workplace law and standards, ethical sourcing and trading standards/objectives • Reduction in health and safety incidents, grievance proceedings etc • Supplier diversity (number of women-owned, minority-owned, small suppliers) • Percentage supply chain monitored and managed for compliance • Supply chain compliance (eg year on year reduction in incidents of non-compliance)	• Diversity and equal opportunity among supplier staff • Minimum working conditions and wages for staff • Compliance with human and labour rights law and standards • Year on year improvements in health and safety record • Percentage supply chain monitored and managed for compliance • Percentage products tested on animals (and adherence to animal welfare standards) • Progress towards sustainability management system or development of CSR policy

3.10 Where an organisation wants to carry out its own sustainability benchmarking, the process may be something like Figure 13.3.

Figure 13.3 *The benchmarking process*

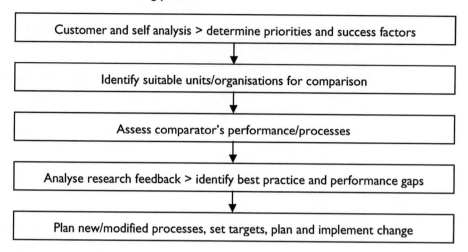

---

4 Cost and whole-life sustainability tools

Cost management

4.1 Public, private and third sector organisations are (albeit with different priorities in regard to profit, surplus, value for money service provision, efficiency targets or stewardship) concerned to manage available resources as efficiently and effectively as possible. It is natural to apply performance measurement systems to the area of cost management – and this is clearly supportive of an economically sustainable operation.

4.2 Cost management strategies are about knowing what the costs really are and then looking at how to reduce them. In other words, we must apply effective cost analysis, with a particular focus on whole-life costing, total cost of ownership or total acquisition costs (discussed below). Then we are in a position to look at eliminating waste, negotiating on price and so on.

4.3 At the level of purchase price, buyers should aim to discover as much as possible about the cost structure of their suppliers, breaking down the supplier's selling price into cost of materials, cost of labour, overheads and profit. Buyers can then compare one supplier with another; monitor changes in price levels over time; work with the supplier to identify areas for cost savings; and challenge the supplier, if it appears that profit levels are unduly high. However, this raises another sustainability issue: what can be considered a 'fair' level of profit that should be allowed to suppliers, in order to protect their financial viability, fairly reward their contribution to the value stream, and protect the security and continuity of supply.

4.4 At an operational level, the procurement function can contribute to cost efficiency and reduction by measures such as the following.

- Reducing the cost of inputs by effective negotiation and/or tendering
- Reducing the cost of purchasing activity and transactions, through process and management efficiencies
- Working with users to improve value analysis and specifications, so that requirements are fulfilled more efficiently and at lower cost
- Managing inventory to minimise the costs of acquiring and holding stock

- Using effective investment appraisal methods (such as whole-life costing) to secure best value over the life of assets.

4.5 At a strategic level, supply chain management may secure cost reductions through measures such as the following.

- *Restructuring*: delayering, downsizing or horizontalising purchasing structures, to minimise labour and overhead costs and maximise process efficiencies (less duplication of effort, fewer managerial/co-ordinatory mechanisms and so on)

- *Centralising purchasing* (to take advantage of aggregated orders and bargaining leverage) or decentralising purchasing (to reduce transport and storage costs)

- *Process engineering or re-engineering*, to streamline and integrate processes, eliminating unnecessary activities and process inefficiencies

- *Outsourcing or off-shoring non-core competencies*: where value can be obtained at less cost, the organisation can divest itself of assets, and internal resources can be more efficiently focused

- *Developing supplier relationships* for cost and price advantages (by using competitive leverage to secure low prices or by developing collaboration to reduce sourcing/transaction costs, encourage mutual cost reduction and so on)

- *Applying ICT and automation technologies* to streamline processes (eg the use of e-procurement tools); increase productivity and reduce labour costs; reduce overheads (eg by 'virtual' teamworking); secure competitive pricing (eg through internet access to global supply markets, or the use of e-auctions); support more efficient planning and decision-making (via computerised planning models), and so on.

Total cost of ownership

4.6 The overall objective of cost management in the private sector is improved profitability, and in the public and third sectors, resource efficiency and value. But profit and value ultimately mean any benefit – including long-term benefits – accruing to the organisation and its stakeholders. This may be far beyond short-term cost and price considerations. Current thinking, as we have seen in previous chapters, emphasises a *total cost of ownership* or *total acquisition cost*, which includes a basket of costs not immediately apparent from the purchase price. 'It is an obvious fact, yet a commonly ignored one, that a low price may lead to a high total acquisition cost.' (Baily, Farmer, Jessop and Jones, *Purchasing Principles and Management*).

4.7 The total costs of ownership can be categorised under six main headings.

- *Pre-acquisition costs*: such as research, sourcing, preparation of tenders and structural changes to allow for the product.

- *Acquisition costs*: including the purchase price, delivery, installation and commissioning etc.

- *Operating costs*: embracing labour, materials, consumables, electricity usage, environmental costs etc.

- *Maintenance costs*: such as spares and replacement parts, servicing, reducing output with age etc.

- *Downtime costs*: lost profit, extra labour costs, costs resulting from non-performance and claims resulting from non-performance.

- *End of life costs*: disposal, ongoing liabilities, decommissioning, sale for scrap, resale etc.

4.8   The broadening strategic remit of purchasing, and the increasing emphasis on strategic alignment, has led to a shift in procurement performance measurement from purchase and inventory cost reduction (in line with purely functional targets) to total cost management: that is, a cross-functional – and cross-supply-chain – approach to controlling and if possible reducing the total costs of ownership. So, for example, while procurement could reduce materials costs by specifying lower quality or taking advantage of bulk discounts, such decisions would be regarded as sub-optimal (and ultimately unsustainable): the savings may be more than outweighed by costs of quality failure or repair, excess inventory and so on.

Whole-life costing

4.9   As we have seen in earlier chapters, the purchase of capital assets illustrates the difference between purchase price and total costs particularly clearly. Such assets by their nature have a long life in use, and will give rise to many costs in addition to the original cost of purchase (delivery, installation, commissioning, maintenance, running costs, time lost to failure/inefficiency, disposal and so on).

4.10   CIPS therefore consider whole-life costing (or lifecycle costing) as a best practice tool for evaluating options for any substantial procurement: establishing the total cost of ownership, and annual spend profile, over the entire anticipated lifespan of the product.

4.11   'In whole-life costing, all costs over the life of goods and services are taken into account. This enables savings in running costs to offset any increase in capital costs. The savings are calculated for each year of the equipment or service contract life. It shows either a simple payback time or the payback during the life of the equipment or service contract. It can be applied to most situations to justify extra expenditure.' (CIPS Knowledge Works Document on Whole-Life Costing)

Product lifecycle analysis

4.12   More generally, the analysis of a product over its total life-span can be used as a tool of risk assessment and management, in support of sustainable procurement. The lifecycle of a product may be defined in different ways.

4.13   Marketers define product lifecycle (PLC) in terms of sales volume and profitability over time, with phases of: introduction, growth, maturity, saturation, decline and withdrawal. The model is arguably of little relevance to sustainable procurement, other than suggesting opportunities (and perhaps a business case) for introducing more sustainable products/services to the portfolio (in order to have a flow of new products entering profitable maturity), or for 'refreshing' declining brands with sustainable attributes, or for sustainable disposal of withdrawn products.

4.14   More relevant might be a product lifecycle model which surveys each stage of a product's progress through various processes: supply of materials, conversion (manufacturing, assembly, processing), storage and distribution, sale, installation, consumption/use, maintenance, decommissioning and end-of-life disposal.

4.15   Using such a model, both purchased products (inputs) and end products (outputs) can be examined – ideally at specification or design/development stage – to identify their economic, environmental and social impacts, risks and benefits at each stage. At what stage of the lifecycle is most energy used, or emissions or wastes created? At what stages can sustainability benefits and 'quick wins' be secured most readily? At what stages can specific measures (such as recycling) be applied? Will downstream, internal or upstream management create the best leverage?

> **Example: Marks & Spencer**
>
> Under its Plan A CSR measures, M & S conducts lifecycle assessments of a range of its retail products and their packaging. It found that some 70% of all energy used in the total life of a clothing garment was accounted for by washing in consumers' homes. In order to apply leverage to the objective of lowering energy consumption (supporting reduced carbon footprint), M & S is manufacturing own-brand clothes that can be washed at lower temperatures, as well as educating customers to wash more energy-efficiently, and engaging them in Plan A pledges to make these changes.

5 Stakeholder and supply chain management tools

Stakeholder mapping

5.1 Stakeholder management was discussed in Chapter 8, as part of the implementation of sustainable procurement programmes. In our coverage, we introduced stakeholder 'mapping' as a tool for categorising and prioritising stakeholders, and identifying appropriate strategies to manage them.

5.2 The most used tool for stakeholder mapping is Mendelow's power/interest matrix: Figure 13.4. We discussed the matrix in Chapter 8, and won't repeat ourselves here: recap the material if you need to.

Figure 13.4: *Mendelow's power/interest matrix*

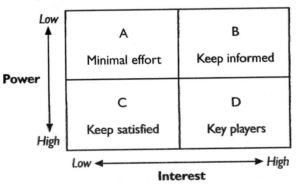

5.3 The purpose of the Mendelow matrix is basically to prioritise stakeholders according to their importance, measured in terms of (a) their power to influence the organisation and its plans and (b) their interest in doing so, or the strength of their motivation to do so. As we saw in Chapter 8, this can support sustainable procurement in the following ways.

- Identifying the stakeholders whose needs and expectations will define sustainable value and shape the sustainability agenda and priorities of the organisation (eg green consumers, influential NGOs and government)

- Identifying the stakeholders whose interests will be most affected by an organisational decision or action, and towards whom the organisation may therefore recognise some moral or legal obligations (eg communities impacted by environmental damage or the withdrawal of services)

- Identifying the stakeholders who will need to be informed, consulted or actively involved in the design and implementation of sustainable procurement policies and programmes (as suggested by the quadrants of the Mendelow matrix)

- Prioritising stakeholder interests, so that resources are not diluted or wasted by trying to 'be all things to all people' (which would be economically unsustainable).

5.4   It may also be helpful to map internal and external stakeholders according to their support for or opposition to sustainable procurement proposals. In another well known model, used in change management, Egan (*Working the Shadow Side*) divides stakeholders in a change or proposal into nine distinct groups, in relation to the leader or agent of change.

- *Partners*: those who support the change agent
- *Allies*: those who will support him or her, given encouragement
- *Fellow travellers*: passive supporters, who are committed to the agenda, but not to the change agent personally
- *Bedfellows*: people who support the agenda, but do not know or trust the change agent
- *Fence sitters*: those whose allegiances are not yet clear
- *Loose cannons*: people who may vote either way on agendas in which they have no direct stake
- *Opponents*: people who oppose the agenda, but not the change agent personally
- *Adversaries*: people who oppose the change agent and the agenda
- *The voiceless*: 'silent' stakeholders who are affected by the agenda, but lack advocates or power to influence decisions (eg future generations, disenfranchised people/workers, and flora and fauna).

5.5   Like other stakeholder maps, Egan's model argues that different stakeholder groups must be managed differently. Supporters (in various groups) need to be encouraged and kept 'on side'; opponents need to be persuaded of the merits of the agenda (or 'converted'); adversaries have to be marginalised or discredited, to reduce their influence for resistance. One of the key principles of sustainability, however, is that the needs of the voiceless must also receive attention, despite their relative powerlessness.

5.6   The Civil Contingencies Secretariat outlines the full range of questions posed by stakeholder mapping as follows.

- What are the potential issues?
- Who will be affected by the risk and consequences of any management decision?
- Which parties or individuals have knowledge and expertise that may be useful to inform any discussion?
- Which parties or individuals have expressed an interest in this particular, or a similar, risk problem?
- Which stakeholders will be prepared to listen to and respect different viewpoints, and might be prepared to negotiate?

Stakeholder communication

5.7   Again, we discussed various tools and mechanisms for stakeholder communication in Chapter 8, and won't repeat ourselves here.

5.8   A stakeholder communications plan might include the following elements.

- A list of all stakeholders and their information requirements
- Communication mechanisms to be used (advertisements, written reports, newsletter, emails, briefing and consultation meetings, workshops, conferences, general meetings, media releases and communiqués, the website, intranets and extranets and so on) — taking into account the need for feedback and dialogue where appropriate

- Key elements of information to be distributed by the different mechanisms, and the level and frequency of communication required

- Roles and responsibilities of key individuals in ensuring that communication is adequate, appropriate and timely

- Identification of how unexpected information from other parties (eg media reports or internet discussion) will be handled within the scope of the activity.

Supply chain mapping

5.9   A supply chain 'encompasses all organisations and activities associated with the flow and transformation of goods from the raw materials stage, through to the end user, as well as the associated information flows. Material and information flow both up and down the supply chain' (Handfield & Nichols).

5.10 Supply chain mapping is a diagrammatic representation of the configuration of a supply chain, including key participants, flows (of materials, products, information and finance) and relationships/linkages. A simplified generic example, in a construction setting, might be as shown in Figure 13.5.

Figure 13.5 *Supply chain map for a construction supply chain*

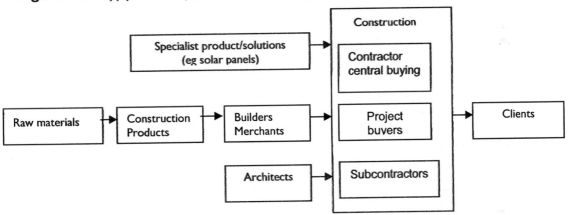

5.11 In a supply network model, there may be a complex web of connections: Figure 13.6.

Figure 13.6 *A simple (!) supply network map*

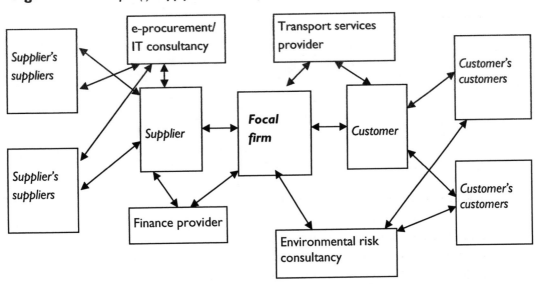

5.12 Like product lifecycle analysis, discussed earlier, supply chain mapping is a tool of analysis and communication, enabling managers to identify:

- Strong and weak linkages in the sustainability chain (eg due to poor relationships; lack of communication; unknown or un-certified sub-suppliers; or supply chain members without sustainability/CSR/ethical policies in place)

- Potential areas of sustainability, compliance or reputational risk (eg due to strong association with high-risk supply chain partners; sustainability risks/issues affecting particular organisation types or stages of the supply process)

- Potential areas of supply risk (eg due to poor supplier relationships, or over-reliance on a small supply base for strategic or bottleneck purchases) and mitigating actions: eg alternative sources of supply, contingency plans, 'just in case' stock levels

- Potential areas of opportunity or strength, arising from network connections or partners with strong capability, resources or reputation for sustainability

- Areas of inefficiency in the supply chain (eg unnecessary movements/transport, processes, or an overly large supply base) which erode economic and/or environmental sustainability. Maps may add elements such as time (eg indicating waiting and idle time) and inventory build up, for the identification of wastes.

- Potential efficiencies (eg for variety reduction, supply base rationalisation or process alignment)

- The breakdown of costs, added value, resource/energy usage and environmental impacts (among other key sustainability factors) at each stage of the supply chain

- Areas in which improved information or resource flows are required for the development of innovation and sustainability (eg feedback from downstream members to support demand and define value for sustainable products)

- Weakness in reverse logistics, or lack of a closed loop supply chain, which may need to be addressed for sustainability (eg for take-back and recycling or disposal obligations)

- Areas in which the organisation may need to move from a 'chain' to a 'network' as the dominant metaphor for supply, in order to develop a wider range of collaborations for sustainability (eg with NGO partners)

5.13 Issues highlighted by the map can be further investigated. If you are interested in this area, you might like to download the *CIPS Good Practice Guide on Supply Chain Mapping*.

Source planning

5.14 One of the activities supported by supply chain mapping is source planning: focusing on priority categories of purchased products or services; conducting a systematic analysis of current and potential sources of supply (in the light of the organisation's sustainable procurement objectives); and planning how the market will be engaged in order to secure requirements most effectively and efficiently.

5.15 We have already discussed the sourcing plan, as part of the procurement cycle, in Chapter 10. A systematic approach to source planning will include the following steps.

- Analysis of business need and requirements
- Gathering key statistics (eg on product/service sustainability measures, current suppliers, allocation of spend and so on)
- Portfolio analysis (eg using the Kraljic matrix) and supplier preferencing to establish priority items and supplier/customer relationships
- Sourcing history

- Price and cost analysis (including the use of lifecycle costing to determine the sustainability of pricing and cost strategies)
- Supply chain and supply market analysis
- Risk assessment (in regard to the supply market, supply base and supply chain relationships)
- Supplier capability and performance appraisal (eg using sustainability measures)
- Options generation and evaluation
- Formulation of an optimal sourcing strategy and plans

6 *Sustainability reporting*

Reasons for transparent sustainability reporting

6.1 This area is not really mentioned in the syllabus, although it could be argued that it is connected to the process of performance measurement and management. However, it is covered in some detail in the guidance published by CIPS for this unit, so we will briefly touch on some key points here – just in case.

6.2 There are a number of reasons for advocating transparency in sustainability reporting.

- Blackburn argues that 'shining a light on performance can produce the heat of accountability, which heightens the likelihood of constructive change'. Sustainability reports spur change because they invite scrutiny, and reaction to performance, from stakeholders.

- Sustainability reports highlight issues, drivers and gaps in performance, creating an impetus for improvement planning and risk management – and enabling the resolution of problems before they escalate.

- The process of preparing reports encourages stakeholder communication on sustainability issues, and educates employees on the issues.

- Examples of good practice may emerge, for use as benchmarks, or as the focus of recognition and reward – reinforcing and motivating improvement.

- Transparency builds stakeholder trust and an organisational reputation for honesty, which may be beneficial in gaining support, resources, reputational/brand capital, goodwill and resilience in the face of PR crises.

6.3 Sustainability reporting may also be a compliance issue. Financial reporting has been a statutory requirement for many years. In the UK, law implementing the EU Accounts Modernisation Directive (AMD) now requires large companies to include a Business Review in their annual reports, including information about the effectiveness of the organisation's sustainability policies, and, where appropriate, an analysis of KPIs related to employee, supplier and environmental matters and social and community issues. Some countries also have detailed pollutant-disclosure laws (eg toxic release inventory reporting in the US), 'right to know' laws, or national registers of environmental emissions.

6.4 There have also been a number of voluntary sustainability reporting initiatives. The EMAS standard (discussed in Chapter 11), for example, requires participating companies to produce a public, externally verified environmental statement, covering environmental policies, programmes, management systems, goals, performance results, and significant environmental impacts and their effects. Another major voluntary framework is the Global Reporting Initiative or GRI, discussed further below.

6.5   An important point to note is the emphasis on 'transparency' – not just 'reporting'. In a 2003 survey of NGOs, reported by Blackburn, less than half of the respondents considered corporate sustainability reports 'believable'. The most effective way to improve credibility was said to be to acknowledge non-compliance, poor performance and significant problems – not just to state policies or boast achievements.

Barriers to sustainability reporting

6.6   Blackburn suggests reasons why many companies do not implement transparent sustainability reporting – and what can be done to overcome the barriers: Table 13.2. This framework might be used within the buying organisation – or to encourage supply chain partners to become more transparent in their reporting.

Table 13.2 *Supporting transparent sustainability reporting*

Barriers to reporting	Ways of overcoming barriers
Embarrassment about performance	Begin with transparency in internal reports
No competitive advantage, if competitors aren't reporting	Draw attention to broad multi-stakeholder support for transparency programmes
Protection of confidentiality	Sell the business case for transparency
Concern about legal liability	Emphasise communicable wins
Concern about negative PR, stakeholder or media responses	Demonstrate resilience of transparent firms: eg Shell, Nike, Johnson & Johnson
Failure to recognise, understand or give priority to the issue	Educate internal stakeholders and demonstrate risks of non-transparency
Belief that cost/effort would be excessive	Reduce costs: start small (scope, frequency), use readily available data and resources, audit internally, combine with other audits or use NGO volunteers

The Global Reporting Initiative

6.7   The GRI was started in 1997 by the Coalition for Environmentally Responsible Economies (CERES) and UNEP, with the aim of promoting reporting on economic, environmental and social performance by all organisations. The Sustainability Reporting Guidelines are applicable across sectors and industries, with sector supplements for specific industries and reporting entities.

6.8   Reporting entities are asked to provide information on strategy, organisational profile, governance, stakeholder engagement, and commitments and management approach on sustainability matters. In addition, specific KPIs are listed across the Triple Bottom Line dimensions, and reporters are required to use those indicators that are material to their stakeholders and decision-making. Blackburn argues that 'although the use of GRI is no substitute for actual dialogue between a company and its own stakeholders, it does offer a perspective even broader than dialogue can produce, helping report writers anticipate issues their own customers, investors and employees may raise in the future.'

6.9   Some 460 organisations are listed as using the guidelines systematically and in full. The number and percentage of companies engaged in GRI reporting – and in sustainability reporting in general – is therefore very small. However, Blackburn identifies a number of drivers in its favour. Some major investment analysts are urging publicly traded companies to prepare GRI reports, for example, to support analysis of underlying risks, liabilities and advantages from corporate activities. Activist shareholders are also pressing for GRI reporting at shareholder meetings.

Accessing sustainability information about suppliers

6.10 In addition to published annual reports and accounts, and voluntary sustainability reports (where available), there are a number of secondary sources of information for assessing the sustainability performance of suppliers, including:

- Credit rating reports and agencies
- Sustainability Indices, such as the Dow Jones Sustainability Index (http://www.sustainability-index.com)
- Awards and directories: eg the Association of Certified Accountants (ACCA) awards for sustainability reporting, and various Top Ethical Brand and Most Admired Company listings
- The Supplier Ethical Data Exchange (Sedex): a web-based non-for-profit organisation for companies wanting to monitor and improve ethical performance in their supply chains – including founding members like Waitrose, Tesco and Marks & Spencer. Members can view supplier data, run reports on their supply chains, report on their own activities, or input data to self assessment questionnaires, depending on membership category.
- Public environmental reports posted under the EMAS standard
- Case studies and reports posted on the websites of relevant standards organisations and NGOs.

Example: Mattel Inc

As befits a global family of market-leading toy brands – a sector under a high degree of scrutiny, due to child safety issues – Mattel Inc has been a leader in transparent CSR, sustainability and governance reporting.

- In 1997, it developed a set of Global Manufacturing Principles (GMP), focused on ensuring the safe and fair treatment of employees in its own and contract factories. Compliance is independently monitored.

- In 2003, it issued its first GRI report, to publicly assess the success of the GMP and commit to improvements.

- In 2003, it also rolled out a Code of Ethical Conduct for all employees.

- In 2004, it issued a public Corporate Responsibility Report: the first to be issued by a toy company. Its website includes public statements on ethics, corporate governance, good corporate citizenship, strategic sustainability initiatives and core values.

- In 2007, it created the post of Vice President of Corporate Responsibility, to take charge of developing and implementing worldwide programmes to underscore Mattel's commitment to business integrity, reporting directly to the CEO.

Chapter summary

- 'What gets measured, gets managed' – so it is important to monitor and measure sustainability performance. Measurement data may be quantitative, qualitative, or both.

- In measuring performance, buyers will often use a formal audit process, whether conducted by internal staff or external experts.

- Audits may be applied to purchasing management, suppliers and the supply chain. Often the aim is to assess environmental credentials.

- The measurement process will normally involve development of critical success factors and key performance indicators.

- Benchmarking can be used to identify any aspect of organisational performance, including environmental and social sustainability.

- Modern thinking emphasises that total cost of ownership is more important than basic purchase price. This has led to the development of whole-life costing.

- Stakeholder mapping, often using Mendelow's matrix, is an important tool in classifying and then managing stakeholders.

- Supply chain mapping is a tool of analysis and communication, enabling managers to identify strengths and weaknesses in the supply chain.

- Increasingly, organisations report their performance in regard to sustainability issues. This helps to educate and to keep such issues high on the corporate agenda.

Self-test questions

Numbers in brackets refer to the paragraphs above where your answers can be checked.

1 Distinguish between quantitative and qualitative data for performance measurement. (1.4)

2 List types of audit relevant to sustainability monitoring. (2.2)

3 List drawbacks to using the audit approach for sustainability monitoring. (2.7)

4 Explain what is meant by a SWOT analysis. (2.20)

5 List advantages of KPIs for supplier sustainability performance. (3.4)

6 Give examples of sustainability KPIs. (Table 13.1)

7 What are the steps in a benchmarking process? (Figure 13.3)

8 List strategic measures by which supply chain managers can achieve cost reductions. (4.5)

9 List six headings under which total costs of ownership may be categorised. (4.7)

10 Draw the Mendelow matrix. (Figure 13.4)

11 List steps in a systematic approach to source planning. (5.15)

12 Give reasons for advocating transparency in sustainability reporting. (6.2)

Further reading

From your 'Essential Reading' list, if you have time, you might look at Blackburn (*The Sustainability Handbook*):

- Chapter 9: Data Systems, Auditing and Other Monitoring and Accountability Mechanisms

- Chapter 10: Transparent Sustainability Reporting

CHAPTER 14

Barriers to Sustainable Procurement

Learning objectives and indicative content

4.1 Evaluate the barriers to achieving sustainable procurement within different organisations and sectors in both the global and local context

- Cost issues such as raw materials, process costs, recycling and re-use, budget and funding restrictions
- Attitudes of key stakeholders including customers, shareholders, employees, donors, suppliers, buyers and the general public
- Policies at international, European Union, government, organisation and department levels
- External cultural factors such as nationality, religion and ethics
- Internal management culture within sectors, industries and organisations
- Level of economic stability: growth or decline, inflation levels and trends, credit restrictions and protectionism

Chapter headings

1 Cost issues

2 Stakeholder attitudes

3 Policy conflicts

4 Cultural barriers

5 Macro-economic barriers

6 Barriers in different sectors

Introduction

The first three sections of the syllabus broadly regard sustainable procurement as a necessary and positive thing, and focus on how it can be developed and implemented. From time to time, we have raised the possibility of a contrary view. In Chapter 1, we asked: is there an argument against sustainable procurement? And in Chapter 6, we noted that not all the implications of sustainable procurement strategy for an organisation are clear-cut or positive: there may be compromises, conflicts and trade-offs to consider.

In this and the following chapters, we explore these issues further. This is the reverse side of our coverage of the drivers for sustainable procurement, in Chapter 5, representing the 'restraining forces' which resist change.

In this chapter, we will look at 'barriers': factors and forces which may obstruct an organisation's progress towards sustainable procurement, or the sustainable procurement agenda in general. In Chapter 15, we will cover 'conflicts' (objectives, options and stakeholder interests which are mutually exclusive) and 'trade-offs' (the compromises that may have to be made to reconcile them). In Chapter 16, we will turn to 'future challenges' in sustainable procurement. Our coverage will necessarily be fairly general: you will need to apply it to the specific circumstances of any case study organisation cited in the exam.

1 Cost issues

The sustainable option may be more expensive...

1.1 One of the biggest challenges faced by sustainable procurement is the perception that it is a more expensive option, and that sustainability fundamentally conflicts with procurement's core aims of cost management and value for money.

1.2 Sustainable options may well be more expensive, for a variety of reasons.

- They may involve the purchase of products and services which are innovative, based on new technologies or new to the market. Most products in the introduction stage of their lifecycle command a price premium, because producers need to cover the costs of research, development and launch marketing. Until sustainable products reach the maturity stage of the lifecycle, with high volume sales and profitability, prices are unlikely to be competitive with established products. Electricity from solar solutions, for example, is currently more expensive than conventionally generated electricity – although prices are steadily falling.

- They may involve more labour and management intensive processes (such as supplier monitoring, independent verification of sustainability standards, sustainable management of forests, organic farming, or disassembly and sorting for recycling). The costs of some sustainability activities will be borne directly by the organisation, while the costs of upstream activity will be passed on to it via the supply chain.

- They may involve additional risks (eg organic, pesticide-free crops, which are more vulnerable to pests and disease), the costs of which are passed down the value chain.

- They may limit the immediate availability of natural resources (eg by imposing limits on unsustainable fishing, logging, mineral extraction or land use), pushing market prices up due to reduced supply. Price premiums for verified or certified hardwood lumber, for example, can be as high as 30% for some Brazilian rainforest woods.

- They may be subject to taxes or price premiums intended to encourage a reduction in consumption (as with tobacco and alcohol products, for example).

- They may prevent organisations from buying opportunistically to secure the best available price (eg because of long-term sustainable contracts) or from pursuing price-maximising strategies (eg because of concerns about fair trading, supplier viability, exploitation of low-cost labour) or from selecting lowest-cost suppliers (eg because of weightings given to diverse, small or local suppliers who lack economies of scale to compete directly on price with larger suppliers).

- They may require the development of new processes and capabilities, and the plant, equipment and systems associated with them: for example, in the area of reverse logistics, disassembly, recycling and re-use of end-of-life or scrap materials.

- They may generally involve significant change (and change management) within the organisation and its supply chain – which also requires investment of resources, possible loss of productivity (during process/technology change and the early stages of the learning curve), investment in training and development, audits and reviews, and so on.

- They may require the organisation to engage in carbon offsetting, or compensatory investment in sustainability projects.

... and 'more expensive' may not be an option!

1.3 The cost barrier may be strengthened by a number of internal and external factors in the procurement environment.

- Organisational performance may be measured by profitability (if not profit maximisation), and procurement performance may be measured by short-term cost reduction and financial value added. In such a case, social and environmental benefits may be undervalued – as may longer-term cost efficiencies based on whole-life costing. There will be no incentive to implement or maintain sustainable procurement.

- There may be lack of understanding or implementation of whole-life costing, with a persistent belief that 'value' and 'efficiency' mean best price and short-term pay-back. This was a finding of the *Procuring the Future* report on public sector sustainable procurement, for example.

- Government subsidies and private sector investment may reinforce the competitive pricing of non-sustainable industries, practices and products. Subsidies currently support mainstream (non-organic) farming, for example, and most planned emissions trading schemes exempt or favour carbon-intensive industries like coal, in order to protect jobs.

- Recessionary pressures may reduce demand for sustainable products, services and commodities. Towards the end of 2008, for example, Far Eastern buyers of UK waste paper for recycling had all but disappeared from the market, and local authorities, supermarkets and printers, among other organisations previously earning revenue from the sale of their waste paper, have been forced to resort to incineration or landfill.

- Budgetary and funding restrictions (and/or cost reduction targets) may make extra expenditure on sustainability impossible – or difficult to justify. This may be a particular problem for third sector organisations, with limited funding from grants and donations. However, it is also a pressure on public sector organisations, with the need to demonstrate value for money and 'economic advantage' in contract award. Meanwhile, in the private sector, the 2008/9 economic recession has similarly imposed severe investment constraints and budget cuts, with the result that sustainability is perceived as a low priority by many purchasers.

1.4 A survey for *Supply Management* (27 August 2009) found that 64% of purchasers are not getting 'significant' financial benefit from sustainable procurement. 'There may be opportunities to benefit from implementing facets of CSR, but at the present time this is quite low on the agenda.' The focus is on economic survival – and although this can be seen as a legitimate sustainability issue, it may create a barrier to other social and environmental sustainability measures.

Overcoming cost barriers

1.5 Cost (and cost perception) barriers can be overcome in various ways.

- Where possible, sell a longer-term view of cost management to shareholders and internal stakeholders. Whole-life costing, for example, can be used to demonstrate that initial investment in sustainability can reap later cost savings in running costs (eg in the case of energy-saving appliances), disposal costs (eg in the case of design for disassembly), and management (eg in the case of sustainable supply relationships based on fair and ethical trading).

- Make the business case for sustainability. Value and return on investment should be re-defined to include reputational and brand strength benefits, future revenue arising from new market opportunities, the management of compliance costs/risks and so on (as discussed in Chapter 1). 'Sustainable procurement is... not the old-fashioned way of buying things as cheaply as possible, but a more rounded approach which gives true value.' (*Supply Management*, ibid).

- Establish TBL or balanced scorecard performance measures, in order to re-orient the corporate culture towards more balanced value/success definitions, including acceptance of the need to invest in sustainability. This will need to be reinforced by senior management championship, incorporation of sustainability in mission and values statements, and various other 'stakeholder buy-in' measures discussed in earlier chapters.

- Build momentum. Start with changes with relatively low cost impacts, and/or quick payback periods: eg energy-saving light bulbs, recycled paper. Emphasise areas in which outlays are actively reduced by sustainable procurement, eg reduced energy and water consumption. Emphasise the concept of 'eco-efficiency'.

- Offset higher prices by seeking efficiencies elsewhere (eg lower transaction costs through efficient procurement systems and long-term contracts, or reduced resource/energy consumption to counteract the higher price of renewables).

- Pass on some of the higher costs of sustainability to consumers, where sustainability is sufficiently valued by the market to command a price premium.

- Access financial grants, subsidies, tax breaks and awards eg for regional development, innovation and sustainability. (One example is the Virgin Group's grants and prizes for innovation and entrepreneurship in renewable energy, resource efficiency and climate change mitigation: Virgin Earth Challenge, Virgin Green Fund and Virgin Unite).

2 Stakeholder attitudes

External stakeholder attitudes

2.1 As we have seen throughout this text, the attitudes, expectations and influence of stakeholder groups can act as a driver and enabler of sustainable procurement – or as a barrier to it.

2.2 External stakeholders might in general be expected to support sustainability, as the intended beneficiaries of its positive effects. However, particular groups may be indifferent to sustainability (creating the barrier of lack of market demand) or actively resistant to it (in defence of their own interests).

2.3 According to the Concerned Consumer Index, three quarters of the population claims to weigh up a company's reputation before buying its products or services, and nearly three in five say they actively avoid purchasing from certain companies because of questions they have about their social, environmental or ethical track record. However, an organisation's customers – and consumers in general – may resist a move towards sustainable procurement because of:

- Price premiums: in other words, they will buy a sustainable product in preference to a non-sustainable product – but only if they are similarly priced. Price sensitivity is inevitably higher in times of economic recession.

- Perceptions of lower functionality or product/service quality: in other words, they will buy a sustainable product in preference to a non-sustainable product – but only if they offer the same performance and desired attributes and benefits. Hybrid cars may be perceived to offer poorer performance, for example; recycled paper may fall short on appearance/texture.

2.4   Shareholders, investors and financiers may equally be resistant to sustainable practices if their primary focus is on short-term profits, dividends or return on investment – particularly since some of the key benefits of sustainability are intangible and hard to quantify.

2.5   Similarly, in the third sector, donors may demand accountability for the use of funds in the particular areas of their concern (say, animal welfare) – at the expense of a more rounded view of sustainable practice (say, labour conditions in the factories supplying the animal welfare charities with fund-raising merchandise).

2.6   Industry stakeholders and interest groups may also resist sustainability in order to protect their interests, or the interests of their members. For example, trade unions representing workers in carbon-intensive industries (such as coal) may resist emissions trading schemes and carbon footprint reduction policies, as a threat to the long-term livelihoods of their members. Similarly, business and industry bodies may resist the sustainability agenda – particularly in times of recession – where a sound business case cannot be made.

2.7   The general public may also resist sustainable practices where their interests or comforts are impacted – despite the fact that sustainability is designed to be in their best interests! Sustainable consumption and lifestyle may be more costly and require more effort (eg recycling or taking public transport). They require change – and, as someone once said, 'We are all for progress: we just don't like change'. They may also be perceived as infringing personal liberties and freedom of choice. Fundamentally, they challenge the prevailing culture in affluent nations, which celebrates consumption.

Internal stakeholder attitudes

2.8   As we saw in Chapter 4, the attitudes and values of internal stakeholders will be crucial in whether sustainable procurement is successfully accepted and embedded in the organisation. The procurement function will have to secure the 'buy-in' of internal customers to sustainability initiatives (including senior management, and clients and partners in internal supply chains and cross-functional projects).

2.9   Managers at all levels may be resistant to sustainable procurement, if:

- It is perceived as being irrelevant to – or, worse, incompatible with – the critical success factors for which they are responsible and accountable (as discussed above, in relation to cost and profitability).

- It is perceived as being 'soft' or subjective, without a sound business case to justify effort and investment

- It is perceived as a public relations or corporate communications exercise: something to which 'lip service' can usefully be paid, without the need for meaningful action

- It is perceived as the preserve of the procurement function, without significant implications for other functions – or as an attempt by the procurement function to bolster its influence and status through additional policy and red tape

- It threatens the *status quo*, established norms and procedures, and established competencies and relationships: in other words, if it involves disruptive change.

Example: Public Sector Food Procurement Initiative (PSFPI)

Following a year of turbulent food prices and significant concern over future food security, the UK government [has emphasised that] the nation must radically rethink the way it produces and consumes food to protect future supplies. Encouraging greater engagement with domestic food vendors will play a big part and the government believes it can use its £2 billion annual spend to lead by example on local and sustainable sourcing.

Efforts are being spearheaded by the Department for Environment, Food and Rural Affairs' (Defra) Public Sector Food Procurement Initiative (PSFPI). Launched in 2003, it encourages government bodies to buy sustainable food and to support domestic suppliers. However, the key word is 'encourages': two recent reports conclude that the government is not doing enough to pioneer good practice. Food policy pressure group Sustain believes it must make the policy mandatory.

Sustain says the issue is not taken seriously. It published an email from a senior buyer at NHS Supply Chain, which suggested the Department of Health's £48 million scheme to increase fruit and vegetable consumption among school pupils will not include sustainability criteria or support local farmers. 'While I would really like to be fluffy and sustainable, I also have to be realistic about the price,' the email read.

Supply Management (27 August 2009)

2.10 Employees in general (and buyers in particular) may similarly resist sustainable procurement if: it is irrelevant to their work and performance evaluation and reward criteria; it threatens established competencies, relationships and ways of working; the issues are not well communicated or understood; the issues are not prioritised, supported and modelled by management; or resources and training are not given to support them in their new responsibilities. Research conducted by the International Finance Corporation (IFC, the private sector arm of the World Bank Group) found that 37% of employees see their company's commitment to sustainability as nothing more than a PR exercise.

2.11 Blackburn identifies five 'camps' into which strong resistors or opponents of sustainability may fall.

- *Antagonists*: oppositional, angry people who are simply resistant to authority, interference or the change agent
- *Overworked*: people who may personally support the sustainability agenda, but are already over-burdened, and see sustainable procurement simply as a further demand on their time
- *Procrastinators*: people who tend to support sustainability, but for whom it is a low priority – and therefore keeps slipping down the schedule
- *Non-believers*: people who have not been persuaded of the business merit, viability, relevance or urgency of sustainable procurement
- *Rocks*: people who simply don't respond, for whatever reason.

2.12 Suppliers may resist sustainable procurement on the same kinds of grounds.

- Externally imposed pressure to change, in areas which may or may not be culturally relevant or commercially viable in the supplier's operating context – and may or may not be adequately supported by co-investment, supplier development or gain/risk sharing by customers
- The costs of developing sustainable products/services, processes, improvements in terms and conditions for workers, and sustainability management systems – which, again, may not be adequately or reliably offset by sales revenue, or gain-sharing by customers

- The costs and risk of buyer-specific innovations and adaptations, where required as part of sustainability standards, which may not be transferable to other customers, and may lock suppliers in to unprofitable customer relationships.

Overcoming stakeholder barriers

2.13 We have already addressed methods of securing stakeholder buy-in, support and commitment to sustainable procurement in Chapters 7 and 8. Broadly, however, stakeholder barriers can be overcome in the following ways.

- Using market, customer and other stakeholder research and consultation to understand stakeholders' fears, concerns, priorities and other sources of indifference or resistance to sustainability
- Stakeholder communication, 'buy-in' programmes and ongoing stakeholder management and issues management
- Emphasising the benefits of sustainability and risks of non-sustainability, as they apply to each key stakeholder group – and ensuring that benefits actually accrue (eg through gain sharing with employees and suppliers)
- Applying incentives and penalties for non-compliance (eg in supplier motivation)
- Co-opting stakeholders who are supportive of sustainability and can influence fence-sitters and neutralise opponents (eg internal champions and coalitions, NGO partners, government policy)
- Integrating and reinforcing sustainability in internal value statements; policies, procedures and practices; and HR systems (recruitment and selection, training and development, appraisal and reward)
- Maintaining consistency in sustainability efforts, so that they become 'business as usual' to internal and external stakeholders, and give time for benefits to accrue.

3 Policy conflicts

Economic growth and development

3.1 Throughout this text, we have cited examples of government (and organisational) policies, legislation and voluntary standards and codes of practice which are designed to support sustainability. The syllabus highlights the fact, however, that policy goals in other areas may conflict with sustainability principles, creating or reinforcing barriers to sustainable procurement – or creating confusion and uncertainty, which erodes the momentum for action. We will outline some examples here.

3.2 National and transnational (eg EU or UN) social policy broadly supports the concept of economic growth and development, as the way forward for enhancing individual and social wellbeing. Economic growth is generally measured by an annual percentage increase in the gross national product (GNP) per head of the population. Economic growth contributes to social infrastructure, enabling technologies, employment and individual and collective wealth – including disposable income, which leads to further investment and consumption, stimulating the economy still further.

3.3 The main advantage of economic growth should be a better standard of living for the population as a whole: one of the aims of sustainable development. However, there are also disadvantages to growth, including the faster usage of scarce and non-renewable natural resources (pushing up energy costs, for example) and more pollution and waste products. It may be argued that there is a fundamental conflict between the concept of economic growth (which requires increasing consumption) and environmental sustainability (which requires decreasing consumption).

Free trade and globalised markets

3.4 Another trend in international policy has been the stimulation of free trade and market globalisation. An increasing number of trading organisations and blocs have been created for this purpose, including: ASEAN (The Association of Southeast Asian Nations); EFTA (The European Free Trade Agreement); and NAFTA (the North American Free Trade Agreement). Trade within each of these three major trading blocs is expanding on a vast scale – although trading between blocs, or indeed with non-members, has tended to decline.

3.5 Meanwhile, the World Trade Organisation (WTO – formerly the General Agreement on Tariffs and Trade, or GATT) is dedicated to promoting free trade between nations. Its main aim is to reduce or remove barriers to trade from tariffs (import taxes and duties) and non-tariff factors (eg quotas, customs red-tape, different regulatory regimes, foreign currency controls, and government subsidies to domestic producers). The usual reason for such barriers is to protect domestic (or trading bloc) industry from the effects of outside competition – a policy called protectionism. It is argued, however, that protectionism inhibits economic growth and leads to political ill will and retaliation between nations, stifling international trade.

3.6 As we saw in Chapter 2, international and global economic integration and free trade can be argued to support sustainable development: prompting investment in infrastructure and skilling in developing economies; encouraging participation in economic activity and the reduction of poverty; promoting economic integration and international peace; raising environmental/labour standards as a condition of participation in free trade agreements; and so on. However, opponents argue that it also:

- Encourages the exploitation of low-cost labour in developing countries (including child and forced labour)

- 'Exports' the developing world's problems of over-consumption, pollution and environmental degradation

- Erodes local cultures and exploits developing markets (eg with the 'dumping' of poor-quality, obsolete or excess product)

- Encourages unsustainable environmental practices (eg mono-culture premium crops for export, leaving little agricultural land – or poor soil quality – for the product of staple foods for the domestic population)

- Disadvantages small and local suppliers in domestic supply markets, who may not be able to compete on price with cheap foreign imports (particularly if also disadvantaged by exchange rates)

- Creates unemployment in the domestic labour market (eg due to off-shoring of production).

Competition

3.7 Another cornerstone of national and EU policy and legislation is the protection and stimulation of free and fair competition in markets. Again, this can broadly be considered a sustainable development objective, but it may militate against specific sustainability policies in areas such as the following.

- Free market practices. For most goods and services, prices are set by the market mechanism of supply and demand, and corporations have the legitimate right to maximise their profits (in the interests of shareholders) if they can. The public sector arguably assures the provision of essential goods and services at affordable prices – but there may still be unsustainable inequities of access (eg private sector firms withdrawing unprofitable services from rural or economically depressed areas).

- Open tendering procedures and economic contract award criteria for public procurement (under the EU Public Procurement Directives). This is intended to protect open competition across the EU, but may also restrict a public authority's ability to impose sustainability criteria that are not directly related to the purchase – such as supplier diversity information.

- Intellectual property protection. This is designed to protect corporations' competitive assets – but may also militate against social or environmental sustainability, by restricting use of proprietary processes, or allowing exploitative pricing of products. Access to proprietary medicines in poorer nations, for example, is a major ethical issue.

Procurement efficiency

3.8 Public sector spending cuts and efficiency policies are similarly both drivers of economic sustainability – and potential barriers to social and economic sustainability. Most obviously, they present cost/funding/budgetary constraints on investment in sustainability measures. In the form of public procurement regulations (eg competitive tendering), they may also hamper the potential to develop long-term supply chain partnerships to develop sustainable procurement.

Organisational and functional policies

3.9 The above are just some of the 'macro' policy factors that may conflict with the sustainable procurement agenda. In addition, the strategies and policies currently being pursued by a given organisation and/or procurement function may create a barrier. Here are some examples.

- An organisation pursuing low-cost sourcing or global sourcing policies may find it difficult to incorporate policies giving preference to local and small suppliers, or paying higher-than-necessary prices to suppliers as part of a fair trade policy.

- An organisation committed to maximising shareholder value might resist any policy for which a strong and immediate business case cannot be demonstrated.

- An organisation whose products or core competences have inherent environmental drawbacks (such as plastic bag manufacturers, oil refineries or airlines) may be limited in its ability to commit to radical environmental sustainability principles.

4 Cultural barriers

4.1 Culture is the shared ways of behaving and understanding that are distinctive to a particular group of people. An influential writer on culture, Geert Hofstede, defines it as 'the collective programming of the mind which distinguishes the members of one category of people from another'. The category of people may be a nation or ethnic group, a social class, a profession or occupation, a gender, or an organisation: each may have its distinctive way of thinking and doing things. These are sometimes called 'spheres' of culture.

4.2 Another influential writer on culture, Fons Trompenaars, suggested that culture operates on different levels. The outward expressions of culture include:

- Behaviour: accepted norms of personal and interpersonal conduct; customs and rules defining the right/wrong behaviour in a given situation; business practices; fashions and fads; and so on.

- Artefacts: products of the culture such as its arts and technology, its myths and heroes, its language and symbols.

- Rituals: patterns of behaviour which have symbolic or traditional value, such as social formalities, ceremonies and rites of passage.

4.3 Beneath these outward expressions, however, there are the values, beliefs and underlying assumptions which give them their special meaning and significance within the culture. These may be explicit in sayings or mottos, but are often not directly expressed so much as reflected in behaviour, artefacts and rituals. Cultural norms are very powerful. Members of the group are 'socialised' to adhere to them by learning, practice and explicit or implicit membership rules: in a culture, you 'fit in or get out'.

External cultural factors

4.4 Different nations and cultural sub-groups (eg different ethnicities and religions) may have significantly different norms, values and assumptions, which influence how they do business and manage people, and how consumers develop product/service preferences and buying patterns. National, ethnic and religious beliefs, values and behavioural norms can support sustainability – or create a barrier to it. A strongly patriarchal culture may be resistant to the imposition of equal opportunity and diversity, for example, while an urbanised, materialistic society may not initially generate significant demand for 'green' products. Paradigm shifts may be required!

4.5 You should be able to think of a range of specific cultural, ethnic or religious norms and values that might create a barrier to the sustainability agenda – particularly in cross-cultural management or trading contexts, where differences may pose a major source of misunderstanding or resistance. For example:

- Cultural or religious norms around gender roles, or ethnic or religious superiority or hostility (often based on historic conflicts), may militate against supplier or workforce diversity policies

- Cultural norms differ in regard to the propriety of personal gifts and hospitality. In some cultures, these are essential for courtesy and relationship development – while in most Western business frameworks, they are considered corrupt and unethical (as potentially being, or being seen to be, an inducement to influence business decisions)

- Cultural norms differ in regard to giving preference in employment and business opportunities to relatives and connections. In some cultures, this is a natural expression of social ties – while, again, in most Western business frameworks, it is considered corrupt and unethical

- Policy, legislation and voluntary standards are artefacts of culture – and can therefore vary according to geography. (One example may be the US's preference for national self-interest and policy-making in the area of climate change, refusing to ratify the Kyoto Treaty.)

- Respect for status and seniority, and the importance of 'face' (eg not criticising those in authority), may create a barrier to performance feedback, problem-solving or employee initiative to support sustainable procurement policies

- Individualistic cultures may generally present more of a barrier to sustainability than collectivist cultures, in which the focus is more naturally on the collective interest and future generations

- Language differences may impede the communication and management of sustainability standards and policies. This includes not just the obvious issue of foreign languages, but the level of education of target audiences, their understanding of technical jargon and terminology, different use of symbols and measures (eg miles or kilometres, pounds or dollars)

- Different communication, relationship and learning styles (eg preferences for rote-learning and rules vs preference for participative, active learning) may impede deployment, training and management efforts.

4.6 In other words, different sustainability issues may have higher or lower priority, or be responded to differently, according to cultural values and geographical imperatives. One culture's definition of unethical behaviour may be a positive value in another. Misunderstandings or unquestioned assumptions about these things may themselves create a barrier to developing and implementing sustainable procurement in cross-cultural supply chains.

Overcoming external cultural barriers

4.7 Cultural education, sensitivity and adaptation may, in itself, be regarded as a social sustainability issue. In every culture, companies enter into an implied contract with society that permits them to pursue commercial interests within certain parameters of conduct. The implied contract constitutes a set of expectations for the role of a company and its managers in that society, and procurement professionals need to be appropriately flexible in order to show respect and maintain goodwill.

4.8 At the same time, certain minimum ethical and sustainability standards may need to be upheld globally, regardless of cultural norms: this is the basis of UN charters, ILO standards, the Kyoto Protocol and other transnational standards discussed in Chapter 11. The focus will then be on the sensitivity, understanding and support with which standards and expectations are communicated, implemented and enforced by procurement professionals in cross-cultural supply chains.

4.9 Schneider and Barsoux (*Managing Across Cultures*) argue that 'rather than knowing what to do in Country X, or whether national or functional cultures are more important in multi-cultural teams, what is necessary is to know how to assess the potential impact of culture, national or otherwise, on performance [and sustainability].'

4.10 At the organisational level, there should be a plan to evaluate this potential impact and to implement programmes to encourage: awareness of areas of cultural difference and sensitivity; behavioural flexibility (being able to use multiple-solution models rather than 'one best way' approaches); and constructive communication, conflict resolution and problem-solving.

4.11 Initial investigation may be required to identify which particular cultures are most relevant to the organisation, and areas in which cultural differences may have most impact. If an organisation is moving into a new market, forming a strategic alliance with an overseas partner, or recruiting significant numbers of staff from a particular ethnic group, for example, the need for education, awareness and communication may be clear.

4.12 Since cultural assumptions are so deeply embedded, the involvement of key stakeholders (suppliers, managers and staff, and perhaps local advisers or NGOs) will be important – both in shifting values and in enhancing ownership and implementation of the sustainable procurement programme.

Organisational and management culture

4.13 Organisation culture is 'a pattern of beliefs and expectations shared by an organisation's members, which produces norms that powerfully shape the behaviour of individuals and groups in the organisation' (Schwartz & Davies). We discussed organisation culture and management attitudes in Chapter 4, as an internal influence on sustainable procurement, and will not go over the same ground again here.

4.14 Essentially, it is worth remembering that attitudes to sustainable procurement (both positive and negative) will be shaped by: the mission and value expressed by senior management and related statements; the mottos, slogans and stories promoted within the organisation; the types of people recruited and promoted within the organisation; the behaviours celebrated and rewarded within the organisation; the behaviours and values modelled by management; and so on.

4.15 What kinds of corporate culture might represent a barrier to the promotion of a sustainable procurement agenda? A corporate culture may:

- Be cynical about the value of sustainability (or see it as purely a PR exercise)
- Be short-termist in its drive for results, supported by short-range corporate planning horizons and shareholder dividend expectations
- Subscribe to a 'greed is good' philosophy
- Have an appetite for (or unconcern about) risk, weakening risk-related drivers of sustainable procurement
- Be highly patriarchal, or dominated by the values of a particular national or ethnic culture, creating a barrier to diversity
- Have an 'unenlightened' view of employee rights and the employment relationship (perhaps supported by laissez-faire employment law, as in the US)
- Be confident (or overconfident) in its brand strength, weakening reputational drivers for sustainability
- Be generally bureaucratic, traditional and averse to change.

4.16 As the syllabus suggests, different sectors, industries and organisations may be prone to different cultural biases. The public sector, for example, may be prone to bureaucracy and resistance to feedback and change. Manufacturing and construction industries traditionally suffer from a 'machismo' culture in which some aspects of sustainability (including health and safety) are seen as 'soft'. Share and commodity trading would tend to be a 'greed is good' culture. And so on.

Overcoming internal cultural barriers

4.17 As we mentioned in Chapter 4, resistant and dysfunctional cultures can be changed – although not easily. Some key areas of leverage for cultural change are as follows.

- Consistent expression and modelling of the new sustainability or CSR values by management (from the top down), leaders and influencers (who may need to be co-opted to the initiative by those in authority)
- Changing behaviours and frameworks for behaviour, by implementing sustainable procurement policies, procedures, rules, incentives and sanctions – and enforcing them. (People often bring their attitudes into line with enforced behaviours, in order to reduce the psychological discomfort or 'dissonance' of the incompatibility.)

- Changing the symbols, rituals and artefacts of the organisation so that they communicate and celebrate sustainability: corporate brand (logos, mottos and so on), mission and value statements, staff awards/prizes, workplace posters, symbolic action (eg involvement in community fundraisers, environmental clean up days or Earth Hour); and so on.

- Changing underlying values and beliefs, through communication, education and involvement; spreading new values and beliefs and encouraging employees to 'own' them (through incentives, co-opting people to teach others and so on); and all the mechanisms of 'securing stakeholder buy-in and commitment' discussed elsewhere in this text

- Use of human resource management mechanisms to reinforce the changes: including new values and behaviours in recruitment and selection profiles; appraisal and reward criteria; training and development planning; and so on.

5 Macro-economic barriers

Economic stability, growth or decline

5.1 As we have already explained in relation to cost and policy issues, a variety of macro-economic factors can present or strengthen barriers to sustainable procurement.

5.2 The International Monetary Fund (IMF) defines the sustainable development issues of economic stability as follows (http://www.imf.org: 'April 2008 Factsheet: How the IMF promotes global economic stability').

- Promoting economic stability is partly a matter of avoiding economic and financial crisis. Economic stability also means avoiding large swings in economic activity, high inflation, and excessive volatility in exchange rates and financial markets. Such instability can increase uncertainty and discourage investment, impede economic growth, and hurt living standards.

- A dynamic market economy necessarily involves some degree of instability, as well as gradual structural change. The challenge for policymakers is to minimise this instability without reducing the ability of the economic system to raise living standards through the increasing productivity, efficiency, and employment that it generates.

- Economic and financial stability is both a national and a multilateral concern. As recent experience in world financial markets has shown, countries are becoming ever more interconnected. Problems in one apparently isolated sector, within any one country, can result in problems in others sectors and spill-over across borders. And global economic and financial conditions have a significant impact on developments in most national economies. Thus, no country is an island when it comes to economic and financial stability.

5.3 Essentially, stable economies are more likely to have the surplus resources, business confidence (enabling future-oriented focus and investment), enabling technologies and management time to support a focus on non-economic sustainability agendas. Unstable economies are too busy 'fire fighting' for economic survival: battling inflation and export-eroding exchange rates, repaying foreign debt, minimising budget deficit in the face of recession and high unemployment – and so on.

5.4 Economic growth (eg an 'over-heated economy') can present a barrier to sustainability by encouraging over-consumption; excessive resource use, wastes and environmental impacts of economic development activity (eg land clearing, urban development); investment risk-taking; over-staffing (creating the risk of redundancies in subsequent downturns); and demand-pull inflation.

5.5 Meanwhile, however, economic decline, downturn and recession create barriers to sustainable procurement by: placing the priority on cost reduction and profitability for business survival; eroding business confidence, leading to reduced investment in projects with long or uncertain payback periods; increasing unemployment (and therefore reducing drivers for above-minimum labour standards); creating a budget deficit (with more unemployment benefits and reduced income tax revenue) which puts pressure on public sector procurement to secure short-term cost reductions; and so on.

Inflation levels and trends

5.6 Inflation is a general, sustained increase in prices over time. This may be the result of:

- Demand for goods exceeding supply, pushing prices up (demand-pull inflation)
- Increases in the costs of production, particularly wages, without increased demand, so that producers have to raise their prices to maintain profitability (cost-push inflation)
- Overexpansion of the monetary supply, which boosts excessive demand by making more money available to spend (monetary inflation)
- A wage-price spiral, where people fear further price rises and seek higher wages and prices to cover them, creating a vicious circle (expectational inflation).

5.7 A high rate of inflation is a sustainability issue for a number of reasons. It disadvantages those on lower (and particularly, fixed) incomes, since their spending power is reduced. It causes uncertainty about the future value of money, which makes it harder for businesses to evaluate future expenditure, or the real value of large-scale capital items over their lifetime, or the likely return on investments. This may act as a disincentive to investment and long-term decision-making. In international trade, if the rate of inflation is higher in the UK than in other economies, exports become relatively expensive and imports relatively cheap: the balance of trade, and local employment, will suffer.

Credit restrictions

5.8 Credit restrictions are the reduced availability of credit from lending institutions, due to more stringent lending guidelines in periods of economic uncertainty, designed to protect the lenders from the risk of debtor default,. The last few years, for example, have seen global 'credit crunch', as inadequately secured mortgage loans in the US market triggered the collapse of major banks and financial institutions, and other lenders took steps to minimise their exposure.

5.9 Credit restrictions can significantly affect the cashflow of businesses, shifting their priorities from long-term sustainability issues (such as environmental and social sustainability) to immediate financial survival. Smaller businesses, in particular, may suffer from reduced access to loan capital – particularly if they are also being squeezed on prices and payment terms by larger customers needing to bolster their own cashflow positions.

Protectionism

5.10 Protectionism is, as we have already explained, the policy of protecting domestic (or trading bloc) industry from the effects of outside competition, by imposing barriers to international trade: tariffs (import taxes and duties) and non-tariff factors (eg quotas, customs red-tape, different regulatory regimes, foreign currency controls, and government subsidies to domestic producers).

5.11 As we noted, protectionism may present a support for sustainability (by halting the unrestrained growth of globalisation), but may also present a barrier to it, to the extent that international trade contributes to the prosperity of developing nations, peaceful international relations and so on.

Overcoming macro-economic barriers

5.12 It is the role of government to manage or control a national economy, in order to provide a stable economic framework from which, ideally, sustainable growth can be achieved. The objective of a government's economic policies may be: to achieve sustainable growth in the economy; to control inflation; to minimise 'boom and bust' cycles in economic activity; to achieve low unemployment levels; or to achieve a balance between exports and imports.

5.13 In order to achieve these objectives, a government will use a number of different policy tools. For example, *monetary policy* is the government's decisions and actions regarding the level of interest rates and the supply of money in the economy; while *fiscal policy* is the government's decisions and actions regarding the balance between taxation revenue and public expenditure.

5.14 Demand-pull inflation and unsustainable growth in an economy can be reduced, for example, by 'slowing down' the economy with measures such as: reduced government spending; higher taxation to reduce consumer spending; or raising interest rates to increase the costs of borrowing for both consumer and business spending. Cost-push inflation can be managed by government intervention to reduce production costs and limit price rises: eg by applying controls over wage and price rises (prices and incomes policy) and encouraging increased productivity in industry (eg by funding technology development).

5.15 Alternatively, unsustainable economic decline or recession can be mitigated by measures to 'stimulate' the economy: increased government spending and investment in infrastructure projects; reduced taxation; lower interest rates; or (as in Australia in 2008/9) direct 'stimulus payments' to taxpayers to encourage consumer spending.

5.16 We would hope that further detail would be beyond the scope of the syllabus...

6 Barriers in different sectors

6.1 Not all of the barriers identified in this chapter will apply, or apply with equal force, to all organisations and industries. The relevance and significance of the barriers for a given organisation or industry will depend on factors such as the following.

- Factors in raw materials costs: the type and quantity of raw materials used, the size of the supply market, the ease of substitution (for less costly and/or more sustainable material) and so on

- Factors in energy costs: the type and amount of fuel/energy used, and the adaptability of technology and processes to renewable alternative energy sources

- The use of whole-life costing, de-emphasising short-term cost barriers in favour of long-term return on investment

- The price sensitivity of the market, and the level of demand for sustainability which may (or may not) support the off-setting of costs with premium pricing

- The strength of drivers and enablers of sustainability (as discussed in Chapter 5), to counteract the significance of any or all of the barriers. For example, as we have highlighted elsewhere in this text, the sportswear industry has had to establish sustainability credentials almost 'at any cost', because of the high degree of scrutiny, consumer activism and reputational risks.

- The internationalisation or globalisation of the organisation's operations and sourcing, and therefore the extent of its exposure to cultural differences, political/economic risk, protectionist policies and so on

- The organisation's asset backing, proportion of loan capital to share capital, reliance on credit for short-term finance and so on, and therefore its exposure to credit restrictions

- The prevailing culture of the organisation and/or industry, which may support or undermine the pursuit of sustainable procurement.

Private sector organisations

6.2 Some of the key barriers to sustainable procurement in the private sector have been summarised by a study reported in *Supply Management* (Neil Jones, 'Breaking through the barriers', 21/6/2007): Table 14.1.

Table 14.1: *Barriers to sustainable procurement in the private sector*

External barriers	Internal barriers
Newly identified:	*Newly identified:*
• Volume of sustainability information	• Lack of knowledge/skills
• Language and cultural differences	• Resource limitations
• Lack of supplier commitment	• Weak processes
• Limiting standards	• Poor communication
	• Scope of audits too wide
Previously identified:	*Previously identified:*
• Customer desire for lower prices	• Lack of roadmap or strategy
• Competitive pressures	• Lack of management commitment
	• Cost reduction focus
	• Other procurement targets
	• Purchasers' abilities
	• Accounting methods

6.3 You should be able, from our coverage so far, to suggest mitigating actions to overcome each of these barriers.

SMEs and third sector organisations

6.4 SMEs and smaller third sector organisations may be particularly prone to cost issues, credit restrictions, resource limitations and lack of knowledge/skills, because of their limited personnel and asset backing – and, generally, because of their focus on financial survival. Third sector organisations may additionally face barriers from their own focus, and donor/volunteer expectations, on particular sustainability issues, at the expense of more general awareness and capability development.

6.5 Sustainability management for small organisations, and NGOs with limited funding, should focus on prioritisation (eg for an NGO, linking sustainability objectives clearly to the mission/vision); pursuing small wins, with small cost impacts; involving staff/volunteers and suppliers; developing a fairly basic sustainability management system; and starting with simple, low-cost sustainability reporting.

Example: Seaview Hotel, Isle of Wight

Blackburn cites this small, 16-room, 40-employee hotel as an example of manageable sustainability policy and reporting.

Seaview has sought to become a model of social responsibility. This strategy has worked well in shaping the hotel's image as a site of operational, social and environmental excellence, an image reinforced by the hotel's location in a picturesque sailing village. The environmental dimensions of its four-page report touch on the hotel's use of locally grown organic produce and its extensive recycling and re-use programs, which include the donation of used curtains and linens. According to the report, heat, light, water and energy are monitored. Low-voltage bulbs and high-efficiency laundry equipment are used. The social dimensions of the document address the hotel's apprenticeship program for underprivileged youth and other initiatives to help children. The economic section describes its participatory structure of management – especially with respect to financial decisions – and discusses its support for local suppliers. Various employee training and development programs are also cited.

Public sector organisations

6.6   The Sustainable Procurement National Action Plan identifies a number of primarily internal barriers to sustainable procurement in the public sector: Table 14.2.

Examples: 'Getting it right'

The following examples of how barriers can be overcome are cited in *Procuring the Future*.

The Canny Buyer, Scottish Executive

Under the Scottish Executive's prudential borrowing regime for public bodies, whole-life costing is mandatory. The City of Dundee Architectural Services Division can apply to the Chief Executive's department for additional short-term (capital) costs of a project where there are lower whole-life (revenue) costs. Currently, schemes with a payback period of 3–6 years are considered appropriate.

North Bristol Health Trust – Patient Transport Services (PTS)

Proactive Logistics were invited to find a sustainable solution to PTS in April 2005. They recognised several missed opportunities, such as the lack of co-ordination or control of transport ordering across directorates and no measurement of service performance. Using their analytical, logistical and change management expertise, costs were reduced by over £240,000 in six months, the project will be self funding within the first 12 months and will achieve full annualised benefits in excess of £500,000. In addition, improvements in the quality and reliability of the service have reduced transport-related delays and vehicle movements were reduced by an estimated 15%, with an equivalent reduction in fuel, pollution and other environmental impacts. One of the key lessons was that a clearly defined plan ensures savings are delivered in line with investment.

Table 14.2 *Barriers to sustainable procurement in the public sector*

Area	Identified barriers	Recommendations
Leadership, clarity and ownership	• Lack of leadership and commitment • Confusion about ownership • Poor incentive systems • Mixed messages to suppliers	• Provide clear policy leadership • Make sustainable procurement integral to public procurement, owned and supported by OGC • Work to clear, measurable targets
Clarity on policy priorities	• Lack of clarity and proliferation of priorities • Lack of cross-government buy-in • 'One size fits all' approach • Guidance overload	• Develop clear policy statement • Rationalise existing policies • Ensure that only real priorities are included in the framework • Establish objectives, targets, monitoring and reporting mechanisms and sanctions for non-compliance
Need to meet minimum standards now, while setting challenging future goals	• Lack of prioritisation • Lack of enforcement of mandatory standards • Failure to signal future trends to the market • Failure to manage supply chain risk	• Create a knowledge base on sustainability impacts of priority items • Benchmark internationally • Set mandatory minimum standards in priority areas • Work with third parties to develop future goals
Developing capabilities	• Lack of helpful information, training and accountability • Ignorance of sustainability • Suspicion about benefits • Confusion arising from mixed messages	• Sustainable procurement delivery team • Management information systems • Upgrade procurement capacity and ensure staff are adequately trained • Targets for attaining Flexible Framework levels
Ensuring budgetary mechanisms enable and support sustainable procurement	• Failure to apply rules on whole-life costing (WLC) • Focus on short-term efficiency saving at the expense of long-term benefits • Concerns re affordability, cost • Inability to offset WLC savings against short-term budget limits • Uncertainty on how to account for non-monetary benefits	• Ensure that the Gershon Review efficiency message is properly interpreted to mean value for money on a whole-life basis • Renewed commitment to implementation of whole-life costing • Find ways to quantify benefits arising from environmental/social factors • Structure tenders to establish best overall proposition for public benefit
Smarter engagement with the market to stimulate innovation	• Supply chain management falling below good private sector practice • Resistance to innovative supplier solutions • Risk aversion • Risk of delivering poor value to taxpayers	• Mechanisms to overcome supplier capability issues (SMEs, third sector) for innovation • Use Flexible Framework to drive innovation • Encourage an informed approach to risk management and supplier relationships • Work with key markets on joint improvement programmes

Chapter summary

- One obvious barrier to adoption of sustainability is that it may be more expensive. But good communication, and emphasis on the 'business case' for sustainability, may overcome this barrier.

- External stakeholders may resist sustainability if, for example, it appears to carry a financial cost that will affect them.

- Internal stakeholders may also be resistant. For example, people may be worried about a threat to the *status quo*, or about possible financial costs or danger to job security.

- There may be conflicts that obscure the case for sustainability. For example, most people are in favour of economic growth and development – but can this be achieved without damage to sustainability objectives?

- There may be cultural barriers to sustainability. For example, different cultures take different attitudes to 'gifts' – perceived in the West as bribery. Internally, too, there may be aspects of an organisation's culture that militate against sustainability.

- There may be economic barriers to sustainability. For example, in a recession the emphasis may be on cost reduction and survival rather than on sustainability measures that, in the short term, are expensive.

- The private sector appears less ready to embrace sustainability, perhaps fearing an adverse effect on the main private sector objective – profit maximisation. The public sector has mostly been seen as leading the way in this area.

Self-test questions

Numbers in brackets refer to the paragraphs above where your answers can be checked.

1　Give reasons why sustainable options may be more expensive, at least in the short term. (1.2)

2　Suggest means of overcoming barriers related to costs and cost perceptions. (1.5)

3　Give reasons why external stakeholders may resist moves towards sustainability. (2.3)

4　Why may internal managers be resistant to sustainable procurement? (2.9)

5　What arguments are made against global economic integration and free trade? (3.6)

6　According to Trompenaars, what are the outward expressions of culture? (4.2)

7　Give examples of external cultural factors that may cause barriers to sustainability. (4.5)

8　Suggest methods of overcoming internal cultural barriers to sustainability. (4.17)

9　Why does economic decline create barriers to sustainability? (5.5)

10　List barriers to sustainable procurement in the private sector. (Table 14.1)

Further reading

If you want to do more reading on barriers to sustainable procurement, the best way to do it may be to browse some online links to a range of sources (mostly relevant to public procurement, but as we have seen, the barriers are substantially the same). You might start at:

- http://www.ukprocurement.com/procurement-guide/sustainable-procurement/barriers-in-achieving-sustainable-procurement.php

CHAPTER 15

Managing Conflicts and Trade-Offs

Learning objectives and indicative content

4.2 Using appropriate tools, analyse the potential conflicts in achieving sustainable procurement for different sectors and industries and suggest how these can be managed

- Tools: forcefield analysis, SWOT
- Economic performance versus social and environmental responsibility
- Sourcing from developed countries versus developing countries
- Local versus international sourcing
- Environmentally friendly products and processes versus product legislation
- Lowest achievable price versus ethical considerations

4.3 Evaluate the potential trade-offs in the achievement of sustainable procurement within the context of an organisation

- Common international supplier standards leading to more competition
- Component and service standardisation allowing less opportunity for product and brand differentiation
- Paying or investing more for an enhanced reputation
- Investment in the short term to protect long-term supply of products and services

Chapter headings

1   Analysing potential conflicts

2   Economic performance versus responsibility

3   Local versus international sourcing

4   Environmentally friendly versus compliant

5   Potential trade-offs in achieving sustainable procurement

Introduction

In Chapter 14, we looked at the barriers to sustainable procurement: potential problems which might prevent or slow its development. In this chapter, we look at the related but slightly different area of 'conflicts' (mutually exclusive objectives or options that may arise when pursuing sustainable procurement) and at the 'trade-offs' or compromises that may be required in order to resolve those dilemmas.

The syllabus distinguishes clearly between barriers, conflicts and trade-offs, so it is important for you to do the same – and to read exam questions carefully. The syllabus also helpfully specifies the key conflicts and trade-offs to be considered, and we will focus on these in our coverage. As usual, you are asked to consider their application 'for different sectors and industries' – and, as usual, we cannot be comprehensive in this: our points will for the most part be general, and you should be able to use them as a framework for examining particular organisations or industries cited in exam case studies, or your own preparation of examples.

1 Analysing potential conflicts

SWOT analysis

1.1 As we saw briefly in Chapter 13, SWOT analysis is a technique of corporate appraisal, used to assess the *internal* resources of an organisation (or procurement function or supply chain) to cope with and/or capitalise on factors in the *external* environment in which it operates.

1.2 In assessing the potential for conflict around sustainable procurement, for example, a multi-disciplinary sustainability team may work together to appraise a comprehensive list of both internal and external factors. SWOT analysis may also be used to identify issues around the implementation of particular sustainable procurement proposals, such as local sourcing or ISO14001 certification of suppliers.

1.3 Internal appraisal of strengths and weaknesses may cover aspects such as: the availability of physical and financial resources; the current product/service portfolio; human resources; the efficiency and effectiveness of functions, operations and systems; organisation structures; distinctive competencies; and measures or enablers already in place for sustainable procurement (if any).

1.4 Opportunities and threats are factors in the external environment that may emerge to impact on the business, such as those discussed at length in Chapter 4 in relation to sustainability. Blackburn suggests a checklist of identified sustainability issues/trends (such as those covered in Chapter 2), against which each can be rated as:

- A *business risk/threat*: legal, financial, reputational, competitive or operational; and/or
- A *business opportunity*: innovation sales, productivity, reputation, employee relations, risk reduction, licence to operate.

1.5 An example of a sustainability SWOT analysis for a supplier was given in Chapter 13: Figure 13.1 The following example (Figure 15.1) shows an analysis for a particular sustainability issue, in an alternative format, drawn from Blackburn. You might like to have a go at drawing up a SWOT grid for a particular sustainability proposal, such as supplier ethical monitoring, or local sourcing.

Figure 15.1: *SWOT analysis*

Issue	Strength	Weakness	Opportunity	Threat	Possible objectives
Supplier labour practices in developing nations	1. Some suppliers are certified 2. Monitoring of key first-tier suppliers	1. Practices of some suppliers are unknown 2. Monitoring programmes not well developed	1. Customers attracted by certified CSR 2. More stable work force, more reliable supply	1. Risk to reputation 2. Labour unrest may interrupt supply	Develop and implement monitoring program at high-risk sites; benchmark to identify best practice

1.6 The following may be useful as a checklist of the kinds of questions that may be asked in preparing a SWOT analysis for sustainable procurement initiatives: Figure 15.2.

Figure 15.2 *SWOT analysis worksheet*

Strengths: What level of support do we have? Do we have a management structure in place? How informed are our management and staff? Do we have an organisational policy? Do we have a procurement policy? Do we have a long-term commitment? What enablers are already in place?	*Weaknesses:* How flexible is our management structure? What barriers/constraints do we face? Does the supply chain understand the issues? Have our staff 'bought-in'? Is sustainability taken seriously? What resources are available? What 'gaps' need to be filled?
Opportunities: Are we maximising the public relations opportunities of sustainability? Are we maximising the benefits of innovation? Are we using our approach as a way of building relationships with suppliers? Can our progressive and pro-active approach be applied in different areas?	*Threats:* How will stakeholders respond? How committed are the funders? How can we respond to changing stakeholder expectations? What will the situation be if we fail to deliver? How can we ensure all those involved are sufficiently aware and trained?

Forcefield analysis

1.7 *Forcefield analysis* (Kurt Lewin) is a technique for identifying forces for and against change, in order to diagnose some of the change management problems that will need to be addressed, and some of the resources and dynamics available to support it. It is thus particularly useful for analysing potential points of conflict within the organisation or supply chain, in relation to sustainable procurement in general — or particular proposals and initiatives.

1.8 As we noted in Chapter 5, at any time in an organisation there exist both forces for change (pushing towards a preferred state) and forces for maintaining the *status quo* (pushing back towards the way things are). At any given moment, the interplay of these forces determines the current state of the organisation (where the forces balance each other out, creating a temporary equilibrium) and the pace and direction of change (if one set of forces is stronger than the other).

- *Driving forces* (for change) encourage people to give up old ways of doing things and to try new behaviours. Examples include: the frustration or unpleasantness caused by customer complaints or inefficient processes; new technology becoming available; or influence/support from a powerful individual or group.

- *Restraining forces* (against change) support the *status quo*. Examples include: shortage of resources; opposition from influencers or cultural values; already-installed technology and established systems; managerial preoccupation with day-to-day matters and so on.

1.9 Forcefield analysis suggests a method of visualising or mapping the forces for and against change using directional arrows, the thickness of which represents the strength of each force. Let's use the introduction of a sustainable procurement policy for a particular organisation as our example – since this is just the sort of thing you might be asked to draft in an exam: Figure 15.3.

Figure 15.3 *Forcefield analysis*

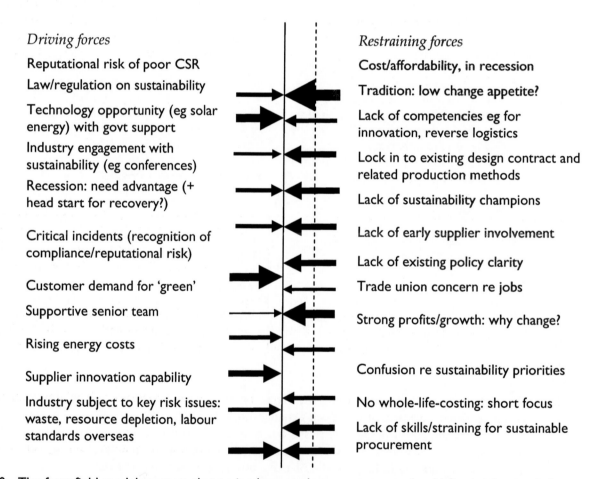

Current state   Preferred state

Driving forces

Reputational risk of poor CSR

Law/regulation on sustainability

Technology opportunity (eg solar energy) with govt support

Industry engagement with sustainability (eg conferences)

Recession: need advantage (+ head start for recovery?)

Critical incidents (recognition of compliance/reputational risk)

Customer demand for 'green'

Supportive senior team

Rising energy costs

Supplier innovation capability

Industry subject to key risk issues: waste, resource depletion, labour standards overseas

Restraining forces

Cost/affordability, in recession

Tradition: low change appetite?

Lack of competencies eg for innovation, reverse logistics

Lock in to existing design contract and related production methods

Lack of sustainability champions

Lack of early supplier involvement

Lack of existing policy clarity

Trade union concern re jobs

Strong profits/growth: why change?

Confusion re sustainability priorities

No whole-life-costing: short focus

Lack of skills/straining for sustainable procurement

1.10 The forcefield model suggests that to implement change, managers should first understand the forces for and against change, and the strength of each. One simple technique is to give a numerical value to each force, on a scale of 0 (neutral) to 4 (strong). If the totals on each side are the same, the *status quo* will be maintained. (You might like to add some scores to the forces in our example – and see whether you think the introduction of sustainable procurement is currently viable or not.)

1.11 Managers can then select change management strategies and styles which concentrate either on strengthening driving forces ('adding forces in the desired direction'), or weakening restraining forces ('diminishing the opposing forces'), or both.

- Driving forces can be strengthened by emphasising the needs and benefits of the change (eg reputational risk from poor CSR); developing people to cope with change (eg buyer training and supplier development); co-opting the support of influencers (including customers, by gathering feedback, say); embedding new values in mission and value statements; and so on.

- Restraining forces can be weakened by participation (involving resistors in diagnosing and solving the problems); education and communication (persuading resistors of the risks and importance of the issues); coercion (applying policy power to silence resistors); or negotiation (offering concessions to buy resistors off).

1.12 Using the numerically-scored technique on our example in Figure 15.3, for example, we might decide on a programme of negotiation with the trade unions (to weaken one of the stronger restraining forces). This might add +1 to the score for 'cost' – but reduce trade union concern by –3. We would need to reinforce customer demand for green products (perhaps partnering with NGOs), to strengthen this factor by +2. Procurement staff could be shown that sustainable procurement gives them more opportunities for development, creating a new driving force of +2. And so on. This would add to the total 'driving' score and lower the 'restraining' score – giving preference to change.

1.13 We will now turn to the specific conflict areas mentioned in the syllabus.

2 Economic performance versus responsibility

Economic performance v social/environmental sustainability

2.1 This is, effectively, the original conflict which sparked the sustainability debate, as discussed in Chapter 1. 'Most societies want to achieve economic development to secure higher standards of living, now and for future generations. They also seek to protect and enhance their environment, now and for their children. Sustainable development tries to reconcile these two objectives.' (HMSO, 1994)

2.2 Although it is argued that economic performance and social/environmental sustainability are potentially mutually reinforcing – rather than mutually exclusive – and although the Triple Bottom Line has been widely recognised, this is still a fundamental conflict for many organisations.

2.3 As we saw in Chapter 14, for example, there are cost implications to social and environmental sustainability. These may be (or may be perceived as):

- An affordability issue, especially where there are budgetary, funding or credit restrictions
- An unjustifiable risk in the face of survival pressures created by economic instability and recession
- An unjustifiable irrelevance, where the organisation seeks to maximise its profits (and shareholder returns), and/or where internal performance measures are focused on profitability and short-term cost management.

In the public sector, they may be perceived (despite policy statements to the contrary) as conflicting with the targets for 'value for money' set by the Gershon efficiency review.

2.4 Moreover, as we saw in Chapter I, the principles of corporate governance dictate that private sector firms are accountable primarily to their shareholders, and that the prime objective of business organisations is economic performance. Economist Milton Friedman famously took the view that 'the social responsibility of business is profit maximisation' – not least because profit maximisation benefits society via corporate taxation.

2.5 Where investment in social or environmental sustainability comes at the expense of economic survival, or shareholders' best long-term interests – or is perceived to do so by corporate management and stakeholders – the conflict will be genuine, and priority may legitimately be given to economic performance.

2.6 We have already discussed ways of resolving the conflict, throughout this text. Fundamentally, organisations will need to make a convincing business case for sustainability: demonstrating the business and 'bottom line' benefits discussed in Chapter I (see Table 1.3); starting sustainable procurement initiatives with quick wins carrying minimal cost implications; emphasising long-term cost savings available from sustainability, and revising costing and accounting procedures to quantify those benefits on a whole-life basis; and crystallising the potential bottom-line value in sustainability (eg through sustainability marketing, eco-efficiencies and so on).

2.7 The main thrust of the sustainable development argument is that economic performance and environmental/social responsibility need not be mutually exclusive – and can, in fact, be mutually reinforcing. However, this concept will have to be 'sold' and demonstrated to key internal and external stakeholders.

Example: HSBC

The guidance published by CIPS for this unit helpfully quotes the Corporate Sustainability statement of global banking giant HSBC, which affirms:

'We have always maintained that a company's first social responsibility is to be successful. Success allows us to invest in new products and services for our customers. It enables us to pay the dividends which form an important part of the long-term saving and pension plans of our shareholders. It allows us to contribute to public services through the taxes we pay to governments. It creates jobs for our colleagues and suppliers.'

Having said this, HSBC is committed to the idea that long-term success and good corporate behaviour are linked.

'At HSBC, our commitment to sustainability means contributing to a stable economy, while managing the social and environmental impacts of our business. We aim to run a sustainable business for the long term. This is about achieving sustainable profits for our shareholders, building long-lasting relationships with customers, valuing our highly committed employees, respecting environmental limits and investing in communities.

The current financial crisis has highlighted how important it is to look ahead to the challenges of the future. We believe that by doing this, we can provide shared value for our shareholders and the wider economy, the environment and society.

As a bank, we manage risk and identify business opportunities every day. We seek to embed social and environmental issues into what we do. Climate change and globalisation are critical trends shaping the way we do business in the future. These trends will affect the world's poorest people most significantly. We aim to mitigate the risks and maximise the opportunities associated with these shifts.'

Lowest achievable price versus ethical considerations

2.8 This area of conflict is clearly related to the previous one, arising from the fact that the responsible/ethical sourcing option may be more expensive. The lowest achievable price for a supply contract may be available as a result of:

- Sourcing from low-cost labour countries, where by definition workers are poorly paid

- Sourcing from high-productivity, low-cost suppliers. In manufacturing, high productivity may be enabled by 'sweatshop' labour conditions, forced or child labour, forced overtime and so on. In agriculture, it may be supported by intensive techniques: intensive farming (exhausting soil), 'battery'-style livestock management and so on

- Sourcing from suppliers whose low prices are enabled by cost-saving short-cuts in quality, safety or environmental standards, which may create downstream risks for customers or workers

- Sourcing from suppliers whose low prices are used deliberately to secure business in the face of poor ethical practices and reputation (and associated reputational risk)

- Using purchasing power to squeeze suppliers' profit margins, and thereby squeezing prices and wages back up the supply chain.

2.9 Ideally, of course, this should not represent a conflict at all: global declarations on human rights, fair trading standards, the Ethical Trading Initiative and other such standards argue that human and labour rights should be a pre-qualifier for all purchase decisions. For organisations adhering to such standards, the conflict may disappear in the face of the pressures for compliance. But the issues are not always so clear cut.

- The economic survival of the firm may still be a priority, and best achievable price may, in the short term, be instrumental in securing it (eg in the face of cashflow crisis).

- The additional costs of ethical procurement may not be borne or offset by the market: customers may not be prepared to pay more for ethical products.

- For very poor people, any employment or economic activity, on any terms, may be better than none at all. Withdrawal of business from suppliers who pose ethical dilemmas or risks, or are unable to comply with ethical standards, may not be an ethical solution!

2.10 Again, the resolution of this conflict will partly come through the management of stakeholder perceptions, expectations and performance indicators. As the Sustainable Procurement Task Force has emphasised for the public sector, 'value for money' must be redefined to include ethical (and other non-financial) benefits, rather than being identified with 'best achievable price'. Price comparisons and evaluations should be made with a keen awareness of the risks and costs associated with unethical sourcing decisions: loss of customer trust; costs of product health and safety failures; supply risk (from the squeezing of supplier profits and wages to the point of non-viability); and, most importantly, reputational risk (or the opportunity cost of wasted reputational capital).

2.11 The resolution of the conflict at the operational level may ultimately, however, have to be a compliance issue, with clear ethical sourcing and trading policies, and ethical standards for suppliers, communicated throughout the organisation and supply chain. These will have to be enforced (with incentives, penalties/sanctions and performance management) and supported (with procurement resources and supplier development).

Example: Sainsburys

In 2007, major supermarket Sainsbury's launched an important environmental sustainability initiative: 'I'm Not A Plastic Bag' shopping bags.

However, activist group Labour Behind the Label (LBL) claimed that the bags were unethically sourced – because they came from China, where workers cannot form unions and where the minimum wage doesn't equate to a proper living wage.

Sainsbury's was forced to reply that it was 'absolutely committed to sourcing with integrity' and 'took the matter seriously at every stage in its production process... The bags were not manufactured with "cheap" labour, nor were local workers exploited. The factory pays almost double the Chinese minimum wage for that province, and complies with all aspects of Chinese labour law.'

The director of the Ethical Trading Initiative reportedly confirmed that 'it is impossible for global-sourcing companies to ignore China: what's important is that they make sure they use their buying power to make a change for the better.'

---

3 Local versus international sourcing

Arguments for and against

3.1 You should be broadly aware of local and international sourcing from your studies for other modules, but to recap:

- Local sourcing implies using suppliers who are 'based within easy reach of the buyer' (*CIPS Knowledge Summary: Using Local Suppliers*), whether geographically or by other measures of accessibility. In the present context, however, it may be taken to mean sourcing within the local region or country – as opposed to international sourcing.

- International sourcing implies using suppliers across national borders – although it can also be distinguished from 'global' sourcing (which implies the co-ordination of requirements among the worldwide business units of a firm).

3.2 The arguments for and against each strategy can be summarised as in Table 15.1. Note that since economic performance is a dimension of sustainability, the business case (profitability, risk, competitive advantage) arguments are part of the sustainability-related conflict between the two approaches, as well as the ethical/ environmental arguments.

Table 15.1 *Arguments for/against local and international sourcing*

Benefits of international sourcing	Drawbacks of international sourcing
Availability of required materials and/or skills: increased supply capacity/competitiveness	Exchange rate risk, currency management issues etc
Competitive price and cost savings (scale economies, low labour costs)	High sourcing and transaction costs (risk management, tariff and non-tariff barriers)
Less onerous constraints/costs re environmental and labour compliance	Cost savings and lower standards may create sustainability/compliance/reputational risk
Leverages technology (eg for virtual organisation, e-sourcing)	Different legal frameworks, time zones, standards, language and culture
International trade (arguably) promotes development, prosperity, international relations etc	Additional risks: political, transport (lead times, exposure), payment, supplier standards monitoring
Public sector: compulsory to advertise contacts within the EU	Environmental impacts of transport/haulage (especially by air freight)

Benefits of local sourcing	Drawbacks of local sourcing
Investment in local community, employment, skills etc (plus reputational/brand benefits)	Materials, skills or capabilities may not be available locally (or may be more costly)
Accessibility for supplier development and contract management (eg site visits)	Ethical/reputational risks of close social ties with suppliers, common spheres etc
Supplier knowledge of local market, sustainability issues, regulatory standards etc.	Smaller suppliers: no economies of scale (higher costs), greater dependency issues
Reduced transport, payment, cultural risks and costs	Local sourcing policy may make local suppliers complacent/un-competitive
Short supply chain eg supporting JIT, fewer environmental impacts of transport	*Public sector:* may not discriminate on basis of geography
Avoids 'evils' of globalisation	*Public sector:* may not offer 'value for money'

3.3 In the private sector, the main sustainability-related conflicts can therefore be summarised as follows.

- The desire for low-cost sourcing, available from low-cost labour, economies of scale, less onerous compliance burdens and resource availability in international supply markets – versus the environmental, social, ethical and risk implications of international sourcing

- The desire to support local businesses (for economic/social sustainability, marketing and PR benefits), and to reap cost/risk advantages of short supply chains – versus uncompetitive costs and ethical issues of dependency

3.4 The public sector faces a particular dilemma in relation to local sourcing. The *CIPS Knowledge Summary: Using Local Suppliers* sums it up as follows.

The public sector must not discriminate on the basis of geography for any contract over the relevant threshold in the EC Procurement Directives.

However, the question of whether or not to buy locally has bedevilled local government for years. On the one hand there is the need to achieve (and be seen to have achieved) value for money and on the other hand, a desire to support local businesses. The dilemma has been brought back into the limelight by a) the introduction of Best Value, which has increased the need for local authorities to demonstrate that value for money is being achieved and b) by the growing influence of e-Commerce which will greatly widen choice in the marketplace and put pressure on local companies to remain competitive.

The current emphasis on Best Value has made it more difficult to justify a decision to try and source purchases locally when, at first sight, the prices being charged would seem to indicate that this would be uneconomical. It is important therefore to calculate the true cost of a purchase, including its impact on the policy outcomes of the authority.

3.5 There is no real 'answer' to this conflict, since both local and international sourcing can be argued on the basis of sustainability. Strategies and policies will have to be developed taking both sides of the argument into account – and carefully implemented and managed to ensure that the drawbacks and risks of the chosen strategy are minimised. For example, an organisation sourcing internationally will have to pay attention to fair pricing, monitoring of suppliers' labour and environmental standards, quality management and transport planning (to minimise carbon footprint). Similarly, an organisation sourcing locally will have to manage issues of supplier complacency (eg via continuous improvement agreements); supplier dependency (eg via supplier development, enabling a wider customer base); and internal cost/value measurement (eg via whole-life costing and TBL accounting).

Example: food supply chains

The following article (posted on environmental news site Ten Bees: www.tenbees.co.uk in May 2007)) suggests how a local sourcing strategy can be sold to stakeholders, in an industry for which sustainability issues (in the form of 'food miles') is a hot topic. (You might note, however, that Waitrose customers will still demand out-of-season imported fruit and vegetables, exotic foods and so on – and that this, too, will form part of the sourcing strategy…)

In line with the Campaign to Protect Rural England (CPRE)'s definition of 'local', local food must be produced within a 30 mile radius of the store in which it is sold.

Waitrose is highlighting its unique local sourcing commitments in a new 40 second television advertisement. The ad features a Waitrose Locally Produced supplier - Moor Organic Apple Juice in Kent - preparing and transporting apple juice a short distance from his orchard to nearby Waitrose store in Ramsgate, where it is sold as part of a range of local produce. Moor Organic Juice is just one of 250 suppliers on the Waitrose Locally Produced Initiative, which now includes over 688 products in Waitrose shops across the country.

Gillian Black, Waitrose Advertising Manager, said: 'Sourcing food from the local area and creating strong links with the community is a key differentiator for Waitrose. Small and independent producers are supplying our shops throughout the country, helping to form a regional identity for each Waitrose branch and reconnecting consumers with their local food and drink industries. We wanted this new ad to celebrate this point of difference, and to further raise the profile of the high quality local food in our branches.'

Shaun Spiers, CPRE's Chief Executive, said: 'We're really pleased Waitrose is making a big thing of selling locally sourced produce in its stores, and using our guidelines for what the 'local' in local foods should actually mean in terms of distances from farm gate to store. We think huge benefits can flow from boosting sales of local food: for consumers, the environment, our countryside and British farming. But for that to happen, local foods have to be promoted compellingly to shoppers. The Waitrose ad is a big step in the right direction.'

Sourcing from developed countries versus developing countries

3.6 If an organisation is involved in, or considering, international sourcing, should it source from developed or developing countries?

- *Developed countries* are industrialised countries, generally characterised by high levels of industrialisation, technological development, educational attainment, health standards and personal incomes.

- *Developing countries* are those countries in the process of industrialisation, with low or middle national income (as defined by the World Bank), and typically with lower levels of technological development and educational attainment and lower living standards. Such countries are found in parts of Africa, Asia, Eastern Europe and South America.

Example: corruption risk

The 2007 Corruption Perceptions Index (published by NGO Transparency International) revealed that more than 40% of 180 countries examined were perceived to have 'rampant corruption' in their public sector procurement. (Supply Management, 4 October 2007).

Meanwhile, a Munich court found German technology firm Siemens guilty of paying bribes to secure contracts in Nigeria, Libya and Russia in 77 cases between 2001 and 2004: the firm accepted full responsibility and agreed to pay a fine of €201 million (€144 million).

The FTSE4 Good Index (the FTSE list of socially responsible firms) has recently added counter-bribery measures to its list of criteria.

- 130 firms, including oil and gas producers and equipment firms, chemicals and mining companies, have been identified as most at risk from exposure to bribery.

- Pharmaceutical businesses, hotels and technology firms have been deemed at 'medium' risk of bribery.

3.7 The advantages and disadvantages of sourcing from developing countries (although, of course, there will be specific considerations in regard to each different nation and culture) may be summarised as in Table 15.2. The arguments for and against sourcing from developed countries will really be the 'flip side' of these points.

Table 15.2 *Sustainability issues in sourcing from developing countries*

Benefits of developing country sourcing	Drawbacks of developing country sourcing
Low-cost labour, competitive pricing, less onerous compliance regimes: cost advantage	Developed country buyers may not be aware of differences, conditions, issues, risks
Supplier and infrastructure development, fair trading etc, can improve living standards	Less onerous standards regimes: little infrastructure to support CSR policies
Reputational and branding benefits may accrue to buyer from contribution to social justice, living standards etc.	Poverty puts focus on survival: low priority for labour standards, wages, environment etc: little support for corporate CSR policies
Focuses attention on need for responsible procurement: development of sustainable procurement awareness, competence	Supply chain standards more difficult to monitor (less ICT/transport infrastructure): reputational risk
Potential to influence supplier development, innovation, infrastructure development proactively to meet requirements	Corruption at all levels endemic in many developing countries: costs/compliance issues of bribes/inducements, diversion of funds etc.
May secure political good will, grants, subsidies or tax breaks for development	May simply 'export' environmental damage, problems of industrialisation

3.8 Again, there is no real 'solution' to this conflict, other than to ensure that strong sustainable procurement policies, principles and systems are used when sourcing from developing countries – as they should be in any sourcing situation – in line with our coverage elsewhere in the text.

3.9 Culturally sensitive ethical codes should also be in place, to support procurement professionals in addressing corruption, managing corruption risk (eg charitable donations being 'diverted' to local officials) – and at the very least, upholding their own professional standards (and, in the public sector, legislative requirements) in relation to bribes and inducements.

4 *Environmentally friendly versus compliant*

4.1 It is ironic that product legislation should conflict with the development of environmentally friendly products and processes, as the syllabus suggests. It is, after all, a key aim of product legislation to support environmental responsibility – just as one of the key drivers for environmental responsibility by organisations is the need to comply with product legislation and other regulations discussed in Chapter 11. For example, think of the regulations on Restriction of Hazardous Substances (RoHS); Control of Substances Hazardous to Health (CoSHH); Registration, Evaluation and Authorisation of Chemicals (REACH); Waste Electronic and Electrical Equipment (WEEE); or End of Live Vehicle (EHV).

4.2 Legislative pressure is cited by as many as 65% of companies as the main incentive to launch environmentally friendly products. As an example, VW and Audi took the lead with catalytic converters in the early 1980s: most companies followed only when legislation was introduced making catalytic converters compulsory.

4.3 However, it may also be argued that product legislation/regulation may have a negative impact on sustainability in various ways.

- It may stifle innovation, because of the perception of compliance risk, the burden of extra compliance costs and the temptation to be satisfied with legislated standards (which often lag behind innovation in fast-changing markets).

- It may limit consumer choice – and interfere with competition in the market, which (among other things) supports environmentally-friendly developments.

- It requires change to products and processes, which may cause sustainability issues in other areas, during the innovation/learning curve (increasing the risk of accidents and quality/reliability problems, say) or as a direct result of changes (eg the use of less effective non-chemical cleaning products, causing hygiene problems; or non-lead soldering techniques, which may damage components; or recycled materials and components, which may compromise reliability).

4.4 Conversely, it may be argued that non-regulatory (eg consumer and competitive) pressures to develop environmentally friendly products and processes may cause compliance risks. The pace of innovation, for example, may lead to inadequately tested products or processes, increasing the risk of environmental impacts (and/or problems with quality, reliability or cost-efficiency). Another example might be the rush to market new products on the basis of their 'green' credentials, which may fall foul of legislation and standards on eco-labelling (to avoid misleading consumers).

Example: consumer electronics

'With heightened public awareness of the energy efficiency of all energy-using products, one debate that is often at the top of the agenda [in the consumer electronics industry] is innovation versus legislation. Many parties believe that the only way to reduce energy consumption is to force manufacturers to comply with government mandates limiting the energy consumption of energy-using products.

However, there is an argument that the implementation of such regulation in regard to consumer electronics would in fact have a negative impact, as it would stifle innovation, limit consumer choice, and interfere with competitive trends in the electronics sector that support energy efficiency. Moreover, existing government-industry partnerships demonstrate that market-oriented solutions can achieve important energy conservation goals while protecting innovation, consumer choice and competition.

Does innovation work?

The overall power consumption of televisions, for example, has been reduced from 400W to 30W since the 1970s: a 92.5% reduction in energy use. Importantly, this progress has been industry led rather than enforced through legislation or regulation.

Voluntary and market-oriented initiatives have also been major drivers in reducing standby power consumption. The international Energy Star programme, for example, is a successful government-industry effort which benefits from strong participation from manufacturers and is well-recognised by consumers. The scheme captures a broad range of consumer electronics product categories and creates a competitive incentive for energy savings.

Why is legislation not the most effective route?

The achievements outlined above would be unlikely and unmanageable under a government mandate. Legislation takes a long time to be drafted and approved. The technology industry is incredibly fast moving, with daily technology developments: legislation would never keep up with the industry, hindering innovation, raising costs for industry and consumers, and generally slowing further improvements in the area of energy efficiency.

In addition, legislation and regulation, usually in place at a national or regional level, often presents new costs and obstacles that can hinder trade and investment. Economies of scale, and lower costs for consumers, are achieved with global markets and global approaches.

Johnson, 'Will legislation improve energy efficiency in consumer products?', *Electronics Weekly*, 12 March 2008

---

5 Potential trade-offs in achieving sustainable procurement

What are 'trade-offs'?

5.1 Trade-offs arise naturally from conflicts. Where an organisation, project or policy has conflicting objectives and success criteria – multiple outcomes which are all broadly desirable, but mutually exclusive – there will have to be a compromise or trade-off between them. Concessions will have to be made in one area, in order to secure the advantages of another.

5.2 This is not inevitably a feature of sustainable procurement. In many cases, objectives (including economic performance and environmental/social sustainability) are compatible or even mutually reinforcing, if seen from a broad enough perspective. The main argument for corporate sustainability is that it is essentially a 'win win' situation. But in some aspects, sustainability is a 'zero-sum' game: that is, you can't have gains in one area, or for one stakeholder group, without losses in another.

5.3 You may already be familiar with the concept of the iron triangle, a tool often used in project management to illustrate the need for trade-offs between equally desirable but mutually incompatible objectives: in this case, cost, time and quality. You can pursue higher quality, but only at the expense of higher cost and longer lead times. You can pursue shorter lead times, but only at the expense of higher cost and/or lower quality. And so on. A similar observation is made by Lysons & Farrington (*Purchasing and Supply Chain Management*) in relation to the 'five rights of purchasing'.

5.4 This is more or less the issue that is raised by the syllabus in relation to certain sustainability elements. Note that these are primarily issues within the context of an organisation: that is, they reflect the priorities and strategic choices made by the organisation. Let's take the trade-offs specified in the syllabus, one by one.

Common supplier standards or competitive advantage?

5.5 The syllabus phrases the trade-off as: 'common international supplier standards leading to more competition'. The dilemma, as we see it, is as follows.

5.6 The sustainability agenda is supported – as we saw in Chapter 11 – by the development of international standards and codes of practice which can be applied to supply chains: eg ISO 14001, SA 8000, the ETI base code and so on.

- Such standards create widespread shared consensus as to minimum standards of environmental, ethical and social management practice.
- They provide a convenient tool for buyers in appraising, pre-qualifying, monitoring/rating, managing and developing suppliers.
- They reduce supply chain risk, and the cost of managing risk, quality and sustainability, by pre-qualifying and assuring supplier management systems.
- They provide a framework for the development of organisational environmental, quality, ethical and social accountability policies, procedures and management systems – and their application in the supply chain.
- They allow credible marketing claims on the basis of certification, compliance or 'benchmarked best practice', which may offer benefits through customer trust, brand positioning and price premiums.
- Their aim is explicitly to raise standards across sectors and industries, to encourage best practice and technology sharing, to offer like-with-like product comparison and

conformity assessment, to offer certified reassurance to buyers (and end users of products and services), and to improve buyer/customer choice by widening competition among suppliers.

5.7 The trouble with this is that while it develops your supply chain's sustainability standards and management capabilities, it also develops those of your competitors' supply chains! By raising sustainability performance across the board, common international supplier standards 'level the playing field'.

- An organisation that has previously differentiated its corporate and/or product brand(s) on the basis of its supply chain's social or environmental sustainability, or ethical sourcing, will lose its source of differentiation and market positioning: competitors will have 'caught up' by adhering to standard – and by being able to claim equal certification status.

- An organisation that has sought to be a CSR/sustainability leader in its market may likewise find that it is no longer so 'cutting edge' in the face of generally raised standards, and widespread claims of certification, standards attainment or 'benchmarked best practice'.

- The organisation may no longer be able to charge a price premium for sustainability excellence.

- There may, as we saw earlier in the case of legislation, be an active disincentive to further innovation or leadership in sustainability excellence, because of the perception that standards attainment (and the marketing claims arising from it) are 'sufficient' to reap the business benefits of sustainability: why invest more than necessary? In other words, standardisation may encourage 'satisficing' ('good enough') performance.

5.8 Another dilemma, not raised by the syllabus, is that international supplier standards promoting sustainable procurement may act against sustainable procurement: for example, if they are so stringent and resource-intensive that they discriminate against small suppliers, or suppliers in developing countries.

5.9 So what is the trade-off? An organisation may need to forgo the marketing and efficiency benefits of claiming that suppliers, products or materials are standards-certified, in order to:

- Preserve unique or differentiated product or performance attributes, and the brand positioning, competitive advantage and premium pricing that come with them

- Develop standards, policies and management systems that position it as an innovator or leader in its market (ie pursuing above-standard performance), for competitive advantage. You might think of Marks & Spencer or Hewlett Packard, for example.

Standardisation or differentiation?

5.10 Much the same argument can be made for – and against – the standardisation of product and service specifications. The syllabus phrases the dilemma as: 'component and service standardisation, allowing less opportunity for product and brand differentiation'. There are various issues here, depending on how one interprets the terms.

5.11 Standard specifications are documents that stipulate or recommend minimum levels of performance and quality of goods and services. Standards may relate to aspects such as: standard use of terms and symbols (BS 208, for example, sets conventions for technical drawings); the dimensions of items (encouraging interchangeability and variety reduction); performance or safety requirements; environmental requirements; and codes of practice. Such standards support sustainable procurement in the following ways.

- Promoting effective and efficient specification of products and services: saving the time and cost of preparing company specifications and related clarifications.

- Allowing accurate comparison of quotations, since all potential suppliers are quoting on the same specifications. This also ensures more equitable access to opportunity for suppliers (reducing reliance on specialist suppliers).

- Promoting efficiency and cost saving in quality management, reducing the need for inspection.

5.12 Standardisation may also mean variety reduction: the reduction of unnecessary variations in specified items. This also supports sustainability, by offering potential for efficiencies and cost savings in the following areas.

- *Specification*: eg use of generic stock items rather than bespoke, own-design or variant items or new buys

- *Purchasing*: eg through the consolidation of requirements (rather than multiple small orders of variant items), bulk discounts and reduced transaction and materials handling costs

- *Transport*: eg using standard load and container sizes to enable inter-modal transport

- *Inventory*: eg through reduced space requirements and risks of obsolescence and deterioration of slow-moving variant items.

5.13 In a third meaning of the term, standardisation may refer to an international marketing strategy of offering the same basic products and brands across all markets – as opposed to a strategy of 'adaptation': adapting the offering according to the local demands and preferences of each market. This, too, can be seen to support sustainability, by respecting cultural distinctions, encouraging local sourcing and employment and so on.

5.14 At the same time, however, as the syllabus points out, standardisation erodes the potential for:

- Competitive differentiation of products, services and brands: the things that make one brand different from another in the eyes of the market, which drive customer preference, choice and loyalty

- Competitive advantage arising from core procurement competencies such as effective product and service specification and quality management

- Competitive advantage in local markets, arising from market- and culture-specific adaptations.

5.15 Differentiation, 'uniqueness' or even 'quirkiness' may be central to an organisation's competitive strategy for a brand; the basis of brand positioning (how the brand is perceived by the market in relation to competitors); the source of brand strength and value; and the ability to charge price premiums or differentials. (Think of Virgin's airline and financial services products for example: their brand strength depends on their not following 'standard' service values.) Global standardised brands may fail because of failure to take account of local sensitivities and preferences, language differences and so on.

5.16 So what is the trade-off? The organisation may have to forgo some of the efficiency and control advantages of standardising components and services, in order to pursue competitive differentiation, brand positioning and price premiums, and local market adaptation.

5.17 One practical solution may be to standardise products, services or components which are less instrumental in customer choice, or which are vulnerable to quality or sustainability risks – and to focus on differentiation, innovation and leadership where these attributes are highly visible and valued by the customer. So, for example, an automotive manufacturer may standardise engine components (for production and maintenance efficiencies) – but differentiate driver controls and visible design features. An airline like Virgin might standardise its maintenance and cleaning procedures – but encourage individuality, flair, humour and initiative in customer service roles.

Example: McDonald's

For many decades, McDonald's pursued a policy of standardisation in its ingredients, products and service, in order to guarantee brand and service consistency from franchise to franchise, worldwide. However, the standards had failed to move with the times on health sustainability issues...

'McDonald's fast food restaurants are slashing their burger menus across Europe to make way for a new range of healthier foods, including chicken salads and chopped fruit. Launched today in the UK, Salad Plus has been dubbed McDonald's 'most significant menu change' in its 30-year history. The move follows the chain's decision last week to phase out 'super-size' fries and drinks in the UK and is a major attempt to fight for the £445 million-a-year prepared salad market.

McDonald's, which has come under increasing pressure from anti-obesity campaigners who claim the company encourages an unhealthy lifestyle, will overhaul menus in 16 European countries by slashing its line-up of burgers for chicken salads, yoghurts and chopped fruits. The chain has already successfully introduced a premium salads range in the US. [The executive vice-president of McDonald's Europe] said the company was also working with nutritionists on a 'smart labelling' system which should be ready by the end of the year.

www.mad.co.uk, 9 March 2004

In a similarly radical re-vamp, McDonald's also now offers regional dishes (eg 'croque monsieur' in France, 'Aussie' burgers in Australia and a spiced chicken 'Maharajah Mac' in India) and uses local produce in different countries.

In the wake of strong public, activist and media pressure (including the film Supersize Me and the notorious 'McLibel' case, in which McDonald's sued a small activist group), McDonald's has developed a very strong corporate responsibility platform. This makes an interesting case study! See:

- http://www.McDonald's.com/usa/good.html
- http://www.McDonald's.co.uk > 'Our world'

For an illustration of the challenges of reaping reputational value from CSR policies, see:

- http://www.mcspotlight.org: "McDonald's spends over $2 billion a year broadcasting their glossy image to the world. This is a small space for alternatives to be heard."

Intangible (reputational) or tangible (financial) benefits?

5.18 The syllabus caption phrases this trade-off as: 'Paying or investing more for an enhanced reputation'. There is a clear trade-off between:

- The immediate, tangible and easily quantifiable benefits of cost reduction, cost savings or profit maximisation and

- The long-term, intangible (and therefore difficult to quantify) benefits of enhanced reputation – and related intangible assets such as the goodwill, loyalty and commitment of suppliers, customers, NGOs, the local community, society and other stakeholders.

5.19 This trade-off arises because, as we have seen, sustainability and ethical sourcing/trading may require significant investment (eg in policy development, implementation and management; innovation; skilling; environmentally friendly processes, equipment and vehicles; and so on) and extra costs (eg for green products, renewable energy, locally-sourced supplies and so on).

5.20 If enhanced reputation (or the management of reputational risk) is seen as the primary business benefit of sustainable procurement, this is a difficult trade-off. Investment in sustainability impacts on the economic bottom line now – and in a tangible and quantifiable way. In contrast, reputational benefits may be seen as:

- *Uncertain*: corporate reputation is a complex perceptual construct. It represents the 'net' affective or emotional reaction – good-bad, weak or strong – of customers, investors, employees and general public to the company's name' (Fombrun). This may depend on all sorts of subjective factors – many of them outside the organisation's control, and not all of them to do with sustainability: a CSR leader can still have a poor reputation or corporate brand, on grounds of poor quality or unfashionability, say.

- *Vulnerable*: corporate reputations are costly and time-consuming to build – but can be lost in a moment, due to a single, perhaps unforeseeable, environmental crisis, product recall, supply chain incident – or 'Gerald Ratner moment' (a reputation-ruining executive speech…)

- *Intangible*: reputational and brand assets are often valued by comparing the 'book' value of the company (tangible assets as shown in the balance sheet) and its 'market' value (or share price) – but it is still difficult to pin this value down, or to ascribe it specifically to reputation.

5.21 For most companies, it will be considered worth some investment in CSR and sustainability management, if only to protect or defend the corporate reputation, and reduce reputational risk. This may be seen less as a 'trade-off' and more as a sound investment, however, if bottom line arguments can be made for reputation management and defence. The economic value of reputation (reputational capital) can be calculated and reported. Reputational risks can be identified, assessed and costed. And so on. If these concepts don't ring a bell, you might like to recap the section on Reputation and Brand Strength in Chapter 4.

Example: Johnson & Johnson

In 1982 and 1986, a few capsules of J&J's top-selling analgesic brand Tylenol were contaminated with cyanide in extortion attempts.

CEO at the time, Jim Burke, considered that immediate and forceful measures were needed: firstly, to ensure public safety and secondly, to restore trust in the company and the product. In an acknowledged best-practice case study of corporate ethical conduct and reputational defence, the company immediately recalled 31 million capsules from shops – and homes – across the US, using full-page newspaper advertisements and television spots to announce the move and keep customers informed.

J&J was publically regarded as demonstrating both concern for its customers and commitment to its own corporate ethical standards, effectively put into action. It already had a strong reputation, and a high level of trust and goodwill – among the public, regulatory agencies and media – enabled it to re-launch Tylenol successfully, after the packing had been redesigned to make it tamper-proof. It swiftly regained 95% of its pre-crisis market share – and J & J continually features near the top of Most Admired Companies rankings.

Was this regarded as a 'trade-off'? J & J has said that 'its actions had been pre-ordained by its widely heralded corporate credo [ethical values]; no other response could even have been contemplated.'

Short or long payback horizons?

5.22 The syllabus phrases this trade-off as: 'investment in the short term to protect long-term supply of products and services'. We have already encountered this tension in our coverage of barriers to sustainable procurement. Essentially, as we have seen:

- Sustainable procurement incurs additional up-front costs and investment.

- Many procurement functions – and organisations generally, under recessionary and/or cashflow pressures – look for short-term return on investment, or short payback periods. (In the public sector, the *Procuring the Future* report found that buyers are often attempting to justify purchases on a 'value for money' basis by securing payback within the current budgetary period.)

- However, the returns on investment from sustainable procurement are often long-term in nature, accruing through whole-life cost savings, improved security (sustainability) of supply and mitigation of supply risks. These returns represent long payback periods – and may, like reputational benefits, be difficult to quantify.

5.23 Nevertheless, like investment in reputation management, investment in security of supply is likely to be a risk management priority for most organisations. One of the key business-case arguments for sustainability, cited by Blackburn, is that: 'by working proactively on sustainability issues with their suppliers and contractors, a company can help assure that critical supplies and services will be available on an ongoing basis and that supply chain costs are properly controlled.'

- Investment in supply chain collaboration can result in more environmentally friendly raw materials, and product and packaging designs that pose less risk and cost in manufacture, handling and use.

- Supplier development and responsible sourcing practices can help minimise the risk of supplier failure, early contract termination and other disruptions to supply – which can be very costly for the buyer in terms of lost production, late delivery to customers, re-scheduling, 'crisis' purchases from alternative sources at penalty cost, and so on.

- Supplier support can also help mitigate the effects of supply disruption.

- Sustainability policies will include collaborative reductions in raw material, and natural resource and energy consumption – thus contributing to the long-term security of supply by ensuring that consumption keeps pace with supply or renewal.

- Sustainable sourcing and supplier management practices ensure that constructive working relationships are maintained for the future: the organisation doesn't 'burn its bridges' by alienating suppliers, to the point that they become merely compliant (without the value-adding potential of goodwill and commitment) – or, worse, charge penalty rates, or refuse to supply the buyer altogether.

5.24 Meanwhile, however, the down side of this trade-off may be minimised, as suggested throughout this text, by the following measures.

- Monitoring, assessing and prioritising supply risk, and focusing investment on bottleneck and strategic/critical purchase items and suppliers

- Costing/quantifying supply risks, where possible, to make a business case for investment in security of supply

- Rolling out sustainable procurement incrementally, with an initial focus on measures with low-cost implications and quick payback periods

- Using whole-life costing to emphasise long-term return on investment.

Example: Toyota

An earthquake in Tokyo in September 2007 suspended Toyota's factory lines for three days, as a key supplier of piston and sealing rings (Riken) was forced to halt production. As part of the firm's philosophy of *genchi genbutsu* ('go and see for yourself'), Toyota provided 200 staff to help Riken with its recovery.

Chapter summary

- A SWOT analysis may highlight possible obstacles to a sustainability programme.

- Kurt Lewin's forcefield analysis may be useful in identifying forces in favour of and in opposition to a sustainability programme.

- Economic factors are often perceived as a barrier to sustainability, but increasingly organisations are taking a long-term financial view so as to give priority to ethical considerations.

- Both local and international sourcing can be supported by sustainability arguments, so there is no simple choice between the two. The same is true of the choice between sourcing from developed countries versus developing countries.

- Paradoxically, product legislation can have a negative impact on sustainability.

- Common supplier standards in relation to sustainability are desirable – but they benefit our competitors as much as ourselves. The same is true of standard specifications.

- Another trade-off is between cost savings (at the expense of sustainability) and reputational benefits (available from investment in sustainability).

Self-test questions

Numbers in brackets refer to the paragraphs above where your answers can be checked.

1   Give examples of driving forces for change (supporting sustainability) and restraining forces for the *status quo* (resisting sustainability). (1.8)

2   How can managers use a forcefield analysis to assist adoption of a sustainability programme? (1.11)

3   How can sustainability be 'sold' to stakeholders in view of its potential costs? (2.7)

4   In what ways may economic considerations tell against adoption of ethical trading? (2.9)

5   Give arguments for and against local and international sourcing. (Table 15.1)

6   Give benefits and drawbacks of sourcing from developing countries. (Table 15.2)

7   In what ways may product legislation have a negative impact on sustainability? (4.3)

8   Explain the conflict between common supplier standards and competitive advantage. (5.6, 5.7)

9   Explain the conflict between reputational and financial benefits. (5.18)

Further reading

You've probably done all the reading you need to, here! If you have spare time, we recommend that you spend it selecting a few organisations that interest you – from different sectors and industries – and browsing their websites. Download relevant sustainable procurement, CSR and ethics information. Google articles about them in online media. Gather case studies from 'portal' sites such as www.csr-supplychain.org or the Global Reporting Initiative.

The aim is to build up a portfolio of case examples that you can use (selectively and where relevant) to support your answers in an exam.

CHAPTER 16

Future Challenges for Sustainable Procurement

Learning objectives and indicative content

4.4 Explore the future challenges for the purchasing profession in the area of sustainable procurement within a global market place

- Sustainable procurement and end-to-end supply chain activity
- Stakeholder priorities
- National and global challenges to successful sustainable procurement
- Supplier development
- Managing for risk and vulnerability in the supply chain
- Making sustainable procurement 'business as usual'

Chapter headings

1   National and global sustainability challenges

2   Challenges of supply chain management

3   Challenges of risk and vulnerability

4   Challenges of commitment

Introduction

In this final chapter, we turn to future challenges of sustainable procurement for the purchasing profession. You will also be able to draw on earlier chapters for this topic. In Chapters 2–5, for example, we looked at trends and influences in sustainability. Many of these presented challenges for sustainable procurement – and, by their nature, these will be projected into the future. The scarcity of non-renewable resources, for example, is a challenge now: it will be even more of a challenge in the future, unless renewable alternatives are developed and adopted. It may not be possible to distinguish meaningfully between present and (continuing) future challenges.

In a sense, any of the issues and measures discussed in this text may present a future challenge, if organisations do not deal with them now. (The development and implementation of a sustainable procurement policy will be a 'future challenge' for an organisation that hasn't yet made a start!) Nor is there a clear distinction between the 'barriers', 'conflicts' and 'trade-offs' discussed in Chapters 14–15 and the 'challenges' raised by this learning objective: unresolved barriers and conflicts will remain challenges for the future, as will the justification of trade-offs, as organisational circumstances and priorities change.

It is also important to remember that new challenges will constantly emerge – and old challenges re-emerge – as environmental conditions change: what is easy in a boom may present a challenge in a recession, for example.

In this chapter, we will simply work through each of the key challenges mentioned by the syllabus.

1 National and global sustainability challenges

1.1 The syllabus actually refers to 'national and global challenges to successful sustainable procurement'. This is a broad and slightly ambiguous category.

- Challenges to sustainable procurement should include factors in the external environment which pose barriers or difficulties for the development and implementation of sustainable procurement strategies (as discussed in Chapters 14 and 15).

- However, the phrase may also refer to factors which pose a challenge for sustainable procurement: that is, challenges requiring successful sustainable procurement – more like the sustainability trends, issues and drivers discussed in Chapters 2–5.

1.2 We will just draw together some points, briefly, here.

National challenges

1.3 Likely future (or ongoing) challenges to successful sustainable procurement at the national level, and suggestions for how they can be managed, are described in Table 16.1.

Table 16.1 *Summary of national challenges to successful sustainable procurement*

Challenge	Comment
The impact of global economic recession on the national economy	As we saw in Chapter 14, cost factors are the primary barrier to the successful development of sustainable procurement.
	In the short term, the need to stimulate and consolidate economic recovery may present the purchasing profession with challenges of affordability and stakeholder resistance. These can be managed (as we have seen) by prioritising affordability and short-term value, and by justifying longer-term investment in sustainability with a strong business case and whole-life costing.
	In the longer term, there may be the challenge of mitigating the risks of 'business cycles'. This may mean adapting sustainable procurement strategies to minimise the destabilising effects of upswings and downswings, where possible: eg through flexible staffing and sourcing policies, demand management and the management of supply risks, and careful whole-life capital investment appraisal.
Conflicting policy objectives	As we saw in Chapter 14, conflicting public policy objectives create a barrier to sustainable procurement in several areas. The trend towards international free trade (eg within the EU) poses a continuing challenge to local sourcing. Policies intended to stimulate economic growth and consumer spending will continue to work against the sustainable procurement objective of reduced consumption, re-use, recycling and the rationalisation of requirements. In the public sector, procurement efficiency and 'value for money' policies are likely to continue to be in tension with the longer-term intangible benefits of sustainability.
	National policy may be outside the organisation's control, but the challenges may be managed by monitoring and shaping stakeholder priorities; clarifying areas of misunderstanding (eg the meaning of 'value for money' and making whole-life costing mandatory in public sector procurement); and perhaps also lobbying and advocating on public policy.
Demographic trends	As we saw in Chapter 2, national demographic trends pose increasing challenges of population growth (and therefore resource consumption and waste products); population ageing (pressure on health and welfare services and funding); population diversity and migration (pressure on cross-cultural marketing and management); and skill development (pressure to develop, attract and retain skills among overseas workforces, immigrants and so on).
	We examined the implications for procurement management in Chapter 2.

Challenge	Comment
Geography	Each nation will have its own challenges to sustainable procurement arising from its geographical position and attributes. The UK is a small island: this creates challenges of land use (eg the need for intensive land productivity); natural resource availability (eg dependence on overseas oil); and carbon footprint (because of the need to import goods and resources by air). Nations in different climate zones will have different drivers and challenges: water management, salination, protection of rainforests and so on. These challenges will have to be managed on a case by case problem-solving basis. They are likely to act as a driver for sustainable procurement, rather than a barrier to it.
Consumer demand	There is a continuing challenge to the success of sustainable procurement arising from the failure of consumer demand to keep pace with the urgency of sustainability issues. In affluent, materialistic societies, a significant paradigm shift is still required to achieve sustainable lifestyles, reduced consumption, recycling and demand for sustainable products. Without support from consumer demand, the business case for sustainable procurement will continue to be weakened. This challenge can be managed to an extent by continuing consumer education, innovation (bringing the prices of sustainable products down), partnership with NGOs in advocacy and marketing and so on.
National targets and commitments	Government policy targets (and targets set under international commitments such as Kyoto) present a challenge to – or driver for – sustainable procurement. Challenging targets are deliberately set: by the government's own purchasing operations (leading by example and using purchasing power to change markets); sustainability targets set for business and the general public (eg in relation to GHG emissions reduction); and sustainable public procurement policies (including targets to move up the Flexible Framework levels of performance). This challenge can broadly be managed by building benchmarking, national targets and continuous improvement planning into sustainable procurement strategies and supply chain relationships. In the public sector, there is a particular challenge in overcoming barriers to sustainable procurement, in order to 'lead by example' for the private and third sectors. Specific recommendations in this respect, by the SPTF, were discussed in Chapter 14.
The pace of legislation	The pace and scope of environmental and social sustainability legislation and regulation is increasing, partly driven by EU directives and international agreements such as Kyoto – and partly driven by increasing awareness of the issues. This poses the challenge of continual industry adaptation to the demands of new legislation such as WEEE, End of Life Vehicles (ELV) and so on, together with ever more rigorous measures on corporate governance and reporting. In broad terms, such challenges can only be managed by: monitoring issues to anticipate legislative measures; pre-empting legislative measures by pursuing best practice; shaping legislative measures through lobbying and voluntary self-regulation; and implementing compliance risk assessment and planning systems.

1.4 In effect, any of the issues and trends discussed in this text, and any of the barriers to successful sustainable procurement discussed in Chapter 14, may represent future challenges for organisations which have not yet taken action to address or overcome them. Some (such as government policy conflicts, economic stability or demographic trends) may present particular ongoing challenges, because they are essentially not within the control of management: issues and risks in these areas will have to be continually monitored and managed

Global challenges

I.5　The essence of globalisation is that markets and economies are increasingly interconnected. In a sense, therefore, national challenges are also often global challenges. (The challenge of the 'credit crunch' in the USA, for example, swiftly transmitted itself to other economies, resulting in a global recession.) Meanwhile, global challenges (such as the need to reduce GHG emissions) become national challenges, through the flow-down of commitments and targets to national policy level.

I.6　Some of the challenges which may be considered genuinely global in scale and scope, however, include: growing demand for finite natural resources; global demographic trends; and climate change. We have already discussed these challenges, and how they can be managed, in earlier chapters.

I.7　The major challenge for (and driver of) sustainable procurement is arguably the general sustainability 'equation': growing demand (arising from global population growth and the increasing industrialisation of developing nations) for finite natural resources, many of which are already scarce, and non-renewable. As we saw in Chapter 2, 'to achieve sustainability of resources, the world must bring back into balance its consumption, technological development resource re-use and recycling, and population growth' (Blackburn).

- For non-renewable resources (such as fossil fuels and minerals), the focus is on developing adequate supplies of alternatives – before the current resources are so depleted as to cause economic or social disruption.

- For renewable resources (such as wood, grain, cotton, fish and other biomass), the focus is on: (a) harvesting at a sustainable rate, not exceeding the rate of replenishment; and (b) consuming at a sustainable rate, not exceeding the combined rate of harvest, re-use and recycling of the resource.

I.8　Resource depletion (and resulting rising costs) can be delayed by reducing the consumption rate. This may involve measures such as support for recycling and re-use; increased resource efficiency (supported by technology); and government policies (eg tax penalties and incentives) for reduced consumption. Government and business can also provide incentives and support to accelerate the research and development of substitutes – and procurement functions have a key role in securing their adoption (initially, perhaps, at higher cost), to stimulate demand for innovation.

I.9　Fundamentally, however, there may need to be a radical shift in cultural norms, to reverse the short-sighted drive for increasing consumption and economic growth. This raises another key challenge to successful sustainable procurement, in the form of stakeholder attitudes and aspirations. This is arguably neither 'national' nor 'global' – but it is pervasive, and may be regarded as a problem for all organisations (and therefore as a 'global' problem in this sense).

- Insofar as internal and external stakeholders (including investors, lenders and consumers) subscribe to sustainability principles and values and appreciate the urgency and priority of the issues, they may act as drivers for sustainable procurement. The challenge then is continually to satisfy their demands and expectations (eg for ethical investment profiles, green and ethically sourced products, CSR and so on).

- Insofar as internal and external stakeholders are ignorant of, indifferent to, or actively resistant to sustainability, they may act as barriers to successful sustainable procurement (as discussed in Chapter 14). The challenge is then to overcome their ignorance, indifference or resistance, by a variety of stakeholder communication, management and 'buy-in' programmes.

Example: Hewlett Packard (HP)

'Global citizenship covers a lot of ground at HP. It is more than a label, larger than a program, greater than any single organisation. Global citizenship is our commitment to balance our business goals with our impacts on society and the planet. It is also one of our corporate objectives, embodied in the commitment and contributions of our employees, and rooted in values core to HP since its founding in 1939.

We believe few companies have HP's capabilities to be a leader in global citizenship. The breadth and depth of our portfolio is at the forefront of the IT industry. Our operations, infrastructure and influence extend worldwide. Collectively, our more than 320,000 employees have unparalleled ingenuity and expertise. And our collaborative stakeholder relationships help us respond to key concerns and promising opportunities.

We focus our global citizenship efforts in five areas: ethics and compliance, human rights and labour practices, environmental sustainability, privacy, and social investment. They span our regions and business units, influencing how we set priorities, respond to customers and engage with stakeholders, run our operations, develop new offerings, and differentiate our brand.'

Hewlett Packard is viewed as a leader in global citizenship. There is a wealth of material on sustainable procurement and related topics on HP's website and via freely available on-line case studies.

---

2   *Challenges of supply chain management*

2.1   The 2006/7 report of the Corporate Responsibility Index, a leading benchmark of responsible business in the UK, suggests that 'supply chain management remains a challenge for companies, although there has been a significant increase in the number of companies working with suppliers to help them improve their social and environmental management and performance'.

2.2   As we saw in Chapter 12, there are significant risks, costs and challenges for the procurement profession in:

- Developing and managing supply network relationships in such a way as to support sustainable procurement: developing close, long-term relationships (to secure continuity of supply and continuous sustainability improvements) – while avoiding the costs and risks of complacency, 'lock in' to limiting or dysfunctional relationships and so on.

- Monitoring and controlling end-to-end supply chain activity in support of sustainability risk management: drilling down to lower tiers of the supply chain (supplier's suppliers), and considering the impacts of the use and disposal of end products (by customers' customers)

- Persuading stakeholders throughout the internal and external supply chain to 'buy into' sustainable procurement principles and programmes – and developing (and maintaining) their motivation and capabilities to contribute to sustainable procurement objectives.

Relationship development and management

2.3   As we saw in Chapter 12, whole-life contract and supply chain management supports successful procurement in managing supply risk; offering economic and cost benefits; leveraging relationships for added value; supporting whole-life costing; and allowing continuous improvement and learning. (You can recap this material if you need to.) For organisations which have not yet developed such strategies, or the relationships and management systems to implement them, the challenge will be to do so.

2.4   As we also saw, however, costs and risks rise where sustainable procurement drives a commitment to long-term contracts and relationships with suppliers, perhaps using a single preferred supplier for the range of product and service purchases relevant to the lifecycle of an asset. The challenge will therefore be to manage the risks of:

- Being locked into a long-term relationship with an under-performing or incompatible supplier or partner: eg by careful supplier selection and management, and the pre-planning of exit strategies

- A long-term contracted supplier growing complacent and ceasing to be competitive on performance, cost or sustainability criteria: eg by the use of incentives, penalties, contract reviews and continuous improvement agreements

- Association with a supplier, who may be (or become, over time) vulnerable to compliance, sustainability or reputational risk: eg by careful collaborative risk assessment and management.

- Excessive dependence on a single supplier or small group of preferred suppliers: eg by avoiding relationship-specific adaptations, pre-qualifying alternative sources of supply, monitoring supply risks and formulating contingency plans.

2.5   In addition, there will be the challenge for the purchasing profession continually to justify long-term relationship development, in the face of the opportunity costs involved. There may be pressure from internal stakeholders to buy more opportunistically or competitively, in order to secure the best available 'deal' for a given requirement.

Managing end-to-end supply chain activity

2.6   In Chapter 13, we explored the use of techniques such as product lifecycle analysis and supply chain analysis, highlighting the fact that sustainable procurement issues and principles apply from the farthest upstream end of the supply chain onwards. The challenge is to monitor, identify and manage sustainability risks 'back' through the tiers of the supply chain (suppliers' suppliers) – right back to the extraction or production of raw materials, if necessary.

2.7   This is a challenge, because (a) supply chains are highly complex, and it is not always possible to identify where purchased items 'ultimately' come from, or through whose hands they pass, and (b) it is costly, time-consuming and potentially unsustainable to monitor and control all tiers of the supply chain. An article in Supply Management (Brown, 'Responsible Technology', 7 July 2005) emphasised that for many organisations fighting for survival with limited resources in an extremely competitive economic environment, pursuing ethical monitoring of the supply chain is likely to be seen as an unattainable luxury. However, it also makes the following points.

- It is possible to prioritise items and supply chains for investment in monitoring, on the basis of reputational risk assessment. We used the example of the sportswear industry, in which public scrutiny is so rigorous that supply chains are risk-assessed right back to the source of fibres. Less 'sensitive' purchases or industries would not require 'drilling down' so far; and supplier assurances and certifications would be sufficient.

- Methods of accessing information on suppliers are becoming increasingly sophisticated... 'In previous eras, checking basic facts about suppliers in the market would have taken days or weeks: now with the right tools, it can be done in seconds [using information technology]'. This also reduces the environmental impact of monitoring activity: eg carbon footprint of travel for the purpose of site visits.

- Procurement professionals can tap into the experience and expertise of organisations which have already developed strategies to identify where there may be problems in the supply chain.

2.8   Meanwhile, in Chapter 9, we saw that sustainability impacts also extend downstream in the supply chain, to customers and customers' customers – all the way to the end users of products and services. The challenge is therefore, increasingly, to manage how products are transported/delivered, advertised, sold (eg via retail outlets), used, returned and/or disposed of. These aspects all reflect back on the producer – and in some cases (such as the disposal of electronic and electrical waste products) are the legal responsibility of the producer.

- Are products transported to distribution outlets or customers in such a way as to minimise environmental impacts and carbon footprint?
- Are products responsibly and accurately labelled: eg with 'eco' standards claims; safety warnings; responsible storage, usage and disposal instructions; and so on?
- Are outsourced services delivered as responsibly as the contracting organisation would wish? How can the procurement function manage the outsourcing contract to support this?
- Are products advertised truthfully, priced affordably and sold on terms which support social responsibility and ethical objectives? How can the organisation educate and influence downstream intermediaries to support this?
- Are products designed to be disassembled, recycled, re-used and/or safely disposed of at end-of-life?
- Does the organisation have recovery (reverse logistics), recycling and disposal capability?

2.9 Managing this challenge requires whole-life sustainability planning and downstream partnerships.

Supplier education and development

2.10 We have included the syllabus caption 'supplier development' here, because we consider it to be part of the challenge of managing sustainability through end-to-end supply chain activity. It will be an ongoing challenge for the purchasing profession to educate, motivate and develop suppliers to buy into, comply with – and contribute proactively to – sustainability objectives. The challenge may be particularly acute in regard to particular suppliers.

- Small suppliers, who may lack the resources, capabilities and skills to implement sustainability standards, and may be unfairly discriminated against in access to contracts if sustainability criteria are too stringent
- Suppliers in developing countries, who may again lack the resources to implement sustainability standards, and may also lack supporting standards and legislative regimes
- Powerful suppliers (eg large in size relative to the buying organisation, or suppliers on whom the organisation is dependent for supply of critical/strategic items), who may lack incentives to achieve above-statutory levels of sustainability performance.

2.11 We discussed supplier development in detail in Chapter 12, and you can re-cap the material if you need to. The essential points in managing the challenge of raising supplier capability and capacity for sustainability can be summarised as follows.

- The need to prioritise purchased items and suppliers for development, on the basis of sustainability-related and supply risks
- The need for a systematic approach to capability/performance appraisal and gap analysis, in order to focus management attention and resources on leverage areas (which should be matched to identified sustainable procurement issues, risks and priorities such as the reduction of resource/energy consumption or GHG emissions, or the development of compliant labour management standards)
- The need for a jointly agreed improvement/development plan to 'close' identified gaps, which may involve a variety of collaborative measures (each of which should be subjected to cost/benefit analysis prior to commitment). Particular challenges may have to be met by different suppliers at different times. In the face of recession and credit

restrictions, for example, development measures may focus on supplier resources and cashflow: supportive staged-payment terms, co-investment, the lending of plant and equipment, or help with low-cost procurement, say. For public sector suppliers, development plans may be driven by the need for Flexible Framework improvements.

- The need to build continuous improvement targets into supply contracts and partnership agreements where possible, in order to incorporate further and emerging sustainable issues and priorities progressively over the duration of the relationship.

Example: Deutsche Post DHL

As an example of the challenges of environmentally sustainable logistics, consider DHL... In its Sustainability Report 2009, the international market leader in logistics and postal services (and the world's sixth-largest employer) outlines its activities in the areas of the environment, employees and corporate social responsibility.

Climate protection

The launch of the Group-wide climate-protection program GoGreen in April 2008 represented a milestone in the commitment of Deutsche Post DHL to the environment. As a result of GoGreen, the logistics service provider became the first company in the sector to set ambitious climate-protection goals: By 2020, the Group intends to improve its CO_2 efficiency in its own business activities and for transports performed by its subcontractors by 30 per cent.

To achieve this goal, investments have been made in fleet optimisation and the replacement of planes and vehicles with quieter-running, more fuel-efficient models. In several projects, alternative drive systems and innovative technologies like dynamic route planning in the SmartTruck project have been tested. Energy-conservation programs and internal programs to mobilise employees are also helping save fuel in many local projects and improve the climate balance sheet. Customers in 20 countries can now choose from climate-neutral products and services. To facilitate the most precise reporting of the environmental improvements and CO_2 emissions, the company has begun to create a carbon-accounting system. In addition, a CO_2 efficiency index was also calculated for the first time.

These efforts have also received recognition from independent groups: DHL is the only transport and logistics service provider to be represented in the Carbon Disclosure Global 500 Leadership Index 2008.

Employees

Two-thirds of the Group's more than 500,000 employees work outside Germany. Common values and a shared corporate culture form the basis for their daily working relationship. One of the future strategic missions of Deutsche Post DHL is to have a variety of talented people as well as to find, support and nurture qualified employees. The company's continuing goal is to become the sector's employer of choice. During the past year, the company achieved outstanding results in various areas, and some of these efforts also received public recognition. For instance, the company's pioneering health-care management program was given the Germany Business Award for Health in 2008. The Global Road Safety Initiative that is designed to increase traffic safety received the international DuPont Safety Award for innovative approach. Employees' inventiveness also played a major role as their contributions to idea management resulted in savings of EUR265 million.

Corporate social responsibility

In the area of corporate social responsibility, Deutsche Post DHL concentrates primarily on the areas of disaster relief, education and the environment. In addition to hundreds of local initiatives started by employees around the world, this commitment is reflected in centrally managed projects. Last year, the global network of disaster response teams coordinated relief supplies sent after Cyclone Nargis struck Myanmar and floods hit Panama, among other places.

In the future as well, sustainable business practices will remain an inseparable part of entrepreneurial activities at Deutsche Post DHL, as CEO Frank Appel stressed at the beginning of March when he introduced the Group's Strategy 2015. 'Despite the worldwide financial crisis and economic challenges, we cannot lose sight of our shared responsibility for the social setting in which we do business around the world and for environment protection. Furthermore, we must not ease off our efforts in these areas', Appel said.

Customer education and development

2.12 One of the key implications of sustainable 'end-to-end' supply chain management is the challenge to educate and develop customers as well as suppliers. We discussed this in Chapter 9, in relation to the management of internal (and external) customer requirements. The purchasing profession can contribute to the development of 'sustainability-intelligent customers' by:

- Challenging the unsustainable requirements, requisitions and specifications of internal customers

- Supporting the design, specification and production of innovative sustainable products (since supply is a driver of customer demand, as well as an effect of it)

- Educating customers in the sustainable storage, use and disposal of products (eg via packaging and labelling)

- Involving customers in sustainability and CSR objectives, eg through feedback and suggestion schemes, voluntary 'pledges' (as with the Marks & Spencer's Plan A programme), or offering carbon off-setting options (as with purchase of tickets from some airlines).

3   *Challenges of risk and vulnerability*

Managing for risk and vulnerability in the supply chain

3.1 As we have emphasised throughout this text, sustainable procurement (like sustainable development, consumption and production) is, essentially, a form of risk management. It is designed to minimise the risk of loss or damage to stakeholders, both in the present and in the future – and the risk of the organisation having to curtail or cease its activities owing to supply failure or disruption, lack of resources, breakdown in stakeholder relationships, or withdrawal of the organisation's licence to operate.

3.2 We have particularly emphasised the importance of the identification and assessment of risk and vulnerability (points of weakness that lead to risk) in prioritising areas for sustainable procurement focus: identifying high-risk supply items, supply chains/suppliers and sustainability issues and performance gaps. This is an ongoing challenge for the purchasing profession, because risk and vulnerability are highly fluid, dynamic and complex: new risks are constantly emerging – and risks change their severity and priority as circumstances change. Globalised, multi-tiered supply chains also create particular points of vulnerability – and challenges in monitoring and managing risk.

3.3 In addition, risk – and, more specifically, risk aversion – has been identified as a key challenge to the innovation which is required to further the sustainable procurement and development agenda. The DTI report *Competing in the Global Economy: The Innovation Challenge* (2003) argued that in the public sector, in particular, there is a tendency to select low-risk, more established solutions. The systematic management of risk, and the confidence it provides, is therefore crucial in enabling innovation.

3.4 You may already have covered risk management in detail in your studies for *Risk Management and Supply Chain Vulnerability*. We will outline some key points here, since we have not had the opportunity to do so elsewhere in the text.

The risk management process

3.5 Risk management may be defined as 'the process whereby organisations methodically address the risks attaching to their activities with the goal of achieving sustained benefit within each activity and across the portfolio of all activities' (Institute of Risk Management). The process of risk management is often portrayed as a cycle: Figure 16.1

Figure 16.1 *The risk management cycle*

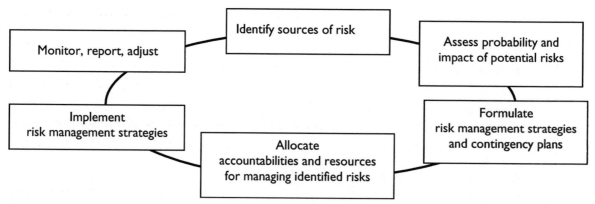

3.6 *Risk identification* is the process of seeking to identify potential problems or areas of uncertainty: in other words, asking 'what could go wrong?' This may be done by environmental scanning and corporate appraisal (PESTLE and SWOT analysis); formal risk analysis exercises; monitoring risk events in benchmark organisations; critical incident investigations and process audits; consulting with key stakeholders and industry experts; or employing third-party risk management consultants. It should be an ongoing process, as the organisation's sustainability risk profile may continually change, presenting new risks or turning slight risks into potential crises (eg if they attract media or NGO scrutiny). A comprehensive list of identified risks should be compiled (eg in a sustainability risk register).

3.7 *Risk assessment or evaluation* is the appraisal of the probability and significance of identified potential risk events: in other words, asking 'how likely is it and how bad could it be?' Risk is often quantified using the basic formula: *Risk = Likelihood x Impact.*

- Risk likelihood is the probability of occurrence, given the nature of the risk and current risk management practices. This may be expressed as a number between 0 (no chance) and 1 (certainty) or as a percentage (100% = certainty), score (1–10) or rating (Low–Medium–High). The more likely the risk event is to occur, the higher the overall level of risk, and the higher priority risk management will be.

- Risk impact/consequence is the likely loss/cost to the organisation or the likely level of impact on its ability to fulfil its objectives. The severity of impacts may be quantified (eg in terms of estimated cost or loss), scored (1–10), or rated (Low–Medium–High). Even if assessed as improbable, high-impact events should be the subject of detailed contingency planning, so that the organisation can respond effectively to the event if it occurs.

3.8 Quantifying the risk allows an organisation to prioritise planning and resources to meet the most severe risks, and to set defined risk thresholds at which action on an issue will be triggered. *Risk management strategies* ('what can we do about it?') are often classified as the Four Ts:

- *Tolerate* (or accept) the risk: if the assessed likelihood or impact of the risk is negligible

- *Transfer* or spread the risk: eg by taking out insurance cover, or not putting all supply eggs in one basket – or using contract terms to ensure that the costs of risk events will be borne by (or shared with) supply chain partners

- *Terminate* (or avoid) the risk: if the risk associated with a particular activity is too great, and cannot be reduced, the activity should not be undertaken. So, for example, suppliers may be rejected on the basis of poor labour management or environmental standards in high-visibility areas.

- *Treat* (or mitigate) the risk: take active steps to manage the risk in such a way as to reduce or minimise its likelihood or potential impact, or both. This may involve measures such as: safety procedures, maintenance schedules, internal governance controls, supplier monitoring, codes of conduct, supplier sustainability policies and standards, supplier certification or pre-qualification, critical incident reporting and analysis, stakeholder feedback gathering, contingency and recovery planning (eg alternative sources of supply) and so on.

3.9 In any case, the organisation will need to make contingency plans in regard to high-impact risks: alternative courses of action, alternative sources of supply, workarounds and fallback positions ('What will we do if...?').

3.10 *Monitoring, reporting and review* ('What happened and what can we learn?') is an important part of risk management, in order to:

- Ascertain whether the organisation's risk profile or exposure is changing, and identify newly emerging or escalating sustainability-related risks

- Give assurance that the organisation's risk management processes are effective, by demonstrating effective avoidance or mitigation of risks. (This may be important in supporting investment in innovation, for example – as well as being a responsible orientation to stakeholder concerns.)

- Indicate where risk management processes need improvement, or where lessons can be learned from critical incidents.

4   Challenges of commitment

4.1 As we have seen throughout this text, long-term commitment and investment are required not just to develop and implement sustainable procurement policies (as discussed in Chapters 6–8), but to maintain them, and ideally also to maintain momentum for continuous progress and improvement over time. It is a significant future challenge for the purchasing profession to avoid sustainable procurement becoming a short-lived 'fad' or 'fashion', easily abandoned in the face of changing strategic priorities or recessionary pressures. To use the words of Blackburn, the challenge is 'to keep the initiative alive' – or to make sustainable procurement itself 'sustainable' in the organisation and supply chain.

Stakeholder priorities

4.2 We have already dealt at length with the idea that successful sustainable procurement requires the commitment of senior management and other key internal stakeholders, and the support, co-operation and – ideally – collaboration of key external stakeholders, including suppliers. We hope that not much more need be said on this subject here (despite its inclusion as a syllabus caption for this learning objective), but we will reiterate two key points.

4.3   Key stakeholder groups may have differing, diverging or even conflicting objectives, interests and priorities. There is therefore a major challenge for the procurement profession in co-opting stakeholder support for sustainable procurement principles and programmes (or minimising resistance to them). The ability to do this depends, in part, on harmonising the interests of different stakeholders as far as possible – which is in itself a key principle of corporate social responsibility. How do you satisfy the desires of shareholders and managers for economic performance – without ignoring the desire of workers and suppliers for better terms, or the impacts of corporate activity on 'voiceless' stakeholders such as future generations and the natural environment?

4.4   Stakeholder concerns, interests and priorities change over time. In recessionary periods, shareholders and management may find a renewed focus on the protection of profits, financial viability and share price – at the expense of 'soft', future-focused interests such as environmental and social sustainability. Consumer, media and activist interests once prioritised animal welfare and the protection of the rainforests – until interest shifted to recycling and 'green' products, and subsequently (it seems, almost overnight, with the release of the film *An Inconvenient Truth*) climate change. A major challenge for the purchasing profession, among others, is therefore to track and anticipate these shifts in priority: to monitor emerging issues over time, through environmental and stakeholder research and analysis.

4.5   In order to maintain sustainable procurement initiatives as an organisational priority, sustainability champions need to:

- Define, articulate and secure 'buy-in' to the organisation's commitment to consider the interests of different stakeholder groups

- Make a business case (on the basis of 'enlightened self interest') for the pursuit of non-economic objectives, such as social and environmental sustainability

- Maintain communication with stakeholder groups, in order to learn what value they seek from sustainable procurement; what issues they are concerned about; what reputational and other risks may arise from stakeholder concern, activism or resistance; what opportunities are available from stakeholder concern, support and commitment; and so on

- Manage stakeholder expectations and perceptions, in order to minimise resistance to sustainable procurement initiatives and to ensure that the potential value and opportunities of sustainable procurement initiatives are realised (in terms of brand strength, customer loyalty, supply chain innovation and eco-efficiencies and so on).

Keeping sustainable procurement initiatives alive

4.6   Blackburn notes that: 'We have all seen inspired efforts go awry in all kinds of organisations. Plans are prepared but not executed. People promise to help, but later move or become sidetracked with other activities. Resources dry up. The excitement dims. Priorities shift. All these problems can plague an organisation's commitment to sustainability, too.'

4.7   Blackburn suggests the following considerations in managing the challenge of 'keeping the initiative alive'.

- *Anticipate the future internally and externally.* 'Are company sales and profits down? If so, the sustainability leader must anticipate working with fewer resources and find ways to emphasise sustainability projects which help the organisation address its problems... Is the organisation planning a big shift in strategy or structure? Then how can sustainability be framed to fit that new environment... A new, highly publicised corporate scandal or disaster is a sure sign that greater public and government scrutiny and expectations of business will follow.' Procurement professionals are ideally placed to gain early warning about evolving issues, both internal and external.

- *Periodically tune the system.* People tend to become blinkered to the strengths and weaknesses of their organisation and established programmes, or complacent with performance. External reviews of the sustainable procurement policy may be required to keep evaluation honest, and improvement planning and priorities 'fresh'.

- *Hone skills and knowledge.* People leave, new people join, lessons fade and sustainability issues and priorities change. Sustainability-focused recruitment, selection, training and development programmes are needed to ensure that current and future team members contribute competently to sustainable procurement, with potential for continual capability- and competence-building.

- *Sustain support and resources.* The job of 'selling' the value of sustainable procurement never ends! Sustainability leaders and advocates must continually be appointed, motivated and resourced to drive sustainable procurement. Success stories, lessons learned, critical incidents and competitor examples must continually be collected to drive the message. Cultural mechanisms (rituals, symbols, communications, HR systems) must continually refresh and reinforce sustainability values.

- *Keep it fresh and inspiring.* When programmes become stale, participants can become apathetic. Participative planning, continuous improvement targets, and creative expressions (eg sustainable procurement awards) can be used to reinvigorate the programme.

- *Collaborate with others.* Procurement professionals are ideally placed to identify opportunities for win-win collaborations with supply chain partners, to offer energy and synergy.

- *Continually improve performance.* The results of sustainable procurement programmes must, as we have emphasised, be continually monitored and measured, lessons learned, and improvement targets (however small-step) formulated, in order to maintain momentum.

Example: IKEA

IKEA has developed a small-step, incremental approach to continuous improvement which it calls 'the Never Ending Job', with a list of improvement areas and targets which it calls 'the Never Ending List'.

'We have decided to help create a world where we take better care of the environment, the earth's resources, and each other. We know that sometimes we are part of the problem. So, we are working hard to become a part of the solution. We are weighing the pros and cons, continually examining and changing things. All these steps, in lots and lots of areas, add up to something big ... and noticeable. The job has already started, and it is a never-ending one.'

Making sustainable procurement 'business as usual'

4.8   In one sense, as we have just seen, it is a challenge to ensure that sustainable procurement doesn't become just 'business as usual' – being taken for granted, unexamined or no longer a priority for innovation, problem-solving, learning and improvement.

4.9   On the other hand, as we saw in Chapter 7, there comes a time when sustainable procurement is no longer in its development and roll-out phase, being given 'special attention', separate layers of responsibility or accountability, launch-level communications and start-up investment and so on. The aim is to integrate it as fully and swiftly as possible into business as usual – or 'standard operating procedure' – for the procurement function and its internal and external supply chains. The spotlight is off the sustainable procurement 'initiative' – and onto sustainable procurement performance, with the understanding that this is not a fad or fashion but an ongoing, natural facet of organisational strategy.

4.10   This is an acknowledged challenge for learning in any setting. The stages of learning are said to progress from unconscious incompetence (you don't know that you can't do something) to conscious incompetence (you're aware that you can't do something) to conscious competence (you have to think carefully about what you're doing in order to do it right) – and finally to unconscious competence (you do it right without thinking). Consider how an individual learns to type or drive a car, for example. The same stages can be applied to corporate sustainable procurement activities: the time comes to progress from conscious incompetence (with the development of policies and procedures) to conscious competence (with their deployment, implementation and early development) to unconscious competence (when sustainable procurement principles are embedded in all decisions and actions).

4.11   In addition, regarding sustainable procurement as 'business as usual' helps to sell and reinforce the concept to corporate management and stakeholders. We saw in Chapter 4, for example, that Blackburn recommends securing buy-in to sustainability principles by emphasising that, fundamentally, the processes required for sustainable procurement are equivalent to the processes of 'sound management' in general. Similarly, Sir Neville Sims (in the foreword to *Procuring the Future*) argues that: 'Sustainable procurement – in short, using procurement to support wider social, economic and environmental objectives, in ways that offer real long-term benefits – is how the public sector should be spending taxpayers' money. Anything less means that today's taxpayer and the future citizen are both being short-changed.'

4.12   The purchasing profession may help to embed sustainable procurement as 'good procurement' by embedding sustainable procurement principles in professional education, and continuing professional development (as CIPS has done via this module and the Knowledge Works bodies of professional resources).

4.13   Procurement professionals may also help to embed sustainable procurement as 'business as usual' in their employing organisations by the following measures.

- Ensuring that sustainable procurement objectives and strategies are vertically and horizontally aligned

- Integrating sustainable procurement policy objectives, principles and standards consistently across all relevant policy documentation, systems, procedures and standard practices (specifications, standard terms, *proforma* tender/contract documents, e-sourcing platforms, pre-qualification questionnaires, tender evaluation forms, framework agreements, call-off contracts, vendor rating forms and so on).

- Recruiting, selecting, training, developing, appraising and rewarding procurement staff using sustainable procurement competencies and criteria

- Embedding sustainability criteria in all documents, procedures and practices in contract, supplier and supply chain management (supplier selection, vendor rating, contract terms, continuous improvement agreements and so on)

- Providing education and training in sustainability principles and practices for internal stakeholders (including non-specialist or part-time purchasers in user departments)

- Implementing whole-life costing (in collaboration with other stakeholders in budgetary control, accounting and financial/management reporting)

- Implementing product lifecycle analysis and end-to-end supply chain risk management (in collaboration with other internal and external stakeholders

- Developing permanent structures for sustainable procurement leadership, consultancy and accountability (in place of deployment-focused task force or change management structures): cross-functional sustainability teams, and all-member responsibility for personal sustainable procurement goals and targets.

4.14 It is useful to study the words of Simon Sperryn, a former Chief Executive of CIPS.

'Sustainable procurement is not a new discipline or a niche activity. It is just "good procurement" that achieves sustainable growth. Businesses that identify sustainability as key to future success will act now and harvest the benefits from efficient procurement systems that are future-proof. Others without an effective procurement strategy will fall victim to changing forces outside of their control.'

Chapter summary

- National challenges to sustainable procurement include the impact of the global recession, conflicting policy objectives, demographic trends, geography, consumer demand, national targets and commitments, and the pace of legislation.

- Global challenges relate to both non-renewable resources (where the focus is on developing alternatives) and renewable resources (where the focus is on harvesting and consuming at a sustainable rate).

- Challenges of supply chain management include developing and managing supply relationships supportive of sustainability, monitoring end-to-end supply chain activity in support of sustainability, and educating supply chain partners.

- It is important to prioritise areas for sustainable procurement focus. One criterion will relate to the level of risk posed by each area.

- Equally, it is important to bring stakeholder influence behind the policy of sustainability. Ultimately, we aim to reach a situation where sustainability is just 'business as usual'.

Self-test questions

Numbers in brackets refer to the paragraphs above where your answers can be checked.

1   Explain how sustainability objectives are challenged by the impact of the global recession and by consumer demand. (Table 16.1)

2   How may stakeholder attitudes impede or support sustainability objectives? (1.9)

3   What are the risks of strategic long-term relationships with suppliers? (2.4)

4   Which particular suppliers may pose problems when we seek to implement sustainability along the supply chain? (2.10)

5   List stages in the risk management cycle. (Figure 16.1)

6   What two aspects of a risk contribute to determining the level of its seriousness? (3.7)

7   List actions that a 'sustainability champion' can take to maintain sustainability as an organisational priority. (4.5)

8   List actions that purchasers may take to embed sustainable procurement in their organisations as 'business as usual'. (4.13)

Further reading

From your 'Essential Reading' list, you might look at: Blackburn (*The Sustainability Handbook*):

- Chapter 16: Keeping the initiative alive

- Chapter 12: Approach to sustainability for small and struggling businesses.

Otherwise, we recommend again that you browse the CIPS website's Professional Resources section for a wide range of papers, Knowledge Summaries and Knowledge Insight guides to responsible procurement, sustainable procurement, corporate social responsibility and related topics.

Subject Index